Christians, Muslims, and Jews in Medieval and Early Modern Spain

Notre Dame Conferences in Medieval Studies
Number VIII

Institute of Medieval Studies
University of Notre Dame

Christians, Muslims, and Jews in Medieval and Early Modern Spain

INTERACTION AND CULTURAL CHANGE

Edited by

MARK D. MEYERSON

AND EDWARD D. ENGLISH

UNIVERSITY OF NOTRE DAME PRESS

Notre Dame, Indiana

University of Notre Dame Press
Notre Dame, Indiana 46556

www. undpress.nd.edu

Published in the United States of America

Library of Congress Cataloging-in-Publication Data

Christians, Muslims, and Jews in medieval and early modern Spain : interaction and cultural change / edited by Mark D. Meyerson and Edward D. English.

p. cm. — (Notre Dame conferences in medieval studies ; no. 8)
Includes bibliographical references.

ISBN 978-0-268-02250-1 (hardback)
ISBN 978-0-268-02263-1 (paperback)

1. Spain—Religion Congresses. 2. Spain—Church history Congressess. 3. Islam—Spain—History Congresses. 4. Judaism—Spain—History Congresses. I. Meyerson, Mark D. II. English, Edward D. III. Series: Notre Dame conferences in medieval studies ; 8.
BL980.S7C48 2000
291.1'72'0946—dc21 99-35905

∞ *This book is printed on acid-free paper.*

In Memory of

JOHN BOSWELL

CONTENTS

Acknowledgments ix
Introduction xi
MARK D. MEYERSON

I. Christians and Jews in Muslim Spain

1. Muḥammad as Antichrist in Ninth-Century Córdoba 3
KENNETH BAXTER WOLF

2. Reading the *Repartimientos:* Modeling Settlement in the Wake of Conquest 20
THOMAS F. GLICK

3. Maimonides and the Spanish Aristotelian School 40
JOEL L. KRAEMER

4. Jewish-Muslim Relations in the Context of Andalusian Emigration 69
STEVEN M. WASSERSTROM

II. Muslims and Jews in Christian Spain

5. Mudejar Parallel Societies: Anglophone Historiography and Spanish Context, 1975–2000 91
ROBERT I. BURNS, S.J.

6. Muslim-Jewish Relations in Crusader Majorca in the Thirteenth Century: An Inquiry Based on Patrimony Register 342 125
LARRY J. SIMON

7. Religious and Sexual Boundaries in the Medieval Crown of Aragon 141
DAVID NIRENBERG

8. History and Intertextuality in Late Medieval Spain 161
ELEAZAR GUTWIRTH

9. Undermining the Jewish Sense of Future: Alfonso of Valladolid and the New Christian Missionizing 179
ROBERT CHAZAN

III. Conversos

10. Crypto-Jewish Women Facing the Spanish Inquisition: Transmitting Religious Practices, Beliefs, and Attitudes 197
RENÉE LEVINE MELAMMED

11. Relations between Conversos and Old Christians in Early Modern Toledo: Some Different Perspectives 220
LINDA MARTZ

12. Conversion and Subversion: Converso Texts in Fifteenth-Century Spain 241
DAYLE SEIDENSPINNER-NÚÑEZ

IV. Moriscos

13. The Moriscos: Loyal Subjects of His Catholic Majesty Philip III 265
STEPHEN HALICZER

14. Moriscas and the Limits of Assimilation 274
MARY ELIZABETH PERRY

15. The Moriscos and Christian Doctrine 290
CONSUELO LÓPEZ-MORILLAS

V. Epilogue

After 1492: Spain as Seen by Non-Spaniards 309
J. N. HILLGARTH

Index 323

ACKNOWLEDGMENTS

The conference from which this volume emerged could not have taken place without the generous support of the National Endowment for the Humanities. I am grateful to John Van Engen, Director of Notre Dame's Medieval Institute, for suggesting that I organize such a conference and to the staff and faculty of the Medieval Institute for their interest and assistance. Special thanks are due to Edward D. English, who worked closely with me in organizing the conference and in editing the present volume. The staff of the Institute for Scholarship in the Liberal Arts at the University of Notre Dame also offered helpful advice in organizing the conference. The splendid papers of the presenters and the contributions of the other participants made the conference a success; to all of them I am especially grateful.

When the conference took place, the late John Boswell of Yale University was in the final stages of a mortal illness. An historian of Mudejars and much else, John Boswell had inspired and assisted a number of the presenters and participants through his scholarship, teaching, and friendship. On the eve of the conference, which was treating issues to which he had devoted so much attention, I wrote him to tell him that he would be in our thoughts. As I write these acknowledgments, he still is. This volume is dedicated to his memory.

INTRODUCTION

MARK D. MEYERSON

The essays comprising this volume were all originally presented at a conference on "Christians, Muslims, and Jews in Medieval and Early Modern Spain: Interaction and Cultural Change," which was held at the University of Notre Dame on February 27–March 1, 1994, and sponsored by Notre Dame's Medieval Institute. The great majority of the papers read at the conference have been included here in revised form.

When I began to organize the conference back in 1993, other conferences that I had attended during the previous two years were very much on my mind. One of them, also sponsored by Notre Dame's Medieval Institute, dealt provocatively with "The Past and Future of Medieval Studies."[1] There I was asked to comment on the papers presented in a session entitled "Judaism, Byzantium, Islam." I wondered aloud, a bit playfully perhaps, how medievalists might move these three fields from a session on what seemed to have been categorized as medieval *exotica* into the disciplinary sessions on history, literature, philosophy, and so on. Considering this marginalization of Jewish, Islamic, and Byzantine studies from the field of medieval studies and its constituent disciplines naturally prompted me to think in this regard about medieval Spain, "the land of three religions." I reflected on how medievalists might integrate Spain more effectively into the field of medieval studies, and on how Hispanists themselves might deal with the three religions, or ethnicities in the sixteenth century, in a more coherent and inclusive fashion. Such questions did not, and still do not admit easy answers, but, with respect to the rationale for the conference that produced this volume, they usefully raised the issue of marginality in a number of different contexts.

It was not so long ago that the study of Spanish history and culture in the medieval and early modern periods had a marginal status vis-à-vis the mainstream of European studies. This was due in no small part to the unwillingness or inability of many Europeanists to give careful attention to a country in whose history and sociocultural formation Muslims and Jews played such a significant role. These peoples, and hence the Iberian peninsula, did not fit easily into the master narrative of European history. More recently, however, as the master narrative is disputed, as new scholarly agendas emerge, and as the discourse of multiculturalism infuses North American campuses, what once rendered medieval Spain almost incomprehensible and was deemed its handicap—its ethnoreligious pluralism—is now perceived as its virtue, its allure. Spain is, as I have heard some students call it, the land of "medieval multiculturalism," or, more pessimistically, it represents the spearhead of European world hegemony, a land where western Christians warmed up on Jews and Muslims before the main event in America, Africa, and Asia. Yet, if the study of Spain is now somewhat more central in university curricula and academic research programs, the move from the margins can bring in its wake other dangers: either a tendency to marvel at the intermingling of Christian, Muslim, and Jewish texts and bodies, or, on the other extreme, a tendency to emphasize persecution and oppression, to revive the Black Legend of Spain for purposes rather different from those of Spain's sixteenth-century enemies.

When considering how scholars approach Christian-Muslim-Jewish relations in Spain, on both interpersonal and intertextual levels, the concept of marginality again comes to the fore—that is, the concept of marginality as a heuristic tool. Concepts like "marginality" or "the other" are frequently bandied about these days, yet it is not clear how useful such concepts are, at least in the manner in which Europeanists often employ them, for interpreting Spanish history and culture. The utilization of the concept of marginality can give rise to two kinds of problematic assumptions. First, if we label Christians and Jews in al-Andalus (Muslim Spain), or Muslims and Jews in Christian Spain, as "marginal groups," then we may be led to assume that the "marginal groups" all maintained the same relationships of power with the Muslim or Christian authorities, or that they all faced the same challenges to their religious identity and cultural integrity—that is, that they all shared the same marginalized or minority experience.

Second, and more problematic, is the very assumption that these groups, Jews and Christians in al-Andalus and Jews and Muslims in Christian Spain, were "marginal." If we understand as "marginal" those groups who eventually converted to the rulers' faith or were forced into exile or otherwise eliminated, then we may be engaging in a retrospective and anachronistic reading of texts and history that obscures the subtleties and complexities of ethnoreligious interaction as the groups and individuals in question experienced it. Or if we label as "marginal" those people who were not members of the religious group holding the reins of political power, then the waters get rather muddy. For it was not at all unusual for members of the so-called "marginal" groups to possess significant power and influence—sometimes more than the coreligionists of the ruler—and to be very much at the center of things, politically and culturally. Although *sharīʿa* defined the status of *dhimmīs* and restricted their activities in certain ways, and the law codes of the Spanish kingdoms did much the same for Muslims and Jews, these groups were not thereby marginated; indeed, often enough the legal restrictions were honored in the breach. Rather than working with ambiguous and ultimately meaningless categories of "marginality" and "otherness," it seems more useful to explore, for instance, how each ethnic and religious group dealt with the tension between power and powerlessness, how and why certain social and intellectual boundaries among groups were established and why at times they were crossed, and how such boundary-crossing caused social tension among and identity crises within groups.

One of the paradoxes of Spanish history, it seems to me, is that the legal, literary, and polemical texts in which the "other" was constructed often were produced because the "other" had become too familiar and hence too dangerous, because the "other" was not "other" at all. For many Europeans outside of the Iberian peninsula the Muslim or Jewish "other" was often a figment of the imagination, a product of second-hand rumor, or a person only infrequently encountered. But in Muslim and Christian Spain the "other" often was a neighbor or a known quantity who had to be rendered "other" if society were to function as rulers and religious elites of all groups desired. For the student of Spain, distinguishing between literary representation and social reality or understanding how literary representation grew out of a given social context and how texts then affected social relations are knottier problems. Hence one may well wonder about the utility of some of the paradigms employed by Europeanists in analyzing Europe's contacts with the "other" for elucidating the Spanish case. Students of the Islamic world, where ethnoreligious pluralism was more common, are on safer ground when they transfer to al-Andalus the methodological assumptions they have developed when studying the rest of Islamdom. In dealing with the textual, historical, and sociological problems associated with ethnoreligious interaction, the Islamicist can stride more confidently and gracefully across the Mediterranean, while the Europeanist may well stumble when crossing the Pyrenees.

The subtitle of this volume, "Interaction and Cultural Change," is thus consistent with this concern about the sometimes distorting and confining discourse of "marginality" and "otherness." In giving the volume this subtitle, I do not mean to suggest that there was anything particularly idyllic or "golden" about Andalusian society or the society of the Spanish Christian kingdoms, or that the social and cultural life of any one religious group was necessarily contingent on its contacts with the others. I am simply indicating the importance, on a more general and human plane, of developing a more refined understanding of the dynamics of social and cultural interchange, whether the result was brilliant literature or horrible violence. And, more specifically, in regard to Spain, I am suggesting how essential it is to analyze the recurring patterns and problems of coexistence, conflict, conversion, assimilation, and cultural transformation, patterns that give Spanish history during the centuries treated here a fascinating and at times tragic symmetry.

Also much on my mind when I organized the conference were the numerous conferences dealing with the tragic and transformative events of 1492: the conquest of Granada, the expulsion of the Jews, and the "discovery" and conquest of America. One can hardly overestimate the value of these conferences for the scholarship they produced, the discussions they generated, and the attention they drew to the field of Hispanic studies. Even so, I experienced a certain disquietude over the almost exclusive emphasis on "1492 and all that." It seemed that Spanish history was being given an excessively retrospective reading and was being framed in such a way that all events, all policies, and all texts were interpreted as leading inevitably to or pointing toward 1492. Certainly there is no denying that the events of 1492 took place, and a reading of inquisitorial records, expulsion narratives, and other sources from the period should quickly disabuse anyone of whatever apologetic notions they may hold. Nevertheless, constantly looking back from the precipice of 1492 gives one the impression of a linear and inescapable decline in the state of Christian-Muslim-Jewish relations; it creates a kind of dysfunctional model of *convivencia.* It is equally important to understand more precisely how the plural societies of medieval Iberia functioned, that is, how these peoples coped with ideological antagonism and negotiated the theological and social boundaries that separated them, and how they coexisted through being enmeshed in complex networks of economic, social, and intellectual interdependence. When we know more about how things worked, we will gain greater insight into how things fell apart.

The 1492 conferences, because they focused almost exclusively on the events surrounding that year, and because they usually dealt exclusively with either Muslims or Jews (or indigenous Americans), severed significant threads of historical continuity and artificially isolated the historical experiences of peoples whose respective fates were more closely linked than is often recognized.[2] In doing so, these conferences merely reflected the unavoidable problem of chronological and disciplinary fragmentation in the study of Christian-Muslim-Jewish interaction in Spain.

Perhaps the most obvious example of chronological disruption is the rather sharp boundary that scholars tend to draw between the medieval and early modern periods, generally around the accession of Fernando and Isabel to the Castilian throne in 1474. Medievalists and early modernists are naturally going to have different perspectives and privilege certain questions over others, but, in dealing with this problem of ethnoreligious interaction, there is much that each school of scholars stands to lose if it does not look across the chronological divide.[3] Early modernists studying the predicament of conversos and Moriscos can clearly profit from a more nuanced understanding of medieval Jewish and Islamic society and culture; at the same time, medievalists exploring the complexities of *convivencia* would find that a consideration of post-1492 social and cultural developments can shed significant light on patterns of change in the medieval period. If conversos and Moriscos responded to Christianity and Christians differently, it was at least partly because the circumstances and behavior of their Jewish and Muslim forebears predisposed them to do so.

The matter of chronological fragmentation is bound up with the nature of the sources available for the study of each period. One hardly needs to comment on the linguistic changes from one period, or from one polity, to the next. But perhaps most significant in terms of our understanding of the social and cultural dynamics of these plural societies is the availability of a vast amount of archival documentation for the period subsequent to the twelfth century. This documentation permits detailed studies of social and economic history at the local level, allows for the use of methods of historical anthropology, and enables the historian and literature scholar to define more precisely the relationship between text and context, representation and reality. Students of al-Andalus do not have such archival sources at their disposal. Yet, by way of careful comparative analysis, they might glean from detailed studies of *convivencia* in Castile and Aragon much that is useful for their own explorations of Andalusian culture and society. In similar fashion, students of the Mudejars (Muslims living under Spanish Christian rule) might learn much from the sources available on the Moriscos, inasmuch as Inquisition records and *aljamiado* literature provide access to the voices and mentality of Hispano-Muslims in a way that the sources for Mudejar studies do not. One must of course be mindful of the Moriscos' unusual predicament and the disorientation and distortions inherent in it.

Thus, in having the conference cover all nine hundred years between 711 and 1610, and in inviting scholars who work in the three distinct settings of Muslim Spain (*ca.* 711–1212), medieval Christian Spain (*ca.* 1100–1492), and early modern Spain, my intention was to provide a framework for a comparative analysis of, for instance, different social and political conditions and the degree to which they facilitated fruitful social and cultural interchange between religious groups or enhanced mutual hostility and aversion.

Also problematic, and equally unavoidable, is disciplinary fragmentation on a synchronic plane, where each scholar is a specialist studying one religious group and sometimes its relations with another, focusing on certain kinds of texts, and utilizing distinct methodologies. It could hardly be otherwise. Consequently, contacts, and collections of essays reflecting such contacts, are all too infrequent between students of Andalusian Jewry and those of Andalusian Christians, or between Mudejaristas and their counterparts studying Castilian and Aragonese Jewish communities, or between historians and students of literature and philosophy. I therefore invited scholars from these different fields to facilitate interdisciplinary contact and to create a forum for discussing, for instance, the differential degrees of acculturation and assimilation of distinct minority groups in the same sociopolitical setting, and the factors that enabled one minority group to maintain its cultural distinctiveness and identity more effectively than another.

This volume has not reproduced the lively discussions that followed the presentation of papers, or the equally stimulating and rewarding exchanges that took place over meals and in hallways. It is, then, left to the reader of this volume of essays, each of which deals admirably with the issues of ethnoreligious interaction and cultural change, to draw her or his own conclusions.

The first two essays in the section "Christians and Jews in Muslim Spain" each deal with issues of cultural change and adaptation in the wake of conquest. Kenneth Wolf shows that Paul Alvarus depicted Muḥammad as the Antichrist in his commentary on the Book of Daniel because Christians in ninth-century Córdoba had been adapting all too well to the culture of their Muslim rulers; by presenting Islamic culture as radically anti-Christian Alvarus hoped to convince Christians to reject it. Focusing on the series of land registers (*Libros de Repartimiento*) produced by the Christian conquerors of Muslim Spain, Thomas Glick discusses how Christian conquest altered the rural landscape of al-Andalus by modifying the function and morphology of castles and the organization and distribution of land in villages.

The last two essays in this section address the remarkable and often fruitful interchange between Jewish and Muslim intellectual elites. Each author is careful to indicate as well the limits to such interchange. Joel Kraemer treats Maimonides as a member of the Andalusian "Aristotelian school," discussing, for example, how Maimonides and his Muslim counterparts confronted the challenge of Ptolemaic astronomy to Aristotelian cosmology, and provocatively questioning whether Maimonides was an Averroist. Steven Wasserstrom looks at circles of Jewish and Muslim emigrants from al-Andalus who shared an interest in "intellectual esoterism," such as Avicennan philosophical mysticism and Sufism of the Murcian school, and suggests that, despite the constraints of ethnocentrism, the intellectual contacts thus cultivated significantly affected the Mediterranean intellectual world.

Reflecting the greater variety of sources available on the plural societies of Christian Spain, the five essays in the section "Muslims and Jews in Christian Spain" treat an especially wide range of topics. Father Robert I. Burns, himself a pioneer in the field of Mudejar studies, charts the remarkable expansion of historiography on the Mudejars in the past twenty years, a development due to Anglo-American interest in issues of ethnic pluralism, the changing agenda of Spanish scholars in the post-Franco era, and the quantity and richness of documentation to be found in Spanish archives. The essays of Larry Simon and David Nirenberg indicate the fascinating material these archives can offer to social historians. Examining just one royal chancery register from thirteenth-century Majorca, Simon is able to study comparatively Jewish and Christian ownership and treatment of Muslim slaves, and thus to shed valuable light on relations of power on the island during the post-conquest decades. Nirenberg deals provocatively with the matter of institutional, judicial violence against Jewish and Muslim men accused of sexual intercourse with Christian women. He explains why the crossing of sexual boundaries caused such anxiety and demonstrates how members of all three groups sometimes strategically employed accusations of miscegenation against their enemies of another or of the same faith.

Eleazar Gutwirth and Robert Chazan turn from archival documents to historical and polemical texts, respectively. Gutwirth pointedly questions the tendency to undervalue medieval Jewish historiography because of its use of biblical allusion, which is often dismissed as merely ornamental. Examining Samuel Çarça's description of the attacks on Castilian Jewish communities in 1366–1368 and Hasdai Crescas's description of the 1391 violence in juxtaposition to contemporary Christian chronicles, Gutwirth demonstrates that in Jewish texts biblical allusion had important and varied historiographical functions, as it sometimes did in Christian texts. Chazan analyzes the efforts of Christian polemicists and missionaries to undermine the Jews' hope for future redemption, and shows more specifically how the Jewish convert Alfonso of Valladolid (formerly Abner of Burgos) first succumbed to this argumentation and then turned it upon his former coreligionists.

The three essays in the "Conversos" section together show the considerable range of sources upon which scholars can draw when treating the issue of converso identity and religiosity and suggest why this issue has become so contentious. Renée Levine Melammed uses records from the tribunals of the Spanish Inquisition to explore the essential role of women in maintaining a Jewish life in the converso community and home in the absence of formal Jewish religious and educational institutions. Linda Martz, however, argues for a greater, though incomplete, converso assimilation into Catholic church and society. She employs ecclesiastical records from Toledo to show how conversos founded nunneries and burial chapels while preserving a degree of ethnic solidarity through their choice of certain churches and nunneries. Through an examination of converso texts Dayle Seidenspinner-Núñez reveals "two opposing converso discourses." On the one hand, converso *letrados* who were royal servants produced a large body of chronicles and political tractates that promoted monarchical authority and "advocated a rationalist adjudication of religious orthodoxy," while, on the other hand, sentimental romances like *Grisel y Mirabella* expressed the growing converso disenchantment with the policies of Fernando and Isabel through a critical and subversive commentary on the tyranny of monarchs and the violence of the judiciary.

The essays in the "Moriscos" section offer equally challenging and fascinating perspectives on the predicament of Spain's baptized Muslims. Both the Moriscos' Old Christian contemporaries and modern scholars have often regarded the Moriscos as a fifth column, but

Stephen Haliczer presents evidence suggesting that at least some Moriscos were loyal subjects of the Spanish monarchy. In an essay strikingly parallel to that of Levine Melammed, Mary Elizabeth Perry highlights the significant role of Moriscas in their families' and communities' resistance to assimilative pressures. Yet she also shows that the experience of Moriscas was by no means uniform and that some chose to assimilate, however imperfectly. Consuelo López-Morillas explores a seemingly odd *aljamiado* text from sixteenth-century Aragon: a Spanish translation of a Quranic commentary on the doctrinal disputes between early Christian sects. She explains why such a traditional text would have been meaningful to Moriscos struggling to maintain an Islamic identity in an increasingly hostile Christian environment.

Jocelyn Hillgarth's essay concludes the volume on an ironic note. He suggests that because of and despite the persistent efforts of the Spanish Inquisition and the Spanish monarchy to rid Spain of its Muslims and Jews, non-Spaniards in the early modern period continued to view Spain as a land full of Muslims and Jews. Hillgarth's essay brings us full circle, for over the centuries this conception of Spain has, for better and for worse, influenced scholarly and popular notions of Spanish history and culture.

NOTES

1. John Van Engen, ed., *The Past and Future of Medieval Studies* (Notre Dame, Ind., 1994).

2. A problem also alluded to by María Rosa Menocal, *Shards of Love: Exile and the Origins of the Lyric* (Durham, 1994), 5.

3. An example of the misconceptions that can result when early modernists treat the ethnoreligious problems of sixteenth-century Spain with apparently minimal consideration of what occurred before 1474 is the recent article of a leading early modern historian, Richard L. Kagan, "Prescott's Paradigm: American Historical Scholarship and the Decline of Spain," *American Historical Review* 101, no. 2 (1996): 439–40. In an otherwise incisive critique of the dominant paradigm of the nineteenth-century historian, William H. Prescott, who emphasized Spanish exceptionalism—its religious fanaticism, tyranny, and indolence—in an effort to explain Spain's imperial decline, Kagan criticizes Américo Castro and his followers for making too much of Spain's Muslim and Jewish heritage, and for giving the conversos "inordinate attention." Conversos, according to Kagan, should be studied in

connection with early modern "Europe's other ethnic and religious minorities"—as if, presumably, their situation paralleled that of Protestants in France, for example. In their anxiety to make Spain appear just like the rest of Europe, Kagan and other early modern Hispanists seemingly ignore the profound transformation of Spanish society that occurred over the course of the fifteenth century and the equally profound social, religious, and cultural transformations that transpired in the sixteenth and seventeenth centuries as Old Christians, conversos, and Moriscos adapted to the new circumstances. One can scarcely understand the life choices made by Moriscos and conversos without a reasonably thorough knowledge of Muslim and Jewish life in Iberia prior to the sixteenth century; such knowledge is far more useful for comprehending early modern Spanish society and culture than comparing conversos and Moriscos with trans-Pyrenean Catholic and Protestant minorities. In their rush to downplay Spanish exceptionalism or persecution, Kagan and like-minded scholars threaten not just to miss important aspects of early modern Spanish society and culture but to present a distorted picture—though no doubt a comfortingly "European" picture—of it as well.

PART I

Christians and Jews in Muslim Spain

I

Muḥammad as Antichrist in Ninth-Century Córdoba

KENNETH BAXTER WOLF

BEATUS OF Liébana's *Commentary on the Apocalypse* is much more famous for the illuminations it would inspire than for the quality of its own exegesis.[1] And justifiably so, for the unbounded creativity of the artwork stands in marked contrast to the slavishly derivative nature of the commentary. Beatus was simply not an innovative exegete. As John Williams recently put it, he was a "cut and paste editor" who fashioned his commentary entirely out of passages drawn from earlier ones, in particular that of the late third-century African exegete Tyconius.[2] As Beatus himself humbly put it, "the things revealed in this book have not been revealed by me, but by the holy Fathers."[3]

But the simple fact that the commentary is so ordinary is, if one thinks about it, rather extraordinary given the general historical context within which it was produced. For it was written, it would appear, in the mid-770s,[4] that is, within two generations after the Muslim conquest of Spain. Given the character and magnitude of the events of 711, it is hard to imagine that a medieval Christian could have read the apocalyptic prophecies without seeing the Muslims on every page. And yet Beatus's commentary reads as if Ibn al-Ṭāriq and Mūsā ibn Nuṣayr had never left Morocco.[5] The interpretations that Beatus offered are, as Williams has observed, consistently "atopical,"[6] offering no realistic hope to the modern reader of connecting what Beatus saw in the text with what was happening in the world around him.

It is possible that the absence of any reference in the commentary to Islam or its leader is simply a function of the chronological limitations of Beatus's sources, the latest of which were the writings of Isidore of Seville. Although surviving Muḥammad by four years, Isidore seems to have known nothing about recent Arabian history. But the fact that the Latin documentation of eighth-century Spain as a whole is practically bereft of references to Islam as a religious phenomenon suggests that Beatus may simply not have regarded Islam as the kind of challenge to the peninsular church that would merit apocalyptic speculation.[7] Could this have indeed been the case?

When we look back to the year 711 from a vantage point almost 1,300 years later, it is hard to resist the temptation to describe the conquest of Spain as a *Muslim* conquest. Our modern perspective encourages us to see this event as the first and decisive step toward the "Islamization" of the southeastern half of the peninsula, a process that involved the slow but steady cultural gravitation of the region from the Latin-Christian world of Europe toward the Arabo-Islamic world of North Africa. As natural as it may seem to assign significance to past events in terms of their perceived relationship to later history, such a retrospective approach can obscure our understanding of how contemporaries, without the benefit of our hindsight, perceived the events as they were occurring. In this particular case to treat the conquest of 711 as a Muslim conquest can prove misleading in two ways. First of all, as Thomas Glick and others have shown,[8] there are real questions as to the religio-cultural status of the men who comprised the invading armies. How Muslim could they have been, given that the bulk of their members were ethnically Berbers who had been brought under Arab domination only a few short years before? What did it mean to be a Muslim anyway at a time when the jurists in the East were still engaged in the process of defining precisely what an Islamic society should or could be? Second, as I have tried to demonstrate on a number of earlier occasions,[9] the conquered peoples of Spain did not immediately conceive of the invaders from Morocco in religious terms. The original settlement of Arabs and Berbers was simply too sparse and, as a result, too militarily insecure to have any major immediate impact on the daily lives of the vastly larger Christian population. When contemporary Spanish Christian observers wrote about the conquest, they concentrated on its military and political consequences, not on its (at least potentially deleterious) effects on the Christian cult. Insofar as Christian authors were concerned about religious issues in the wake of the conquest—and the few surviving letters from the century after the invasion suggest that they were[10]—Judaizing and heresy dominated their concern, just as had been the case when Spain was ruled by the Christian kings of Toledo. When viewed from this perspective, the conquest of 711 might well not have prompted immediate associations in the minds of Latin intellectuals between the political subjection of the Christian population and the activities of Antichrist.

But by the ninth century things were changing. The conquerors, their numbers swelled by immigration, had not only managed to hang onto their Iberian conquests, but had established thriving urban centers in the Guadalquivir and Ebro valleys, as well as along the coastal littoral that connected the two. Commercial ties among these cities and those of North Africa and the Mideast brought not only material goods but cultural commodities that many Ibero-Christians found attractive. Because full participation in the culture and society of al-Andalus was, at least theoretically, restricted to Muslims, many urban Christians converted to Islam. Many others, it appears, participated in various aspects of Andalusian culture while retaining their Christianity.[11]

This was a tendency that at least some Christians living under Muslim rule found disturbing. In their efforts to stem the tide of cultural absorption, they did what they could to draw attention to its hidden dangers. A number of Cordoban Christians over the course of the 850s engaged in public denunciations of Muḥammad and his teachings and were put to death for blasphemy. This series of executions, known today as the "Cordoban Martyrs' Movement," disturbed many of the more assimilated Christians, who had managed to achieve a comfortable *modus vivendi* within the Arabo-Islamic society of Córdoba. They responded by denouncing the would-be martyrs as fanatical suicides. It was in response to the denigration of the executed Christians by their coreligionists that the priest Eulogius and his lay friend Paul Alvarus applied their literary talents to a defense of the martyrs. This defense required that the two apologists construct an unambiguously derogatory image of Islam, not only to justify the radical actions of the martyrs, but to embarrass those Cordoban Christians who felt at ease working within the framework of Arabo-Islamic society.[12]

Given the rigidity of the Christian intellectual framework within which these authors operated, it is not surprising that the tools they used to erect their negative images of Islam were for the most part those used by previous Christian polemicists for disparaging earlier threats to Christianity. Thus Eulogius concentrated his efforts on casting the Muslims as persecutors of the church of the classical pagan Roman type[13] and depicting Muḥammad as a false prophet who, like Arius, had challenged the divinity of Christ.[14] For his part Alvarus followed the parallel but distinct path of identifying Muḥammad with the Antichrist, by reinterpreting key passages in scripture. It is this equation of Muḥammad and Antichrist—the first of its kind in Latin literature—that is the subject of this essay. The creativity and "topicality" of Alvarus's exegesis—which stands in marked contrast to the derivative and ahistorical efforts of Beatus—allow us to treat his work as an artifact of the particular place and time in which he wrote. Thus Alvarus's commentary can be used to reveal not only something of how a medieval mind in general went about processing new information in terms of traditional patterns, but how much the medieval mind of Alvarus in particular knew about Islam.

Alvarus's commentary comprises the latter half of a treatise, called the *Indiculus luminosus,* that he wrote in 854 in defense of the Christians who were being executed for religious offenses against Islam.[15] The first half, which resembles the apologetic portions of Eulogius's own *Memoriale sanctorum* and *Liber apologeticus martyrum,*[16] attempts to vindicate the actions of the martyrs by creating a context within which those actions would make sense. Alvarus approached this task from two different directions. On the one hand, he underscored the duty of every Christian to confront religious error with the truth of the gospel and accused those who hesitated of being no better than collaborators.[17] On the other, he insisted that the restrictions placed upon the Cordoban Christians by the Muslim authorities amounted to a form of persecution no less significant than that sustained by the church in pagan Roman times. As such they merited the same martyrial degree of resistance on the part of good Christians.[18]

The second half of the *Indiculus luminosus* is dedicated to the scriptural reinterpretation in question. The first part treats passages drawn from chapters seven and eleven of Daniel, passages which had been identified in Jerome's *Commentarium in Danielem* as referring to Antichrist. A second portion focuses on the descriptions of the Behemoth and Leviathan found in Job and patristically explicated by Gregory.[19] Though significantly shorter, the section devoted to the Danielan prophecies is considerably more fecund when it comes to specific information about Islam. This may be due in part to the fact that Alvarus commented on the Daniel section first and simply wanted to avoid being redundant when he turned to Job. Or it may be that because Alvarus felt compelled to say something about each word of the rather lengthy Jobean descriptions of the two monsters, he found himself with no time to develop any single image. Be that as it may, I will be concentrating on the more promising initial portion related to Daniel.

My approach will be to offer an *explication de texte* of this portion of the *Indiculus luminosus* that will not only reveal the extent of Alvarus's knowledge of Muḥammad and his teachings but also demonstrate how he fit this information into a polemically serviceable framework. Alvarus began by quoting from the seventh chapter of Daniel:

> The fourth beast, which you have seen, shall be the fourth kingdom, which shall be greater than all the kingdoms. . . . The ten horns of the same kingdom shall be the ten kings. And another king shall rise up after them and he shall be more powerful than the previous ones, and he shall humble three kings and he shall speak words against the Heavenly and he shall destroy the saints of the Most High. And he shall think that he is able to change the times and the law. And they shall be surrendered to his hand for a time, times, and half a time.[20]

Alvarus then set out to connect this prophecy to what he knew about Islamic history and doctrine. The Muslim armies had clearly "humbled" many kings; the three that Alvarus picked were the emperor of the Greeks, the king of the Visigoths, and—for reasons that are not nearly as obvious, given what we are told about Charles Martel's good fortune at the Battle of Poitiers—the king of the Franks. Moreover Muḥammad had certainly "spoken words against the heavenly God":

> balancing things lofty and weaving them together with things murky, things that truly are antecedents of Antichrist and adverse to our humble religion; hoping to envelop in a nebulous fog the law of the Lord, shining with the light of miracles; weaving for his followers, with ridiculous audacity, as if by some command from God on high, unsubstantial stories worthy of laughter; fabricating fabulous things with a false pen, an impure façade, and theatrical favor, lies girded with neither truth nor the vigor of reason.[21]

Somewhere in the midst of this rather dense rhetorical flourish are clear indications that Alvarus knew that Muḥammad claimed to have received revelations from God and that they had been recorded for his followers. There is also an awareness that these revelations were reminiscent of Christian ones, insofar as Alvarus acknowledged that "lofty" things were being mixed with murky ones, and a "shining" law was being shrouded in fog.

That this Antichrist was "destroying the saints of the Most High" was, given the circumstances that elicited the *Indiculus luminosus* in the first place, obvious to Alvarus, "confirmed more by the evidence provided by [his] own eyes than by the eloquence of any exposition." Indeed one might interpret the defense of the martyrs in the first half of the treatise as an elaboration on this particular aspect of Muḥammad's biblically foreseen role. Alvarus took the opportunity provided by the last line of the prophecy to speculate as to when this ongoing "persecution" might end once and for all. The way Alvarus figured it, a "time" equaled seventy years (as Psalm 89:10), so one time plus two times plus one half time added up to 245 years. If, according to his sources, Muḥammad "rose up" in 625 and Alvarus was himself writing in 854, only sixteen years of the original 245 remained. In other words, Muslim persecution, presumably meaning Muslim domination, would end in 870.[22]

Alvarus did not take the time to elaborate on the significance of this calculation. Instead he turned quickly to Daniel 11:36–37: "He shall be lifted up and shall magnify himself against every god, and he shall speak great things against the God of gods. . . . And he shall make no account of the god of his fathers." All of this was rather easily adapted to fit Islam. Alvarus gave Muḥammad some credit for "making no account" of the idols that the Arabs before his time had worshipped. But in the same breath he chastised him for "composing a law . . . in his own name at the instigation of demons and, through dishonest pilfering, weaving a false third testament [the Qur'ān] for those who followed him."[23]

Nothing up to this point in this concise and relatively restrained commentary could prepare the reader for the extended and passionate (in more ways than one) diatribe that the next line from Daniel—"And he shall follow the lust of women"—would elicit. "Is there anyone," asked Alvarus, "who does not see how this passage refers precisely to this shameless one?" In the event that there might be, Alvarus took it upon himself to offer a detailed and singularly immodest "exposé" of the sexual profligacy that he felt characterized both Muḥammad's life and his law.

> In their disturbing teachings, these ones [that is, the Muslims] recount and babble, as if proclaiming something noble, that this pimp of theirs, preoccupied with the activity of seduction, had obtained the power of Aphrodite in excess of other men; that he had received as a gift from his god a more abundant "will of Venus" than others; that he had a greater quantity of liquid for his foul activities than the rest; that he could distribute this fluid with less effort than could other men; and that he had been given the endurance in coitus and indeed the abundance of more than forty men for exercising his lust for women. The foul, fertile abundance of his rank loins [came] not from God, the begetter of all things, as this most evil robber dreamed, but from Venus, the ridiculous mate of Vulcan, that is, from the wife of fire. She is called *Afrodin* on account of this foamy liquid and it is to her that venereal activity is ascribed. This shameless one [Muḥammad] called her *alkaufeit*. Excellent praise indeed! What an elegant gift of great carnality![24]

Where did Alvarus come up with all this? It is possible that he had access to Greek Christian works of anti-Muslim polemic, such as, for instance, al-Kindi, which is the only other known source of this time to devote so much attention to Muḥammad's sexuality.[25] But it is not essential to posit eastern influence, given the fact that by the ninth century Andalusian Christians had at least as many reasons and opportunities to develop their own critiques of Islam as their eastern counterparts did.[26] Alvarus could have discovered on his own that the deities worshipped in pre-Islamic Mecca included goddesses, the most prominent of which were al-Lāt and al-Manāt.[27] Given his desire to package the Muslims as pagan-style persecutors, and to discredit them as sexual deviants, it made perfect sense to identify pre-Islamic goddesses with the Greco-Roman goddess of love so familiar to Alvarus's audience.[28]

In any case Alvarus knew the story of Muḥammad's marriage to Zaynab, the former wife of his disciple Zayd, and proceeded to recount it, holding it up as the first and formative case of Muslim polygamy, a practice which, of course, Alvarus could not distinguish from adultery.

> All of those who come to the sect of this most foul one are transformed into pimps and adulterers, for in accordance with [his] orders, they break their marriage vows and come together again in adultery to their greater shame. By multiplying their mistresses and being subject to three or four wives, these seducers, or better yet pimps, all become whinnying horses and braying asses. Thinking it shameful to refuse any request, they applaudingly make licit for themselves everything they seek regarding women, usurping natural laws and seeking—woe is me!—new paths for their lust.[29]

The reference to horses and asses comes straight from Ezekiel and Jeremiah: "She was mad with lust to lie with them, whose flesh was like the flesh of asses and whose fluid was like the fluid of horses."[30] And "They became horses lovesick for their mares, each one whinnying after his neighbor's mate."[31]

Alvarus confessed to his reader at this point that "the redness of [his] cheeks" would not permit him to go on. He did not want "to lose, by means of [his] own words, the modesty which [the followers of Muḥammad] lack."[32] But that having been said, he immediately launched into yet another diatribe, even more titillating than the ones that had just made him blush, against the apparent carnality of the Islamic afterlife.

> There is no one so lost to his lusts and so soiled with the dirt of his sty as this pimp polluted with putridity. As we said, he enjoys the wives of other men like a pimp, concealing the scabbiness of his filth behind an angelic command, promising as a gift for those who believe in him harlots for the taking, scattered about in the paradise of his god; harlots bound by no limit in coitus so that the extreme heat [of passion] is not terminated in the usual space of one hour, but is multiplied by seventy times for the enjoyment of men—the same sort of flowing enjoyment that is typically associated with asses. The lethargic inhabitant of this paradise will have an increased [quantity of] fluid and a heightened sexual desire. And the virginity lost [by the harlot] through each act of coitus in the course of this prolonged villany will be restored, despite the perforation [of the hymen] by the inflexible reed, so that it may be of [further] service to those enjoying it. And neither the tearing of the ruptured hymen nor its remending will inflict terrible pain on those who undergo it, but will delight both [partners] with the sweetness of pleasure, furnishing their minds with even more desire to engage in it again, thus not curtailing but extending their renewed and ardent gluttony.[33]

The point of departure for this parody of the Islamic afterlife is, of course, the descriptions of *jannah,* or paradise, in the Qurʾān. In these celestial oases there will be "maidens, chaste, restraining their glances, whom no man or jinn before them has touched."[34] Alvarus would not have needed much more information about the *jannah* to unleash this diatribe, given the age-old tendency for Christian polemicists to account for the popularity of dissident movements by recasting divine inspiration as diabolic corruption and charismatic appeal as sexual attraction.[35] It should be noted that even after this mini-dissertation on Islamic sexuality, Alvarus still felt there was more to be said on the subject. Hence his promise to pursue the matter in a separate book dedicated entirely to this subject, "if God grants [us a long enough] life." Apparently God did not.[36]

Pushing on through Daniel 11, Alvarus came to verses 38 and 39: "He shall worship the god Maozim in his place . . . and he shall do this to fortify Maozim with a strange god, whom he has known." Now Alvarus knew from his reading of Jerome[37] that "maozim" meant "great" in Hebrew. And he knew, perhaps from his own independent investigation, that "*Allāh akbar,*" the most common repeated Arabic affirmation at the time of prayer, meant "God most Great." This was all that he needed to connect the two terms:

> Everyday they cry out, in this rite of savages, with an enormous and monstrous roar, shouting like madmen from their smoky towers, their dissolute lips and jaws thrown open as if belching, "so as to fortify Maozim with a strange god whom he has known."[38] Thus he has fortified Moazim with a name of veneration, calling him "Cobar" [*Akbar,* from *Allāh akbar*], that is, "the greatest." And [he has fortified him] with a strange god, that is, with the demon that appeared to him under the guise of Gabriel, so that he could conceal his error from the hearts of his believers and extoll, in the name of the great God, this ritual of shouting, and, through this superstitious effort, infect the souls of noble men with the evil spirit.[39]

Alvarus's demonization of Gabriel, whom the Muslims identified as Muḥammad's heavenly interlocutor, may simply reflect his reliance on "boilerplate" polemics inherited from previous champions of Catholic Christianity. It was certainly not unusual to see demons at work behind the authors of religious error. On the other hand, Alvarus may have been indirectly inspired by the Qur'ān, which contains occasional *apologiae* aimed at convincing its audience that Muḥammad was not inspired by the forces of darkness: "Your Companion is not one possessed," reads sūra 81:22–23, "and without doubt he saw him [that is, Gabriel] in the clear horizon."[40]

Alvarus had still not exhausted the exegetical potential of the term "Maozim."

> Consider how up to this very day they use the same word to refer to those days, dedicated to the same rite, on which they consecrate their insanity in the temple of their idol. Due to the fact that the Arabic language differs only slightly from the Hebrew in many words, these festivals are called "Almozem" [*al-mawsim*].[41]

The word "mawsim" originally meant "market," but because the great pilgrimage to the Kaʿbah was always, even in pre-Islamic times, associated with a great market or fair, the word came to mean "festival." Here the word is of interest to Alvarus primarily because of its phonetic similarity to "Maozim." In light of a recourse, similar to the practice of Isidore, to false etymology, it is interesting that Alvarus made nothing out of the similarities between "Maozim" and "muezzin" (*muʾadhdhin*), though his reference to prayer leaders "belching forth" from their "smoky towers" may have been all that his readers needed to make the connection for themselves. Alvarus continued:

> At this same time [each year], from long ago, this same people, placed among the nations, has hastened forth from all regions to the abovementioned idol, just as now the same lost multitudes rush to the same demon—which they regard as having been extracted from that place by the magnitude of their faith—and they serve it every year. They have worshipped Maozim "in his place"—just as the prophet [Daniel], [inspired] by the divine spirit, said [they would]—up to the present time, and they refer to these days by the accustomed name and call that month "Almorram," just as the worshippers of the idol previously established, so these ones today, with more abundant perfection—or so it seems to them—advance all the way to heaven.[42]

Again the sophistication of Alvarus's understanding of Islamic tradition radiates through the hostile rhetoric. Aside from correctly identifying the first month of the Muslim calendar (*al-Muḥarram*), he knew that the Kaʿbah, the goal of the Muslim hajj, had been the focus of pre-Islamic worship and that Muḥammad had appropriated the shrine in the name of Islam. This was all very convenient from Alvarus's polemical perspective, of course, since it allowed him to claim that Islam represented nothing more than a thin veil covering the kind of idolatry that had always been inimical to the Judaeo-Christian tradition.

Taking Alvarus's commentary on Daniel as a whole, it can, at one level, be dismissed as a gross manipulation of Islamic beliefs and practices. At another it must be appreciated as evidence for a remarkably detailed understanding of Islam on the part, not only of its author, but of his Latin Christian audience as well. For such a sophisticated parody would not have been necessary or even meaningful if the Christians whom Alvarus was trying to sway had little or no familiarity with Islamic culture or if they were already predisposed to reject it out of hand. This is an extremely important consideration for anyone seeking an accurate understanding of Christian views of Islam. For although the hostile polemics of an Alvarus or an Eulogius dominate the extant documentation pertaining to Christian-Muslim interaction in ninth-century al-Andalus, such sources cannot in fact be taken as typical of Andalusian Christian attitudes toward Islam. For such polemical works were written precisely to counteract attitudes that were less critical, even accepting, of Islamic culture, attitudes that we can assume were widespread even if they remained unrecorded. In this sense the context is more significant than the text, even though the text itself is essential for recreating the context.

Having considered in some detail the exegetical process by which Alvarus transformed Muḥammad into Antichrist, we have yet to weigh the possible apocalyptic implications of this identification. Can we take Alvarus's re-reading of Daniel as evidence that he thought the End was at hand? Here it is important to recognize that, long before Alvarus came along, Christian thinkers had developed two distinct traditions regarding the historical role of Antichrist. On the one hand, there was *the* Antichrist, the powerful figure who would play a dramatic role in the final act of Christian history. On the other hand, there were the Antichrists, or more technically, the *types* of the Antichrist, who would emerge from time to time throughout history as persecutors of the "chosen people," prefiguring the decisive persecution that would be implemented by the ultimate Antichrist.[43]

Jerome, Alvarus's principal model, had been very clear about this distinction in his own commentary on Daniel. He regularly distinguished between passages that described *the* Antichrist and those which were more properly understood as referring to Antiochus IV Epiphanes, the notorious Seleucid ruler who outlawed Judaism and desecrated the Temple in 168 B.C.E. For Jerome was well aware that historically the book of Daniel was a product of this particular period of persecution and revolt even if prophetically it could also speak of ages yet to come.

Alvarus accepted Jerome's *historical* identification of the eleventh king of Daniel 7 as Antiochus Epiphanes and told his readers as much. But he did not hesitate to recycle the same prophecy and apply it to Muḥammad as yet another "type" of Antichrist. For, as Alvarus pointed out at some length in the *Indiculus luminosus,* "many events from different time periods can be revealed in a single passage. . . . Indeed it befits better the wisdom of God and the Catholic doctrines that we keep [to say this], than if we were to say that the history of this insane man or of other kingdoms had not been prophetically foreseen."[44] Alvarus's effort to extend the category of Antichrist was assisted by the first epistle of John which noted that "even now," on the eve of the advent of the final Antichrist, "there are many Antichrists."[45] Hilary's treatise *Against the Arians* picked up on this theme and showed Alvarus how the term could be used against heresiarchs as well as kings and emperors: "We acknowledge, on the basis of the preaching of the apostle John, that there are many Antichrists. Whosoever denies Christ as preached by the apostles is an Antichrist. It is in the nature of the name Antichrist that he should be contrary to Christ."[46] It was for Alvarus simply a matter of perspective: "I think that Antiochus [Epiphanes], Nero, and the others whom the blessed doctors [identified] were indeed precursors of Antichrist. But if [these same doctors] lived in our time, they would also consider this one [Muḥammad] to be an instrument of Antichrist."[47]

That Alvarus followed faithfully in Jerome's footsteps, interpreting Muḥammad as a new "type" of Antichrist in the Antiochus tradition, is readily apparent when we compare his exegesis of the "he shall follow the lust of women" passage with that of Jerome. Jerome had begun his explication by pointing out an ambiguity in the original Hebrew text which allowed the same passage to be rendered "he understood nothing about lust for women." Jerome concluded that the ambiguity was deliberate, so as to allow for both historical possibilities. Jerome would go on to say:

> If we read and understand that "he understood nothing about lust for women," the easiest interpretation is that this refers to *the* Antichrist, because he will simulate chastity so as to deceive many. If, however, we read this as "he shall follow the lust of women," it fits [the specific figure of] Antiochus better, for he is said to have been most lustful, and to have arrived at such a level of shamelessness through the violations and seductions of his royal dignity, that he copulated in public with entertainers and prostitutes, satisfying his lusts in the presence of other people.[48]

For his part, Alvarus paraphrased Jerome's point about the ambiguity of the wording, agreeing that it was intended to cover both eventualities. He then proceeded to fit Muḥammad into precisely the slot that Jerome had prepared for Antiochus, albeit with considerable creative amplification.

Alvarus's decision to opt for Muḥammad as a type of Antichrist rather than as the Antichrist himself suggests that Alvarus was more concerned with disparaging Islam than he was with identifying his own times with the End. His very use of Daniel and Job, rather than the Book of the Apocalypse—perhaps a more obvious choice for anyone interested in interpreting contemporary history in light of eschatological prophecy—is itself suggestive, for both Daniel and Job offer descriptions of Antichrist that can be considered apart from predictions about his future cosmic role. Alvarus's decision to cut short his treatment of Daniel 7 after verse 25 also fits this hypothesis nicely, since, had he continued, he would have had to say something about the rendering of judgment after the fall of the "eleventh horn." Even Alvarus's algebraic calculation of the duration of Muslim rule lacks apocalyptic punch, again offering no speculation as to what one might expect to happen after those sixteen years had elapsed.

The point of Alvarus's commentary, in short, was less to make Muḥammad the Antichrist than to make the Islamic society within which he lived seem "Antichristian." Its purpose was not to suggest to its readers that their troubles as Christians living under the yoke of Antichrist were about to end with the coming of a New Age. It was to make them see that the Muslim-dominated world to which they had begun assimilating was antithetical to their identities as Christians, and that it had, therefore, to be summarily rejected. This is where Alvarus's famous lament, which is to be found at the very end of the *Indiculus luminosus,* fits in.

> What educated person, I ask, can be found today among the laity of our faith who, attentive to the holy Scripture, explores the Latin volumes of any of the doctors [of the church]? Who is there who burns with evangelical, prophetic, or apostolic love? Do not all the Christian youths, handsome of face, fluent of tongue, conspicuous in their dress and gestures, outstanding in their knowledge of gentile erudition, and sublime in their ability to speak Arabic, most avidly pull down the volumes of the Chaldeans, read them most intently, discuss them ardently, and, collecting them with great zeal, make them known far and wide

> with the praises of their tongues, while at the same time remaining ignorant of ecclesiastical beauty and disdainful of the rivers flowing from the paradise of the church as if they were something vile.[49]

Faced with what we, from our modern vantage point, might consider to be an inevitable process of cultural absorption, Alvarus fought it the only way that he knew how. He reconstructed the apparent attractiveness of Arab-Islamic culture as a diabolically inspired threat to Christian culture; and he interpreted the signs of assimilation that he must have seen around him every day—the clothing, the language, the literature—as the "marks of Antichrist." Hence he placed value on the examples set by the Christians who were being executed for publicly blaspheming Muḥammad. Their resistance to the enticements of an "antichristian" culture was every bit as heroic as that of the martyrs who suffered at the hands of the Romans.

In the end we are left with a polemical treatise in the guise of an apocalyptic one, one that is in its own way as useless as Beatus's *Commentary on the Apocalypse* for assaying the impact—if indeed there was any—of the Muslim invasion on Iberian eschatology. For if the work of Beatus is clearly apocalyptic, it lacks specific reference to the events of Beatus's own day. On the other hand Alvarus's commentary on Daniel is full of historical reference points, but its use of apocalyptic imagery appears to have been deliberately subsumed to the specific needs of a treatise aimed at defending the martyrs and criticizing the assimilated Christians. In the end it would seem that Beatus and Alvarus are more alike than they might, at first glance, appear. For neither one of them really knew what to do with Islam in the grand scheme of sacred history.

NOTES

1. For a recent and intelligent overview of the commentary and the interpretive issues it raises, see John Williams, "Purpose and Imagery in the Apocalypse Commentary of Beatus of Liébana," in *The Apocalypse in the Middle Ages,* ed. Richard K. Emmerson and Bernard McGinn (Ithaca, 1992), 217–33.

2. Ibid., 218–19. Though a Donatist, Tyconius set the pace for Latin treatments of the Apocalypse by charting a middle course between exclusively allegorical and narrowly historical interpretations. For a discussion of the influence of Tyconius's commentary, see Paula Fredriksen, "Tyconius

and Augustine on the Apocalypse," in Emmerson and McGinn, *The Apocalypse,* 20–37.

3. Henry A. Sanders, ed., *Beati in Apocalipsin libri duodecim* (Rome, 1930), 1–2.

4. Ibid., 221.

5. As Williams has pointed out, at the very least we might have expected some mention of Islam in the section enumerating Christian heresies at the beginning of the second book ("Purpose and Imagery," 227).

6. Ibid., 219.

7. Kenneth Baxter Wolf, "The Earliest Spanish Christian Views of Islam," *Church History* 55 (1986): 281–93.

8. Thomas Glick, *Islamic and Christian Spain in the Early Middle Ages* (Princeton, 1979), 165–93.

9. Kenneth Baxter Wolf, *Conquerors and Chroniclers of Early Medieval Spain* (Liverpool, 1990), 28–45; Wolf, "Earliest Spanish Christian Views," 281–93.

10. Juan Gil, ed. *Corpus scriptorum mozarabicorum* [hereafter *CSM*], 2 vols. (Madrid, 1973), 1:55–124.

11. For a recent analysis of the Islamization of Spain, see Mikel de Epalza, "Mozarabs: An Emblematic Christian Minority in Islamic Al-Andalus," in *The Legacy of Muslim Spain,* ed. Salma Khadra Jayyusi (Leiden, 1992), 159–60.

12. For detailed treatments of the Cordoban Martyrs' Movement, see Kenneth Baxter Wolf, *Christian Martyrs in Muslim Spain* (Cambridge, 1988); Franz Richard Franke, "Die freiwilligen Märtyrer von Cordova und das Verhältnis der Mozaraber zum Islam (nach den Schriften des Speraindeo, Eulogius und Alvar)," *Gesammelte Aufsätze zur Kulturgeschichte Spaniens,* 26 vols. (Münster, 1928–71), 13.1–170; and Edward P. Colbert, *The Martyrs of Córdoba (850–859): A Study of the Sources,* doctoral dissertation, Catholic University of America, 1962.

13. Colbert, *Martyrs of Córdoba,* 77–85.

14. Wolf, *Christian Martyrs,* 88–91.

15. Paulus Alvarus, *Indiculus luminosus* [hereafter *IL*] in *CSM* 1:270–315.

16. *CSM* 2:363–459, 475–95.

17. *IL* 1, 8–11, *CSM* 1:272–73, 280–85.

18. *IL* 3–7, *CSM* 1:274–79.

19. Gregory, *Moralia in Job,* 31.28; 32.17; 33.10, 14, 18; 34.19.

20. Daniel 7:23–25.

21. *IL* 21, *CSM* 1:294.

22. *IL* 21, *CSM* 1:294–95.

23. *IL* 22, *CSM* 1:296.

24. *IL* 23, *CSM* 1:296–97.

25. Both refer to Muḥammad as having the virility of forty men (Franke, "Die freiwilligen Märtyrer," 128). For an effort, albeit an often strained one, to uncover the possible eastern influence on Alvarus's polemical work, see Feliciano Delgado, "Albaro y la polémica contra el Islam," *Axerquía* 12 (1984): 237–48.

26. As far as we know, this began with Alvarus's teacher, Abbot Speraindeo (Wolf, *Christian Martyrs*, 532–33).

27. *Shorter Encyclopaedia of Islam*, ed. H. A. R. Gibb and Johannes H. Kramers (Leiden, 1974), 287, 325.

28. John of Damascus, among other anti-Muslim polemicists in the East, also made the connection between the Kaʿbah and the worship of Aphrodite (*De haeresibus*, 101). According to Franke, this refers to *al-kaukaba*, Arabic version of Syriac *kawkabta:* "female (or morning) star;" but this seems to me to be quite a stretch (Franke, "Die freiwilligen Märtyrer," 128–29).

29. *IL* 23, *CSM* 1:297.

30. Ezekiel 23:20.

31. Jeremiah 5:8.

32. *IL* 23, *CSM* 1:29.

33. *IL* 24, *CSM* 1:297–98.

34. Sūras 37:48, 38:52, 44:54, and especially 55:56.

35. See Norman Cohn, *Europe's Inner Demons* (New York, 1975), 1–15.

36. *IL* 24, *CSM* 1:298.

37. Alvarus admits elsewhere that he did not know Hebrew (*Epistola* 16.4, *CSM* 1:237).

38. Daniel 11:39.

39. *IL* 25, *CSM* 1:298–99.

40. Qurʾān 81:22–23.

41. *IL* 25, *CSM* 1:299.

42. Ibid.

43. Richard Kenneth Emmerson, *Antichrist in the Middle Ages: A Study of Medieval Apocalypticism, Art, and Literature* (Seattle, 1981), 21–33.

44. *IL* 22, *CSM* 1:295.

45. 1 John 2:18.

46. Hilary of Poitiers, *Contra Arianos* 2.

47. *IL* 34, *CSM* 1:312.

48. Jerome, *Libri commentariorum in Danielem*, 11:37.

49. *IL* 35, *CSM* 1:314–15.

2

Reading the Repartimientos: *Modeling Settlement in the Wake of Conquest*

THOMAS F. GLICK

IN THE WAKE OF the conquest of al-Andalus, the kings of Aragon and Castile set in motion a total reordering of the rural landscape.[1] From the time of the conquest of Majorca (1231) on, this reordering was documented in a distinctive series of land registers called the *Llibres del Repartiment/Libros de Repartimiento,* which are certainly unprecedented in any country of medieval Europe because they provide a moving picture over four centuries which documents a cross-cultural transfer of landscape. In a certain sense, so does the *Domesday Book,* inasmuch as that famous inventory was supposed to establish the pattern of English land tenure as it had been in the time of the Anglo-Saxon King Edward. But *Domesday*'s rationale was quite different: it was first and foremost an instrument whereby the king might know what feudal dues were owed him. But both series share the registration of landholds across a cultural divide.[2] A prime distinction here, however, is that while *Domesday* records fiefs, many *Repartimientos* record the lowest level of landholding, down to individual peasant parcels (or to units—*cuadrillas*—of peasant parcels). This was because, unlike the situation in England where ceorls/villeins remained on their ancestral holds, the Castilian and Aragonese monarchs had to replace, in many places, one entire population by another. This is especially true of Andalucía, where the kings of Castile attempted to implant a free peasantry. Thus the usability of houses and estates by settlers was perhaps the overriding criterion of the *Repartimientos.*[3]

The *Domesday Book* records two very different principles of settlement and land distribution, one seigniorial, the other territorial.[4] While the distinction also appears in the *Repartimientos,* the emphasis is on territorial rather than seigniorial space, although there is some notational overlap, to be sure. We can also recognize that the *Domesday* series is generally richer in the kind of raw economic and social data that medievalists like and are familiar with. (The historical geographer H. C. Darby was said to have boasted he'd counted every pig in England.[5]) Much of this information is lacking in the *Repartimientos,* except perhaps in some later registers for Andalucía where fruit trees are enumerated.[6]

Culturally, England remained substantially Saxon, whereas Spain underwent a profound cultural change. As a result, and in view of the general lack of detailed local records in Arabic, the *Repartimientos* are invaluable as a source for both re-creating the lost landscape of al-Andalus and evaluating the ensuing modal change in the ordering of the countryside.

Here I will comment on how these books have been used to further that re-creation, to what extent they document an Andalusi model of landholding, and in what ways they reveal (or do not reveal) the replacement model that the Christian conquerors imposed on the conquered landscape. In this endeavor, I will rely primarily upon the registers dealing with Majorca, Valencia, Orihuela, Murcia, Seville, and Loja.[7] I will also comment on the early modern books of *Apeo* and *Repartimiento* of Granada in which were recorded the land transfers taking place after the expulsion of the Moriscos from the kingdom and which, both technically and conceptually, represented a continuation of the same process of landscape change already described.

THE *ḤIṢN/QARYA* MODEL

That *Repartimientos* have not been used to their fullest potential is owing to the fact that there was no model of the agrarian landscape of al-Andalus until the 1980s when medieval archeologists working mainly in Majorca, the Valencian region, and the province of Almería generated one which has proven susceptible to confirmation by historians working from the documentary record. This model, which I will call the *ḥiṣn/qarya* complex portrays a rural landscape whose nodal points are fortified structures or castles (*ḥuṣūn;* singular, *ḥiṣn*), which served as security for a number of villages or *alquerías* (*qarya;* pl. *qurà*), generally six to ten.[8] These *alquerías,* at least in their formative periods, were settled by clans or tribal segments, mainly Berber, which held and worked their territories collectively, according to tribal norms well understood in anthropological literature. Thus in Majorca and Valencia in particular, there was a profusion of *alquerías* with place-names in the form of Beni-, "sons of," indicative of settlement by a clan.[9] Furthermore, in the three areas studied, there was a statistically significant tendency for such *alquerías* to practice irrigation agriculture, whatever other elements of agriculture—dry farming, arboriculture, or pastoralism—they may also have practiced. Alongside *alquerías,* particularly in the environs of cities, were parcels called *rahal*/s, which were private estates owned by wealthy individuals, usually associated with state offices.[10]

Here I would like to make a brief historiographical digression. The practice of "extensive archeology," which concentrates on surface features rather than on traditional stratigraphic methodology and which has produced such striking, even revolutionary, results in the survey areas mentioned, was the result of the energies unleashed by Pierre Toubert's conception of *incastellamento* (which was an invitation to look at castles as a social phenomenon) and the famous Rome meeting of 1978.[11]

In Spain, these energies were diffused by French scholars working under the aegis of the Casa de Velázquez (Pierre Guichard, André Bazzana, Patrice Cressier), and their perspective then spread to historians working in eastern Spain and Granada. This revolution took place at the same time as the old "liberal" doctrine of feudalism associated with Sánchez Albornoz was being overthrown in the 1970s and 1980s. Therefore the reassessment of feudalism in Catalonia and Valencia, closely tied to Pierre Toubert and *incastellamento,* was expressed in an explanatory framework whose centerpiece was the contrast between the function of castles in feudal Catalonia/Valencia on the one hand, and non-feudal, "tributary" al-Andalus on the other. Among Castilian medievalists, however, the reassessment of feudalism took place in isolation from the *incastellamento* debate, and therefore the break with the "liberal" model has been conceptually more narrowly focused on issues of dependency, rather than on overall social organization.[12]

This model has generated a fierce polemic which in its general contour has pitted the archeologist/historians against Arabists and which has its roots in the professional cultures of the contending groups of scholars. Arabists are trained philologically and practice a kind of hypercriticism which makes it easy to defeat almost any etymology, particularly a Berber one. They also tend to support a reflexive, pre-packaged view of medieval Islamic society that discounts the significance of tribalism in the organization of tributary states and views the countryside as organized around cities whose culture is purely Arabic and whose social organization is absolutely standardized.[13]

In the *ḥiṣn/qarya* model, the *ḥiṣn* is non-feudal in character; that is, its primordial function is not to control the surrounding countryside, except in a limited sense of sporadically functioning as a center for tax collection, but rather to serve it as a refuge in times of danger. This function was initially deduced from the morphologies of the *ḥuṣūn:* they had huge open spaces within their walls, called *albacar/*s, capable of holding considerable populations both of people and livestock, while the castle itself was not fitted for housing permanent garrisons. The *qā'id* in charge of a *ḥiṣn* normally did not reside there, except in certain frontier situations.

When one looks at *systems* of *ḥuṣun,* rather than just local configurations, it becomes clear that they were not primarily defensive in the usual sense of the word. Even in an area like the presentday province of Castellón which was permanently exposed to military incursions from Catalonia and Aragon, the castles were not, as a group, oriented towards the fighting frontier.[14]

Virtually all elements of the model have been attacked by Arabists, including the function of *ḥiṣn* and *albacar;* the nature of governmental control in a tributary state; the veracity of a tribal model of settlement and, thus, the meaning of the Beni-toponyms, and so forth. Yet, now after approximately fifteen years have passed since the model was formulated, its high heuristic value in the interpretation of documents has led an ever-expanding circle of medievalists to conclude that the model is basically true, particularly as current research continues to identify new *ḥiṣn/qarya* complexes and incidences of *alquerías* with Beni- names in many parts of the peninsula. It is now time to put an end to these skirmishes and invest more energy in testing the model.

REPARTIMIENTO BEFORE THE *LIBROS*

I will begin my review of the *Repartimiento* literature with a brief discussion of the partition of property in Toledo following upon the conquest of that city, a process which was accomplished without the compilation of such registers or which did not require them to be preserved, even if some must have been generated at the time.[15] The area south of Toledo, as described by Julio González, consisted in large part of *alquerías* which had been abandoned for so long that the names of the former owners were not known and the structure of property was difficult to determine. *Repartimiento* was accomplished by *Juntas de Partidores* in Toledo and in the towns that adopted its *Fuero*. These *Juntas* held inquests and dispatched surveyors (called *sexmeros, quinoneros, cuadrilleros,* etc.) whose job was to break down larger units into smaller ones.[16] González notes that in large *secano,* wheat-farming *alquerías,* the fields were undivided or with only a few divisions. If such *alquerías* were donated whole, they were divided into halves, thirds, or fourths, with further subdivision left up to the grantee. There was also a tendency in the time of Alfonso VII to join two *alquerías* together to make villages of a certain size and density, a process which, according to González, broke the structure of quite a few *latifundios* encountered by the Castilians.[17]

What González appears to have been describing here, but was unaware of, was territory which had no *metes* and bounds not because it was comprised of *latifundia* but which rather consisted of *alquerías* that had been held previously by clan groups farming collectively. It is probable that even in this dry-farming region, the countryside had been organized in *ḥiṣn/qarya* complexes. González documents a number of place-names within *ḥiṣn,* such as Exnavexore, or Aznaron (= *ḥiṣn Hārūn*), as well as the descriptive use of the word: the citadel of Toledo was called Alhicen; houses were donated in Monzón, *in illo alhizen de illo castello* (1090), and in Calahorra (1074), within the Alhicen.[18]

González's account of the rural landscape of New Castile is similar to his earlier account of the *Repartimiento* of Seville, which also suffered from the lack of a model of agrarian space in al-Andalus. Here, in spite of the massive documentation afforded by that *Repartimiento,* González's description of the rural landscape is strangely disjointed. There is no sense of a hierarchy of settlements. His definition of *alquería* here is "A rural entity which maintained unity, at least partial, of property. The majority were preserved whole." The concept of unity is basic for appreciating not only the physical deployment of the settlement (boundaries, parcellization patterns), but also to the built areas.[19] This unity of structure, however, he associated with Roman centuriation (the prevalence of lots of thirty *yugadas* suggested a regularity of partition within the logic of centuriation).

Rather than bracketing Andalusi history and presuming such scarcely unchanged Roman surveying patterns, it is more to the point to associate the features he describes with *alquerías* which, in origin at least, had been undivided. Certain *alquerías* or parts thereof did indeed have Beni- names, for example Quintos Abençunit, a barrio of Benimahmut.[20] There are also a number of suggestive *ḥiṣn* placenames within the *alfoz* of Seville, including Aznalfarache, Aznarcóllar, and Aznalcázar.[21] What the *Repartimiento* of Seville describes is an Islamic landscape, deprived of its social basis, in the process of losing its coherence, as *alquerías* were merged, absorbed into the city, and so forth. González also describes, without fully understanding their significance, parcels called *machar* (Ar. *majshar*), which were compounded with personal names, such as Machar Almanzor or Machar Alcadi (*machar* of the judge).[22] These *cortijos* seem to be the equivalent of the Valencian and Murcian *rahal:* a single estate owned by a wealthy or prestigious individual, presumably associated with the state.

González in both the cases of New Castile and of Seville gives an account of the pre-existing landscape which is too undifferentiated to provide any conceptual basis for analyzing the change in model. He realizes there must have been some underlying organizational model and chooses, inappropriately in my view, a Roman one.

THE *REPARTIMENT* OF MAJORCA

The baseline for the evaluation of the Andalusi rural landscape is established in the earliest of the books of *Repartimiento,* that of

Majorca, which survives in Arabic, Latin, and Catalan versions.[23] In the *Repartiment,* all the measures are given in jovates (1 = 11.36H), so it is possible to derive ratios among different kinds of settlements. Poveda Sánchez compared *alquerías* to *rahal*/s and found that the former were considerably larger (7 versus 4 jovates, or 83.7 v. 49H). The distinction between *alquería* and *rahal* was not clear to the Catalans and almost immediately they lost their specific meanings.[24] He then looked at *alquerías* with Beni- names (92 of them from the *Repartiment,* plus 98 more from complementary documentation; 65 *rahal*/s also had Beni- names), and found that in area they clustered around the mean for all *alquerías* of 7.63 jovates. That means that statistically, Beni-named *alquerías* represent the mean type of exploitation.[25] The proper names compounded with Beni- suggest that the majority of these settlements were Berber due to the late occupation of the island and known waves of Berber settlement under the Almoravids and Almohads.[26]

The Christians changed the agrarian landscape immediately. In Majorca, wherever there was a preponderance of irrigation agriculture, there is a general presumption of a retrocession of irrigation, not because Christian peasants did not know how to irrigate or were not as adept at it, as the myth goes, but because feudal rent, which was normally taken in measures of grain, was the tail wagging the dog of peasant settlement. The feudal tax structure, that is, demanded a certain level of investment in cereal-culture. Whether such crops were irrigated or not (as they certainly were in Aragon) is another question.[27] The demand for grain also set up a situation of positive feedback where the need for additional water for milling acted as a further constraint on irrigation. Nor was there any land in Muslim Majorca specifically set aside for grapevines, which were considered just another garden crop. The lords did not like garden vegetables which were difficult to commercialize. Hence they did not tax village *horts,* a further indication of how changing tastes and values can force a severe shift in agrarian regimes. Land use in thirteenth-century, post-*Repartiment* Majorca was approximately 31 percent in irrigation, 30 percent in vineyards, 30 percent in arboriculture, and an unknown amount in dry-farmed cereals. We can deduce, since Christians for all intents introduced grapes, that Muslim agriculture had been split between irrigated *horts,* where some cereal grains were grown, and arboriculture.[28]

In terms of the morphology of rural settlement, grants were in the form of dispersed fragments; the process of *repartimiento* tended towards parcellization of *alquerías* presumably encountered in the form of undivided, communally worked fields.[29]

THE *REPARTIMENT* OF VALENCIA

The Valencian *Repartiment* covers the entire kingdom.[30] In Valencia both *alquerías* and *rahal/*s are well defined. *Alquerías* typically had ten to fifty houses: in irrigated areas they were quite small (half a square kilometer to two and a half), while some of the mountainous arboriculture *alquerías* were quite large, nine kilometers square (e.g., Benilloba, 9.26K; Benasuau, 9.5K). Of 150 agricultural places in the *huerta* of Valencia mentioned in the *Repartiment,* two thirds are *alquerías,* one third *rahal/*s. The latter were much smaller than the former and had personal names.[31] *Alquerías* were collectively worked and had no fixed territorial limits—what Robert I. Burns refers to as the "amorphous *qarya.*"[32] Christian settlers were normally granted three jovates (*ca.* 9 hectares), which were agriculturally mixed, including some *huerta* and vineyards near the settlement, cereal fields farther away. Whenever it was the rule to mix land use in the composition of lots, that implied in practice the maintenance of parcellary dispersion and of the size of preexisting parcels.[33] Therefore, the Christian post-*Repartimiento* agrarian landscape tended to physically resemble the Muslim one preceding it. But land tenure was quite a different matter. Directly after the *Repartiment* immediate social stratification ensued under conditions of a very active market in land. The atomization of parcels that followed made the Islamic *alquería* unrecognizable, as individual ownership replaced collectivity as the organizing principle of tenure. As had been the case in Majorca, Christian cultivators concentrated their efforts on cereals and grapevines, to the prejudice of *huertas* (even though these were mainly free of dues). It was at this point, in Torró's view, that Mudejars, in order to pay their taxes, began irrigating wheat, in that wheat could be dry-farmed.[34]

In a masterful study of the feudal transformation in Alcoi, Torró shows how this new town, of Christian foundation, rose on the same space formerly occupied by a *ḥiṣn/qarya* complex. Of twelve newly delimited agricultural zones surrounding the town, six corresponded to old Andalusi *alquerías,* occupying from between 72–90 hectares (quite close to the mean of 83.7 that Poveda Sánchez had found in Majorca). These settlements were irrigated by the *Acequia de Barxell* whose course wound around under the *ḥiṣn,* now known as El Castellar. Forty percent of the parcels granted out to Christian settlers were small, irrigated ones, half of which were in the Horta d'Alcoi. Grapes were planted on terraces that were lower with respect to *huertas* and irrigated with excess water. There was a vast expansion in cereal cultivation over what the Muslims had formerly cultivated. As elsewhere, there was an immediate tendency towards fragmentation of holdings and dispersion of parcels.[35]

With respect to *alquerías,* there were two modes of partition. Either they were seigniorialized, granted whole to lords, or they were apportioned by small parcels. The latter mode was much more disturbing to Mudejar society. Even when, directly after the conquest, Muslims remained in place, their *alquerías* were atomized into single family units: the original undivided and unbounded *alquerías* were now surveyed and parceled out.[36] Thus, although the *Repartiment* may give a sense of continuity of population in Mudejar rural communities, discontinuity was apparent: the parcellization of *alquerías* represents a formal pressure towards social destabilization (detribalization).

Orihuela and Murcia

These were *Repartimientos* ordered by Alfonso X, even though Orihuela soon after became part of the Crown of Aragon. In Orihuela there was a wholesale replacement of the Muslim population by Christians. There was a general policy of aggregating two, three, and up to six *alquerías* to make a *cuadrilla* which became the basis for a new administrative unit. An interesting aspect of the *Repartimiento* of Orihuela is that the royal officials found substantial tracts of land which had "never been surveyed in the time of the Moors." All of this land lay in *alquerías* with Beni- names: Benmira, Benamoquetib, Benijües, and so forth. One settler is recorded as wanting to fence (*tapiar*) his property, another indication of an *alquería* that had previously been undivided. The fields in question were in the limits between the *huerta* and the sea, marshy land that is difficult to stabilize for irrigation.[37]

In Murcia, where the *Repartimiento* only covers the *huerta* itself, there was a high incidence of *minifundios* (that is, parcels of no more than 200 square meters), reflecting the high level of parcellization typically prevailing in highly productive irrigated areas of al-Andalus.[38] Here again, the traditional *alquería* array was broken by the composition of *cuadrillas* as the basis of a new administrative order. Here we detect something like what F. W. Maitland, in reference to *Domesday*, called "notional movability" of parcels.[39] That is, some *cuadrillas* never acquired the designed judicial independence, but were integrated into neighboring ones. These *cuadrillas* were organized to fit the irrigation system; each one was dependent on a specific *acequia* which acquired the name of the parcels it irrigated.

ANDALUCÍA

To return to the *Repartimiento* of Seville: it is mainly a rural document which shows (according to González Jiménez) the concentration of property in a few hands in Almohad times.[40] Once again, I must express my doubts about Muslim "latifundia" and wonder whether or not these same documents can be read for evidence of undivided *alquerías,* which is just what one would expect of recently settled Berber tribesmen, as in Majorca, for example. The same author's account of the modal change in agrarian settlement would seem to support the later view: with so much Muslim emigration in the wake of conquest, the old settlement pattern of rural population based on many small population nuclei, *alquerías,* disappeared and was replaced by a much more concentrated pattern. Of 160 *alquerías* recorded in the Aljarafe, for example, only thirty were repopulated. Hence, the *Repartimientos* did not create *latifundia.*[41]

There are only a few places in the *Repartimiento* of Seville where *metes* and bounds of village *términos* are recorded, leading to the supposition that *alquerías* tended not to be demarcated in al-Andalus into the thirteenth century.[42] Between the *Repartimiento* of Seville and that of Loja (1486), where *metes* and bounds are provided for many places, it is clear that the nature of land tenure in al-Andalus had been changing, evolving towards individual ownership, juridical definition of *alquerías,* and towns, associated no doubt with the breakdown of tribal society and its typical modes of land tenure and village organization. By the end of the fifteenth century, *alquerías* (in Nasrid Granada) had lost their homogeneous and communal nature, endogamy yielded increasingly to exogamy, and as a result *alquería* parcels were increasingly dispersed, a trend enhanced by the ever-growing roster of parcels held by *habices* or religious trusts.[43] When Christian *repartidores* surveyed Loja in 1487 along with a half dozen Muslim former residents sent by the king of Granada, it is clear that boundary markers between *términos* were already in place, as the Muslims guided the Christians from one to another. In both Loja and Comares *término* boundaries were determined not only by obvious markers like *atalayas,* towers and wells, but by the broad contours of watersheds, with water flowing in one direction marking the bounds of one town, that in the opposite direction, its neighbor.[44] It is also clear in the case of Comares, that grazing land—still communal—had never been surveyed, inasmuch as the Christian *repartidores* are depicted as placing markers along *cañadas* and measuring them with cords (*sogas*).[45]

The fifteenth-century Granadan *Repartimientos* reveal an increasing pace of privatization of agricultural property resulting in a modal change in the organization of *alquerías* in the Nasrid kingdom. The other two elements of the *ḥiṣn/qarya* complex, the castle and the irrigation systems, had also changed. First, more castles may have been permanently garrisoned because of defense considerations. Second, the privatization of water rights documented in the *Libros de Habices* suggests substantial degradation in the Berber communal model of rights, although it did not influence the operating procedures of irrigation systems.

Questions of tenure aside, the Christian conquest of Granada appears not to have induced much change in the Muslim agricultural system. With regard to the eastern mountains (Yznalloz, Piñar, and Montexicar), Peinado finds no evidence that Castilian settlers eliminated fruit trees, nor did they consider *regadío* to be cereal space. The Nasrids themselves had encouraged the irrigation of cereals in order to reduce chronic flour deficits. Thus the agricultural style later attributed to the Castilians already existed in this area before they arrived.[46]

In the two centuries that intervened between Ibn al-Khaṭīb's description of Granada and the early sixteenth century, the number of *alquerías* in the vega diminished from 300 to 71.[47] After the Christian conquest, Morisco *alquerías* continued to be characterized by the predominance of clans, by the cultivation of fields according to traditional techniques, and the communal use of pastures. However, the clan was not the strong tribal segment of old and family groups tended to disperse and to own property in more than one *alquería.* There was an enormous admixture of lineages throughout fifteenth-century Granada, to the point where the correspondence between the founders of a place and its current population had practically disappeared, even though Luna Diaz found some *alquerías* in which one family owned between a quarter and a half of the land. Once undivided family property was fragmented by inheritance, dowry, or sale. Social status came to rest increasingly on wealth rather than on lineage.[48] From fifteenth- as well as sixteenth-century evidence, therefore, it is clear that as tribalism broke down, privatized landholdings emerged, as demonstrated by the availability of private properties for religious trusts.

Luna Diaz found the mean number of houses in Granadan *alquerías* of the sixteenth century to be 140, with a density of 125 persons per square kilometer in irrigated areas, 13 for unirrigated. He found tremendous parcellization of agricultural land throughout the vega: in *alquerías* near the city the average parcel size was 2.9 square meters, with average holdings of around .82.[49]

After the second Alpujarras revolt, the Moriscos were expelled from the kingdom of Granada and all their possessions passed into royal ownership by a provision of February 24, 1571. A supplementary *Cédula,* issued on September 27, stipulated that previously existing agricultural practices were to be preserved: new settlers had to farm according to the custom of their new place of residence and to preserve irrigation arrangements intact.[50] Barrios and Burriel reached three general conclusions regarding the nature of agrarian change and continuity across the process of *Repartimiento.* First, the typical Morisco *minifundio* was attenuated as individual *suertes* were generous. Second, there was initial equality among the settlers, according to social class, just as had been characteristic of the medieval *Repartimientos.* Third, the process of accumulation and fragmentation (together with the typical land market which, we have seen, arises after *Repartimientos*) favored certain groups more than others and introduced inequalities. But, they go on to say, these changes were not accompanied by any significant change in the pattern of parcellization. Since the rules laid down by the king specified that each lot had to have a mixture of parcels, the general dispersion and size of parcels was maintained.[51]

I have deliberately followed the fortunes here of only one element of the *ḥiṣn/qarya* complex. The other two elements also suffered changes across the transition. The *ḥuṣun* themselves were made over to reflect the reality of feudal organization. When Christians took them over they generally rebuilt them to be able to house a castellan and permanent garrison whose function was to dominate the zones of *alquerías,* politically and economically. When new castles were built, they were much smaller, lacking the huge *albacar*/s of the Muslim *ḥuṣūn.*[52]

The third element was irrigation. Here there is a paradox: even in those places where there was retrenchment of irrigated garden agriculture and where its share of the total sector lost out to cereals and vineyards, the distribution regimes were kept intact. In some cases, instructions regarding irrigation arrangements were included in the *Repartimiento* itself, as in this passage from that of Orihuela:

> [It is ordered] that all the property owners of Orihuela, not only those who have grants, but also the other residents, be made to clean and repair the drainage ditches and the large and small irrigation canals of the territory of Orihuela, so that the water might flow without impediment just as it flowed in the time of the Moors. And let them apportion the water by *tahullas* to each one as he had it, just as they lawfully had in the time of the Moors. We order them to seize the properties of those who do not wish to obey and give them to whoever will uphold custom and neighborly duty. And if anyone should force the irrigation officers [*acequieros*] to give them water, let them forfeit their persons and everything they have to the king.
>
> Furthermore we order that no one dare to plant grapevines in those irrigated places that are for cereals. Those who so plant, let it be taken for the king.[53]

It is particularly clear in this passage, that it was royal policy "to uphold custom," in this case, that of the antecessor Muslim irrigators.

In other instances, discrete inquests were held, such as the one conducted by Peregrín de Atrosillo in 1244, after the conquest of Gandía, in which Atrosillo quizzed Muslim irrigators regarding the apportionment of water among the various communities irrigating from the Serpis river.[54]

Operating procedures thus displayed considerable continuity, even though the tribal model of governance that everywhere prevailed in the irrigation communities of the Muslim world had to be replaced by one modeled on guild organization. In Bizar, a Muslim *alquería* near Guadix known by the Christians as Policar, a dual system of water rights arose in the 1490s, a Muslim one dating to a twelfth-century apportionment of water and a Christian one based on a royal decree of 1494 establishing guidelines for water officials (*alcaldes de aguas*). Litigation ensued between the two groups of irrigators.[55] But this kind of dispute was quite rare in post-conquest irrigation.

Various of the *apeos* made after the expulsion of the Moriscos from the kingdom of Granada in the 1570s recorded irrigation procedures and water rights. An *apeo* of Tafira Zufla, a Morisco *alquería,* in 1574 included an enumeration of irrigation rights on its final day. The following year Loaysa's *apeo* of Aindamar, a district of the city of Granada, was designed to determine water rights in order that there be a return to the "order and custom prevailing in the times of the Moriscos."[56]

The *Repartimientos,* considered as a chronological series, reflect changing land tenure patterns in al-Andalus which have yet to be analyzed.[57] They also record a tenurial revolution of major proportions where Christians replaced Muslims, although the impact of the latter upon the agrarian landscape, with respect to morphology of fields, parcellization, and dispersion of parcels, was less disturbing and is still felt today.

Although I am in general agreement with the new doctrine of feudalism which holds that the level of peasant dependence in Spain was about on a par with that of countries of the feudal heartland,[58] I must also agree with Pierre Guichard and Manuel González Jiménez that the *Libros de Repartimiento* do not reflect it. They are not feudal documents. As I remarked above, they overwhelmingly document topographic rather than seigniorial space. Only Majorca, with its detailed list of the appurtenances of the fief of Nunyo Sanç, for example, approaches the quality and tenor of classical feudal land registers.

Overly zealous avatars of the new feudalism see the malevolent tentacles of feudal aggression spreading everywhere. Yet the *Repartimientos* are decidedly non-feudal both in character and objectives.[59] Thus, in Valencia, Guichard notes the large segment of free property that the kings of Aragon sought to implant in the form of *hereditates* granted free and quit of any royal or seigniorial dues. If that freedom weakened towards the end of the thirteenth century with the steady progression of seigniorialism, that does not obviate the original objectives of the *Repartiment* to implant free townsmen and peasants.[60] Likewise, González Jiménez, with respect to Andalucía, criticizes those who posit reflexively that conquest led necessarily to seigniorialization. The overwhelming mass of settlers were free men, free from archaic feudal services, with no substantial noble inroads until the end of the thirteenth century.[61] Thus in both Valencia and Andalucía, we can perceive a gradient of feudalization, as the original objectives of the *Repartimientos* were submerged, against the original intent of royal policy, by the rising tide of seigniorialism, by the harshness of frontier life, and by a voraciously active land market that did not favor the small, rural freeholder.

NOTES

1. For a more extensive survey of the *Repartimientos,* see my book *From Muslim Fortress to Christian Castle: Social and Cultural Change in Medieval Spain* (Manchester, 1995), chapter 6.

2. There has been some interest by *Domesday* scholars in the land registers of Norman Sicily, but only with regard to what in my view is a minor point. They wanted to know if Normans elsewhere relied on pre-conquest land registers, whether Saxon or Arab. Clearly, there are more interesting questions to be asked of Sicilian registers. See Dione Clementi, "Notes on Norman Sicilian Surveys," in *The Making of Domesday Book,* ed. Vivian H. Galbraith (Oxford, 1961), 55–58; Sally Harvey, "Domesday Book and Its Predecessors," *English Historical Review* 86 (1971): 765.

3. Julio González notes ruined vills or houses in New Castile: Julio González, *Repoblación de Castilla la Nueva,* 2 vols. (Madrid, 1975–76), 2.284–88. See also Manuel Barrios Aguilera, *Libro de los Repartimientos de Loja* (Granada, 1988), 59: "alcaria caida." There is an analogy here with *Domes-*

day which notes whether a field or vill is devastated (*wasta est terra, mansiones vastatae,* etc.), but again the particular interest is in value, not usability per se (Henry Clifford Darby, *Domesday England* [Cambridge, 1977], 234, 236, 238).

4. See Robin Fleming, *Kings and Lords in Conquest England* (Cambridge, 1991), 154–62.

5. Whether or not the story is apocryphal, the warrant for it comes directly from the Anglo-Saxon Chronicle's boast that "nor even . . . an ox, nor a cow, nor a swine was left that was not set down in his writing."

6. As in the *Repartimiento de Almería,* ed. Cristina Segura Graíño (Madrid, 1982). The counting of trees revives a tradition of the Roman census wherein, according to the *Digest,* the number of vines and olive trees were counted (John Percival, "The Precursors of Domesday: Roman and Carolingian Land Registers," in *Domesday Book: A Reassessment,* ed. Peter Sawyer [London, 1985], especially pages 12ff).

7. A much expanded version of this essay comprises chapter 6 of my *From Muslim Fortress to Christian Castle.*

8. See both for Valencia and Almería: André Bazzana, Patrice Cressier and Pierre Guichard, *Les châteaux ruraux d'Al-Andalus* (Madrid, 1988). Guichard points out that the two terms are so tightly linked that the same place may be described as *ḥiṣn* in one Arabic source, *qarya* in another. *Ḥiṣn* implied a group of *qarya*/s (Pierre Guichard, *Les musulmans de Valence et la reconquête [XI*^e^*–*XIIIe siècles], 2 vols. [Damascus, 1990–91], 1.189).

9. The polemics over the significance of Beni- names, whether they are Arab or Berber, whether they date to early times or only to the more recent period of Almoravid and Almohad settlement, or whether these tribal entities continued to segment in the thirteenth century, are all irrelevant to the nature of land tenure the Christians found there, namely unbounded, unsurveyed *alquerías* which can be presumed to have been worked, in some fashion, collectively.

10. Pierre Guichard, "A propos des rahals de l'Espagne orientale," *Miscelánea medieval murciana* 15 (1989): 11–24.

11. See the Spanish edition of selected articles from that meeting: Pierre Bonnassie et al., *Estructuras feudales y feudalismo en el mundo mediteráneo* (Barcelona, 1984).

12. Peter Linehan's assessment of the new doctrine of feudalism is wide of the mark, in part because he takes the story only to 1980 and in part because he comments only on Castilian historiography which he deems victimized by "academic Marxists." He regards it as ironic that medieval León/Castile is now regarded as a fully feudalized society, just when for the rest of Europe "the twin dogmas of normative feudalism and the fundamental uniformity of feudal institutions have been abandoned" (*History and Historians of Medieval Spain* [Oxford, 1993], 191–200, especially p. 197). Most of

Linehan's critique of the historiographical revolution in Spanish feudalism is tendentious and unsubstantiated.

13. See in this respect, María Jesús Rubiera and Míkel de Epalza, *Xàtiva musulmana* (Játiva, 1987), and María Jesús Rubiera, *La Taifa de Denia* (Alicante, 1985). In both cases, the view of urban life presented is stereotypical and based on the supposition that life in any medieval town was identical to life in any other. The model of urban society presented is generic and similar to that of Gideon Sjoberg, *The Preindustrial City, Past and Present* (New York, 1960).

14. André Bazzana and Pierre Guichard, "La frontière du Sharq al-Andalus," in *La Marche supérieure d'Al-Andalus et l'occident chrétien* (Madrid, 1991), 82–83; where the population was most dense (in the south of Castellón), so was the network of *ḥuṣūn.* The frontier with Aragon was defended by only three *ḥuṣūn,* that with Catalonia, four.

15. There is also a technological reason for the lack of any *Libro de Repartimiento* and why the *Repartiment* of Valencia (1238) was the first such register: the "paper revolution" that had such a profound effect on royal administration began only after the Muslim paper mills at Játiva had fallen into King Jaume's hands (Robert I. Burns, *Society and Documentation in Medieval Valencia: Diplomatarium of the Crusader Kingdom of Valencia: The Registered Charters of Its Conqueror, Jaume I, 1257–1276, I: Introduction* [Princeton, 1985], 48–50, 151–61). The *Repartiment of Mallorca* (1232) like the eleventh-century *Domesday Book,* is written on vellum.

16. González, *Repoblación de Castilla la Nueva,* 2.162, 164, 174, 175, 180ff.

17. Ibid., 2.176, 178, 311. The amalgamation of small holdings into more viable units and "the combining of divided vills into a single holding" were hallmarks of the *Domesday* grants (Fleming, *Kings and Lords,* 122, 150).

18. González, *Repoblación de Castilla la Nueva,* 2.224, 291. Houses *in* the *ḥiṣn,* suggesting that an *albacar* is meant.

19. Julio González, *Repartimiento de Sevilla,* 2 vols. (Madrid, 1951), 1.396.

20. Ibid., 1.416, 2.44.

21. Ibid., 1.388. Note the curious semantic doubling in Aznalcázar (= *ḥiṣn al-qasr*).

22. Ibid., 1.423, 2.45. See also a *Rahal al-qāḍī* in Valencia (Guichard, *Musulmans de Valence,* 2.384).

23. For the Arabic version, see Jaime Busquets Mulet, "El códice latino-arábigo del Repartimiento de Mallorca" (texto árabe), in *Homenaje a Millás Vallicrosa,* 2 vols. (Barcelona, 1954–56), 1.243–300. Busquets also published the Latin text: "El códice latinoárabigo del Repartimiento de Mallorca (parte latina)," *Bolletí de la Societat arqueològica lul.liana* 30 (1947–52): 6–55. For the Catalan version, Ricard Soto i Company, ed., *Còdex català del Llibre*

del Repartiment de Mallorca (Palma de Mallorca, 1984). Although the conquerors must have had access to Arabic land *dīwān*/s in some places, this is the only surviving Arabic specimen, although it covers only Palma and its immediate environs. All three versions have the limitation of covering only royal land. Hence, a good complementary document is the register of lands granted to an important magnate (*La remembrança de Nunyo Sanç: una relació de les seves propietats a la ruralia de Mallorca,* ed. Antoni Mut Calafell and Guillem Rosselló Bordoy [Palma de Mallorca, 1993]).

24. Angel Poveda Sánchez, "Introducción al estudio de la toponimia árabe-musulmana de Mayurqa según la documentación de los Archivos de la Ciutat de Mallorca (1232–1278)," *Awraq* 3 (1980): 96.

25. Ibid., 84–85, 95–96.

26. Ibid., 83, 95.

27. See, in this regard, Pierre Ponsot, "Les Morisques, la culture irrigué du blé et le problème de la décadence de l'agriculture espagnole au XVIIe siècle," *Mélanges de la Casa de Velázquez* 7 (1971): 237–62.

28. Ricard Soto i Company, "Repartiment i repartiments: l'ordenació d'un espai de colonització feudal a la Mallorca del segle XIII," in *De Al-Andalus a la sociedad feudal: los repartimientos bajomedievales* (Barcelona, 1990), 1–51, especially 37–38.

29. Ibid., 30.

30. *Libre del repartiment del Regne de Valencia,* ed. María Desamparados Cabanes Pecourt and Ramón Ferrer Navarro, 2 vols. (Zaragoza, 1979).

31. According to Pierre Guichard in *Nuestra historia* (Valencia, 1980), 2.269ff and *Musulmans de Valence,* 2.375–85.

32. Robert I. Burns, *Muslims, Christians and Jews in the Crusader Kingdom of Valencia* (Cambridge, 1984), 215–23. Of course, the *qarya* was not amorphous, just unbounded. Thus it appeared inchoate to Christian eyes.

33. Manuel Barrios Aguilera and Margarita M. Burriel Salcedo, *La repoblación de Granada después de la expulsión de los Moriscos* (Granada, 1986), 52. I believe this rule holds true for medieval, as well as for early modern *Repartimientos.*

34. Josep Torró, *Poblamenti i espai rural: transformacions històriques* (Valencia, 1990).

35. Josep Torró, *Alcoi: la formació d'un espai feudal (de 1245 a 1305)* (Valencia, 1992), 45, 50, 162, 208, 211–12, 265.

36. Guichard in *Nuestra historia,* 3.29; Josep Torró, "Sobre ordenament feudal del territori i trasbalsaments del poblament mudèjar. La *Montanea Valencie* (1286–1291)," *Afers* 7 (1988–89): 107.

37. Juan Torres Fontes, "Los Repartimientos murcianos del siglo XIII," in *De Al-Andalus a la sociedad feudal,* 88; Juan Torres Fontes, ed., *Repartimiento*

de Orihuela (Murcia, 1988), 89 ("Fue fincada por mala terra que negun la quiso tomar en las otras particiones et auya y dellas mucha que en tempo de moros nonqua foron sogueadas . . . ").

38. Torres Fontes, "Repartimientos murcianos," 76. The text of the *Repartimiento* was edited by Juan Torres Fontes, *Repartimiento de Murcia* (Madrid, 1961), 33.

39. Fredric W. Maitland, *Domesday Book and Beyond: Three Essays in the Early History of England* (Cambridge, 1907; reprinted London, 1961), 33.

40. Manuel González Jiménez, "Repartimientos andaluces del siglo XIII: perspectiva de conjunto y problemas," in *De Al-Andalus à la sociedad feudal,* 102.

41. Ibid., 106–107, 113.

42. Thus the *hereamiento* of Alcalá de Guadayra is one of the few places to be described with *metes* and bounds, suggesting it had been surveyed in Muslim times (González, *Repartimiento de Sevilla,* 2.128). See also a grant by Alfonso X specifying that the *término* of this place will be the same as it had been in the time of the Moors (p. 359).

43. Antonio Malpica, "De la Granada nazarí al reino de Granada," in *De Al-Andalus a la sociedad feudal,* 122, 133.

44. Barrios Aguilera, *Libro de los Repartimientos de Loja,* 56, 59 (see also note 2). Francisco Bejarano-Robles and Joaquín Vallvé, ed. *Repartamiento de Comares (1487–1496)* (Barcelona, 1974), 2–4, 42ff.

45. Bejarano-Robles and Vallvé, *Repartimiento de Comares,* 64ff.

46. Rafael G. Peinado Santella, *La repoblación de la tierra de Granada: los montes orientales (1485–1515)* (Granada, 1989), 103–104.

47. Juan Andrés Luna Diaz, "La alquería: un modelo socio-económico en la vega de Granada. Aproximación a su estudio," *Chrónica nova* 16 (1988): 81.

48. Ibid., 92, 95; Antonio Malpica Cuello, *Turillas, alquería del Alfoz seixitano* (Granada, 1984), 15–16, 22–23; Manuel Acién Almansa, "Reino de Granada," *Historia de los pueblos de España: tierras fronterizas, I: Andalucía, Canarias,* ed. Miquel Barceló (Barcelona, 1984), 49.

49. Luna Diaz, "La alquería," 89, 92.

50. Barrios and Burriel, *Repoblación de Granada,* 32, 39.

51. Ibid., 51–52.

52. Pierre Guichard, *Estudios sobre historia medieval* (Valencia, 1987), 120, 201.

53. Torres Fontes, *Repartimiento de Orihuela,* 51.

54. Roque Chabás, *Distribución de las aquas en 1244 y donaciones del término de Gandía por D. Jaime I* (Valencia, 1898).

55. Manuel Espinar Moreno, "Bizar: una alquería musulmana y el paso al dominio cristiano (siglos XII–XVI)," *Actas del V Coloquio internacional de historia medieval de Andalucía* (Córdoba, 1988), 707–18.

56. Manuel Barrios Aguilera, *Moriscos y repoblación en las postrimeras de la Granada islámica* (Granada, 1993), 138–39, 188.

57. In *From Muslim Fortress to Christian Castle,* I survey the *Repartimientos* in chronological order, from that of Majorca to those of sixteenth-century Granada, after the expulsion of the Moriscos. By so doing, I was able to perceive changes in Muslim land tenure regimes reflected through the Christian surveys.

58. Thomas F. Glick, *Cristianos y musulmanes en la España medieval* (Madrid, 1991), 277–82. Since writing that, a better acquaintance with the *incastellmento* literature has deepened my commitment to a view of a substantially feudalized Spain. Compare the views expressed in my *Islamic and Christian Spain in the Early Middle Ages* (Princeton, 1970), 210–14, which I no longer accept.

59. Again, if one compares the *Repartimientos* as a whole with the *Domesday Book,* there can be no doubt of this assertion.

60. Pierre Guichard, "Quelques notes à propos du repeuplement de Valence," in *Coloquio de la V asamblea general de la Sociedad española de estudios medievales* (Zaragoza, 1991), 131.

61. Manuel González Jiménez, "Repartimientos andaluces del siglo XIII: perspectiva de conjunto y problemas," in *De Al-Andalus à la sociedad feudal,* especially p. 117; and "Conquista y repoblación de Andalucía, Estado de la cuestión cuarenta años después de la reunión de Jaca," in *Actas, V Asamblea,* especially pp. 245–46.

3

Maimonides and the Spanish Aristotelian School

JOEL L. KRAEMER

ANDALUSIAN AFFINITIES

Abū ʿImran Mūsā ibn Maymūn al-Qurṭubī (al-Isrāʾīlī al-Andalusī), as Maimonides was known to Arab authors, was in the core of his being—as legal scholar, physician, and philosopher—an Andalusian. He lived in Egypt for nearly forty years and gained new vistas there, and he was totally immersed in the cultural life of his Arab-Islamic milieu, moving in the highest intellectual and ruling circles of Cairo. Friend of Saladin's erudite vizier al-Qāḍī al-Fāḍil and of the eminent judge and poet al-Qāḍī ibn Sanāʾ al-Mulk, Mūsā ibn Maymūn also served as physician in the royal entourage. But however assimilated to Egyptian life and manner, coming from the West, his speech, dress, and demeanor surely betrayed him as a foreigner—an Andalusian.

Like his fellow Cordoban Averroës, he was proud of his Andalusian heritage, conscious of his Andalusian origins. Maimonides lived in al-Andalus (Andalusia) for only ten years (1138–1148), but he spent another twenty-five in the Maghrib; and Andalusia and the Maghrib formed a single *Kulturkreis.* Indeed, when Maimonides uses the expression *ʿindanā fī l-maghrib* ("*chez nous* in the Maghrib") concerning legal practice or linguistic usage, he thinks of "Maghrib" as including Andalusia.[1]

Maimonides places himself squarely in a Spanish tradition of learning at the beginning of the *Letter to Yemen,* where he gently ripostes his interlocutors' innocent flattery by modestly proclaiming his inferiority to his countrymen: "I am the least of the sages of Sefarad whose adornment has been brought low by Exile." He looked to the sages of Sefarad as his authorities in legal matters.[2] Foremost among his Andalusian masters in jurisprudence (along with his father) were the esteemed Rabbi Isaac Alfasi and his great Lucenan heir Rabbi Joseph ibn Megas, whom Maimonides reverently called "my teacher." For Maimonides, Andalusian scholars had virtually eclipsed the Babylonian geonim. Jewish scholarship had been transported from the East to Andalusia, and Córdoba rivaled Baghdad in intellectual splendor, much as learning in the Islamic world had been transferred from East to West in the tenth century. By the twelfth century, Andalusian culture in Arabic and Hebrew was well racinated, and Abū al-Walīd ibn Rushd and Mūsā ibn Maymūn were confident, but their Andalusian insistence may still have been tinged by what the literary scholar Harold Bloom called an "anxiety of influence," expressing itself as a quest for independence and superiority over influential past authorities.

Maimonides extols the philosophical heritage of Andalusian Jews because they quite properly kept philosophy and theology asunder. Discussing philosophy and *Kalām,* he observes (expressing an *odium theologicum* for the latter):[3] "As for the Andalusians among the people of our nation,[4] all of them cling to the affirmations of the philosophers and incline to their opinions, in so far as these do not ruin the foundation of the Law. You will not find them in any way taking the paths of the *Mutakallimūn.*" The statement is hardly true; for Andalusian Jews, like Joseph ibn Saddiq and Baḥya ibn Paqūda, wandered down some Kalamic paths.[5] Maimonides' hyperbole merely accents his cultural bias and intellectual *parti pris.*

In medicine, Maimonides displays a Western orientation. He studied medicine in the Maghrib before coming to Egypt, had high regard for Maghrebi physicians, and refers in his medical works to practices he witnessed there.[6] His *Sharḥ Kitāb al-ʿUqqar* is a product of an Andalusian—but also Egyptian and common Mediterranean—environment. He gives the names of pharmaceuticals in Arabic, Greek, Spanish (even colloquial), Berber, and vernacular Egyptian, whilst omitting Hebrew.[7]

Maimonides' knowledge of mathematics and astronomy also locates him in an Andalusian ambience. Among works on mathematics which Muslim authors ascribe to Maimonides,[8] al-Qifṭī mentions Maimonides' revision of al-Muʾtamin ibn Hūd's *Istikmāl.* The author, a scholar and scientist (d. 1085), was of the Hudid dynasty of Saragossa, of the *mulūk al-ṭawāʾif* (*reyes de Taïfas*) in eleventh-century Spain. A member of the Ibn Hūd family taught the *Guide* to a circle of Jews in Damascus.[9] Maimonides studied astronomy in Spain and was in touch with a student of Ibn Bājja and with a son of the astronomer Jābir ibn Aflaḥ, and edited an astronomical treatise of Jābir.[10]

Maimonides' Andalusian moorings come to vibrant expression in his fervor for language and fondness for poetry. This observation may be for some a shock or revelation since the current scholarly portrait of Maimonides as serious and solemn, indeed somber, has obscured the vivacity of his wit. However, to overlook the humor and irony in Maimonides is to miss something precious and essential. Intrigued by contradiction and paradox, he could say that if you ascribe emotions and deficiencies to God (like anger), he will be *angry* with you.[11] As we shall see below, the dilemmas and puzzles—the *aporiai*—embedded in the fabric of the heavens, built into the nature of the universe, engendered in him an aptitude for skeptical wonder and suspension of belief.

His *jue d'esprit* is vivid in his correspondence with his pupil Joseph b. Judah.[12] Teacher and disciple exchanged allegorical letters written in rhymed prose, linguistically embellished with subtly irreverent biblical allusions (by way of desacrilization of the text) and even the *de rigeur* (for Andalusians) erotic connotations. This was a scintillating scholarly battle of wits. One must relish the Andalusian ambience to savor this properly.

Maimonides' familiarity with poetry is confirmed by a letter discovered in the Cairo *Geniza.*[13] A friend writes, expressing longing and love (*maḥabba*) for Maimonides, conveying his feelings by citing a poem of friendship with erotic overtones written by Judah Halevi for *Moses* ibn Ezra. We know that Maimonides was familiar with Judah Halevi's theological work *al-Kuzari.* We now have evidence (if it was needed) that he also knew Halevi's poetical oeuvre. Indeed, he cites a line of verse from a poem ascribed to Halevi in his letter to Samuel ibn Tibbon: "[If they knew his ancestors, they would say]/It is an excellence transferred from father to son."[14]

The newly discovered letter thus features a facet of Maimonides' personality generally slighted—his poetic, emotional, and spirited side.[15] Scholarly consensus mistakes Maimonides' occasional disapproval of poetry as evidence that he held this literary genre in disdain.[16] For an Andalusian, disdain for poetry is *prima facie* implausible. Maimonides' exquisite rhymed prose, evident in his letters to Rabbi Anatoli, to the Sages of Lunel, and in his letters to Joseph b. Judah, show his skill in this medium.

Maimonides ascribes his fondness for poetry to his Sefardic upbringing. In a charming digression in a letter to the Sages of Lunel Maimonides apologizes (*soi-disant*) for writing in rhymed prose. He refers to ways that are not right in his eyes, the ways of female and male singers and words of enigmas and parables—"for all our brethren, the men of Sefarad, turn to [the way of singers], and our Sages have said, "If you enter a town, follow its customs—*in 'alt le-qarta hallekh be-nimuseh.*"[17] Maimonides apologized here for rhymed prose, but consider that he also wrote poetry.[18] Maimonides' *esprit* is quintessentially Andalusian. He was moored in Andalusia in more ways than one.

In the philosophical domain, our paramount concern, Maimonides remained anchored to problems that he first encountered in Andalusia and the Maghrib.[19] In his letter to Samuel ibn Tibbon, where he directs the young man's studies, Maimonides intimates his own philosophical priorities. He is strongly Aristotelian, participant in the Andalusian revival of Aristotle initiated by Ibn Bājja, a legacy which reverts in some of its features to al-Fārābī in the East. Maimonides scans the field, from al-Fārābī and Ibn Sīnā in the East to the Andalusian philosophers in the West.[20] He silently omits his Andalusian Jewish predecessors (Ibn Gabirol, Abraham ibn Ezra, Abraham ibn Daud), with the exception of Joseph ibn Saddiq, whom he respected, without however seeing his work. This part of the letter we may cite verbatim because it places his Aristotelianism and Andalusian affinities in proper perspective.[21]

> Be careful not to study the works of Aristotle without the commentaries on them, the commentary of Alexander [Aphrodisias] or that of Themistius, or the commentary of Ibn Rushd. However the books you mentioned to me that you have with you, including the *Book of the Apple*

and the *Book of the House of Gold,* are all drivel, inane and vapid. These two books are spurious works ascribed to Aristotle. The *Book of Divine Wisdom,* which [Abū Bakr] al-Rāzī wrote, is authentic, but it is useless, for al-Rāzī was merely a physician. The same is true of the *Book of Definitions* and the *Book of Elements,* which Isaac Israeli composed; they too are drivel, inane and vapid, for Isaac Israeli was also only a physician. However, the *Book Microcosm,* which R. Joseph ha-Saddiq composed, I have not seen, but I knew the man and his discourse,[22] and I recognized his eminence and the value[23] of his book, for without doubt he followed the system of the Sincere Brethren.[24]

In general, I say to you: Do not concern yourself with books on logic except for what the philosopher Abū Naṣr al-Fārābī composed; for all that he wrote in general, and in particular his *Principles of the Existent Beings,* is wheat without chaff, and one should pay attention to his words and understand what he says, for he was exceedingly wise. Likewise, Abū Bakr ibn al-Ṣāʾigh is a great philosopher, and his words and compositions—"all are straightforward to the intelligent man, and right to those who have attained knowledge."[25]

The books of Aristotle are the roots and principles for these compositions on the sciences, and they are not understandable, as we have mentioned, except with the commentaries on them, the commentary of Alexander or Themistius, or the commentary of Ibn Rushd. But as for other compositions, such as the books of Empedocles, the books of Pythagoras, the books of Hermes, and the books of Porphyry—all these are ancient philosophers on which it is not worth wasting one's time.

The discourse of Plato, the teacher of Aristotle, in his books and compositions, contain enigmas and parables and are also dispensable for an intelligent man; for the books of Aristotle his pupil serve for all that was composed before them. And his opinion—I mean to say, the opinion of Aristotle—is the ultimate of human opinion, save for those who received the divine emanation so that they attained the rank of prophecy, which is the highest rank. The books of ʿAlī ibn Sīnā, although they are accurate and contain subtle speculation, are not like the books of Abū Naṣr al-Fārābī. His books are nevertheless useful. He too is a man whose discourse you should study and whose compositions you should scrutinize. I have guided and instructed you concerning what you should study and wherein you should occupy your precious mind. May your peace, my friend, son and pupil, increase; and may salvation be at hand for a poor and miserable people. Written by Moses, son of R. Maimon, the Sefardi, may the memory of the righteous be a blessing, on 8 Tishre 1511 S.E. Peace.

Maimonides wrote this letter after having completed the *Guide*. His high commendation of al-Fārābī and Ibn Bājja, his emphasis on Averroës' commentaries on Aristotle, and his assessment that Avicenna was *useful* indicate from where he was coming.

THE TWELFTH-CENTURY ANDALUSIAN SCHOOL OF ARISTOTLE STUDIES

Maimonides belonged to the twelfth-century Spanish school of Aristotelian philosophy, which (for the most part) traced itself embryonically to al-Fārābī rather than Avicenna.[26] The pioneer of the Aristotelian revival in Spain was Abū Bakr ibn Bājja (Avempace) (d. 1139), and he was followed by Ibn Ṭufayl (d. 1185) and Ibn Rushd (Averroës, d. 1198). These Spanish Aristotelians were translated into Latin and had a vital impact on Latin Scholastic philosophy.[27]

This Spanish Aristotelian school shared a common Aristotelian matrix; it was not a school in the formal or institutional sense. It shared a system of ideas, similar source material, and terminology, a common set of definitions and problems, and a shared method of discussing these problems.[28] A Neoplatonic component influenced Aristotelian metaphysics, and the concept of "Neoaristotelianism" is quite appropriate.[29] Moreover, the political philosophy of the Spanish school was emphatically Platonic.

Philosophy under Wraps

Maimonides alerted the reader to his esoteric philosophical style, explaining his aim and providing us with keys to decipher his meaning. He was not unique in using this rhetorical device. An exoteric-esoteric binarity pervades medieval Arabic and Hebrew thought and is well represented in the Spanish experience. Frank Talmage viewed the polarity of *nigleh* (*ẓāhir*) and *nistar* (*bāṭin*), or exoteric and esoteric, as a dominant binarity in the medieval Jewish world influenced by Islamic culture—in Spain, Provence, and (by extension) Italy—calling allegory not simply a hermeneutic mode but "a state of mind, and not merely a way of looking at the world but a way of constructing the world." And Talmage cites Maimonides' splendid embellishment of the verse in Proverbs 25:11: "A word fitly spoken is like apples of gold in settings of silver," and the Sage's interpretation of this: "a saying uttered with a view to two meanings is like an apple of gold overlaid with silver filigree—work having very small holes."[30]

The biblical commentaries of Abraham ibn Ezra and Moses ben Nahman (Nahmanides) bristle with esoteric allusions. Ibn Ezra's esotericism was rational, with allegorical references to philosophical meanings; and Nahmanides' esotericism was mystical, intimating mythical and theosophic ideas and ushering us into the atmosphere of the Andalusian esoteric work par excellence—the *Zohar.* Philosophical and mystical esotericism is native to Muslim Andalusian culture from the time of Ibn Masarra and his school through the great Ibn ᶜArabī and his followers. Andalusian poetry, whether in Arabic or Hebrew, tends to vacillate imperceptively from love objects that are male to those that are female, and from human to divine. Layers of silver filigree have to be peeled away to reach the apples of gold.

The Marrano experience of Jews in late medieval Spain instances this duality of inward and outward and makes sense against the background of the rhetorical esotericism of philosophers and the prudent dissimulation (*taqiyya*) practiced by minorities in the Islamic world. Thus the question of Spinoza's esotericism and whether it should be understood against his family's Marrano background becomes almost impossible to answer. The medieval sources he read so avidly, like Maimonides and Ibn Ezra (whose esotericism he well understood), placed him in that mode and mentality even if we prescind from any Marrano effect. The classical esotericist maneuver of equivocating between a philosophical concept and a more popular and religiously acceptable one, which Spinoza adopted, had been used to good effect by Maimonides. Moreover, the pervasive influence and power of late medieval Jewish Averroism, not to mention Cartesianism, was sufficiently potent to contribute toward Spinoza's kind of rationalism and naturalism, his pantheism and immanentism.[31] Marrano esotericism was existential, like Shiᶜite *taqiyya;* Spinoza's esotericism was philosophical, not existential. Spinoza did not practice a Marrano-like existential esotericism but rather lived as he believed, without presenting a mask of devout Judaism or Christianity to the world. I raise this point here because it seems to me proper to view Spinoza in a broader Spanish context rather than against the special backdrop of the Marrano experience. We may well place him in the tradition of Andalusian esotericism and Averroistic naturalism and rationalism for which we have ample documentary evidence.

Esotericism was a mode of expression that fit many needs. When history is viewed as typological, as a congeries of prefigurations and fulfillments; when nature is regarded as emblematic and reflective of higher realities; when the words of Scripture are considered as vessels bearing deeper meanings—esoteric communication becomes natural and even inevitable.

Philosophical writing was done with circumspection because of the threat of persecution. Owing to the atmosphere of danger, Andalusians pursued philosophy with caution, the target audience being an elite, privileged coterie. We have explicit evidence for this in the Spanish environment. The eleventh-century judge and litterateur Ṣāᶜid al-Andalusī wrote: "All who were active in the study of philosophy reduced their activities and kept, as secret, whatever they had pertaining to these sciences."[32]

And so the twelfth-century Spanish school labored under strenuous conditions of suppression in a region straining under a long tradition of persecution. After the cultural burgeoning in the days of ᶜAbd al-Raḥmān III and his son al-Ḥakam II, at the time of the latter's son Hishām, a certain Abū ᶜĀmir ibn Abī ᶜĀmir, the *ḥājib* (chamberlain), who became, in effect, head of state, campaigned against freedom of thought, purging al-Ḥakam's library of works offensive to religious scholars.

The ominous precedent is related in detail by al-Ṣāᶜid al-Andalusī. He tells that the *ḥājib* Abū ᶜĀmir usurped the power of Hishām and confiscated the libraries of his father al-Ḥakam.

> Those libraries held the previously mentioned collections of famous books as well as others; he showed these books to his entourage of theologians and ordered them to take from them all those dealing with the ancient science of logic, astronomy, and other fields, saving only the books on medicine and mathematics. The books that dealt with language, grammar, poetry, history, medicine, tradition, *ḥadīth*, and other similar sciences that were permitted in Andalus were preserved. And he ordered that all the rest be destroyed. Only a very few were saved;

> the rest were either burned or thrown in the wells of the palace and covered with dirt and rocks. Abū ʿĀmir performed this act to gain the support of the common people of al-Andalus and to discredit the doctrine of Caliph al-Ḥakam. To justify this deed, he proclaimed that these sciences were not known to their ancestors and were loathed by their past leaders. Everyone who read them was suspected of heresy and of not being in conformity with Islamic laws. All who were active in the study of philosophy reduced their activities and kept, as secret, whatever they had pertaining to these sciences.[33]

Those Andalusians who pursued philosophy were, in fact, persecuted. Muḥammad ibn Masarra (d. 931), an early practitioner of philosophy, theology, and mysticism in Andalusia, was ostracized, his books removed from circulation, his followers condemned and persecuted.[34] The great theologian, jurist, and litterateur Ibn Ḥazm of Córdoba was banned, his works torched. Al-Ghazālī's books were burned by order of the chief judge of Córdoba.

Among philosophers, Ibn Bājja was twice imprisoned on charges of treason and heresy. Ibn Rushd fell out of favor with the caliph (*ca.* 1195); his books were burned and he was banished to Lucena along with other scholars. An interdiction prohibited the study of subjects dangerous to religion. Ibn Rushd was later reinstated and the caliph himself resumed studying philosophy.

Under these restrictive conditions Andalusian philosophers became ardent, albeit circumspect, defenders of philosophy, giving it preeminence over religion. The Almoravid and Almohad dynasties (eleventh to thirteenth centuries) engineered an official state theology and intensified ideological oppression, imposing strict limitations on free thought. Nonetheless, somewhat paradoxically, great intellectuals flourished during their rule in the twelfth and thirteenth centuries. Though official ideology was suppressive, rulers occasionally supported scientific and philosophical endeavors *sub rosa,* publicly denouncing philosophy, privately extending it patronage, just as caliphs publicly condemned wine drinking and clandestinely imbibed to their heart's content.

The perilous situation of philosophy in Judaism and in Islam was a blessing in disguise for philosophy. This precarious status guaranteed philosophy's private, reclusive character and its freedom from supervision. The situation of philosophy in the Islamic-Jewish world resembled its position in classical Greece. As Greek society was totalitarian, the one activity that was private and trans-political was philosophy. The philosophical schools were taught by private men, people without authority or power. Islamic and Jewish philosophers were aware of similarities between their situation and that of the Greeks, and compared the philosophical life to the life of the recluse. On the other hand, when philosophy receives official sanction, it may be bent to ulterior purposes. The official acceptance of philosophy in the Christian world subjected it to ecclesiastical supervision.[35]

Scholars pursued the philosophical life in private, surrounded by an intimate coterie of students. There were no institutions for studying philosophy or formal, public courses of study. Philosophy was the solitary pursuit of the individual soul. But paradoxically the Andalusian philosophers, while pursuing their human *telos* by withdrawal from this world and abstention from politics, extolling the life of contemplation and solitude, were all actively engaged in communal and political affairs.

Ibn Bājja, author of the *Regime of the Solitary,* led an active and turbulent life, serving even as vizier for the Almoravids. He was engagé and versatile: philosopher, physician, poet, musician, and statesman. Ibn Ṭufayl, who had studied medicine and philosophy at Seville and Córdoba, served in the court of the Almohad caliph Abū Yaʿqūb Yūsuf, sponsor of the sciences, patron of philosophy. Ibn Ṭufayl presented Ibn Rushd to the caliph. When in 1184 his sponsor died, Ibn Ṭufayl retained his station at court under the caliph's son and successor until 1185. Ibn Ṭufayl introduced Averroës to the caliph Abū Yaʿqūb in 1169 in a celebrated meeting. He was also qāḍī of Seville and chief qāḍī in Córdoba, later becoming physician to the Almohad court in Marrakesh, succeeding Ibn Ṭufayl in 1182.[36] Maimonides, a man who craved solitude, became head of the Jewish community in Egypt (*raʾīs al-yahūd*) and was a court physician.

These philosophers belonged to different religious communities. They acquiesced to the rites, rituals, and symbols of their respective religious traditions. But they also transcended the closed circle of national and religious myth, which is by nature exclusivist and parochial, and which leads to confrontational theologies and bloodshed (e.g., the Crusades).[37] The philosophers were united in a common aporetic endeavor. They were joined in the philosophic enterprise by "the ecumenical power of antiquity" and by "the internationality of science."[38]

No other endeavor could so unite men of diverse religious persuasions, certainly not mysticism, which, qua mythical, was freighted by particularistic motifs; indeed, a system like that of the *Zohar* absolutizes or universalizes what is particularly and narrowly Jewish. The Aristotelian philosophers solved the issue of sameness and difference, the universal or rational and the particular and mythical, in an impressively elegant manner.

The harmony was not, of course, a monotonal unanimity. Shared cultural themes broke down on the highest level of thought into distinctive patterns. Still, the cultural contacts among Muslims and Jews, whether by personal communication or by literary citation, exemplify the *convivencia* which Américo Castro found in medieval Spanish culture.[39]

The True Puzzle

The Aristotelian resurgence in medieval Andalusia was tested by a severe crisis which threatened the Aristotelian paradigm of celestial physics and that subverted the foundations of science—the challenge to Aristotelian cosmology by Ptolemaic astronomy.[40] This predicament was undoubtedly one of the most powerful demands that Maimonides' Andalusian heritage made on him.[41] And it shook his confidence in our ability to have proper knowledge of what is beyond the realm of physics: astronomy, cosmology, metaphysics.

Aristotle represented for Maimonides the summit of human knowledge. But Maimonides was aware that Aristotelian cosmology could not satisfactorily explain celestial phenomena, specifically the irregular motion of the planets. For this a more adequate paradigm had to be invoked—the Ptolemaic system of epicycles and eccentrics. But this (for then) elegant solution was highly problematic because the Ptolemaic hypotheses conflicted with Aristotelian postulates. Furthermore, brilliant as the Ptolemaic solutions were, they left many questions unanswered.

Ptolemy's epicycles and eccentrics, Maimonides observes (*Guide,* 2.24, pp. 322–23), conflict with reasoning (*qiyās*) and with all that has been expounded in physics.[42] Ptolemaic astronomy subverts Aristotelian natural science, according to which there must be some immobile entity about which circular motion takes place. For Aristotle, celestial bodies can only have a single, uniform, cyclic motion of homocentric spheres concentric with the earth's center. But the circular motion of the Ptolemaic epicycles is not about something immobile. Aristotle's physics required that the earth be motionless at the center of the universe; and he defined bodies as being heavy and light or in motion and at rest with respect to earth.

Maimonides objected to the Ptolemaic model primarily because it conflicted with reason. Islamic astronomers prior to Maimonides, like Ibn al-Haytham, had already raised doubts (*shukūk*) concerning Ptolemaic astronomy, and Andalusian astronomers and philosophers were astute critics of the Ptolemaic paradigm. Ibn Bājja, Ibn Ṭufayl, Ibn Rushd, and the astronomers Jābir b. Aflaḥ and al-Biṭrūji raised doubts concerning the Ptolemaic hypotheses.[43] Maimonides had contact with pupils of Ibn Bājja and with a son of Jābir b. Aflaḥ, and was familiar with the objections of other scientists.[44] And he shared some of their misgivings about the Ptolemaic system. But he could not deny the power of the Ptolemaic mathematical model for explaining planetary motions, nor could he gird himself with sword and buckler to defend the Aristotelian system. In this respect he differed from his great older contemporary Ibn Rushd, the arch-representative of medieval Andalusian Aristotelianism; for Ibn Rushd took up cudgels in defense of Aristotle and strove with might and main to buttress the crumbling pillars of his cosmology.

Averroës contended, using an Aristotelian argument, that the existence of eccentric spheres and epicycles is contrary to nature.[45] They contravene nature by positing a center other than the earth, for the center of the deferent bearing the epicycle does not coincide with the center of earth and the universe. Averroës accepted the possibility of replacing these mechanisms with "spiral motions" which, he said, Aristotle posited following a theory of his own predecessors.

Averroës believed that there was an ancient, pre-Aristotelian, astronomy which was true according to physical principles, and that it was based on the postulate of a single sphere rotating around a single center and different poles, thus producing acceleration, retardation, accession, and recession of planets, which Ptolemaic astronomy could not adequately explain. In his youth Averroës had hoped to work this out, but in his old age he felt he must leave it to someone else to inquire further into these matters. And he added that in "our time" there was only agreement about calculations and not about what exists; that is, astronomers concurred about mathematical explanations but not about physical models of the universe.[46]

Unlike Averroës, then, Maimonides offered no defense of Aristotle, nor did he look back wistfully to some ancient physically true astronomy that had been lost, though he propounded the idea of an ancient lost wisdom existing among his religious community that had perished in the course of time (*Guide,* 1.71, p. 174). Maimonides maintained that there had been progress in the sciences, and he emphasized the difficulties inherent in Aristotle's system, putting them in a glaring way. Maimonides posited that the science of mathematics was not perfected in Aristotle's time, who was thus limited in his knowledge of astronomy.[47] Aristotle's natural science cannot explain the various motions of the heavenly bodies. Aristotle's principle that motion is circular, uniform, and perfect conflicts with appearances, which can only be explained if we use epicycles and eccentrics. Maimonides believed that the principles of Ptolemaic astronomy were justified by the precision of calculations relating to the course of the moon, eclipses, and retrograde and other motions of stars.[48] Now, it is quite telling that in *Guide,* 1.72, where he adumbrates the principles of physics and astronomy, he simply accepts the Ptolemaic system.[49] And he welcomes the Ptolemaic system in the *Mishneh Torah,* where he explicitly speaks of epicycles (though not eccentrics) as physical configurations of celestial phenomena not merely as mathematical models.[50]

Although Maimonides relied less on Aristotle than did Averroës and granted the explanatory power of the Ptolemaic hypotheses, he considered the Ptolemaic system inadequate. For how, Maimonides asked, is it possible to conceive of a rolling motion in the heavens or a motion about a center that is not immobile? This, he added, is "the true puzzle" (*al-ḥayra al-ḥaqīqa*).[51] By signifying an astronomical dilemma as the true puzzle, Maimonides implicity downplays the *aporiai* of creation versus eternity of the world and the initial *aporia* of the *Guide*—the confict between the biblical text and science.

Like Jābir ibn Aflaḥ and other Andalusians, he was disturbed not only by Ptolemy's violation of Aristotelian principles but by the intrinsic deficiency of Ptolemaic astronomy, its lack of mathematical consistency and comprehensive explanatory power.

Maimonides tried to solve the puzzle by claiming (*viva voce* to his pupil Joseph b. Judah) that the function of the astronomer is not to explain how the spheres are *in reality* but to devise an astronomical model that corresponds to *appearances,* whether things are this way or not.[52] By resorting to this methodological rescue operation ("saving the appearances"), Maimonides sought to reduce the conflict between the Aristotelian and Ptolemaic paradigms.

Maimonides revered Aristotle, but he was not the hard-bitten apostle that Averroës was. I. A. Sabra classifies the "Aristotelianism" of Averroës' *Tafsīr* passage as extreme, explaining it (in cultural or psychological terms) as Andalusian self-assertiveness, the creation of a distinctively Andalusian system of ideas in opposition to the Eastern part of the Islamic world. Vaunting Andalusian culture, Averroës accused al-Ghazālī and Avicenna of corrupting the true doctrine of Aristotle, "the first philosopher," who was perfect.[53]

Maimonides does not present Aristotle, "the chief of the philosophers," as consummate, but as an earnest seeker of the truth who propounds plausible theories in a tentative way—an *aporetic philosopher.*[54] His characterization of Aristotle as an aporetic philosopher reflects his own view of what philosophy is: a *quest* for the truth and a way of life.

The paradigm conflict, the true puzzle, drove Maimonides to skepticism about our ability to have scientific knowledge of cosmology and to give adequate explanations of astronomical phenomena. Aristotle's natural science accords with reasoning (*qiyās*) because physical phenomena have known causes. "However, regarding all that is in the heavens, man grasps nothing but a small measure of what is mathematical" (*Guide,* 2.24, p. 326). Maimonides did not infer from the collapse of Aristotelian cosmology that his natural science might also be shaken. But had he been consistent, he would have concluded that the indeterminacy of the center of the universe obstructed Aristotelian physics as well.

Shlomo Pines called attention to aspects of Maimonides' skepticism.[55] Pines believed that Maimonides wanted to reap a theological harvest from this skepticism, as did Kant after him, by overstating his misgivings so as to cast doubt on Aristotelian science and, by implication, on the eternity of the universe. It strikes me rather that Maimonides' skepticism rose from genuine perplexity about the way the world is.[56] He recognized the legitimacy of conflicting claims and acknowledged the contradictions and paradoxes inherent in the nature of being. His skepticism emerged out of relentless intellectual integrity.[57]

Maimonides, then, was immersed in the epistemological eddies which swept his Andalusian colleagues; but they were (1) inclined to jettison the Ptolemaic system and (2) eager to save Aristotle, while he was prepared to leave the *aporia* in place, offering an interim mathematical solution, anticipating some future physical resolution. In this "true puzzle" and the antinomy of creation versus eternity, he embraced a stance of *dialectical skepticism.*[58]

MAIMONIDES' AVERROISM

Post-Maimonidean Jewish philosophers and commentators often interpreted the master in an Averroistic direction.[59] The attraction of Jewish philosophers to Averroës is intriguing.[60] The career and fate of Averroism offers the fascinating paradox that it was embraced by Jewish thinkers and had a profound effect on Latin Scholasticism but made hardly a ripple in Islamic thought.

But was Maimonides an Averroist? In his letter to Samuel ibn Tibbon, Maimonides twice commends Averroës' commentaries on Aristotle. To be sure, this does not make him an Averroist.[61] The question of Maimonides' knowledge of Averroës is inevitable.[62] Averroës was Maimonides' older contemporary and fellow Cordoban; however there is no evidence of any connection between the two.[63]

What did Maimonides know of Averroës' writings?[64] In a letter to his pupil Joseph b. Judah, the recipient of the *Guide,* Maimonides writes: "As for the rest of the sciences, I do not find time to study any of them. I am deeply aggrieved by this circumstance. Right now I have received all that Ibn Rushd wrote pertaining to the books of Aristotle except *De Sensu et Sensibili.*[65] In my opinion, he has hit the mark well. I have not found time to peruse all his books until now."[66] By saying that he lacked time to read *all of his books until now,* Maimonides implies that he had read *some* of them previously. This is an important point because it means that he may have been familiar with Averroës' works when he wrote the *Guide.*

The prevalent assumption is that when Maimonides wrote the *Guide,* he did not know Averroës.[67] For example, Harry A. Wolfson avows that there is no evidence for Maimonides having been familiar with the writings of Averroës when he wrote the *Guide,* and that a "sort of argument from silence" indicates that the *Guide* was written "in complete ignorance of the works of Averroës."[68]

Some connection of Averroës with the *Guide* is actually signified in an allegorical letter that Maimonides' pupil Joseph b. Judah wrote to him. The disciple protests that he had legally married Pleiades, the daughter of Maimonides, before two witnesses, Ibn ᶜUbaydallāh[69] and Ibn Rushd (Averroës), who are called "friends." Yet (he goes on) under the marriage canopy, Pleiades took other lovers, without the father protesting, and perhaps with his encouragement. Joseph demands that his wife be returned to him, saying that he is a prophet or will become one.

The allegory probably means, as Baneth has suggested, that the master Maimonides had promised to give his daughter (Pleiades = the *Guide*) to his favorite pupil, Joseph b. Judah, but had let the work be disseminated among others before Joseph received his copy. In his reply, Maimonides ascribes the accusation to envy, admonishing the pupil for linking him and Ibn Rushd and for calling himself a prophet.

Medieval commentators did, in fact, ascertain an Averroistic component in the *Guide.* And Shlomo Pines, in his "Translator's Introduction," stresses aspects of the *Guide* containing a naturalistic Aristotelian Averroism. Pines was surely aware that this Averroism coexists with a Neoplatonic and Avicennian tenor. He assumes, however, that had Maimonides been more familiar with Averroës when he wrote the *Guide,* he would have trimmed the book's Neoplatonic and Avicennian boughs. Does Maimonides' tepid commendation of Avicenna in his letter to Samuel ibn Tibbon, written after completion of the *Guide,* mean that he had changed his mind and veered in the direction of Averroës in his thinking? This would accord with Pines' view in his "Translator's Introduction." Or did he take a more Neoplatonic turn at a later stage when he was in Egypt and under the influence of Ismāᶜīlī Neoplatonism?

The obvious solution to the coexistence of an Aristotelian or naturalistic Averroism with a Neoplatonic or mystical Avicennianism is to assume that Maimonides modified his views. Now, it is true that Maimonides constantly revised his writings. This is clear from autographs of his *Commentary on the Mishnah* and from the manuscript tradition of the *Mishneh Torah.*[70] Indeed, we should speak of versions rather than editions of his works. He changed his mind often, constantly altering the text. It comes as no surprise, therefore, that recipients of his books complained of a faulty text. The *Guide* was not exempt from authorial editing. Samuel ibn Tibbon objected, when his translation was criticized by Maimonides, that the master's students had sent him an inferior text.

Thus, we should steer a middle course between the (Straussian) claim that contradictions in the *Guide* were deliberate and the philologian's avowal of shifts in viewpoint and a dynamic evolution of the text.[71] If we assume revision, the question is whether Maimonides revised the *Guide* in a more Averroistic, naturalistic way or in a more mystical, Neoplatonic direction.[72]

Maimonides may have come under Neoplatonic influences in Egypt where he came under the impact of the Fatimid dynasty and Neoplatonic Ismāᶜīlī theology. But he may easily have been familiar with these currents previously, for Andalusia was a haven for Neoplatonism. Neoplatonic works, such as the treatises of the Ikhwān al-Ṣafāᵓ and the Arabic Plotinus material, were imported into Andalusia by Muḥammad b. ᶜAbdallāh ibn Masarra, Maslamah b. Ahmad al-Majrīṭī, Abū al-Ḥakam ᶜAmr al-Kirmani, and others.[73] And Andalusia was the home of Jewish Neoplatonists like Ibn Gabirol and Abraham ibn Ezra.[74]

We may safely say that all the elements which infiltrated the *Guide* and Maimonides' other theological writings were available to him in al-Andalus. Andalusian writings on Kalām, Neoplatonism, Sufism, Aristotelian philosophy, and science were available to Maimonides before he settled in Egypt and had access to its great libraries.

Maimonides held Aristotelian or Averroistic naturalistism and Neoplatonic or Avicennian transcendentalism in equipoise, in *dialectical equilibrium.* Shlomo Pines, in his "Translator's Introduction," represents Maimonides as close to Averroës and a step away from Spinoza, anchoring him firmly within the parameters of the Spanish Aristotelian school and its "naturalistic hard-headedness." This naturalistic hard-headedness was expressed in the physical theory of the

Spanish school. Following Aristotle and Alexander of Aphrodisias, they avoided the natural world of Neoplatonists like Proclus who denigrated nature and treated physics as inferior to metaphysics, and rejected Ibn Sīnā and the injection of mystical conjectures into physics.[75]

For Ibn Rushd, the Aristotelian proof for a Prime Mover has its necessary starting point in physical data such as the nature of motion; it presupposes physical phenomena; and God, the principle object of metaphysics, can be proved to exist only by reference to physics. For Ibn Sīnā, the Necessary Existent (= God) may be proved to exist without any reference to physical phenomena. For Ibn Sīnā, God is transcendental, distinct from the intellect of the outer sphere; whereas for Ibn Rushd, God is identical with the intellect of the outer sphere and thus enmeshed in the workings of nature.

Ibn Rushd carefully pruned Neoplatonic (Avicennian) branches from his Aristotelian tree and went through several phases leading him to a more naturalistic Aristotelianism. Maimonides, however, unlike his Cordoban confrère, does not refrain from characterizing God as the Necessary Being and invoking proofs for God's existence depending on the Avicennian distinction between essence and existence, anathema to Ibn Rushd. Pines explains that Maimonides tolerated Avicennian ideas because he was unfamiliar with Ibn Rushd's attempt to eradicate Ibn Sīnā's accretions, and therefore uses the Avicennian term Necessary Existent and the distinction between essence and existence.[76] Even so, Pines says, this proof, like others, is not purely metaphysical; for all of Maimonides' proofs are predicated on the existence of motion or change and thus concur with Ibn Rushd (and Aristotle). Indeed, Maimonides says (*Guide,* 1.70), that the motion of the heavenly sphere is the most powerful proof of God's existence. And elsewhere (*Guide,* 1.71, p. 183), he states that there is no inference possible proving God's existence save those deriving from the totality of this existent and its details.

However, in my view, Maimonides' adoption of Ibn Sīnā's Necessary Existent belongs to a broader scope of Avicennian thought in the *Guide.*[77] Maimonides adopts the crucial Avicennian distinction between essence (quiddity) and existence and the concomitant view that existence is an accident accruing to essence. For example, Maimonides states (*Guide,* 1.57, p. 132) as something known[78] that "existence is an accident appended to what exists, and therefore superadded to its essence. This is true of everything which has a cause. Only God has no cause for his existence. His existence is necessary and is identical with His essence and His true reality; and His essence is His existence."[79]

And so, in Avicennian terms, there is a distinction between what is necessary in itself, or absolutely, and what is necessary by something else, harboring in its essence the category of the possible.[80]

Ibn Sīnā distinguished in the heavenly spheres between potentiality and actuality, matter and form, and made them necessary existents only vis-à-vis the First Cause or God.[81]

In this vein Maimonides says (*Guide,* Int. 1.22, p. 238) that every body is necessarily composed of matter and form and is accompanied by accidents of quantity, shape, and position. As Munk noticed, Maimonides adopted here the view of Ibn Sīnā who ascribed matter and form also to the heavenly bodies.[82] This ascription of possible being to the heavenly bodies is antithetical to Aristotle and was refuted by Ibn Rushd who considered the heavenly bodies as simple bodies having their form or entelechy in separate intelligences, and not as composed, as are bodies in the physical world, of form and matter.

I see no justification for concluding that Maimonides admitted Avicennian views because he was ignorant of Averroës' more consistent Aristotelian principles. He had his reasons for arguing (1) that the deity was the Necessary Being whose existence was identical with his essence and who transcended the physical world; and (2) that the existence of the heavenly bodies was merely contingent and possible. And he would have done so whether or not he knew Averroës' views on these issues.

We cannot say that Maimonides was an Averroist. Nevertheless, there are naturalistic positions he adopted that bring him close to Averroës and, indeed, to Spinoza. There is no need to assert that Maimonides derived these views from Averroës and used his writings when he wrote the *Guide,* although this is a possibility.

In several passages Maimonides identifies God with the system of nature. For instance (*Guide,* 3.32, p. 525): "If you consider the divine actions—I mean to say the natural actions—the deity's wily graciousness (*talaṭṭuf*) and wisdom (*ḥikma*), as shown in the creation of living beings . . . "[83] By a deft use of the phrase "I mean" Maimonides establishes the equivalence of divine with natural, which inevitably reminds us of Spinoza's *deus sive natura.*[84] The equation of the divine and the natural relates to God's wily graciousness and wisdom in creation of living beings, and in the chapter Maimonides stresses the wondrous and gracious arrangement of the human body, explained by Galen in *De usu partium humani corporis.* It is this expression of divine wisdom and providence that Maimonides discerns in natural phenomena but not in the heavens where apparent chaos invades order. That the divine actions are equivalent to the natural actions is implied in *Guide,* 1.54, p. 125, where Maimonides designates God's ways (*derakhim*) and characteristics (*middot*) as his actions in the world, so that we apprehend the kindness (*lutf*) of his governance (*tadbīr*) in the production of human embryos, which we call mercy. The knowledge of God's attributes of action, the divine activities in the world, which Moses achieved (1.54), is the only positive knowledge concerning God possible to human beings. The study of the order of nature is the only way for us to have positive knowledge of God.[85]

Pines believed that this knowledge of the system of nature may signify the essence of God, and that this may be the meaning of the judgment that God apprehends us by the same light by which we apprehend him (3.52), implying, in harmony with the Aristotelian assumption of the unity of the subject and object of intellection, that God is identical with the system of natural sciences, and that man too may gain this identity.[86]

But this interpretation, while attractive, prescinds from the transcendance of the God who is beyond attribution and human comprehension—above the system of nature. The dialectical equipoise sustained between the Averroistic and Avicennian visions is not accidental; it reflects the two aspects of the deity: the God whose actions are manifested in nature and the God who is beyond nature, who is radically and wholly other, beyond attributes, serenely above knowledge or description.

Whatever the course of composition of the *Guide,* the finished product—by a "canonicial reading"—sustains both immanence and transcendance, a balance Maimonides wished to profess. All else but God is contingent, tentative, evanescent, even (especially) the celestial bodies. Only by eliminating the transcendental deity can we arrive at a totally naturalist, immanentist philosophy. And this is precisely what Spinoza does.

NOTES

1. The Arabic expression *ʿindanā* has no proper English equivalent; it means something like "by us" or "with us." For the sense, see Joshua Blau, "'At Our Place in al-Andalus,' 'At Our Place in the Maghreb,'" in *Perspectives on Maimonides: Philosophical and Historical Studies,* ed. Joel L. Kraemer (Oxford, 1991), 293–94.

2. See Isadore Twersky's *Introduction to the Code of Maimonides* (*Mishneh Torah*) (New Haven, 1980), 8–9.

3. See *Guide of the Perplexed,* trans. Shlomo Pines (Chicago, 1963), 1.71, page 177. References to the Arabic text are to *Dalatat al-harʾirin,* ed. Solomon Munk and I. Joel (Jerusalem, 1930–31). Prior to this passage Maimonides criticizes some geonim, placing them in the dubious company of the Karaites as having adopted theological arguments from the Islamic *Mutakallimūn* (176).

4. Text: *min ahl millatinā,* "people of our religious community."

5. See *Le guide des égarés,* 3 vols., trans. Solomon Munk (Paris, 1856–1866), 1.338–39, and note 1. And see, in general, on Jewish philosophers in Spain, Colette Sirat, *A History of Jewish Philosophy in the Middle Ages* (Cambridge, 1990), *passim;* Georges Vajda, "La philosophie juive en Espagne," in *The Sephardi Heritage: Essays on the History and Cultural Contribution of the Jews of Spain and Portugal, Vol. 1: The Jews of Spain and Portugal after the Expulsion of 1492,* ed. Richard David Barnett (London, 1971), 81–111.

6. I discussed Maimonides as a physician (and his Maghrebi roots) in the symposium "Maimonides as Physician, Scientist, and Philosopher" in Jerusalem, October 29–31, 1990.

7. See Max Meyerhof, *Sharḥ Asmaʾ al-ʿUqqar (l'explication des noms de drogues): un glossaire de matière medicale composé par Maïmonide* (Cairo, 1940), xxiii, lxv–lxvi. The work was copied by a non-Jew, Ibn al-Baytar, which may explain the lack of Hebrew terms.

8. Ibn al-Qiftī, *Taʾrīkh al-ḥukamāʾ,* ed. Julius Lippert (Leipzig, 1903), 317–19, notes that he had a mastery of mathematics (*wa-ahkama al-riyādiyyāt*), and is followed in this (and other matters) by Bar Hebraeus, *Taʾrīkh mukhtaṣar al-duwal* (Beirut, 1986), 239, who mentions his "fine treatises on mathematics." See Tzvi Langermann, "The Mathematical Writings of Maimonides," *Jewish Quarterly Review* 75 (1984): 57–65.

9. This was the Sufi scholar Abū ʿAlī al-Ḥasan b. ʿAdud al-Dawla b. Hūd al-Judhami (d. 1300), a nephew of al-Muʾtamin. See my "The Andalusian Mystic Ibn Hūd and the Conversion of the Jews," *Israel Oriental Studies* 12 (1992): 59–73.

10. See *Guide,* 2.9 (trans. Shlomo Pines, p. 268): "In fact, Ibn Aflaḥ of Sevilla, whose son I have met, has written a celebrated book about this [that Venus and Mercury are above the sun]. Thereupon the excellent philosopher Abū Bakr ibn al-Ṣā'igh, under the guidance of one of whose pupils I have read texts, reflected on this notion and showed various ways of argumentation—transcribed by us from him—by means of which the opinion that Venus and Mercury are above the sun may be shown to be improbable. . . . " And see Richard P. Lorch, "The Astronomy of Jābir ibn Aflaḥ," *Centaurus* 19 (1975): 88–90; Langermann, "Mathematical Writings," 65.

11. *Guide,* 1.36, p. 84; cf. 1.24; 3.28.

12. David Hartwig Baneth, *Epistles,* 2nd ed. (Jerusalem, 1985), no. 5, 27–30.

13. The letter is preserved in MS. T–S 10 K 8.14; see my "Six Unpublished Maimonides Letters from the Cairo Genizah," *Maimonidean Studies* 2 (1991): 80–87.

14. Edited by Isaac Shailat (Yitshak Shilat), *Letters and Essays of Moses Maimonides* (Maᶜale Adummim), 2 vols. with consecutive pagination (5747–48 [1985/6–1988/9]), p. 530. The verse is also ascribed, however, to Solomon ibn Gabirol; see the *Diwan of Judah ha-Levi,* ed. Heinrich Brody (Berlin, 1894–1930), 1.129, with notes. Maimonides refers to "the ancient poem" (*ha-shir ha-qadmoni*).

15. Baneth remarks on Maimonides' wittiness and esprit (*Epistles,* 17). I once commented on this side of Maimonides' personality to Professor Pines and was rewarded with one of his Olympian smiles. On the other hand, an Orthodox colleague insisted that this allegorical letter was spurious because it did not fit Maimonides' seriousness—a fine example of circular reasoning.

16. See for instance, Salo W. Baron, "The Historical Outlook of Maimonides," *Proceedings of the American Academy for Jewish Research* 6 (1934–35): 8 n. 4. And see Twersky, *Introduction,* 250–51, but see note 29, where "Maimonides' rather complicated attitude" is noted and also p. 409 n. 135.

17. This is an Aramaic equivalent of "When in Rome do as the Romans." See Shailat, *Letters and Essays,* 501. The quotation appears as a proverb in *Bereshit Rabba,* 48:14; *Shemot Rabba,* 47:8; *Midrash Bereshit,* 48:20 (it is cited in connection with the biblical Moses). On similar sayings, see A. A. Hallewi, *ᶜOlamah shel ha-Aggadah* (Tel Aviv, 1947), 121–28.

18. For Maimonides' poems, see Moritz Steinschneider, "*Moreh Meqom ha-Moreh,*" in *Kobez al Jad* 1 (1885): 1–31; Wilhelm Bacher, "Hebräische Verse von Maimuni," *Monattschrift für geschichte und Wissenschaft des Judentums* 53 (1909): 581–88; Schirmann, "Ha-Rambam we-ha-shirah ha-ᶜivrit," *Moznaim* 3 (1935): 433–36.

In a *Geniza* manuscript in Cambridge (MS. T–S J 2.39), I came across a copy of the poem by Maimonides that stands at the head of the *Guide* (trans. Pines, opposite page 3): "My knowledge goes forth to point out the way,/To pave straight its road.// Lo, everyone who goes astray in the field of Torah,/ Come and follow its path.// The unclean and the fool shall not pass over it;/It shall be called Way of Holiness." It is in Maimonides' own handwriting, and thus should be added to the collection of his holographs. The poem appeared on the outside flyleaf of the work. Consider also his appreciation of the poems and *maqamas* of Joseph b. Judah, sent from Alexandria, in the Arabic letter accompanying the *Guide* (Baneth, no. 2, p. 7; trans. Pines, p. 3). It was in these poems that Maimonides observed Joseph's "powerful longing for speculative matters."

19. Pines, "Translator's Introduction," cix.

20. See A. Marx, "Texts by and about Maimonides," *Jewish Quarterly Review* 25 (1935): 374–81; Shailat, *Letters and Essays,* 552–54; Pines, "Translator's Introduction," lix–lx.

21. I have used the text edited by Shailat in *Letters and Essays.* My translation has been prepared for a volume of translations of Maimonides' letters being prepared for the Yale Judaica Series.

22. See 2 Kings 9:11.

23. Text: *maᶜalat.* MS *toᶜelet.*

24. The famous Ikhwān al-Ṣafā᾽, whose encyclopedia was very popular. Maimonides, by implication, praises them here. The Hebrew translation *ba᾽ale ha-te᾽arim* is presumably an error, reading *sifat* for *ṣafā᾽*. See Sarah Stroumsa, "Note on Maimonides' Attitude to Joseph ibn Saddiq," in *Shlomo Pines Jubilee Volume,* 2 vols. (Jerusalem, 1988–90), 2.33–38.

25. See Prov. 8:9.

26. Pines, "Translator's Introduction," ciii.

27. Pines believed that Ibn Ṭufayl "was preoccupied with the mystical or semimystical aspects of Avicenna's thought" and therefore had no apparent influence on Maimonides ("Translator's Introduction," cviii). Ibn Bājja was quite important for Maimonides, but as this has been treated rather fully elsewhere, by scholars such as Alexander Altmann and Lawrence V. Berman, I shall focus here on Ibn Rushd.

28. Paul Oskar Kristeller in *Renaissance Thought: The Classic, Scholastic and Humanist Strains* (New York, 1961), 32, characterizes late medieval Aristotelianism in similar terms.

29. See Philip Merlan, *Monopsychism, Mysticism, Metaconsciousness: Problems of the Soul in the Neoaristotelian and Neoplatonic Tradition* (The Hague, 1963).

30. Frank Talmage, "Apples of Gold: The Inner Meaning of Sacred Texts in Medieval Judaism," in *Jewish Spirituality: From the Bible through the Middle Ages,* ed. Arthur Green (New York, 1986), 314–15; *Guide,* "Introduction," 11.

31. See Yirmiahu Yovel, *Spinoza and Other Heretics: The Marrano of Reason*

(Princeton, 1992). Yovel ascribes Spinoza's duality and esotericism to his Marrano background, though he recognizes that Maimonides was his "chief mentor" in rhetorical matters and the multitude (143). Primary in philosophical rhetoric is the use of "metaphoric-systematic equivalence," in which the real sense of the first formulation is given in the second. Maimonides used phrases like "I mean" or "it means." See also Spinoza's *vel magis proprie loquendo,* cited there by Yovel.

32. Ṣāʿid al-Andalusī, *Ṭabaqāt al-Umam,* trans. Semaan I. Salem and Alok Kumar as *Science in the Medieval World: Book of the Categories of Nature* (Austin, 1991), 61–62.

33. Ibid.

34. See Miguel Cruz Hernández, "Islamic Thought in the Iberian Peninsula," in *The Legacy of Muslim Spain,* ed. Salma Khadra Jayyusi (Leiden, 1992), 779.

35. Leo Strauss, *Persecution and the Art of Writing* (New York, 1952; rpt. Chicago, 1980), 21.

36. In Book 4 of "De partibus animalium" he points out the duties of his post and his separation from books.

37. The philosopher in Judah Halevi's *Kuzari* (1.1), reflecting the views of Ibn Bājja (according to Shlomo Pines), says that philosophy's supreme goal is purity of heart and knowledge, not religion and worship, or language and actions. The Khazar King then asks why then if rituals and actions are negligible have Christians and Muslims divided up the world waging wars. The philosopher replies that the philosophers' credo precludes killing because they only cultivate the intellect.

38. See Werner Jaeger, "Die Antike im wissenschaftlichen Austausch der Nationen," *Humanistische Reden und Vorträge,* 2nd ed. (Berlin 1960), 180–81; *Die Antike und das Problem der Internationalität der Geisteswissenschaften,* in *Inter Nationes,* Jahrgang I (Berlin 1931), 93b. And see Thomas F. Glick, *Islamic and Christian Spain in the Early Middle Ages* (Princeton, 1979), 251.

39. Américo Castro, *The Spaniards: An Introduction to Their History,* trans. Willard F. King and Selma Margaretten (Berkeley 1971), 584.

40. See George Saliba, *A History of Arabic Astronomy* (New York, 1994), 22–26; A. I. Sabra, "The Andalusian Revolt against Ptolemaic Astronomy," in *Transformation and Tradition in the Sciences,* ed. Everett Mendelsohn (New York, 1984), 133–53, reprinted in his *Optics, Astronomy, and Logic: Studies in Arabic Science and Philosophy* (London, 1994), no. XV. And see Bernard R. Goldstein, "The Status of Models in Ancient and Medieval Astronomy," *Centaurus* 24 (1980): 132–47; Francis James Carmody, "The Planetary Theory of Ibn Rushd," *Osiris* 10 (1952): 556–86; Louis Gauthier, "Une réforme du système astronomique de Ptolémé tentée par les philosophes arabes du XIIe siècle," *Journal asiatique* (1909): 483–510.

41. See Pines, "Translator's Introduction," cix–cxi. Although I have discussed this previously in "Maimonides on Aristotle and Scientific Method," in *Moses Maimonides and His Time,* ed. Eric L. Ormsby (Washington, D.C., 1989), 76–84, I wish to develop further certain points here.

42. Pines states (*Guide,* 322 n. 1) that the word *qiyās* used here means "syllogism" and more broadly "reasoning" or "analogy." It is possible that *qiyās* here means demonstrative proof.

43. See the fine discussion by Sabra on this point ("The Andalusian Revolt," 134ff).

44. In *Guide* 2.24, Maimonides mentions also Thabit ibn Qurra and al-Qabisi. Langermann, "The 'True Perplexity,'" 161, raised the question whether Maimonides knew Ibn al-Haytham's *al-Shukūk ʿalā Batlamyus;* see the edition by A. I. Sabra and Nabil Shehaby (Cairo, 1971). He notes that Maimonides does not mention the work, and that there is no firm evidence that he was familiar with it.

45. See the text in his Great Commentary on the Metaphysics (*Tafsīr Ma Baʿd al-Tabiʿa*), ed. Maurice Bouyges, 3 vols. (Beirut, 1948), 3.1661–64 and the discussion by Sabra in "The Andalusian Revolt," 140ff.

46. See also his statement in his commentary on Aristotle's *De caelo,* cited by Carmody ("Planetary Theory," 572).

47. See *Guide,* 2.24, pp. 326–27.

48. Cf. Otto Neugebauer, "The Astronomy of Maimonides and Its Sources," *Hebrew Union College Annual* 22 (1949): 336.

49. See also Pines, "Translator's Introduction," cxi.

50. See *Hilkhot Yesode ha-Torah,* III, 1–11; Tzvi Langermann, "The 'True Perplexity': *The Guide of the Perplexed,* Part II, Chapter 24," in Kraemer, *Perspectives on Maimonides,* 162–64, 169. To be sure, he may have avoided subtle explanations of mathematical models out of consideration for his audience.

51. Maimonides calls the issue *al-ḥayra al-ḥaqīqa* in *Guide,* 2.24, (ed. Munk-Joel, 23b). The word *ḥayra* is of the same root as *haʾirin* in the title of the *Guide,* translated "Perplexed." But *ḥayra* often renders Greek *aporia,* meaning "puzzle" or "difficulty" or "problem." And I shall favor the translation "puzzle" here. I suggest that we get away from the language of perplexity and substitute terms closer to the Aristotelian sense of aporetic and aporematic. Maimonides was not a builder of philosophical systems but an aporetic philosopher, and the *Guide* is an aporetic work; it raises *aporiai* and attempts to resolve them; but many rest unresolved. On *al-ḥayra al-ḥaqīqa,* see Langermann, "The 'True Perplexity'," in Kraemer, *Perspectives on Maimonides,* 159–74.

52. See the discussion in Goldstein, "The Status of Models," 139.

53. Sabra, "The Andalusian Revolt," 143–44.

54. I have argued this in "Aristotle on Scientific Method."

55. See Shlomo Pines, "The Limitations of Human Knowledge according to al-Fārābī, ibn Bājja, and Maimonides," in *Studies in Medieval Jewish History and Literature,* ed. Isidore Twersky (Cambridge, Mass., 1979), 82–109. It is generally surmised, perhaps correctly, that Pines changed his mind from the time he published his "Translator's Introduction" (published in 1963) to the time he wrote his "Limitations" article and others stating his position. Herbert A. Davidson has taken issue with Pines in "Maimonides on Metaphysical Knowledge," *Maimonidean Studies* 3 (1992–93): 49–103. Whether Pines changed his mind or not does not have bearing on the value of the presentation in his "Translator's Introduction" to his translation of the *Guide,* which is a masterpiece and a catalyst for many subsequent studies on Maimonides.

56. Consider Maimonides' discussion of the irrationality of Π in *Mishnah ᶜEruvin,* 1.5, ed. Jospeh Kafih (Jerusalem, 1963), 2.98; Langermann, "The 'True Perplexity'," 165. The ratio of the diameter of the circle to its circumference cannot ever be known due to its own nature, not to our ignorance.

57. He writes (Pines, 327): "It is possible that someone else may find a demonstration by means of which the true reality of what is obscure (*ashkala ᶜalyayya*) for me will become clear to him. The extreme predilection that I have for investigating the truth is evidenced by the fact that I have explicitly stated and reported my perplexity (*ḥayra*) regarding these matters as well as by the fact that I have not heard nor do I know a demonstration as to anything concerning them."

58. I mean by "dialectical skepticism" a stance of philosophical doubt occurring when an *aporia* cannot be scientifically decided by either one of two opposing arguments. In the creation-eternity antinomy Maimonides ostensibly preferred the creationist hypothesis theologically by an act of volition; in the astronomical crisis he favored the Ptolemaic system as a superior mathematical model.

59. See Georges Vajda, "A propos de l'Averroïsme juif," *Sefarad* 12 (1952): 3–29. Maimonides appears to have accepted the doctrine of the unity of the intellect in the afterlife, elaborated by Ibn Bājja (see *Guide,* 1.74, p. 221) and espoused by Ibn Rushd, whence it was adopted in Latin Averroism and by Jewish Averroists who correctly interpreted Maimonides this way; see Pines, "Translator's Introduction," civ.

60. The Sultan Abū Yaᶜqūb Yūsuf banished the elderly Averroës to the mostly Jewish town of Lucena near Córdoba. This gave rise to legends that Ibn Rushd sought refuge with his disciple Maimonides; see Solomon Munk, *Mélanges de philosophie juive et arab* (Paris, 1955), 425.

61. Cf. Kristeller, *Renaissance Thought,* 33: "If we understand by Averroism the use of Averroës' commentary on Aristotle, every medieval Aristo-

telian including Aquinas was an Averroist." Kristeller adds two additional criteria: first, a neat distinction between reason and faith, and secondly, the unity of the intellect in all men. In fact, Maimonides presumably meets these standards.

62. See the discussion by Pines in his "Translator's Introduction," cviii–cxxiii. Miguel Cruz Hernández, *Abū-l-Walīd Ibn Rushd (Averroës): vida, obra, pensamiento, influencia* (Córdoba, 1986), 407, cites a number of studies bearing on Averroës and the Jews, inter alia, David Gonzalo Maeso, "Averroës y Maimónides (1135–1204), does glorias de Córdoba," *Miscelánea de estudios arabes y hebraicos* 16–17 (1967–68): 139–64.

63. One may fantasize them as children playing chess or marbles together in the area between the great mosque (mesquita) and the Jewish quarter (*harāt al-yahūd*). And later, whilst Averroës was sitting on his veranda, overlooking Córdoba, above the gardens, the orchards, and the busy Guadalquivir, (as depicted) in the lovely story "Averroës's Search" by Jorge Luis Borges, puzzling over the terms "tragedy" and "comedy" in Aristotle's Poetics, something revealed to him their meaning, to wit, "panegyrics" and "satires and anathemas." One may indulge one's fancy and picture Mūsā ibn Maymūn passing by and trying to help his colleague fathom the arcane utterances from a distant culture.

64. See Pines, "Preface," lxxx, cviii.

65. The Arabic title is *Kitāb al-Ḥiss wal-Maḥsūs.* The Compendium or Epitome of Ibn Rushd (completed in 1170 in Seville) of what Greek editions call the *Parva Naturalia,* includes six of the nine Aristotelian treatises, the first being *De sensu et sensibili.* See Peters, *Aristoteles Arabus* (Leiden, 1968), 46; the edition of Abdurrahman Badawi, in *Aristutalis fi l-nafs* (Cairo, 1954); that of Helmut Gätje, *Die Epitome des Parva Naturalia des Averroes* (Leiden, 1961); and Gätje's, *Studien zu Überlieferung der Aristotelischen Psychologie im Islam* (Heidelberg, 1971); the Arabic-Hebrew version of Moses ibn Tibbon, *Averrois Cordubensis Compendia librorum Aristotelis qui Parva naturalia vocantur,* ed. Henry Blumberg (Cambridge, Mass., 1949).

66. Baneth, *Letters,* no. 6, p. 70.

67. See Alexander Altmann, "Essence and Existence in Maimonides," *Bulletin of the John Rylands Library* 35 (1952–53): 294, note 3; also in his *Studies in Religious Philosophy and Mysticism* (Ithaca, 1969), 109 n. 3.

68. Harry A. Wolfson, *Crescas' Critique of Aristotle* (Cambridge, Mass., 1929), 323.

69. See Baneth, *Letters,* no. 4, p. 23. ʿAbdallāh or ʿUbaydallāh (Heb. Obadiah) was the progenitor of the family who gave it its name, and so Maimonides is Ibn ʿUbaydallāh. The family name today would be Obadiah.

70. Joshua Blau and Aexander Scheiber, *An Autograph of Maimonides from the Adler Collection and the Leningrad Library* (Jerusalem, 1981).

71. See Pines, "Preface," cxiv, who notes that the notion that God is the soul of the universe is disconcerting because this was a Sabian doctrine; see *Guide,* 3.29. On earlier and later strata, see now the attempt by Hannah Kasher, "Is There an Early Stratum in the *Guide of the Perplexed?*" *Maimonidean Studies* 3 (1992–93): 105–129.

72. This is what Alfred Ivry suggests in a number of publications on the Neoplatonic features of the *Guide.* See most recently "Ismā ʿīlī Theology and Maimonides' Philosophy," in *The Jews of Medieval Islam: Community, Society, and Identity,* ed. Daniel Frank (Leiden, 1995), 271–99.

73. Majid Fakhry, *A History of Islamic Philosophy* (New York, 1983), 258–59.

74. See Herman Greive, *Studien zum jüdischen Neuplatonismus: Die Religionsphilosophie des Abraham Ibn Ezra* (Berlin-New York, 1973). And see *Neoplatonism and Jewish Thought,* ed. Lenn E. Goodman (Albany, 1992).

75. Pines, "Translator's Introduction," cxi–cxii.

76. Ibid., cxiii.

77. In discussing the subject of metaphysics, Pines ("Translator's Introduction," cxii) sees the Avicennian view on essence and existence and the subject of being as treated merely cursorily in the *Guide;* he tends to notice but underplay Avicennian traces, whereas Wolfson (see note 68 above) downplayed or eliminated Averroistic themes and stressed Maimonides' reliance on Avicenna.

78. Altmann, "Essence and Existence," 294, takes the reference to the theory as being well known and commonly accepted as indicative that Maimonides did not know Ibn Rushd's criticism of Ibn Sīnā's doctrine.

79. See the long note in Munk, *Le guide des égares,* 1.231, note 1. And see Altmann, "Essence and Existence in Maimonides," 294, 296, *et passim;* and *Guide,* 2.18. This, as Joseph Owens points out, is a Platonic admission of ideas or forms that are preexistent. Accordingly, the entity's existence is not derived from its own nature but from another entity and ultimately from the ultimate cause of existence (Joseph Owens, "The Relevance of Avicennian Neoplatonism," in *Neoplatonism and Islamic Thought,* ed. Parviz Morewedge [Albany, 1992], 44). And see *Guide,* "Introduction," 19th proposition (p. 238). This and the two subsequent propositions are Avicennian.

80. See Munk, *Le guide des égares,* 2.18, note 3.

81. Munk notes that Ibn Sīnā refers to Aristotle who expressed the idea of Necessary Existent; Met. ix, 8. Cf. Caelo I, 2. Ibn Rushd rejected this in many of his works; cf. *Mélanges,* 358–59.

82. On the heavenly bodies, see *Guide,* 2.20 and Munk, *Le guide des égarés,* 2.20 n. 1. Munk cites Aristotle, *Metaph.* ix, 8 and xii, 2; and see Munk, *Mélanges,* 4 n. 1, and 18 n. 1.

83. See Pines ("Translator's Introduction," lxxii–iv) on wily graciousness and Hegel's *Vernunft;* and Amos Funkenstein, "Maimonides: Political Theory and Realistic Messianism," in *Die Mächte des Guten und Bösen: Vorstellungen im XII. und XIII. Jahrhundert über ihr Wirken in der Heilsgeschichte,* ed. Albert Zimmermann, Miscellanea mediaevalia, number 11 (Berlin, 1977), 81–103.

84. See Pines, "Translator's Introduction," xcvi n. 66.

85. Ibid., cxv; *Guide,* 1.54, and 68.

86. Pines, "Translator's Introduction," cxv.

4

Jewish-Muslim Relations in the Context of Andalusian Emigration

STEVEN M. WASSERSTROM

THIS ESSAY CONCERNS interconfessional circles among Spanish emigrants in the central Muslim lands, as well as in Spain itself, particularly during the late twelfth and thirteenth centuries. My focus rests on intellectuals who were, one might say, *interconfessional despite themselves.* Specifically, it was through the shared passion for certain intellectual subsystems—Sufi, Ismāʿīlī, Ishrāqi, Kabbalistic—that intercourse between Spanish Jews and Muslims flourished. And it was specifically Spanish emigrants who shipped a propensity for *convivencia* with them in their luggage, as it were, and who maintained such characteristically Spanish conversations abroad. The resulting interactions were sufficiently extensive, I think, to allow us to speak of interconfessional circles of Spanish intellectuals.

Some of the contacts that I will discuss did take place on Spanish soil. When they did not, they were still experienced by men who considered themselves to be Spanish. Pride of origins was sufficiently common that, as Joshua Blau notes, "[Maimonides] always considered himself a Spaniard, attached to the Judeo-Spanish ways of life and extolling Judeo-Spanish customs."[1] Keep in mind, too, that two figures central to the following discussion, Ibn ʿArabī and Maimonides (who called himself "ha-Sepharadi") were adults when they left Spain, Ibn ʿArabī at age thirty-five and Maimonides in his early twenties.

An additional consideration to keep in mind concerns the oscillation between the old center in Spain and newly embraced centers in the East. At least one circle which I will address, the Murcia school of Sufism, operated both on Spanish soil and subsequently in exile. Such Arabophone early Kabbalists as Abraham Abulafia, Isaac of Acre, and Joseph ben Shalom operated both in East and West.[2] Rabbi Isaac of Acre, a student of Nahmanides for a time, subsequently emigrated to eastern Islamicate lands, as did many of the figures under discussion here. He gained firsthand knowledge of Sufism and eventually had a substantial impact on the origins of Kabbalah.[3] The Nahmanides circle demonstrably was Arabophone.[4] It was through students of Nahmanides that Ramon Llull seems to have gotten his knowledge of Kabbalah as early as the 1270s.[5] This two-way street continued into the fourteenth century.[6]

STIMULI AND CONSTRAINTS OF INTERCONFESSIONALISM IN EXILE

However much the needs of impersonal science and desires of personal attraction drew Jews and Muslims together, doctrine and chauvinism held them apart. From the Jewish confessional standpoint, contacts were fraught with dangers, as indeed the incidence of conversion in these circles proves. Jewish "philosophical converts" of the twelfth and thirteenth centuries include Abuʾl Barakāt al-Baghdādī, Ibn Kammūna, Samauʾal al-Maghribī, Abū Sayyid al-Isrāʾīlī, Sāʿīd ibn Ḥasan, and Isaac ibn Ezra.[7] On the other hand, common activities drew them together. If there was any one *deformation professionelle* which distinctively shaped the careers of Jewish and Muslim philosophers, it was that of the physician-scientist.[8] Jewish-Muslim physician friendships could develop such intensity that the Muslim Ibn al-Qifṭī (d. 1248) and the Spanish emigrant Jew Ibn ʿAqnīn, who died in the early thirteenth century, were said apocryphally to have vowed "that whoever preceded the other in death would have to send reports from eternity to the survivor."[9] Both formal and informal friendships between Muslim and Jew, moreover, are well known from a variety of sources.[10] Correspondence survives, for example, between the influential Spanish-Muslim refugee philosopher Ibn Bājja (a major player in the following discussion) and his friend, the logician and converted Jew, Yūsuf ibn Hasdai, the great-grandson of the famous Spanish-Jewish dignitary, Hasdai ibn Shapruṭ.[11] Jewish and Muslim philosophically oriented physicians, then, could become friends who both met together and corresponded with one another.

Within the context of such general dynamics of danger and enticement, attraction and repulsion, I should now like to address four subsystems of intellectual esoterism: Ismaᶜilism, Ishrāq, Sufism, and Kabbalah.[12]

Judeo-Ismaᶜilism

The first subculture I want to address is Ismaᶜilism. The theoretical writings of Sevener Shiᶜites attracted Jewish thinkers in part because they provided particularly vivid means of conceptualizing group-pride, a kind of ontology of supremacy. The greatest Spanish-Jewish thinkers of the period of "creative symbiosis," Judah Halevi and Maimonides, utilized Ismāᶜīlī teachings in this sense.[13] Maimonides' followers, like Isaac ibn Laṭīf, did so undeniably.[14]

Recent scholarship has begun to confirm Scholem's assertion, identifying aspects of common interest between Ismāᶜīlīs and Jews.[15] The phenomenon of Jewish Ismaᶜilism, while not marginal in its scope of influence, seems, however, largely to have been a function of shared religious interest in speculation, for example, in support for a quasi-biologistic prophetology. These features spoke to a common cause of sorts, but do not seem to have arisen, in this case, from an extensive or immediate social nexus. Ismaᶜilism survived as a still-potent component of the *theoretical* or speculative literature of the day. I include it here not only because this Muslim theology had an impact on Andalusian Jews like Judah Halevi and Maimonides, but because recent research suggests it also enjoyed a surprising impact on more than one form of Spanish Kabbalah. Moreover, the negative theology of the Judeo-Ismāᶜīlī milieu stimulated imagery leading, it has been argued, to the *Ein Sof* of Kabbalah. In all cases, finally, the synthesis was then carried abroad and disseminated there. It was even picked up in this century by the theologian Franz Rosenzweig.[16]

Ishrāq

By contrast to the relatively rarified impact of Ismāᶜīlī thought, perhaps no subculture was as demonstrably reciprocal as that which produced the Avicennan philosophical mysticism known as "Illumination" (*Ishrāq*). Three Muslim philosophers were particularly implicated in the social context of *Ishrāqī* thought, to which Jewish (or Jewish-convert) philosophers also seem markedly to have been drawn. These Muslim philosophers, Suhrawardī (d. 1192), Ibn Ṭufayl (d. 1185), and Ibn Sabʿīn (d. 1270), explicitly were beholden to the still mysterious *Oriental Wisdom, al-Ḥikma al-Mashriqiyya,* of Avicenna.[17] For purposes at hand, *Ishrāqī* subculture may be said to have been significantly interconfessional in at least four senses. First, the curriculum, so to speak, of these thinkers was one distinctively (though not exclusively) cultivated over several centuries in Jewish-Muslim circles. Second, some of these Muslim philosophers both met with Jewish philosophers and initiated Jewish students: their circles were intertwined with those of contemporaneous Jewish philosophers in certain fundamental respects. Third, they occasionally studied and sometimes even taught Jewish works. Fourth, a number of their works were popular among Jewish philosophers for several centuries.

This combination of factors, taken as a whole, serves to highlight a significant and still little-studied intercultural context for Spanish philosophy, which therefore deserves to be treated in more detail. The first of these factors, that of a certain shared curriculum, may be discerned, for example, in the interconfessional reception-history of such neo-Platonic classics as the *Theology of Aristotle* and the *Liber de Causis.* The *Theology of Aristotle,* particularly in the so-called "Longer Version," seems to have emerged into Islamicate philosophical discourse out of a context at once Ismāʿīlī and Jewish.[18] The text-history of the *Liber de causis* also seems striking in this regard. Its primary readers were al-ʿĀmirī, an exponent of Pseudo-Empedoclean traditions heavily favored by Andalusian Jewish philosophers; Moses ibn Ezra, whose son became a "philosophical convert"; ʿAbd al-Laṭīf al-Baghdādī, who studied the *Guide for the Perplexed;* and Ibn Sabʿīn, who both studied and cited Maimonides' masterwork.[19]

Second, the philosophers associated with *Ishrāq* met and taught Jews, Jewish converts, and Judaizing Muslims. The martyred mystical philosopher Suhrawardī initiated (with the *khirqa*) one Najm al-Dīn ibn Isrāʾīl, who taught, along with an appropriately Muslim confessional doxology, non-Muslim confessions as well.[20] A leading commentator on Suhrawardī, the scientist Qutb al-Dīn Shīrāzī, gave the *ijāza* to Abū Bakr Muḥammad ibn Muḥammad al-Tabrīzī in 701/1301–02: this would appear to be the same al-Tabrīzī who wrote a celebrated gloss on sections of the *Guide for the Perplexed.*[21] Ibn Ṭufayl's biography is extremely scanty, but he could have met Moses Maimonides at the court in Fez, where Ibn Ṭufayl served as vizier precisely at the time when Maimonides was passing through on the road to Cairo. Fellow Aristotelians strongly influenced by Ibn Bājja, these fellow Spanish exiles would have had much to discuss.[22] And Ibn Ṭufayl's pioneering novel was translated and analyzed by Maimonidean mystical Jews in the thirteenth century, like Moshe Narboni, who also wrote a commentary on *The Guide for the Perplexed.*[23]

The third aspect to the interconfessional context of "Illuminationism" (*Ishrāq*) which deserves mention is the Muslim study and teaching of Jewish philosophical works.[24] Ibn Sabᶜīn used the work of Maimonides, as did ᶜAbd al-Laṭīf al-Baghdādī, who, like Ibn Sabᶜīn, was a hermetically oriented philosopher.[25] ᶜAbd al-Laṭīf al-Baghdādī, interestingly enough, is the only Muslim author known to have cited the "Long Recension" of the *Theology of Aristotle,* which may have been originally redacted in Arabic by a Jew, and which is a fundamental text in the development of a Jewish-Muslim doctrine of the "negation of attributes."[26] ᶜAbd al-Laṭīf al-Baghdādī is also significant because Ishrāqi circles were markedly Hermetic. Suhrawardī, Ibn Sabᶜīn, and ᶜAbd al-Laṭīf al-Baghdādī included Hermes in their intellectual *isnāds.*[27] The first Jewish philosophers to claim this spiritual genealogy, Moses ibn Ezra, Judah Halevi, and Abraham ibn Ezra, were twelfth-century Spanish members of the same circle.[28] In this way, the figure of Hermes stood for a transconfessional wisdom, a universal revelation, which doctrine further endorsed Muslim study of Jewish works.

Two works of Maimonides have been said to bear some relation to the *Ḥayy ibn Yaqẓān* of Ibn Ṭufayl. Although this likelihood has been suggested for many years, a systematic investigation of the relationship between the contemporaneous classics, the *Guide* and *Ḥayy,* has not been undertaken.[29] The second text has not been proven conclusively to belong in the Maimonidean oeuvre. But this work, the *Perakim be-Hazlaha* (*Chapters on Beatitude*), cites *Ḥayy ibn Yaqẓan,* and emerges from this milieu, if not from the hand of Maimonides himself.[30] It should be noted that Ibn Ṭufayl explicitly identifies himself with the "*Ishrāq*" tradition in his epistolary introduction to *Ḥayy ibn Yaqẓān* (which provides the rhetorical framework for the book, just as an epistolary introduction frames the *Guide*).[31] Nonetheless, clarifying the relation between the two must proceed on the basis of internal evidence, inasmuch as neither one cites or even alludes to the other. Thus Dominique Urvoy may be accurate in his recent observation that, for Maimonides, "the Almohad background consituted a framework . . . he comes close to the Avicennism of ibn Ṭufayl in juxtaposing a strictly deductive method in the details of the analysis with the concept of metaphysical knowledge known as illumination, but without revealing the link between the two."[32]

Finally, works by Muslim philosophers which emerged from this interconfessional context were studied and annotated by Jews for centuries. Suhrawardī emphatically influenced the Jewish converts Abuʾl Barakāt al-Baghdādī and Ibn Kammūna, and a century later still had a powerful effect on R. David b. Joshua Maimonides, the "last of the Maimonidean Negidim."[33] Ibn Ṭufayl enjoyed an impact on Jewish philosophers from Moshe Narboni (1300–1362) to Yohannan Alemanno, Baruch Spinoza, and Ernst Bloch.[34]

The Murcia School of Sufism

A third intellectual subculture shared by Spanish emigrant Muslims and Jews was that of Sufism. In this case, I am interested less in the remarkable phenomenon of Jewish Sufism, whose centers were in Cairo and the Yemen, than I am in the approach to Jews on the part of Spanish emigrant Sufis.

Joel Kraemer recently has spoken of "the Sufī school of Murcia."[35] Ibn Sabʿīn of Murcia not only cited Maimonides' *Guide for the Perplexed* in his *Risāla al-Nūriyya* and displayed further knowledge of Maimonidean thought in his correspondence with the Emperor Frederick II, but produced disciples like Ibn Hūd of Murcia, who taught the *Guide* to Muslims and Jews alike.[36] Ibn Sabʿīn also was followed, moreover, by another Murcian disciple in Damascus, ʿAlī al-Ḥarrālī, whose father was a Jewish convert.[37] Louis Massignon went so far as to argue, in fact, that Ibn Sabʿīn possessed an "interconfessional plan" and even spoke of "Ibn Sabʿīn and the Hallajian conspiracy in Andalusia and the Orient in the thirteenth century."[38] Apparently, expatriate colonies of Murcian activists were transplanted to Fez and Damascus.[39] Still, Massignon was an enthusiast of genius, and we should not feel constrained to follow him in ascribing conspiratorial plans to the Sabᶜīniyya.

The followers of Ibn ᶜArabī spread far more widely than those of Ibn Sabᶜīn, but here again one need not resort to conspiracy theory. In the present context, the *Shaykh al-Akbar, The Great Master,* is certainly the most important figure in terms of impact, and yet he remains the least known in terms of his relationship to Jews and Judaism. Let me begin with an intriguing example. Ibn ᶜArabī's theory of divine names bears a suggestive similarity to certain Jewish notions, as Vajda noted some years ago.[40] For example, in the *Guide for the Perplexed,* Maimonides glosses the traditional name *hey ha-ᶜolamim,* "the Life of the worlds"; while Ibn ᶜArabī places *ḥayy al-ᶜālim,* the *Life of the World,* as the first of seven Prototypes (*ummahāt*), an important cognate term in Jewish-Muslim philosophy.[41] Indeed, Ibn ᶜArabī's theory of "eternal exemplars" may have some bearing on the development of the *sefirot* of Kabbalah, but this comparison remains to be explored.[42]

Ibn ᶜArabī's sources, likewise, remain to be investigated systematically. But indications suggest that he drew on sources heavily favored by Spanish Jews. For example, in his extraordinary vision of a youth by the *Kaabah*—one of the climactic passages in his vast corpus—he cites the *Theology of Aristotle.*[43] It is even more striking that he twice explicitly cites Ibn al-Sīd al-Baṭalyawsī (1052–1127).[44] This twelfth-century Spanish Muslim philosopher was studied, it appears, almost exclusively by Jews, who produced at least three Hebrew translations of his *Book of the Circles.*[45] Other Jews who cited him include the Spanish Kabbalists Abraham Abulafia and Moshe de Leon.[46] Ibn ᶜArabī's use of such sources as the *Theology of Aristotle* and the *Book of the Circles* may amplify our knowledge of the interconfessional circles in which he circulated.

Ibn ᶜArabī's social circumstances do not preclude contacts. It should be noted that both Ibn ᶜArabī and Maimonides, Spanish emigrant philosophers, resided in Cairo in 1203 and again in 1206.[47] That they could have met is not farfetched: Ibn ᶜArabī, like Maimonides, visited the few small circles of philosophers, and had already met, for example, Ibn Rushd.[48] In fact, Ibn ᶜArabī describes meeting a rabbi in his *Futūhāt,* just as we have actual protocols of Maimonides' meetings with Muslim scholars.[49] Moreover, Ibn ᶜArabī's circles, in addition to those just mentioned, also had other Jewish contacts. Al-Būnī, the thirteenth-century Egyptian magician and follower both of Ibn Sabᶜīn and Ibn ᶜArabī, included the Jewish angel Metatron in his repertoire, along with other Jewish motifs.[50]

The influence of the "Sufi school of Murcia" rolled through the early modern period. Ibn Sabᶜīn's disciple al-Ḥarrālī wrote a work which stimulated al-Biqāʾī, perhaps the first Muslim scholar to consult a written Arabic translation of the Bible.[51] The Majorcan itinerant, Ramon Llull, under the impact both of Ibn Sabᶜīn and of his student al-Shustarī (d. 1269), went on to influence Nicholas of Cusa (d. 1464), thereby providing a significant stimulus to the metaphysics of the European Renaissance.[52] And the influence of Ibn ᶜArabī simply may have been as deep and as broad as that of any Muslim thinker after the thirteenth century.[53]

Jewish Esoteric Elites

The last subculture is that of Arabophone Kabbalists with a philosophical orientation. From Southern Spain two thirteenth-century Jewish philosophers, Judah ben Nissim ibn Malkah and Judah ben Solomon ha-Cohen ibn Malkah (b. 1215), must be singled out in this regard.[54] Judah ben Nissim, Arabophone, perhaps originally Spanish, strongly influenced by Ismāᶜīlī thought, is closely associated with Judah ben Solomon ha-Cohen.[55] This latter connection may be significant, for Judah ben Solomon served as Jewish informant at the court of the Emperor Frederick II, with whom Ibn Sabᶜīn corresponded.[56] Judah, Judah, Ibn Laṭīf, and Abraham, operating between 1240 and 1280 in the largely Arabic milieu of Spain and Morocco, were Maimonideans influenced by Sufism whose interpretation of Kabbalah formed a distinct mystical approach. This form of Kabbalah would be incomprehensible without understanding its interconfessional contacts, particularly those in Spain.

A few words are in order concerning the meaning of this phenomenon. These four circles operated on the blurry line somewhere between *mythos* and *logos*. Largely Avicennan and Neoplatonic, they shared an increasing tendency to resort to narrative depictions of ratiocination.[57] No sooner had angels commonly come to be identified with Intelligences or Intellects—by the year 1200 a fact in all three traditions—than the road to seraphic reason circled back on itself. Imaginative representations of conceptual materials by means of the hybrid genre of philosophical allegory now enjoyed a brief but intense ascendency—Suhrawardī's "visonary recitals," Ovadya Maimonides' *Treatise of the Pool,* the pseudo-Maimonidean *Chapters on Beatitude,* Ibn Ṭufayl's pioneering novel, *Ḥayy ibn Yaqẓān.* What we have, in short, was an interconfessional renarrativization of Abrahamic religious thought. Along with other fictionalizing tendencies—return to pseudepigraphic conceits and the use of dialogues (like Judah ben Nissim ibn Malkah's *Uns al-Gharīb*)—this narrative turn paved the way, ultimately, for a full-blown theosophical remythologization. Spanning thirteenth-century Spain, this remythologization produced the theosophic masterworks of Abrahamic monotheism: the *al-Futūḥāt al-Makkiyya* of Ibn ᶜArabī, the *Zohar* of Moshe de Leon, and the *Art* of Ramon Llull.

What did this renarrativization have to do with interconfessionalism among emigrants? Jewish and Muslim Andalusians shared a common Christian enemy, for one thing. As I have noted, they also shared a class and professional basis, grounded in a common language, curriculum, and often occupation. But most pertinently, they shared a regnant esoterism. I leave aside the question of whether *falsafa* (philosophy) or *taṣawwuf* (Sufism) as such encouraged transgression of confessional boundaries. It is enough to observe that esoterism flourished among elites who believed that they alone actualized the theory of philosophy and perfected the practice of mysticism.

Intellectuals abroad sought out familiars from the "old country." The isolation of the exile, emigrant or itinerant, could only be compounded by being an intellectual. Isaac of Acre, commenting on Judah ben Nissim ibn Malkah's dialogue *Consolation to the Stranger* (*Uns al-Gharīb*) put it succinctly: "The author means by [the term "stranger"] to designate the body and the soul that are strangers here below, especially the soul whose place of origin is the heaven but presently resides on this earth like a person who sojourns in a strange land." This symbolic conflation of intellectual quest and geographical homelessness spoke succinctly to the plight and to the self-glorification of these refugees.[58] It would be worthwhile to reflect further on the acute rhetorical shaping of thought in these subcultures. We will not understand these social changes, I think, unless we understand *emigration and the art of writing.*[59]

CONCLUSION: SCHWELLENKUNDE

In the twelfth and thirteenth centuries, Jewish and Muslim migrants from Spain brought with them a "philosophy of combat," to transpose Professor Hillgarth's characterization of Ramon Llull's project. That is, they engaged opposing thought systems from a firm ethnocentric foundation, and not out of some anachronistically misplaced ecumenical spirit. That being said, they were, nonetheless, interconfessional despite themselves (as was the case with Llull).[60] Jewish-Muslim relations, of course, were constrained by polemic, conversion, mission. And yet other realities of the social life of intellectuals—the cravings of scholarship and the curiosity of science, to be sure, but also the chauvinism of nativity and devotion of friends—could override these fundamental oppositions. Once overridden, and learning occurred, the ostensible polemicist inwardly could be "turned," could take on the images, motifs, approaches, of the nominal enemy. Through contacts cultivated in these circles, information, translations, books, but most importantly, living dialogue on matters of the mind, moved from Muslim to Jew, Jew to Muslim.

The results were considerable. By the end of the thirteenth century, we find that the revolutions identified with Maimonides and (differently) with Ibn ʿArabī cleaved a kind of caesura in time.[61] We arrive at a new threshold, as we leave the long period of symbiosis and renaissance behind. The epochal greatness of the Spanish emigrants, in fact, may be sensed as a matter of thresholds: they operated between East and West, between ancient and modern, between philosophy and mysticism, and between Muslim and Jew. This export of *convivencia,* with its veritable connoisseurship of thresholds (*Schwellenkunde*), unmistakably reshaped the Mediterranean intellectual world.[62]

NOTES

1. Joshua Blau, "Maimonides, Al-Andalus, and the Influence of the Spanish-Arabic Dialect on His Language," in *New Horizons in Sephardic Studies,* ed. Yedida K. Stillman and George K. Zucker (Albany, N.Y., 1993), 203,

with special reference to his use of ᶜ*indanā fi-l-andalus*. See more generally Norman Roth, "Maimonides as a Spaniard: National Consciousness of a Medieval Jew," in *Sobre la Vida y Obra de Maimonides: I Congreso internacional* [Córdoba, 1985], ed. Jesus Pelaez del Rosal (Córdoba, 1991), 463–72.

2. Moshe Idel, *Kabbalah New Perspectives* (New Haven, Conn., 1988).

3. Seth Brody reviews the literature in "Human Hands Dwell in Heavenly Heights: Contemplative Ascent and Theurgic Power in Thirteenth-Century Kabbalah," in *Mystics of the Book: Themes, Topics, and Typologies,* ed. Robert A. Herrara (New York, 1993), 156 n. 23. Moshe Idel also notes that Isaac of Acre was active in Damascus, where followers of Ibn ᶜArabī and Ibn Sabᶜīn were simultaneously active (*Kabalah New Perspectives,* 307 n. 72). For more on this context, see Louis Pouzet, "De Murcie à Damas: le chef des Sabᶜiniens Badr ad-Dīn al-Ḥasan ibn Hūd," in *Actes du XIᵉ Congrès de l'union européenne des arabisants et islamologues,* ed. Adel Sidarus (Evora, 1986), 317–30, and Louis Pouzet, *Damas au VIIᵉ/XIIIᵉ siècle: vie et structures religieuses d'une métropole islamique* (Beirut, 1988).

4. Raphael Jospe, "*Ranban* (Nahmanides) and Arabic," *Tarbitz* 57 (1987): 67–93 [in Hebrew]. For even later survivals of Spanish-Jewish knowledge of Arabic, see Eleazar Gutwirth, "Hispano-Jewish Attitudes to the Moors in the Fifteenth Century," *Sefarad* 49 (1989): 237–62.

5. Jose Maria Millàs Vallicrosa, "The Doctrine of the 'Lullian Dignities' and the *Sefiroth,*" in *Yitzhak F. Baer Jubilee Volume,* ed. Salo W. Baron, B. Dinur, S. Ettinger, I. Halpern (Jerusalem, 1960), 186–90 [in Hebrew]. Like the Spanish Hebrew writers studied by Ross Brann, Ramon Llull similarly was a "compunctious poet" (Anthony Bonner, trans., *Selected Works of Ramon Llull [1231–1316],* 2 vols. [Princeton, 1985], 1.13–15, on his conversion) and was also indebted to Ibn ᶜArabī. Miguel Asin Palacios, *The Mystical Philosophy of Ibn Masarra and His Followers* (Leiden, 1978), 138–40.

6. For example, Moshe Idel has argued that there was a "magical renascence among some members of the Jewish elite of 14th century . . . Castile, [who] were acquainted with Arabic literature and inclined, in some instances, to a philosophical interpretation of Kabbalah. . . . [T]he significant change that took place among the cultural elite during the 14th century was a reorientation to a philosophical-magical understanding of magical texts that was deeply influenced primarily by Islamic, and only rarely by Christian, magical sources" (Moshe Idel, "An Astral-Pneumatic Anthropoid," *Incognita* 2 [1991]: 10–11).

7. Sarah Stroumsa, "On Apostate Jewish Intellectuals in the Early Middle Ages under the Rule of Islam," *Peamim* 42 (1991): 61–76 [in Hebrew], and Gerson D. Cohen, "The Soteriology of R. Abraham Maimuni," in *Studies in the Variety of Rabbinic Cultures* (Philadelphia and New York, 1991), 228–29. Fischel spoke of "a wave of conversions which swept over the intellectual strata of Babylonian-Persian Jewry in the second part of the 13th century"

(Walter J. Fischel, "The Court Jew in the Islamic World" [= "New Introduction" to reprint of the 1937 edition] in *Jews in the Economic and Political Life of Mediaeval Islam* [New York, 1969], xx n. 26). See also Joel L. Kraemer, "The Andalusian Mystic Ibn Hūd and the Conversion of the Jews," *Israel Oriental Studies* 12 (1992): 59–73.

8. Speaking of "cooperation between adherents of different religions belonging to the same class or group of occupations," Goitein noted that "physicians and druggists [as representatives of Greek science] were to a large extent Jewish and Christian, which again was a most important factor promoting interconfessional contacts" (Shlomo Dov Goitein, "Interfaith Relations in Medieval Islam," *The Yaacov Herzog Memorial Lecture,* delivered at Columbia University, October 22, 1973, p. 26). For Maimonides as a physician, see now Mark R. Cohen, "The Burdensome Life of a Jewish Physician and Communal Leader: A Geniza Fragment from the Alliance Israélite Universelle Collection," *Jerusalem Studies in Arabic and Islam* 16 (1993): 125–37. For the health sciences more generally, see Sami K. Hamarneh, *Health Sciences in Early Islam: Collected Papers of Sami K. Hamarneh,* ed. Munawar A. Anees (San Antonio, n.d.). For Muslim scholars among the sciences, see Abdelhamid I. Sabra, "The Appropriation and Subsequent Naturalization of Greek Science in Medieval Islam: A Preliminary Statement," *History of Science* 25 (1987): 223–43. And for Jewish participation in the sciences see now Gad Freudenthal, "The Place of Science in Medieval Hebrew-Writing Jewish Communities: A Sociological Perspective," in *RASHI, 1040–1990: hommage à Ephraim E. Urbach* (Paris, 1993), 599–613.

9. David Kaufmann, "Maimonides's *Guide* in World Literature," in *Studies in Jewish Thought: An Anthology of German Jewish Scholarship,* ed. Alfred Jospe (Detroit, 1981), 225.

10. Shlomo Dov Goitein, "Formal Friendship in the Medieval Near East," *Proceedings of the American Philosophical Society* 115, no. 6 (1971): 484–89.

11. D. M. Dunlop, "Philosophical Predecessors and Contemporaries of Ibn Bājjah," *Islamic Quarterly* 2 (1955): 111–12; Shlomo Pines, "La Dynamique d'Ibn Bājja," in *Mélanges Alexandre Koyré publiés à l'occasion de son soixante-dixième anniversaire, 1: l'aventure de la science,* 2 vols. (Paris, 1964), 1.444. See also Shlomo Pines, "A Tenth-Century Philosophical Correspondence," *Proceedings of the American Academy for Jewish Research* 24 (1955): 134 n. 107, for more on early philosophical contacts across denominational lines.

12. These subcultures may be considered *intellectual esoterism* in order to avoid the misleading dichotomy of philosophy versus mysticism. Under this broader rubric one would include, then, some intellectuals who conventionally are considered philosophers and others commonly designated as mystics. Features in common to *intellectual esoterism* include: the fabrication of a comprehensive system of thought, whose stated goal is nothing less than "perfection"; appropriation of Aristotelian and Neoplatonic concepts, how-

ever much their implementation is mythological, theosophical, or hermetic; an appeal to the élite (*khawāss*); and the consequent practice of "the art of writing" in the rhetorical sense made famous by Leo Strauss.

However, just as the boundaries between philosophy and mysticism were blurry, so too were the delimitations of subsystems of intellectual esoterism. They were, in fact, profoundly interpenetrated, and distinctions between them accordingly should be posed purely for heuristic purposes. That is not to say that we are dealing with socially marginal subcultures. Rather, these were intellectual élites, who were keenly aware of their elevated position in the hierarchy of thought.

13. Ivry speaks of "an entire pattern of sympathy which Maimonides harbors towards Ismaʿīlī methodology and even doctrine." See "Islamic and Greek Influences on Maimonides' Philosophy," in *Maimonides and Philosophy,* ed. Shlomo Pines and Yiiahu Yovel (Dordrecht, 1986), 144. Scholem even asserted that "there is no essential difference between so radically spiritualistic a doctrine as the prophetology of the Ismaʿīlī and a rationalistic theory like that of Maimonides" (Gershom Scholem, *On the Kabbalah and Its Symbolism* [New York, 1965], 10).

14. Ibn Laṭīf utilized (apparently) Ismāʿīlī motifs of "the first created thing," of worldyears, and of prophetology. See Sarah Heller Wilensky, "The Guide and the Gate: The Dialectical Influence of Maimonides on Isaac ibn Laṭīf and Early Spanish Kabbalah" in *A Straight Path: Studies in Medieval Philosophy and Culture,* ed. Ruth Link-Salinger (Washington, D.C., 1988), 266–78; the original Hebrew version appears in *The Shlomo Pines Jubilee Volume on the Occasion of His 80th Birthday* (Jerusalem Studies in Jewish Thought 7 [1988]: 289–306); Sarah Heller Wilensky, "On the 'First Created Thing' in the Origins of Kabbalah and Its Philosophical Sources," in *Studies in Jewish Thought,* ed. Sarah Heller Wilensky and Moshe Idel (Jerusalem, 1989) [Hebrew].

15. Ivry, "Islamic and Greek Influences," summarizes this material (141–43). I deal with this question in my *Between Muslim and Jew: The Problem of Symbiosis under Early Islam* (Princeton, 1995).

16. Moshe Idel, "Franz Rosenzweig and Kabbalah," in *The Philosophy of Franz Rosenzweig,* ed. Paul Mendes-Flohr (Hanover, 1988), 67.

17. Suhrawardī capitalized (in the words of Fakhry) "to the utmost on the anti-Peripatetic sentiments of Ibn Sīnā and the mystical and experiential aspirations which he and kindred spirits had sought to satisfy" (Majid Fakhry, *A History of Islamic Philosophy: A Second Edition* [New York, 1983], 294); Ibn Ṭufayl explicitly enjoined that "whoever wishes to learn the Pure Truth should consult [*Ḥikma al-Mashriqiyya*]" (Miguel Cruz Hernández, *Historia de pensiamiento en el mundo islámico 2: desde el islam andalusi hasta el socialismo árabe* [Madrid, 1981], 308); while Ibn Sabʿīn similarly asserted that *al-Ḥikma al-Mashriqiyya* was "closer to the truth than all the rest" (Miguel Cruz Hernández, "Islamic Thought in the Iberian Peninsula," in *The Legacy of Muslim Spain,* ed. Salma Khadra Jayyusi [Leiden, 1992], 789, 798).

18. Paul B. Fenton, "The Arabic and Hebrew Versions of the *Theology of Aristotle*," in *Pseudo-Aristotle in the Middle Ages, The Theology and Other Texts,* ed. Jill Kraye, W. F. Ryan, and Charles B. Schmitt (London, 1986), 241–64.

19. Richard C. Taylor, "A Critical Analysis of the Structure of the *Kalām fi mahd al-khair* (*Liber de causis*)," in *Neoplatonism and Islamic Thought,* ed. Parviz Morewedge (Albany, 1992), 11–12.

20. Pouzet, *Damas au VIIe/XIIIe siècle,* 220.

21. For the *ijāza,* see John Walbridge, *The Science of Mystic Lights: Qutb al-Dīn Shīrāzī and the Illuminationist Tradition in Islamic Philosophy* (Cambridge, Mass., 1992): 174 n. 14. For the gloss on the *Guide,* see Harry A. Wolfson, *Crescas' Critique of Aristotle* (Cambridge, Mass., 1929), 19–23; and Mehdi Mohaqqeq, *Tabrīzī's Commentary on the Twenty-Five Premises from* The Guide of the Perplexed *by M. Maimonides,* trans. Jacfar Sajjādī (Tehran, 1981). Shīrāzī was part of the circle which corresponded with the Emperor Frederick II. Ivry notes that Moshe Narboni and Tabrīzī identified the undivided soul with the intellect. See Alfred Ivry, "Moses of Narbonne's 'Treatise on the Perfection of the Soul': A Methodological and Conceptual Analysis," *Jewish Quarterly Review* 57 (1967): 292 n. 43.

22. Heschel, for one, raises the possibility of a meeting in Fez: Abraham Joshua Heschel, *Maimonides: A Biography,* trans. Joachim Neugroschel (New York, 1982), 20. The influence of Ibn Bājja on Maimonides was explicit and fundamental: Shlomo Pines, "The Limitations of Human Knowledge According to al-Farabi, Ibn Bajja, and Maimonides," in *Studies in Medieval Jewish History and Literature,* ed. Isadore Twersky (Cambridge, Mass., 1979), 82–109. For Ibn Ṭufayl, see Dunlop, "Philosophical Predecessors," 115: "The impression left is that Ibn Ṭufail . . . regarded ibn Bājja as among the greatest if not the greatest, of Spanish philosophers who had hitherto appeared."

23. Maurice R. Hayoun, *Moshe Narboni* (Tübingen, 1986), and "Le commentaire de Moïse de Narbonne (1300–1362) sur le *Ḥayy ibn Yaqẓān* d'Ibn Ṭufayl (mort en 1185)," *Archives d'histoire et du litterature du moyen âge* 60 (1988): 23–98.

24. The converted Jew Abuʾl Barakāt al-Baghdādī influenced certain conceptions of Suhrawardī, while one leading commentator on Suhrawardī, Ibn Kammūna, was a Jewish convert. For details see my discussion, "The Social and Cultural Context: The Islamic Context" in *Routledge History of Jewish Philosophy,* ed. Daniel Frank and Oliver Leaman (Routledge, 1996).

25. See the discussion in Paul B. Fenton, *The Treatise of the Pool* (London, 1981) 65 n. 100, on the famous report by Ibn Abī Uṣaybiʿa. See also Samuel M. Stern, "A Collection of Treatises by ʿAbd al-Laṭīf al-Baghdādī," *Islamic Studies* 1 (1962): 60–61, on ʿAbd al-Laṭīf's familiarity with Ibn Shamʿūn, the pupil for whom Maimonides wrote his *Guide.*

26. Fenton, "The Arabic and Hebrew Versions," especially p. 256.

27. Louis Massignon, "Inventaire de la littérature hermétique arabe," ap-

pendix III to *La Révélation d'Hermès Trismégiste I: l'astrologie et les sciences occultes* (Paris, 1944), 384–400.

28. "Hermeticism and Judaism," in *Hermeticism and the Renaissance: Intellectual History and the Occult in Early Modern Europe* (Washington, D.C., 1988), 72 nn. 28–30.

29. Though Lenn E. Goodman has made a start. See his "Maimonides' Responses to Sa^cadya Gaon's Theodicy and Their Islamic Backgrounds," in *Studies in Islamic and Judaic Traditions* (Atlanta, 1988), 2.21 n. 50, and 22 n. 69; and Lenn E. Goodman, "Ordinary and Extraordinary Language in Medieval Jewish and Islamic Philosophy," *Manuscrito* 2 (1989): 70–71. I thank Professor Goodman for sharing these articles with me.

30. David H. Baneth [Hebrew translation and annotation] and H. S. Davidowitz, ed. *The Chapters on Beatitude Ascribed to R. Moses Maimonides* (Jerusalem, 1939), 33, line 21. In his recent English translation, Fred Rosner reviews the considerable consensus that this work is a pseudepigraphon (*Six Treatises Attributed to Maimonides* [Northvale, N.J., 1991], 12–13). Still, even if not the work of Maimonides himself, this treatise was written by another nearly contemporaneous Jewish philosopher familiar with Ibn Ṭufayl's work. The judgment of Vajda is representative: "Le mystère de [*Perakim be Hazlaha*] n'est pas encore éclairici; en tout cas, il fait partie de l'ensemble de productions judéo-arabes d'inspiration tant maimonidean que néoplatonique, tendant au mysticism me plus soufique que kabbalistique (en gros) qui constituera, en Egypte, en Syrie, et au Yémen, la pensée spéculative, non sans certaine variété, des Juifs arabophones postérieurement à Maimonide" (Georges Vajda, "La philosophie juive du moyen âge . . . " [Part II], *Hebrew Union College Annual* 45 [1974]: 223 n. 66).

31. Ibn Ṭufayl, *Ḥayy ibn Yaqdhān, roman philosophique d'Ibn Thofail,* ed. and trans. into French by Louis Gauthier, 2nd ed. (Beirut, 1936), 17. For a discussion of Ibn Ṭufayl in light of *Ishrāq* and other philosophical currents, see the forthcoming article of Bernd Radtke, "How Can Man Reach the Mystical Union? Ibn Ṭufayl and the Divine Spark." I thank Professor Radtke for sharing a preprint of this article with me. Miguel Cruz Hernandez also comments on this specific comparison ("Maimonnides como Faylasūf," in *Sobre la Vida y Obra de Maimonides: I Congreso internacional, Córdoba, 1985,* ed. Jesus Pelaez del Rosal [Córdoba, 1991], 83).

32. Dominique Urvoy, *Ibn Rushd (Averroës)* (London and New York, 1991), 123.

33. Originally misidentified in an otherwise superb study by Franz Rosenthal, "A Judaeo-Arabic work under Sufic Influence," *Hebrew Union College Annual* 15 (1940): 433–87. The work has now been translated and annotated closely, with special reference to the influence of Suhrawardī in Paul B. Fenton, *Deux traités de mystique juive* (Paris, 1987).

34. Hayoun, *Moshe Narboni;* Hayoun, "Le commentaire de Moïse de Nar-

bonne"; Moshe Idel, *Golem: Jewish Magical and Mystical Traditions on the Artifical Anthropoid* (Albany, 1990), 167 and 187 n. 10; Ernst Bloch, *Avicenna und die Aristotelische Linke* (Berlin, 1952), 25–30.

35. Kraemer, "The Andalusian Mystic Ibn Hūd," 68 n. 34.

36. For the citation of the *Guide for the Perplexed* in the *Risāla al-Nūriyya*, see Ibn Sabᶜīn, *Rasāʾil Ibn Sabᶜīn*, ed. A. Abdurrahmnan Badawi (Cairo, 1965), 157. This citation is noted by Chodkiewicz, *Le sceau des saints*, 106 n. 1. For a comparison of Ibn Sabᶜīn and Ibn ᶜArabī, see Michel Chodkiewicz, trans., *Epître dur l'Unicité Absolue* (*Risāla al-Ahadiya*) by Awhad al-dīn al-Balyânî (Paris, 1982). For the Maimonidean questions which Frederick II posed to Ibn Sabᶜīn in their correspondence, see Solomon Munk, *Mélanges de philosophie juive et arabe* (reprint of 1855–65 edition, Paris, 1988), 144–45 n. 2; and Kaufmann, "Maimonides's *Guide*," 232. For Ibn Hūd, see Pouzet, "De Murcie à Damas"; Pouzet, *Damas au VIIᵉ/XIIIᵉ siècle*," 218–19; and especially Kraemer, "The Andalusian Mystic Ibn Hūd."

37. Pouzet, *Damas au VIIᵉ/XIIIᵉ siècle*, 218–19; Claude Addas, Ibn *ᶜArabi ou la quête du soufre rouge* (Paris, 1989), 229, 230, 294, 302; Emile Dermenghem, *Vies des saints musulmans* (Paris, 1981), 276–88. Al-Ḥarrālī exerted a strong influence on al-Biqāʾī, one of the only medieval Muslim authors known to have studied a written (Arabic) text of the Torah. He also worked with a Jewish informant. See Hava Lazarus-Yafeh, *Intertwined Worlds: Medieval Islam and Bible Criticism* (Princeton, 1992), 128 n. 62. However, al-Biqāʾī was a violent opponent of Ibn ᶜArabī. See Michael Chodkiewicz, *An Ocean without Shore: Ibn Arabi, the Book and the Law* (Albany, 1993), 19 and Alexander Knysh, "Ibn ᶜArabī in the Later Islamic Tradition," in *Muhyiddin ibn ᶜArabī: A Commemorative Volume*, ed. Stephen Hertenstein and Michael Tiernan (Shaftesbury, Dorset, 1993), 316–17.

38. Louis Massignon, "Ibn Sabᶜīn, et la 'conspiration hallagienne' en Andalousie, et en Orient au XIIIᵉ siècle," in *Études d'orientalisme dédiées a la mémoire de Lévi-Provençal, tome II* (Paris, 1962), 671.

39. Isaac of Acre operated in Damascus for a time, as did Ibn Hūd, ᶜAbd al-Sayyid al-Isrāʾīlī, and others. See note 3 above. As I have noted above, Maimonides could have met Ibn Ṭufayl in Fez and Ibn ᶜArabī in Cairo. Fez, for a time, seems to have sustained a certain interconfessionalism. According to Ibn Kaspī, in 1332, Muslims studied the *Guide for the Perplexed* in a Fez *madrasa*. See Fenton, *Deux traités*, 107 n. 231.

40. Georges Vajda, *Juda ben Nissim ibn Malka* (Paris, 1956), 73.

41. *Guide*, 1.69; 1.72. Vajda cites this verse but does not make the connection between Maimonides and Ibn ᶜArabī, but he deals more directly with the parallels between Judah ben Nissim and Ibn ᶜArabī elsewhere (*Guide*, 1.84). See also Alexander Altmann, "Maimonides' Attitude toward Jewish Mysticism," in *Studies in Jewish Thought: An Anthology of German Jewish Scholarship*, ed. Alfred Jospe (Detroit, 1981), 219 n. 62, citing *Guide*, 1.69 and

1.72. For more on the "life of the worlds," see also Gershom Scholem, *Origins of the Kabbalah* trans. Allan Arkush (Princeton, 1987), 157. For the *ummahāt* in Ibn ʿArabī, see, for example, Franz Rosenthal, "Ibn ʿArabī between 'Philosophy' and 'Mysticism'," *Oriens* (1988): 28.

42. Some hints are provided by Paul B. Fenton, "The Hierarchy of the Saints in Jewish and Islamic Mysticism," *Journal of the Muhyiddin ibn ʿArabī Society* 10 (1991): 32 n. 36, for a provocative comparison of respective hierarchies of saints, represented on a graph.

43. Fritz Meier, "The Mystery of the Kaʿba: Symbol and Reality in Islamic Mysticism," in *The Mysteries: Papers from the Eranos Yearbooks* (New York, 1955), 156; Henry Corbin, *Creative Imagination in the Sufism of Ibn ʿArabī* (Princeton, 1969), 385; Chodkiewicz, *An Ocean without Shore*, 28, 79, 156.

44. Claude Addas, *Quest for the Red Sulfur: The Life of Ibn ʿArabī*, trans. Peter Kingsley (Cambridge, 1993), 137.

45. Alexander Altmann, "The Ladder of Ascension," in *Studies in Religious Philosophy and Mysticism* (Ithaca, 1969), 48. It may be added to Altmann's magisterial discussion that Ibn al-Sīd's work agrees with the *Theology of Aristotle* in identifying the active intellect with the cosmic intellect (Herbert A. Davidson, *Al-Fārābī, Avicenna, and Averroës, on Intellect: Their Cosmologies, Theories of the Active Intellect, and Theories of Human Intellect* [New York, 1992], 154 n. 139; and Fenton, "The Arabic and Hebrew Versions," 260 n. 2).

46. For Abulafia, see the provocative discussion in Moshe Idel, *Studies in Ecstatic Kabbalah* (Albany, 1988), 23 n. 34. For Moshe de Leon, see Altmann, "The Ladder of Ascension," 67–68, where he provides "decisive proof" of this borrowing.

47. Michael Sean Ryan, *Empty Bodies on Ruined Thrones: Politics in the Thought of Ibn ʿArabī*, doctoral dissertation, Harvard, 1981, 72–73.

48. Egbert Meyer, "Ibn ʿArabī begegnet ibn Rušd: Variationen zum Thema Gotteskenntnis," in *Zeitschrift für Geschichte der Arabischen-Islamischen Wissenschaften* 3 (1986): 280–334. On the other hand, Avicenna and Ibn Ṭufayl find no trace in Ibn ʿArabī (Addas, *Ibn ʿArabī*, 177).

49. *Futūḥāt I*, 837, cited in Addas, *Ibn ʿArabī*, 139 n. 1. For an example of Maimonides' meetings, see Sholmo Dov Goitein, "The Maimonides–Ibn Sanāʾ al-Mulk Circle (A Deathbed Declaration from March 1182)," in *Studies in Islamic History and Civilization in Honour of Professor David Ayalon* (Leiden, 1986). It has been suggested that Ibn ʿArabī may have borrowed some elements of his theory of the *insan kamil* (Perfect Man) from Maimonides (Ronald Kiener, "Ibn al-ʿArabī and the Qabbalah: A Study of Thirteenth-Century Iberian Mysticism," *Studies in Mystical Literature*, and Roger Arnaldez, "Ibn ʿArabī," in *Encyclopedia of Islam*, 2nd ed., 3.1239.

50. See Vajda, "De quelques éléments juifs et pseudo-juifs dans l'encyclopédie magique de Buni," in *Ignace Goldziher Memorial Volume I* (Budapest,

1948), 387–92. Rosenthal spoke of the "apparent lack of influence on al-Būnī by ibn ᶜArabī" (Franz Rosenthal, *The Muqaddimah: An Introduction to History,* 2nd ed., 3 vols. (Princeton, 1967), 3.172 n. 807). But Chodkiewicz now notes that Būnī "mentions Ibn ᶜArabī in his chains of transmission" (Chodkiewicz, *An Ocean without Shore,* 9). For a fuller treatment of Būnī and Ibn ᶜArabī, see Denis Gril, "La hiérarchie des lettres," in *Les illuminations de La Mecque/The Meccan Illuminations,* selected texts trans. Michel Chodkiewiz et al. (Paris, 1988), 430–32.

51. Lazarus-Yafeh, *Intertwined Worlds,* 128 n. 62.

52. Charles Lohr, "Christianus arabicus, cuius nomen Raimundus Lullus," *Freiburger Zeitschrift fur Philosophie und Theologie* 31 (1984): 57–88; and "Metaphysics," in *The Cambridge History of Renaissance Philosophy* (Cambridge and New York, 1988). On Shustarī, see now Omaima Abou-Bakr, "The Symbolic Function of Metaphor in Medieval Sufi Poetry: The Case of Shustarī," in *Alif 12: Metaphor and Allegory in the Middle Ages* (1992), 40–58. On the influence of Shustarī, see Dominique Urvoy, and Marie-Therese Urvoy, "Les thèmes chrétiens chez ibn Sabᶜīn et la question de la spécificité de sa pensée," *Studia islamica* 44 (1976): 99–121, especially 119–21.

53. Chodkiewicz, *An Ocean without Shore,* 1–18.

54. They are grouped together and discussed perspicuously but cursorily by Colette Sirat, *A History of Jewish Philosophy in the Middle Ages* (Cambridge, 1985), 250–59. The most important recent work, after that of Vajda, on Judah ben Nissim is that of Moshe Idel, "The Beginning of Kabbalah in North Africa? A Forgotten Document by R. Yehuda ben Nissim ibn Malka," *Peamin* 43 (1990): 4–15 [in Hebrew].

55. Sirat, *A History of Jewish Philosophy,* 250–59.

56. Collette Sirat, "La Qabbale d'après Juda b. Solomon ha-Cohen," in *Hommage à Georges Vajda,* ed. Georges Nahon and Charles Touati (Louvain, 1980), 191–202.

57. Peter Heath, *Allegory and Philosophy in Avicenna (Ibn Sīnā), with a Translation of the Book of the Prophet Muḥammad's Ascent to Heaven* (Philadelphia, 1992), 9: "From the perspective of the sociology of knowledge, the commitment of philosophers to logos as their preferred form of narrative and discourse constitutes a fundamental element in what Ibn Khaldūn (d. 808/1406) would call their ᶜaṣabiyya, or 'feeling of group solidarity'. . . . Not surprisingly, this philosophical ᶜaṣabiyya has tended to make experts in other fields nervous and defensive." See also James Morris, "Situating Islamic 'Mysticism': Between Written Tradition and Popular Spirituality," in Herrara, *Mystics of the Book,* 332, n. 55, on Avicenna's general influence on theoretical mysticism.

58. Vajda, *Juda ben Nissim,* 11 n. 1; cf Ex. 19.

59. Heath, *Allegory and Philosophy,* and Leo Strauss, "Persecution and the Art of Writing," in *Persecution and the Art of Writing* (Glencoe, Ill., 1952). See

also Kraemer, "The Andalusian Mystic Ibn Hūd," for some allusive suggestions concerning these circles. See also James Morris, "Ibn ʿArabī's 'Esotericism': The Problem of Spiritual Authority," *Studia islamica* 71 (1990): 37–64 and Morris, "Situating Islamic 'Mysticism'."

60. Anthony Bonner, "The Current State of Studies on Ramon Llull's Thought," *Catalonia Review* 2 (1989): 147: "he was obliged to develop a totally autonomous abstract system, based on points which were equally acceptable to all three religions. . . . [I]t has no specifically Christian points; all are equally acceptable to the three monotheistic religions, all equally the heirs of the same Greek science."

61. Compare the current "Akbarian Renaissance" (Chodkiewicz, *An Ocean without Shore*) with the equally current "Rambamian Renaissance" (Warren Zev Harvey, "The Return of Maimonideanism," *Journal of Jewish Studies* 42 [1980]: 249–68).

62. I borrow this phrase from Winfried Menninghaus, *Schwellenkunde: Walter Benjamin's Passage des Mythos* (Frankfurt a.M., 1986).

PART II

Muslims and Jews in Christian Spain

5

Mudejar Parallel Societies: Anglophone Historiography and Spanish Context, 1975–2000

ROBERT I. BURNS, S.J.

A CONSIDERABLE SCHOOL of medieval historians in the United States has been studying Spain for many years; it is only fair that Spain has now begun studying us. The first such turnabout is Ángel Galán Sánchez's volume on *A Vision of "Spanish Decline": Anglo-Saxon Historiography on the Mudejars and Moriscos (18th to 20th Centuries)*.[1] Only a rare scholar among my non-Spanish colleagues would submit to the disconcerting description "Anglo-Saxon"; John Boswell, Anwar Chejne, Thomas Glick, Elena Lourie, Angus MacKay, and I are among those analyzed under the Mudejar rubric as Anglo-Saxon. We charitably understand, however, that "Anglophone" is meant. Galán's book is welcome on two counts. He is well informed and careful in his analysis of authors, drawing upon serious historiographical studies in both English and Spanish. And his work implicitly invites us to pause in our production to reflect upon our common motives, assumptions, and thematic directions in the history of Spain's Mudejars—Muslims living under their Christian conquerors. No other field of medieval study, except for the crusades, is so largely the work of Anglophone scholars. But just as our view of a Spanish phenomenon from the outside can result in distortions, lacunae, and idiosyncrasies, so a Spaniard's view of us historians may also need correction and amplification.

Unlike continental historians, we are far less likely to have a conscious theory or a common theory, or to follow a dominant mentality in shaping and interpreting our materials. More exactly, we are likely to be pragmatic and changeable, adopting techniques, approaches, and viewpoints as they catch our fancy. However vulnerable our partialities, they are not usually programmatic or too firmly held. This is in marked contrast to literary scholars in North America, whose contentious factions rally passionately under their respective banners of theory. Nor should much be made of a connection with England and its anti-Spanish traditions. The ethnic transformation of the United States by our lifetime, the influence of German historiographical practice, and above all the influx of exile scholars during and after Hitler's war broke any English continuum and radically reshaped America's intellectual and academic landscape. Galán Sánchez presents the twentieth-century Anglophone historiography under the title "From a Polemical Vision to the Influence of the Social Sciences," a perspective that needs to be qualified. American historians generally resist identification with the social sciences and are ambivalent about adapting their paradigms and methodologies. Historians value their use for bridging gaps in the data and for opening novel perspectives, but they also mistrust the static structure of such disciplines in a constantly changing world as well as their shallow foundations on theory. Historians do use elements from the social sciences but gingerly and as auxiliary aids toward new insights. We look to the provocative instead of the ideologic, to the exploratory rather than the fixed.

Experience and common sense nonetheless warn us that contemporary mentalities and assumptions as well as personal evolution, preoccupations, and attitudes to some degree direct and color our researches. Since these influences in their aggregate differ with each different person, like the unique fingerprint or visage, a more useful historiography might issue from autobiographical reflection by a cast of both senior and junior contributors to the Mudejar field. This would trace the origins and development of the individual's attraction to and immersion in the world of Spain's three communities, the talents, training, and pedagogical influences, and finally the personal characteristics, life contexts and experiences, and simple accidents that have affected his work. If history is at bottom biographies, so also is historiography.[2]

There were many kinds of Mudejar communities, whose structures and externals were analogous but whose contexts and experiences varied widely, according to place and time. These changing faces of Mudejar society are not yet reflected adequately in the many research works coming on stream, but a promising beginning has been made. Mudejar historiography itself displays many faces, however, and these invite a recapitulation. A thorough review is not possible except in book form. But we can draw a simple map showing where our generation started (both Hispanic and "Anglo"), where we are now, and how we got here. When I began my own medieval studies almost a half-century ago, and indeed up to the year 1960, only one serious book existed on the Mudejars in any language, and it had been published a hundred years before—Francisco Fernández y González's *Estado social y político de los mudejares de Castilla.*[3] This is astonishing when one reflects that conquered Muslims had constituted significant parallel societies over many generations in many parts of Spain. Moriscos had always attracted attention, of course, as much for the human tragedy of their story as for the relative abundance of their more modern sources. In a shadowy way too, the mere existence of conquered Muslims formed part of everyone's romantic perception of medieval Spain as pluri-cultural and somehow a "tolerant" society.

Some twenty-five years further into my work, however, it was possible to survey the startling rise of a new field, as I did in my 1977 *Viator* article "Mudejar History Today."[4] Where a handful of articles had long constituted our Mudejar knowledge, by scholars such as Francisco Macho y Ortega (1922), Felipe Mateu y Llopis (1942), Leopoldo Piles Ros (1949), Miguel Gual Camarena (1949), Francisco Roca Traver (1952), and Leopoldo Torres Balbás (from the 1950s), the decade of the 1960s gave us José M. Lacarra's pioneering book on the Mudejars of Aragon proper (1960) and Miguel Angel Ladero Quesada's book on Isabeline Mudejars (1969). This modest start was accompanied by still more articles, notably by Juan Torres Fontes opening up the subfield of Murcia's Mudejars (1961). Articles were now becoming numerous enough, of high quality, and of a widening range of interest, so that by the end of the 1960s one could properly speak of a maturing field.[5]

The 1970s saw a bibliographical revolution in Mudejar scholarship. The decade opened with Thomas Glick's *Irrigation and Society in Medieval Valencia* (1970) and closed with his *Islamic and Christian Spain in the Early Middle Ages: Comparative Perspectives on Social and Cultural Formation* (1979). Though neither book was focused directly on Mudejarism, they both involved that society tangentially, and they both proposed provocative models and perspectives about mutual acculturation of Muslim and Christian in the Mudejar situation. Glick's article on "*Muḥtasib* and *Mustasaf*" was similarly comprehensive in its data and provocatively original in its arguments for mutual acculturation or feedback between those institutions.[6] My own first two books on Mudejarism appeared then—*Islam under the Crusaders: Colonial Survival in the Thirteenth-Century Kingdom of Valencia* (1973), and *Medieval Colonialism: Postcrusade Exploitation of Islamic Valencia* (1975).[7] The first attempted a comprehensive view of the Mudejar society taking form in the first generation or so after the crusader conquest. It owed something to the *Annales* approach to social history which then offered new visions and patterns, but there was no systematic application of principles (if indeed the founders of that approach ever envisaged the relentless system that evolved) and it did not exclude an eclectic inspiration from other historians. My previous training in ethnohistory under R. Rahman at the Anthropos Institut, then attached in exile to the University of Fribourg, in Switzerland, had resulted in a separate doctorate and series of publications, and that certainly exercised some influence.[8] *Islam* and *Colonialism* were not strongly theoretical, but rather a pragmatic effort to recover the myriad archival details, to arrange them in the widest possible context of other data, and to approach the emerging society from as many perspectives as time allowed. The fiscal or tax documentation proved so overwhelming that it demanded the second book to explore how far such material could illumine Mudejar structure and daily life all by itself.

An important and permanent contribution appeared at mid-decade, John Boswell's Harvard dissertation published under the title *The Royal Treasure: Muslim Communities under the Crown of Aragon in the Fourteenth Century* (1977).[9] Boswell moved Mudejar research boldly into its late fourteenth-century context, a critical time in both Iberian and Mudejar history. The stage widened to encompass all the realms of Arago-Catalonia except the Balearics. Boswell focused on the decade between 1355 and 1366, the years of savage war between Pere the Ceremonious and Castile's Pedro the Cruel, as a time of general social crisis that illumines the Mudejar condition. With archival resources so formidable for this later period, from municipal and notarial to the range of ecclesiastical corporations, Boswell's practical strategy was to confine his energies to the register and patrimonial sections of the crown archives at Barcelona. He marshaled his findings in eight chapters: the Mudejar population (relation to lord or king, serfs, slaves, wealthy class, occupations); community organization (housing pattern, prostitution and gambling, minor officials and major, notaries, butchers); legal system (loss of autonomous jurisdiction, role of each Christian authority, fines, torture); military obligations (draft, service, mixed units, cavalry), taxes and finance (tax nomenclature, wartime exploitation, exemptions, emigration); rights (erosion of religious privileges, restricting mendicancy, armsbearing, sales, inheritance, travel); oppression (enslavement, wartime seizure, rapacious officials, sexual exploitation, harassment, grievances presented by communities); acculturation, loyalty, and the war (mixing with Christians, mutual hostility, increase in European surnames, language as acculturative index, wartime dislocation and destruction); and a documentary appendix.

A Princeton dissertation by Donald Thaler, unpublished but still available from Xerox University Microfilms, also appeared at this time (1973): *The Mudejars of Aragon during the Twelfth and Thirteenth Centuries.*[10] Though the author attempts too large a review for two hundred typed pages, both chronologically and geographically, he does present a useful survey as well as novel data, suggestive interpretations, and transcribed documents. After a chapter on sources, published and archival, and a chapter on the Reconquest and Mudejarism, Thaler offers three chapters: social organization by *aljama,* economic activity (crops, tenure, trades, rents), and relations with Christians. The last is an inconclusive essay, which sees intermixing and formal correctness along with an alarming increase of troubles between the two peoples from the fourteenth century, and in general a slow decline from the end of the Reconquest.

In 1978 my Variorum reprint collection *Moors and Crusaders in Mediterranean Spain* selected seventeen of my articles, particularly those in *Speculum* and *The American Historical Review.*[11] The decade had seen a generous spate of articles, of course, including Elena Lourie's revisionist *Speculum* study on "Free Muslims in the Balearics under Christian Rule in the Thirteenth Century" (1970) from her Oxford dissertation, the starting point for all future work on Majorca's Mudejars.[12] The scope and quality of that decade's books in English on Mudejars would alone have made it a memorable time in Mudejar Studies. Even halfway through the decade, it seemed imperative to survey all the recent advances in articles and books to inform medievalists of the burgeoning field.[13] The Anglo-Saxons had arrived.

It would expand this presentation inappropriately to take in supporting fields, but it is necessary to note that an Anglophone medieval Hispanism was part and parcel of the Anglophone Mudejarism. Joseph O'Callaghan brought out his comprehensive *History of Medieval Spain* in 1975 and Jocelyn Hillgarth his *Spanish Kingdoms 1250–1516* in 1978, with summary histories coming from Gabriel Jackson (1972), Angus MacKay (1977) and Derek Lomax (1978).[14] Others would follow later, notably Roger Collins's survey, *Early Medieval Spain: Unity in Diversity, 400–1000* (1983), and Bernard Reilly, *The Medieval Spains* (1993).[15] Anglophone Hispanists by the 1970s encountered each other in formal conferences, reviewed each other's books, came together in sociable interchanges, and in 1975 established the Academy of Research Historians on Medieval Spain. That organization, numbering about 150, became an affiliate of the American Historical Association, with a national newsletter and two large conference-programs annually. It offered both a platform for frequent Mudejar papers and the supporting function of critique and reflection such a peculiar required. To a lesser degree the more general Society for Spanish and Portuguese Historical Studies, from 1975, was hospitable to a measure of medieval history and presented some Mudejar offerings. Of use too from the late 1950s, though resolutely literary in its main issues, was the North American Catalan Society.

The patterns of availability of Mudejar documentation tended to draw its practitioners into Catalan archives and Catalan historical contexts. The rise of a vigorous Anglophone school of Catalan history, both medieval and modern, is therefore relevant to the contemporaneous rise of a parallel Mudejar school. I have reviewed "Catalan Studies in North America: Medieval History" elsewhere, however, so the movement's rise from the 1940s into the 1990s, and its many younger scholars, need not detain us here.[16] Anglophone Hispanists, Catalanists, and Mudejarists alike now turned up each year in

Spain's archives and congresses. People began to speak of Hispanist "schools" at Toronto and UCLA, picking up the torch of medieval Hispanism from the pioneering Charles Julian Bishko of the University of Virginia. It was in 1975, too, that Bishko published his monograph-length recapitulation of the "Spanish and Portuguese Reconquest, 1095–1492" in the giant Wisconsin history of the crusades.[17] And in 1976 the Institute of Medieval Mediterranean Spain opened its doors in a high-rise office building in Playa del Rey, a pleasant beachside adjunct to Los Angeles. Its library of Catalan history and microfilm manuscripts has increased considerably with each passing year.[18]

Though special attention is given here to Anglophone contributions, Spain itself increased its own output of Mudejar articles strongly in that decade, while France contributed the early works of Pierre Guichard, especially his important study on the Mudejar fief of Crevillente.[19] The defining event in the origins and evolution of Mudejar Studies at large came appropriately at mid-decade—the International Symposium of Mudejar Studies, convened at Teruel in 1975 among that city's treasures of Mudejar towers and art. Sponsored by the Spanish government, opened by public dignitaries, covered by television and journalists, and attended by some two hundred participants, this became the first in a permanent series, each producing a large volume of variegated studies. The symposia both marked the coming of age of this field and provided the necessary stimulation and visibility for its further progress. Ironically, the Anglophones were usually sequestered in their classrooms when the several symposia convened, and in any event they were inhibited by the expense of the voyage. Actual publication of the symposia did not come out until the 1980s, so their content will be considered below, but a detailed report of the first symposium appeared in UCLA's *Viator,* outlining the framing disquisitions or *ponencias* by Lacarra, Ladero Quesada, Torres Fontes, and others, including my own presentation of ten positions or conclusions on the state of Mudejar research.[20] After the bleak landscape on Mudejars in the 1950s, and the modest quickening of the 1960s, the surge of the 1970s may well have evoked in the breasts of the more impressionable Mudejarists a Wordsworthian emotion that "Bliss it was in that dawn to be alive." The best, however, may yet to be.

The 1980s and 1990s, which may be expressed as an artificial decade 1984–1994, have witnessed a transformation and epiphany. The field has at last been institutionalized, with a government-sponsored Center for Mudejar and Morisco studies ensconced at Teruel. An ongoing bibliography, centered on eastern Spain but with a generous peninsular horizon, has exhaustively collected Mudejar items both old and new, with topical index and annotations. This is the work of Míkel de Epalza, the University of Alicante's Arabist, who is also involved in the Center. His *Moros y moríscos en el levante peninsular (Sharq al-Andalus): introducción bibliográfica* in 1983 began with over two thousand entries on Spain's Muslims, Mudejars, and Moriscos.[21] He also founded a journal in 1984 as an annual volume—*Sharq al-Andalus: estudios árabes*—which carries Mudejar articles among its wider coverage and a regular appendix updating his original bibliography. The number of bibliographical entries had reached over 5,126 by the volume for 1992. While this bibliographical wealth was coming from the University of Alicante, the University of Oviedo in 1989 began its bibliographical bulletin *Aljamía* on Mudejar and Morisco themes, under the direction of Alvaro Galmés de Fuentes with the assistance of Epalza and others. It publishes bibliographies, reviews, reports on conferences, accounts of works in progress, and news of the field. Epalza's own articles, an unceasing flow, are listed in these bibliographies and are always worth consulting—original, erudite, and often establishing new directions, ranging from properly Arabist topics up through the Moriscos. Mudejar studies are deeply indebted to his insights.

So rich is the book and article bibliography on Mudejars now, a very sea of publications, that it would be impossible to present in one sitting the kind of overview I was able to offer in 1977. Selective regional or topical surveys are commissioned for the successive volumes of the Teruel symposia, and occasionally appear elsewhere as with Maria Teresa Ferrer i Mallol's 1992 thematic review of publications on the Mudejars of the realms of Aragon.[22] The wider field of Iberian Mudejar bibliography was covered in a 1989 bibliographical booklet by Paz Fernández.[23] Without reduplicating those efforts, it is both possible and necessary to note representative works that have appeared in the decade 1984–1994, where the transformation of the field, its current directions, and its promise are most visible. In this *decada mirabilis* the Anglo-Saxons continue their valuable contributions, though now with more formidable competition from Spain, France, and even Japan. Subjective perspectives shape such lists, and apologies may be owing to excellent works bypassed in the choosing here.

The decade began with Mercedes García Arenal's archival reconstruction of the Mudejar society of Navarre,[24] and with María Carmen Barceló Torres's ambitious tome on surviving Arabic documentation for the Valencian Mudejars and their dialect, a linguistic study which also reviewed the historical and cultural scholarship to date.[25] Akio Ozaki was now publishing, in Japanese and Spanish, sections of his archival dissertation on Navarre's Mudejars. In 1986, for example, he produced a long study on Mudejar taxes and occupations there.[26] The year 1987 brought Maria Teresa Ferrer i Mallol's remarkable history-cum-*documentarium* covering the Mudejars in the fourteenth-century realms of Aragon, and 1988 her similar book on the Mudejar society of Orihuela as well as a third book on Mudejars and Christians in fourteenth-century Valencia. The collection of documents in transcription in each volume constitutes an invaluable resource for all future work in the field. Topically there are few aspects of Mudejar life and culture untouched there, while chronologically the trilogy fills the major outlines of a hitherto neglected century, where Boswell had stood almost alone. I presented a long analysis of this magisterial set of works in *Speculum* for 1991, so I need not repeat its findings here.[27]

In 1987, too, Pierre Guichard collected a number of his many articles on Muslim and Mudejar Spain in a handy volume, notably on fortifications and the organization of rural society.[28] In 1987 and 1988, three of my own books came out in Catalan translation in inexpensive editions widely reviewed and received.[29] In 1989 María Blanca Basáñez Villaluenga brought out a companion volume to the trilogy of Ferrer i Mallol, a history and extensive transcripts of charters on the Mudejars of Huesca in Aragon.[30] Like its predecessors a treasure trove of unpublished new materials, it also surveyed every aspect of that *aljama* visible in those and other archival sources. A number of studies on Castilian Mudejars at the end of the decade and start of the 1990s enlivened that rather moribund field. J. C. de Miguel Rodríguez brought out a booklet on this Castilian community (1988).[31] Serafín de Tapia Sánchez followed his "notes" on Extremadura Mudejars (1989) with a large book on Avila's community (1991).[32] And amid smaller contributions by others, Manuel González Jiménez surveyed the social and economic life of Andalucía's Mudejars in the fourth *Symposio* noted above (1991).[33] Steady production of articles on Mudejars of Aragon proper continued also, with some notable exemplars during this same turn of the decade.[34]

In 1990 a small archival-based book slipped into libraries almost unnoticed; an original monograph, it was buried in a volume of the author's previously published articles. This was Elena Lourie's "Anatomy of Ambivalence: Muslims under the Crown of Aragon in the Late Thirteenth Century," throwing special light on such topics as the Minorca Mudejars, the plight of Mudejar women, and a comparison with the local Jews.[35] Those of us who have discovered and used the work fondly hope that translation one day as a book in its own right in Spain may give it more visibility and influence. The year 1990 saw another unusual book, a biography of the great Mudejar physician in thirteenth-century Valencia, Muḥammad al-Shafra, by Francisco Franco Sánchez and María Sol Cabello.[36] This in turn recalls the intensive researches by Luis García Ballester and Michael McVaugh on the history of physicians and medicine in the medieval realms of Aragon, which included and revealed the role of Mudejar practitioners.[37]

In 1991 Mark Meyerson's revisionist history of fifteenth-century Valencian Mudejarism not only filled a great lacuna between books on thirteenth- and fourteenth-century Mudejars and the bibliography on sixteenth-century Moriscos, but also argued a non-linear evolution of Mudejarism in general, a point discussed below.[38] Thomas Glick assesses the Meyerson book "as a model case-study of the multiple dimensions of intergroup relations" in the late Middle Ages, "particularly cogent on the distinction between social and cultural phenomena as they effect the dynamics of ethnic relations." Thus "the judicial and economic integration" which painlessly eroded their autonomy in the fifteenth century, implied acculturation but "did not at all imply assimilation: social distance was maintained."[39] The year 1991 also saw my *Foundations of Crusader Valencia,* the first set of five hundred charters transcribed from the Arago-Catalan crown archives, out of some three thousand projected, offering a *Diplomatarium* of Valencian Mudejars and their colonial overlords.[40]

In 1992 Josefa Mutgé, another contributor on Ferrer i Mallol's Consejo Superior de Investigaciones Científicas staff, presented us with a splendid documentary history of Catalonia's main Mudejar aljama, at Lérida.[41] As with the Ferrer and Basáñez books, this divided between a comprehensive review of that society under many rubrics and a transcription of two hundred selected charters. The year 1993 saw Pierre Guichard's long-awaited history of Islamic and Mudejar Valencia in two large volumes, summing up his three decades of labor in that demanding field.[42] The same year also brought Pere Balañà i Abadia's erudite *Els musulmans a Catalunya (713–1153),* not directly a study of Mudejars but rather of the impact and traces of Muslims and presumed Mudejars in Catalonia proper, from language to genetics.[43] Also notable were two articles of 1993 by Carmen Díaz de Rábago Hernández on Mudejar access to Christian justice and on the long-lived *aljama* of Chivert, as well as a huge homage volume for María Luisa Ledesma Rubio containing important Mudejar studies as well as a thorough bibliography of her own Mudejar and other contributions. Finally, 1993 saw David Nirenberg's pioneering analysis in *Viator* of "Muslim-Jewish Relations in the Fourteenth-Century Crown of Aragon." A fitting close to the Anglophone archival histories of the decade 1984–1994 was David Abulafia's treatment of the Balearic Mudejars in his *A Mediterranean Emporium: The Catalan Kingdom of Majorca,* which both reviews and advances that historiography.[44]

The 1990s have also seen the first synthesis of all Iberia's Mudejars to 1300, the multi-author *Muslims under Latin Rule* edited by James Powell, including Portugal and even nearby Sicily as well as ecclesiastical policies, all in comparative perspective.[45] In the same year (1990) the distinguished Arabo-Hispanist Leonard Patrick Harvey devoted nearly half the chapters of his *Islamic Spain, 1250 to 1500* to the Mudejar communities as seen in current scholarship.[46] And the Mudejar story has also entered in detail some of the wider medieval syntheses, such as Robert Bartlett's *Medieval Frontier Society* (1989, reissued in paperback 1992).[47]

If the "Anglo-Saxons" continue to hold a prominent place in their surprising flow of major books, they do not really compete with Spanish authors in the quantity and quality of articles in journals, conference acta, and book chapters, and notably in Teruel's International Symposium of Mudejar Studies series, seen above. Overwhelmingly by Spanish scholars, the *Simposio* volumes have all come out in the 1980s and 1990s—respectively so far in 1981, 1982, 1986, 1990, 1991, and 1996, an intensifying rhythm of publication boding well for their continuance.[48] The series heavily stresses Mudejar art as well as history, most of the volumes divided between these two themes. This emphasis was clear from the beginning. The first symposium had twelve studies on Aragon, ten of them on art; six studies on Andalucía, three of them on art; six on Castile-León, five of them on art; two on Latin America, both on art; and two on Valencia, neither on art.[49] The second symposium concentrated entirely on art, forty-two articles in all, mostly on woodworking but not excluding studies on ceramics, castles, iconography and the like. The third divided equally—twenty-four works on history, twenty-four on art. The particularly hefty fourth volume redressed the balance, its fifty studies devoted to socio-economic topics, such as artisans, agriculture, administration, debt, rents, slave sales, and taxes. These fell into regional patterns, with Aragon, Granada, and Valencia receiving the most pages but with Castile and Murcia well represented and Navarre not neglected. The mix as always included position papers, monographic topics, and *Kleinschrift* bits and pieces.

Symposium five returned to the split formula but with focused themes: eight art papers on plaster techniques and seventeen papers (double the number of art pages) on lordship and fiscality. The number of participants in this symposium series fluctuated usually above 200, though the second meeting boasted 325 and the fifth only 130. Their attention to Mudejar art underscores the lack of interest in that subject by Anglophone historians. This may owe something to not living among the treasures of that art, and something perhaps to the separation between art history programs and history in North America. Of particular use to historians are the up-to-date bibliographical surveys, as in the 1984 volume where Miguel Ladero Quesada discussed Castile, Mercedes García-Arenal covered Navarre, and Manuel Ruzafa García reviewed Valencia. All future work on Mudejars must begin with this ongoing series.

To the symposia might be added the many Mudejar articles appearing in the multiplying regional journals as at Murcia and Alicante, in the proliferating local *asambleas* and conferences,[50] in the new Arabist journals, and even in the innumerable university master's theses or *tesinas.*[51] Among the most promising in this output is the *Congreso internacional: Encuentro de las tres culturas,* going forward from the 1980s as a joint venture of the University of Tel Aviv and the Ayuntamiento of Toledo.[52] Its fourth meeting, held at Toledo in 1985 and published there (simultaneously with the third meeting of 1984) in 1988, presented seventeen papers by symposiasts from Israeli and Spanish universities on Jewish, Mudejar/Arabic, and mixed themes, including a disquisition on the vexed term "Mudejar" itself, tracing its etymology and use through the centuries. A successful collaboration between a new journal and a new conference series was *The Intercultural Debate in the Thirteenth and Fourteenth Centuries,* which became volume nine in 1989 of Gerona's *Estudi general,* constituting the first *Jornades* of Catalan philosophy and mingling Arnau de Vilanova, Ramon Llull, Jewish authors, and Islamic currents.[53] Foreign conferences involved Spanish scholars, as in the "Minorities and Marginalized" colloquy held at Pau in the Pyrenees and published in 1986.[54] An example of conferences now taking new directions is that which centered on Muslims, Christians, and Jews in twelfth- and thirteenth-century Toledo, and specifically on "learning and tolerance," published both in French in 1991 and Spanish in 1992 under the direction of Louis Cardaillac.[55] It deals with Mudejar art, for instance, as a novel creation involving all three religions, and with tolerance from several novel perspectives.

New journals that have carried innovative studies on Mudejars include *Afers* (especially volume seven, 1988–89),[56] Valencia University's *Revista d'història medieval* (begun 1990),[57] *Estudis castellonencs* (begun 1983),[58] the *Miscelánea medieval murciana* (begun 1973) with its articles by Emilio Molina López,[59] the *Anales* of the University of Alicante in the Medieval History issues (since 1982),[60] Barcelona's *Miscel•lània de textos medievales* (since 1972),[61] and of course the more established Spanish journals such as the *Anuario de estudios medievales,*[62] the *Bolletí de la Societat arqueològica lul•liana, Saitabi,* or the *Mélanges de la Casa de Velázquez.* Controlling this swelling bibliography, even with aids such as the lists in *Sharq al-Andalus* and *Aljamía,* promises to become yearly more challenging, as the items take refuge in scattered and relatively less accessible journals.

Here in the United States, where journals hospitable to Mudejar articles are much fewer, major established reviews such as *Speculum, Viator,* and *The American Historical Review* have made their contributions and have now been joined by a new generation of journals open to this field. Most promising of these is Brill's *Medieval Encounters,* dedicated to a cross-cultural, cross-disciplinary examination of the medieval cultures of Judaism, Christianity, and Islam; its inaugural issue appeared in 1995. The *Anuario medieval,* now in its fourth issue from St. John's University in New York, accepts Mudejar materials among its Spanish medieval literary, historical, and especially textual articles.[63] Similarly *Al-Masāq: studia arabo-islamica mediterranea,* from the University of Leeds in England, has a special interest in cross-cultural themes such as Mudejars and Moriscos, since its inauguration in 1988. New Arabist journals in Spain have also welcomed Mudejar materials—not only *Sharq al-Andalus* but *Al-Qanṭara,* successor to *Al-Andalus, Qurṭuba,* and *Awrāq* (the last currently turning more to modern themes).

Mudejar historiography must take into account the affiliated historiographies that supply its wider contexts. These too are in continual change. The past quarter-century has seen a revolution in our understanding of the Middle Ages and of medieval Spain in which the Mudejars had their existence. Paradoxically, to understand the Mudejars we must understand the Christian culture through whose documentation we see them, and in whose assimilative/hostile pressures their life flowed as between two banks. New directions in agrarian history, feudalism, canon law, and mentalities or sensibilities are all therefore relevant also to Mudejar studies. To take the topic of Mudejars as a minority, for example, one must realize that "an enormous body of excellent scholarly work" has now appeared on European minorities, from heretics and prostitutes to lepers, Jews, and Gypsies, as increasingly a "chronologically and conceptually unified phenomenon."[64]

The history of Islam in Spain has equally undergone a sea-change as new contributions and novel interpretations multiply in a ferment of their own. The names of Dominique Urvoy, Rachel Arié, and especially Míkel de Epalza immediately come to mind, as well as Miquel Barceló for Majorca and the castellology explorations by André Bazzana and Pierre Guichard.[65] Olivia Remie Constable's *Trade and Traders in Muslim Spain: The Commercial Realignment of the Iberian Peninsula, 900–1500*[66] adds new dimensions and detail to a field opened so brilliantly by Charles Dufourcq in 1966.[67] The Mudejars were a society of Islam, with a religious continuity passing from free Islam to colonial Islam to Moriscos. Though the very word "continuity" paralyzes historians who think in polarities of total change or total identification, Mudejar society was a transformed Muslim society, a subspecies of Islam. Whatever penetration is achieved in studying the processes and changes in the Maghrib, to which the Mudejars related, will also further clarify the Mudejars. Epalza has particularly insisted upon Islam as the bottom-line identity of the Mudejar, a continuity overriding all sociological deformations, not allowing us a dominantly materialistic definition of Mudejarism as essentially a socioeconomic phenomenon.

Jewish studies in Spain, especially in the realms of Aragon, have also taken on new life and interpretations, a growing volume of books, archival catalogs, and monographic studies. To manage the influx and wed it to the older bibliography, Enrique Cantera Montenegro has organized five hundred major items into a discursive essay-booklet.[68] The new journal *Calls* and the book series under the direction of Yom Tov Assís in Jerusalem (who also has a history of the Jews of the realms of Aragon in press), as well as the works of David Romano and Jaume Riera, are indicators for Catalan lands of this widespread movement. Norman Roth, as part of his multi-volume project on the interrelations of Jews, Christians, and Muslims in medieval Spain, has a revisionist and provocative study on the character and evolution of the Jewish converso movement in the fifteenth century.[69] All this inevitably crosses and lends new meanings to the study of the parallel Mudejar society. David Nirenberg's pioneering new work focuses on Mudejar-Jewish relations.[70] The much wider discussion of Muslim-Jewish relations in the Middle Ages (the myths of Islamic tolerance and the countermyth of persecution) has been explored by Mark Cohen.[71]

Comparison can constitute a context too, the *dhimma* experience in Islam and its "Mozarabic" subspecies inviting not so much a structural as an anecdotal exploration, as analogous episodes in social history. The Twelfth Medieval Conference in 1982 at the University of British Columbia focused on the Mozarabic enigma and stirred wide interest in it by us Anglophones. A recent symposium has also caught the attention of Mudejar scholars—*Indigenous Christian Communities in Islamic Lands, Eighth to Eighteenth Centuries* (1990).[72] Comparative studies of every kind are needed; a small contribution has been my paralleling the conversionary movements of medieval Spain against Mudejars with the expansionist movement in the nineteenth-century United States at the expense of the Indians, directly involving missionary work.[73] To enter upon such supporting bibliographies, however, would expand our present task impractically.

If the professional and bibliographical structures of the Mudejar field, even taken in isolation from supporting fields, have been changing very rapidly and promise to change even faster, what of content itself, our view of the Mudejar communities? Content changes are even harder to chart briefly, but some illustrations may serve. An example at hand in the present book is Thomas Glick's summary of how the agrarian-social transition from Islamic subject to colonial Mudejar may well have progressed.[74] A more startling penetration into patterns is Mark Meyerson's reversal of received wisdom as to the linear decline of the Mudejars in the kingdom of Valencia—from a position of strength at the moment of conquest to an inevitable culmination of persecution and eventual expulsion. In place of that universal understanding, he has persuaded us to see a cyclical reality of ups and downs, and to understand how both foreign and domestic pressures on the rulers could result in simultaneously contradictory policies toward Mudejars of the Crown of Aragon as against the Crown of Castile's Mudejars.[75]

Indeed, the major reversal of traditional Mudejar studies (as reflected in Francisco Fernández y González's work that held the field a century ago) has been appreciation of how different and differently acculturated the many Mudejar regions were. Catalan experience was not the Aragonese experience; Aragon differed from Valencia, and both from the Balearics. Moreover, there was no single Mudejar experience within Castile, or for that matter in the kingdom of Valencia. Differences by region, as well as differences by chronology, are intrinsic to the Mudejar story. It is heartening to see how the

Teruel symposia struggle to give equal time to each region of Spain, despite the very unequal availability of primary sources. It is less comforting to note how easily historians' accounts continue to favor the structural data and program of the Mudejars, those general patterns fairly common in the abstract to all Mudejar communities. In terms of charter evidence, the differences may often be in the details—the telling *obiter dicta* or sudden odd glimpses that reveal particular patterns and behaviors. The reconstruction of Mudejar attitudes and daily living are more likely to come from such items, considered as "representative singular" experiences. This is not a process of random selection or of curiosities but rather a sifting of routine and replicative public documentation for revelation of obviously or probably normal private actions, shown to be such by the contact of audience, stated circumstance, apparently quotidian character, or micro- or macro-historical contexts.

New directions in the content of Mudejar studies come not only from new perspectives or newly applied contexts but also from the simple accumulation of data. As seen above, a number of recent regional histories such as those by Maria Teresa Ferrer i Mallol and her C.S.I.C. staff have transcribed a mass of unpublished charters. Manuel Vicent Febrer i Romaguera has collected (1991) the surrender or basic constitutions granted to each Valencian *aljama.*[76] For Seville, Klaus Wagner has summarized over four hundred documents on Mudejars and Jews of the region, surviving in the notarial archives there.[77] María Jesús Viguera has called for closer attention to the "internal documentation" by Mudejars themselves, noting too some unpublished documentation in Aragon currently being studied.[78] On a lesser but steady scale, the increasing number of Spanish scholars interested in Mudejars has been rescuing odd documents from local archives. In Spain's tricultural experience, too, it is a mistake to concentrate too closely on the Mudejars alone. The colonial overlords were themselves acculturated by the environment into which their settlers moved, cheek-by-jowl with the Other. The Dutch sociologist Rob Kroes argues (1992) "that transplanted cultures often develop the way Creole languages do—away from the mother tongue, they assimilate alien elements quickly and hospitably and take on newer and more variegated features, becoming, as they do so, markedly different from the original language."[79] Authors such as Joan Fuster have investigated the differences marking the resulting Valencian character, but more reflection directly on the question as denoting Muslim influence is needed. The closing chapter of the present book, by Jocelyn Hillgarth, stresses how universally other Europeans saw a Muslim-Jewish component later in Spanish society at large.[80]

Some other directions over the past quarter-century have already been indicated when noting particular works. Certainly the archeological movement, by teams such as the Butzers (1986)[81] or that of André Bazzana and Pierre Guichard,[82] is a notable new approach. The attention to language, both as a barrier to acculturation by the Christian conquerors and as a prominent element of Mudejar culture, has been greatly advanced by the work of Barceló Torres and others, not excluding researches of wider compass such as those of Ana Labarta and Federico Corriente.[83] In this connection Barceló's edition of a Mudejar *Book of the Sunna and Sharīʿa* (1989), composed in Catalan around 1408, is an intriguing landmark both as an exemplar of acculturation and as a window into Mudejar society and law.[84] Fiscality, land tenure and taxes, and in general the economic relations between Mudejar and Christian, while by no means neglected previously, have been marvelously expanded and are still being industriously researched by many hands. And owing especially to the symposia series, the range of Mudejar art has been displayed far more publicly to historians of Mudejarism, while detailed contributions have been multiplied until one can almost speak of a field in itself. Hopefully the two fields will no longer be pursued in isolation.

A major shift of viewpoint, issuing from many studies and reflection, has been the weakening of our Enlightenment concept of "tolerance" and "intolerance" as a qualifier of Mudejar-Christian history. Américo Castro's *convivencia* too is not so often heard in the land. We grope for a more realistic terminology—parallel societies, accommodation, symbiosis. There is still a tendency toward Whiggish judgment, and toward beginning as romantics but ending as moralists, bootlegging our current values and concepts into the past. Maria Teresa Ferrer i Mallol's splendid recent volume on the Mudejars of the fourteenth-century realms of Aragon, for example, carries a major conclusion in its subtitle: "Segregation and Discrimination." Mutual retreat by the three peoples from contamination by the Other, or worse from assimilation, was a given in Spain, as three distinct worlds were created and tenaciously held, along with a mutual rhetoric of hostility. Actual persecution by the dominant society was also recurrent, from the Valencian riots of 1276 to the destruction of Valencia city's Muslim quarter in mid-fifteenth century. Shifting economic pressures and social realignments within the larger society distorted or even destroyed Mudejar communities. And a pervasive dislike of Mudejars by the Christian populace, even against converts as Ramon Llull noted, balanced against all the informal contacts which worked to mitigate hostility. In short, hostility has a history. Its gradations were differently experienced in urban and rural settings, or from the seignorial class to the plebs, or from one setting of time and circumstance to another. Mutual withdrawal could become true segregation, for example, as when King Sanç of Majorca decreed ghettoization for the Jews. On the other hand, the pervasive slavery on which all three societies to some degree rested, was not seen by any of them as mistreatment or an inhumane activity.

The anatomy of hostility and prejudice calls for, and has been receiving, reflection from new perspectives. Even in a given individual, this could be very complex. James the Conqueror, for example, displays a confusion of attractions and rejections. As citizen of a Christian polity, he could not conceive of Muslims as sharing fellow-citizens. As military defender of his kingdom, he distrusted his Muslim populations as endangering it from within. He deployed a full-throated rhetoric of expulsion as his goal, and easily contemned the "filth" (*spurcitia*) of Mudejar Islam. Yet he boasts of his knowledge of and sensitivity to Muslim ways in dealing with Mudejars. He reassures them by stressing his faithful adherence to the traditional pro-Mudejar policies of his whole dynasty. He energetically imported Muslims into his Valencian farms to maximize tax profits, despite papal rebukes. As a king of the three religions, he avenged his Mudejars against the mobs, notably so in the late 1270s. As a diplomat he welcomed and housed the last of the Almohad dynasty as pawns for negotiation. He expressed admiration and respect for Muslims as faithful to their word and as fighting men. And he had around him Muslim army contingents, barbers, painters, musicians, and courtiers. In the course of his very long life, he had occasion to let one or another of these attitudes rise to color and affect his policies, as changeable in this as most men become under pressure of circumstance.

A dramatic marker for the maturity of the Mudejar field in the mid-1990s is the revitalization of Teruel's Center for Mudejar and Morisco studies, with an expansive publishing program and doctoral courses in Mudejar history and culture. The 1995 courses, for example, offered twenty hours of seminar instruction under six basic themes of Mudejarism, moderated by professors from the University of Alicante, the University of Navarre, and the University of Seville. Corresponding sets of twenty hours under other professors from Spain and abroad took up Mudejar art, Mudejar ceramics, and Morisco resistance.[85] An accompanying indicator of maturity is the name change and consequent reorientation of the lively journal *Sharq al-Andalus,* whose subtitle shifted in 1995 from *estudios árabes* to *estudios mudéjares y moriscos.*

Instead of pursuing further the defining contexts of Mudejarism, or usurping the ongoing task of general bibliographical reportage now assumed by *Sharq al-Andalus,* we may return to our core concern, Anglophone contributions to Mudejar historiography. A *tour d'horizon* of representative current productions from 1995 on will illustrate their range and continuing importance. That year saw an ambitious examination of the early and influential Aragonese solution to the Mudejar dilemma, William Clayton Stalls's *Possessing the Land: Aragon's Expansion into Islam's Ebro Frontier under Alfonso the Battler (1104–1134).* Here the formation of Mudejar policy is part and parcel of the wider colonialist story.[86] In 1995 too, Thomas Glick presented his controversial *From Muslim Fortress to Christian Castle: Social and Cultural Change in Medieval Spain,* a theory of Islamic rural-agrarian organization and its radical transformation during the transition to Mudejarism.[87] My commissioned monograph in 1995 for E. J. Brill's new journal *Medieval Encounters: Jewish, Christian, and Muslim Culture in Confluence and Dialogue* explored the neglected phenomenon of passports that tied together the Mudejar, Muslim, Jewish, and Christian societies—"The *Guidaticum* Safe-Conduct in Medieval Arago-Catalonia: A Mini-Institution for Muslims, Christians, and Jews."[88]

Iberia and the Mediterranean World of the Middle Ages: Essays in Honor of Robert I. Burns, S.J. came out in two volumes, respectively in 1995 and 1996, its thirty-five articles offering such relevant studies as Mark

Meyerson's revisionist "Religious Change, Regionalism, and Royal Power" under Fernando and Isabel, Paul Padilla's "Transport of Muslim Slaves in Fifteenth-Century Valencia," Míkel de Epalza's "Islamic Social Structures in Muslim and Christian Valencia," and Larry Simon's "Church and Slavery in Ramon Llull's Majorca."[89] A particular gift in 1996 was David Nirenberg's prize-winning *Communities of Violence: Persecution of Minorities in the Middle Ages,* a revisionist historiography on the episodes of persecution in the Crown of Aragon and Occitania against Jews, Mudejars, lepers, and the like, which were "processes of negotiation and contextualization that shaped the general charges to local needs," each episode showing its own "dynamic relationship between collective anxieties and individual action," where violence becomes not the antithesis of medieval tolerance but paradoxically its underpinning.[90]

Also welcome in 1996 was a Variorum collection of eighteen articles on irrigation and hydraulic matters by Thomas Glick, many related to Valencia's Muslims/Mudejars.[91] Mark Meyerson contributed a lengthy pair of articles in *Medieval Encounters* for 1995 and 1996: "Slavery and the Social Order: Mudejars and Christians in the Kingdom of Valencia," and his "Slavery and Solidarity: Mudejars and Foreign Muslim Captives in the Kingdom of Valencia." Together with the ambitious study by Stephen Bensch in *Viator* in the previous year, "From Prizes of War to Domestic Merchandise: The Changing Face of Slavery in Catalonia and Aragon, 1000–1300," the Meyerson articles reflect a growing interest among Anglophones in the Muslim slaves who were not quite Mudejars but under Christian domestic control, a population reinforcing the Mudejar presence at the very hearths of the conquerors, a randomly documented presence inviting exploration by new methodologies and approaches.[92] Four items of my own may close the 1996 list: documentation on the last *wāli* of Islamic Valencia who became the foremost Mudejar until his conversion to Christianity; an examination of "the many crusades" constituting Valencia's conquest, including those summoned to repress Mudejar revolts; a study of Mudejar community scribes; and a revisionist assessment of the Mudejars' role in introducing paper to Europe, including Játiva's clear precedence over Italy's Fabriano in the process.[93]

The chronological limits of the present study as 1276 to 2000 were originally devised with tongue in cheek, since publication had been envisioned for 1994. The extension has been felicitous, as embracing many more items, but it will still leave a gap at the lip of the millennium. A *tour d'horizon* of representative projects and pregnancies visible into 1999 can serve as bridge to that onrushing future. Bold spirits will doubtless eventually tally a multiplying Anglophone contribution far into the new millennium. A handy example of end-of-old-millennium trends is the present book itself, including pertinent articles by Mark Meyerson, Larry Simon, and myself. Simon's own book is now ready for publication, the first sustained treatment of the Balearic Mudejars, eagerly awaited by an international clientele. He has disseminated Mudejar themes not only by his own presentations at history conferences, but through the panels he has arranged as a main organizer for the annual international congress of medieval studies at Western Michigan University. Professor Simon has just been appointed editor of the journal *Medieval Encounters: Jewish, Christian and Muslim Culture in Confluence and Dialogue,* published by Brill from Leiden, in which regular Mudejar components are now envisioned.

Younger scholars are also moving about on the horizon. Brian Catlos in the doctoral program at Toronto University is well advanced with his archival dissertation on the Mudejars of the upland Kingdom of Aragon proper in the twelfth century. Isabel Bonet O'Connor has finished her archival dissertation for the U.C.L.A. doctorate, "A Forgotten Community: The Mudejar Aljama of Xàtiva, 1244–1327." This ambitious work draws on archives at Játiva, Barcelona, and elsewhere to trace the flowering and later downfall of that "stronghold of Mudejar identity." Among her current articles drawn from this thesis are two in the *Sharq al-Andalus: estudios mudéjares y moriscos.*[94] A student of David Abulafia at Cambridge University in England is completing her dissertation from many Italian archives to bring into focus an intriguing analog of Spain's Mudejars, the Lucera community established by the thirteenth-century emperor Frederick II Hohenstaufen, when he expelled the last 20,000 Muslims from Sicily to isolate them and bind them to the soil.

An even more pioneering doctoral dissertation illumines the similar "Mudejar" analog in Hungary, Nora Berend's "Non-Christians in a Medieval Frontier Society: Jews, Muslims and Pagans in Thirteenth-

Century Hungary," already accepted at Columbia University in New York but as yet unpublished. Given the influence of the Hungarian wife of James the Conqueror in his Valencian policies and politics, this study may have direct as well as analogical implications for Mudejars. Though without charters of privilege, "these Muslims lived in their own communities and had a collective status, which included rights and obligations." Ecclesiastics complained there about the "too favorable status" of these Muslims and their comingling with Christians.[95] Finally, many young as well as senior Anglophone scholars have contributed to the comprehensive *Encyclopedia of Medieval Iberia*, now ready for publication at Garland Publishers, with much material relevant to Mudejarism.

Paul E. Chevedden, Míkel de Epalza, and I have collaborated on an interdisciplinary study going into galleys at Brill Publishers: *Negotiating Cultures: Bilingual Treaties in Muslim-Crusader Spain under James the Conqueror.* By intensive focus on Arabic and Latin/Romance texts, the book reconstructs and explores the mental processes behind the treaty dialogues by which the Mudejar world was formed. The main title is deliberately ambiguous, of course, the two cultures not only operating by negotiations with their neighbors but also bargaining away elements of their identity to create acceptable situations of subjection. The ever-widening circles of context, from Quranic to military draw surprises from the negotiating texts that illumine the general Mudejar situation.

Mudejar studies have evolved in the past twenty-five years from a curiosity or marginal theme in Spanish history into a full-fledged freestanding field. A small grove has luxuriated into a forest. From now on we shall have to turn to computers in order to control the bibliography and sift the variety of themes. For the first time too, it has become possible to attempt at least a preliminary general history of the peninsula's Mudejar societies. So many and talented are the researchers in the field, and so promising are the approaches already laid out, that the chronology of progress in this chapter's title, as from 1975 up to 2000, does not seem overconfident in its implicit prediction for the immediate future. For the long run, however, all of this is only a beginning. Plentiful unexamined data still lie hidden in Spain's many archives; in timely fashion archival finding aids have been multiplying, even for obscure collections,[96] to encourage the search. The Mudejar catalog for the fourteenth-century realms of Aragon, going forward under Maria Teresa Ferrer i Mallol, is a splendid example of such finding aids.[97] Fresh conceptualizations and perspectives are also needed, and to some degree are in evidence, in order to take advantage of kinds of documentation hitherto recalcitrant, or to extract new visions and meaning from the materials already at hand. We shall not exhaust that archival treasure for generations. From all present indications, we "Anglo-Saxons" of all countries and races will continue to play a role in that adventure. In a Mudejar-history Olympics we would surely have won a gold medal or two by now and a clutch of silvers or bronzes.

NOTES

1. Ángel Galán Sánchez, *Una visión de la "decadencia española": la historiografía anglosajona sobre mudéjares y moriscos (siglos XVIII–XX)* (Málaga, 1991). Ángel Galán Sánchez recently published *Los mudéjares del reino de Granada* (Granada, 1991).

2. A full bibliography of my own works to 1993 will be found in *Medieval Spain and the Western Mediterranean: Essays in Honor of Robert I. Burns, S.J.*, ed. Paul Chevedden, Donald Kagay, Paul Padilla, and Larry Simon, 2 vols. (Leiden, 1995–96), 2.xxi–xxxvii. Besides Ángel Galán Sánchez's assessment of my work (*Historiografía anglosajona,* 134 n. 137, 151, 152 and especially 155–65), others include the brief academic biography and selected bibliography by Jill R. Webster in the *Anuario de estudios medievales* 21 (1991): 647–61; Antoni Ferrando Francés, "Les interrelacions lingüistiques en la València doscentista: comentaris a les aportacions de Robert I. Burns," *Afers: fulls de recerca i pensament* 7 (1988–89): 216–29; also in *Zeitschrift für Katalanistik* 2 (1989): 115–89; Ernest Belenguer, *Jaume I a través de la història,* 2 vols. (Valencia, 1984), a historiographical analysis (see the thirty entries in the index under "Burns"), especially 2.107–10; three historians in separate studies as "Debat: a propòsit de l'obra de R. I. Burns," *Revista d'història medieval* 1 (1990): 217–47; Felipe Mateu y Llopis, "La obra investigadora valenciana de Robert I. Burns S.J.," *Anales del Centro de cultura valenciana* 37 (1977): 115–19; Michael Kammen ed., *The Past before Us: Contemporary Historical Writing in the United States* (Ithaca, 1980), 56 n., 66–67, 376; José Hinojosa Montalvo, "En torno a los judíos valencianos," *Hispania* (Madrid) 175 (1990): 921–40.

3. Madrid, 1866, reprint 1985. The title omits the usual accent on *mudéjares.* Isidro de las Cagigas's seductively titled *Los mudéjares,* 2 vols., in his *Minorías étnico-religiosas de la edad media española,* 4 vols. of projected twelve, 1947–49 (Madrid, 1948–49), is only a history of the Reconquest, with Mudejar history deferred to the never-published volume 3 (see the revised plan,

facing title page of volume 2). It nevertheless continues permanently to encumber Mudejar bibliography. Other older authors such as Anne M. J. A. Circourt, *Histoire des mores, mudéjares et des morisques* . . . , 3 vols. (Paris, 1845–48, reprint 1986) and Florencio Janer, *Condición social de los moriscos* . . . (Madrid, 1857, reprint 1987), are virtually useless on the Mudejars. Celestino López Martínez, *Mudéjares y moriscos sevillanos: páginas históricas* (Seville, 1935, reprint 1994), is a light confection of no great use; see also José Pedregal y Fantini, *Estado social y cultural de los mozárabes y mudéjares españoles* (Seville, 1898).

4. "Mudejar History Today: New Directions," *Viator* 8 (1977): 128–43, an address at the opening session of the annual convention of the Society for Spanish and Portuguese Historical Studies, held at Johns Hopkins University in 1976.

5. These authors are cited and discussed in "Mudejar History Today."

6. Glick, *Irrigation* (Cambridge, 1969); "*Muḥtasib and Mustasaf:* A Case Study of Institutional Diffusion," *Viator* 11 (1971): 59–81; and *Islamic and Christian Spain* (Princeton, 1979).

7. *Islam* (Princeton, 1973). *Colonial Survival* (Princeton, 1975); see too my study, "Le royaume chrétien de Valence et ses vassaux musulmans (1240–1280)," *Annales: économies, sociétés, civilisations* 28 (1973): 199–225.

8. My major publication of those years but not irrelevant to the later Mudejar work was *The Jesuits and the Indian Wars of the Northwest* in the Yale Western Americana Series (New Haven, 1966; reprint Moscow, ID, 1985).

9. New Haven, 1977.

10. Ann Arbor, Mich., University Microfilms [Princeton University dissertation], 1973.

11. London, 1978; it includes seven articles from *Speculum* and two from *The American Historical Review.*

12. *Speculum* 45 (1970): 624–49. Now given wider readership by inclusion in her *Crusade and Colonisation: Muslims, Christians and Jews in Medieval Aragon* (Aldershot, 1990), chapter 5.

13. Cited above in note 4.

14. O'Callaghan (Ithaca, 1975); Hillgarth, 2 vols. (Oxford, 1978); Jackson, *The Making of Medieval Spain* (London, 1972); MacKay, *Spain in the Middle Ages: From Frontier to Empire, 1000–1500* (London, 1977); Lomax, *The Reconquest of Spain* (London, 1978).

15. Collins (New York, 1983); Reilly (Cambridge, 1993). Of the many general medieval non-Anglophone histories of the past quarter-century, special note should be taken of Charles Dufourcq and Jean Gautier-Dalché, *Histoire économique et sociale de l'Espagne chrétienne au moyen âge* (Paris, 1976), much improved in the Spanish edition, *Historia económica y social de la España cristiana en la edad media* (Barcelona, 1983) by a bibliography of over 2,500

selected items. More recent is Adeline Rucquoi, *Histoire médiévale de la péninsule ibérique* (Paris, 1993). Spanish manuals old and new are in good supply.

16. In *Proceedings, First Catalan Symposium,* ed. Josep Solà-Solé (New York, 1993), 15–27.

17. Bishko, in *A History of the Crusades,* ed. Kenneth M. Setton, 6 vols. (Madison, 1969–89), 3.396–456. Central to the ferment between 1975 and 1985 in this country were such medieval Hispanist historians as James Brodman, Heath Dillard, Paul Freedman, Lawrence McCrank, James Powers, Bernard Reilly, and Jill Webster, though none were involved in Mudejar studies. The list could easily be extended for North America and of course by adding British colleagues, such as David Abulafia, Richard A. Fletcher, Peter Linehan, and Alan Ryder.

18. Notice was taken of the Institute by the *Gran enciclopèdia catalana,* 15 vols. (Barcelona, 1969–80). Supplementary, 162. It is not a private professorial library shared temporarily, but a systematic general collection on Catalan history that will eventually lodge permanently at the University of San Francisco.

19. "Un seigneur musulman dans l'Espagne chrétienne: le ʿraʾisʾ de Crevillente," *Mélanges de la Casa de Velázquez* 9 (1973): 283–334.

20. See above, note 4.

21. Co-authored with María Jesús Paternina and Antonio Couto (Alicante, 1983).

22. "Les mudéjars de la couronne d'Aragon: origine de la population mudéjare," *Revue du monde musulmane et de la Méditerranée* 63–64 (1992): 179–94.

23. Paz Fernández, *Mudéjares: repertorio bibliográfico,* Cuadernos de la biblioteca islámica Felix María Pareja 18 (Madrid, 1989).

24. With Béatrice Leroy, *Moros y judíos en Navarra en la baja edad media* (Madrid, 1984). This is a double book, each author independently treating her own minority and appending a generous selection of transcribed charters. The influential interpretive study by Dolors Bramon, *Contra moros i jueus: formació i estratègia d'unes discriminacions al país valencià* (Valencia, 1981) also demands notice as formative for the scholarship of the 1980s.

25. María Carmen Barceló Torres, *Minorías islámicas en el país valenciano: historia y dialecto* (Valencia, 1984).

26. "El regimen tributario y la vida económica de los mudéjares de Navarra," *Anuario de estudios medievales* 16 (1986): 319–68. See also his "Mudejars of the Kingdom of Navarre [in Japanese]," *Seiyo-shigaku* 137 (1985): 1–20. On Portuguese Mudejars and their sources, see Antonio Losa, "Les 'mourarias' portuguaises au XVe siècle," in *XIII Congresso dell'Union européene d'arabisants et d'islamisants,* Quaderni di studi arabi, 5–6 (1987–88), 457–58.

27. *Els sarraïns de la corona catalano-aragonesa en el segle XIV: segregació i discriminació* (Barcelona, 1987): *La frontera amb Islam en el segle XIV: cristians i sarraïns al país valencià* (Barcelona, 1988); *Les aljames sarraïnes de la governació d'Oriola en el segle XIV* (Barcelona, 1988). The review is in *Speculum* 66 (1991): 152–56.

28. *Estudios sobre historia medieval* (Valencia, 1987). In 1980 Guichard also published an extensive popular survey of Valencian Mudejarism into the early fourteenth century, in the collection *Nuestra historia,* ed. Miguel Mas-Ivars, 7 vols. (Valencia, 1980), 3.13–107.

29. Burns, *Moros, cristians i jueus en el regne croat de Valencia* (Valencia, 1987); *Colonialisme medieval: explotació postcroada de la València islámica* (Valencia, 1987); *Societat i documentació en el regne croat de Valencia* (Valencia, 1988); and "Els mudejars del regne de València de la generació posterior a la croada," an original survey commissioned for the multi-volume *Història del país valencià,* ed. Ernest Belenguer, 5 vols. (Barcelona, 1989–90), 2.139–67.

30. *La aljama sarracena de Huesca en el siglo XIV* (Barcelona, 1989).

31. Juan Carlos de Miguel Rodríguez, *Los mudéjares de la corona de Castilla* (Madrid, 1988).

32. Serafín de Tapia Sánchez, "Los mudéjares de la Extremadura castellano-leonesa: notas sobre una minoría dócil (1085–1502)," *Studia historica: historia medieval* 7 (1989): 95–125; and his *La comunidad morisca de Avila* (Salamanca, 1991).

33. Manuel González Jiménez, "La condicón social y actividades económicas de los mudéjares andaluces," IV Teruel *Simposio,* 411–425. His volume on thirteenth-century Andalusia, adumbrating the Mudejar story there, appeared in 1980 and in a second edition in 1988—*En torno a los orígenes de Andalucía: la repoblación del siglo XIII* (Seville, 1988). See also his work on Castile below in note 47. The difficulties of writing Castilian Mudejar history from the exiguous sources can be seen in Juan Carlos de Miguel Rodríguez's clever *La comunidad mudéjar de Madrid: un modelo de análisis de aljamas mudéjares castellanas* (Madrid, 1989). See too Julio Valdeón Baruque, "Judiós y mudéjares en tierras palentinas: siglos XIII–XV," in *II Congreso de historia de Palencia,* 6 vols. (Palencia, 1990), 2. 359–75. On Granada's Mudejars, see Ángel Galán Sánchez above in note 1 (1991).

34. See as exemplars: (1) María Luisa Ledesma Rubió, "Los mudéjares aragoneses: de la convivencia a la ruptura," *Destierros aragoneses* (Zaragoza, 1988), 171–88. (2) Ovidio Cuella, "Los mudéjares de la comunidad de Calatayud a fines del siglo XIV y comienzas del XV," *II Encuentro de estudios bilbilitanos* (Calatayud, 1989), 209–19; and Concepción de la Fuente Cobos, "La morería de Terrer hasta comienzos del siglo XV," *II Encuentro de estudios bilbilitanos,* 251–57. (3) María Luisa Ledesma Rubió, "Marginación y violencia: Aportación al estudio de los mudéjares aragoneses," *Aragón en la edad*

media 9 (1991): 203–24. (4) Francisco Javier García Marco, "Fiscalidad, feudalismo, y señorió en el mudejarismo aragonés a través del ejemplo de las comunidades del Jalón y del Jiloca medios (siglos XII al XVI)," *Simposio internacional de mudejarismo* 5 (Teruel, 1991), 41–63; cf. below, note 48 and text.

35. In her *Crusade and Colonization: Muslims, Christians, and Jews in Medieval Aragon* (London, 1990), section VII, 1–77.

36. *Muḥammad aš-Šafra, el médico y su época* (Alicante, 1990).

37. See for example their *Medical Licensing in Fourteenth-Century Valencia*, Transactions, number 79:6 (Philadelphia, 1989), and García Ballester's earlier *Historia social de la medicina en la España de los siglos XIII al XVI: la minoría musulmana y morisca* (Madrid, 1976).

38. *The Muslims of Valencia in the Age of Fernando and Isabel: Between Coexistence and Crusade* (Berkeley and Los Angeles, 1991); see also his summary statement, "The War against Islam and the Muslims at Home: The Mudejar Predicament in the Kingdom of Valencia during the Reign of Fernando 'El Católico'," *Sharq al-Andalus* 3 (1986): 103–13; also his "Prostitution of Muslim Women in the Kingdom of Valencia: Religious and Sexual Discrimination in a Medieval Plural Society," in *The Medieval Mediterranean: Cross-Cultural Contacts*, ed. Marilyn J. Chiat and Kathryn Reyerson (St. Cloud, 1988), 87–95; and below, note 72.

39. *Speculum* 67 (1992): 725–26.

40. *Foundations of Crusader Valencia: Revolt and Recovery, 1257–1263*, volume 2 of the *Diplomatarium of the Crusader Kingdom of Valencia: The Registered Charters of Its Conqueror, Jaume I, 1257–1276* (Princeton, 1991).

41. *L'aljama sarraïna de Lleida a l'edat mitjana: aproximació a la seva història* (Barcelona, 1992). A far less comprehensive interpretive essay but still useful is Rodrigo Pita Mercé, *Lérida morisca* (Lérida, 1977).

42. *Les musulmans de Valence et la reconquête (XIe–XIIIe siècles)*, 2 vols. (Damascus, 1990–91). On his contributions see also notes 19 and 28 above, and notes 58 and 65 below, with texts.

43. Subtitled *Assaig de síntesi orientativa* (Sabadell, 1993).

44. Carmen Díaz de Rábago Hernández, "La justicia cristiana ante los mudéjares: los Bocayo, una familia valenciana del siglo XV," *Boletín de la Sociedad castellonense de cultura* 69 (1993): 201–209; and her "Introducción al estudio de la aljama musulmana de Xivert durante la edad media," *Centro de estudios del Maestrazgo: Boletín* 41–42 (1993): 63–72. *Homenaje a la profesora emérita María Luisa Ledesma Rubio* (Zaragoza, 1993), also issued as the journal *Aragón en la edad media* 10–11 (1993). Nirenberg, "Muslim-Jewish Relations," *Viator* 24 (1993): 249–68.

45. *Muslims under Latin Rule, 1100–1300*, ed. James M.. Powell (Princeton, 1990). Joseph O'Callaghan covers Castile and Portugal, I cover the Crown

of Aragon, David Abulafia Sicily, Benjamin Kedar the Frankish Levant, and James Powell the papacy and the Muslim frontier.

46. Chicago, 1990. Leonard Harvey has also briefly summarized the topic in "The Mudejars," in *The Legacy of Muslim Spain,* ed. Salma Khadra Jayyusi (Leiden, 1992), 176–87.

47. Ed. Robert Bartlett and Angus MacKay (Oxford, 1989, reissued in paperback 1992). Chapter 2, by Manuel González Jiménez, deals with Castile's frontier and settlement between 1085 and 1350. Chapter 6 by José Enrique López de Coca Castañer studies the institutions of the Castilian-Granadan frontier between 1369 and 1482. Chapter 11, by Angus MacKay, is on religion, culture, and ideology on that frontier. And in chapter 13, I discuss conquered Valencia in terms of the Turner frontier thesis.

48. *Simposio internacional de mudejarismo at Teruel:* 1 (1981), 2 (1982), 3 (1984), 4 (1987), 5 (1991), 6 (1996). See below for further discussion.

49. "Los mudéjares sevillanos" in the first *Simposio,* by Antonio Collantes de Terán Sánchez (pp. 225–35), was revised and expanded also as "La aljama mudéjar de Sevilla" in *al-Andalus* 43 (1978): 143–62, while awaiting the delayed *Simposio* publication.

50. One example of conference papers would be Pilar Pérez Viñuales, "El señorío de Alfajarín en el siglo XV: fiscalidad mudéjar y cristiana," *Congreso sobre señorío y feudalismo (siglos XII–XIX),* in press. In the same vein, see her "Los contratos de arrendamiento de rentas señoriales como fuente para el conocimiento de la fiscalidad mudéjar y cristiana: documentación notarial aragonesa del siglo XV," in *Metodología de la investigación científica sobre fuentes aragonesas* (Zaragoza, 1992), 183–92. She has also published on the pace and nature of Mudejar emigration. Typical of local items are Enrique Cantera Montenegro's "Las comunidades mudéjares de las diócesis de Osma y Sigüenza a fines de la edad media," *Espacio, tiempo y forma: revista de historia medieval* 1 (1988): 137–73; and Vicente García Edo, "Un plet per les aigües del riu de Sonella entre la vila d'Onda i l'aljama mora de Tales (1310–1322)," *Miralcamp: butlletí d'estudis onders* 3 (1987): 75–110.

51. Recent licentiate theses have included J. M. López Ortiz, *La encomienda mudéjar de Valle de Ricote (siglos XIII–XVI)* (Universidad de Murcia, 1990). A *tesina* unpublished since 1972 but maintaining a place and influence in the bibliography is Roser Argemi, "Els tagarins a la Ribera d'Ebre al segle XIII" from the Semitic languages section of Barcelona University's philological faculty. Maria Teresa Ferrer i Mallol has noted, among University of Barcelona doctoral dissertations nearing completion, "a thesis on crime among the Saracens of the Crown of Aragon in the fourteenth century."

52. *Encuentro,* ed. Carlos Carrete Parrondo: 1 (1983), 2 (1985), 3 (1988), 4 (1988), 5 (1991).

53. *El debat intercultural als segles XIII i XIV* (= I Jornades de filosofia catalana, *Actes*) (= *Estudi general,* vol. 9) (Gerona, 1981).

54. *Minorités et marginaux en Espagne et dans le midi de la France (VIIe–XVIIIe siècles),* (*Actes du Colloque de Pau, 1984*) (Paris, 1986).

55. *Tolède XIIe–XIIIe: Musulmans, chrétiens et juifs, le savoir et la tolérance,* ed. Louis Cardaillac (Paris, 1991); translated by José Luis Arántegui as *Toledo, siglos XII–XIII: Musulmanes, cristianos y judíos: La sabiduría y la tolerancia* (Madrid, 1992).

56. *Afers: fulls de recerca i pensament* 1 (1985). Volume seven (1988–89) is almost entirely on Valencian Mudejars, including articles by Karl and Elizabeth Butzer on irrigation systems, Pierre Guichard on the Berber legacy, Jaume Coll i Conesa on ceramics, Manuel Ruzafa Garcia on a Mudejar merchant family, Antoni Ferrando Francés on assessment of linguistic interrelations, and so on.

57. See for example Manuel Ruzafa García, "Los mudéjares en el desarrollo mercantil valenciano del cuatrocientos," *Revista d'història medieval* 2 (1991): 179–89.

58. At Castellón de la Plana. María Carmen Barceló Torres has a statistical study there, around Mudejar Arabic documents, for a "Revisión del panorama mudéjar valenciano," *Estudis castellonenes* 1 (1983): 365–97. Pierre Guichard and André Bazzana explore "Habitats et sites defensifs" (in the same issue, 611–93), a version of their article in note 65 below. And Carmen Díaz de Rábago Hernández has an archival analysis of Castellón's Mudejar *aljama* in that issue: 483–90.

59. See for example his article on Zayyān's rule in Murcia, *Miscelánea medieval murciana* 7 (1981): 157, 182; cf. 4 (1978): 63–86.

60. For example Joaquín Navarro Reig, "Los mudéjares contestanos [Cocentaina] en el siglo XIII," *Anales* 6 (1987): 175–206; and Josep Torró, "El problema del hábitat fortificado en el sur del reino de Valencia después de la segunda revuelta mudéjar (1276–1304)," *Anales* 7 (1988–89): 53–81.

61. For example, Pascual Ortega, "De mudéjares a moriscos: algunas reflexiones en torno a las relaciones sociales de producción y la conflictividad religiosa: el caso de la Ribera d'Ebre (Tarragona)," *Miscel·lània de textos medievales* 4 (1988): 319–33.

62. Most recently and originally, Manuel Vicent Febrer Romaguera, "Los tribunales de los alcadíes moros en las aljamas mudéjares valencianas," *Anuario de estudios medievales* 22 (1992): 45–77. Some idea of both the flood of newer Catalan journals and the continuing older staples can be gathered from the list of journals with articles pertinent to Catalan history and culture in *Arxiu de textos catalans antics* 10 (1992): Appendix, "Taules dels volums I–X," 35–57, covering 550 periodicals both Spanish and foreign, including collections and symposia. The *Arxiu* itself (1 [1982]) is invaluable for its

comprehensive abstracts of articles and books on Catalan peoples, including Mudejars.

63. For example, my "The Changing Face of Muslim Spain: Mudejar Foundations of the Morisco Tragedy," *Anuario medieval* 4 (1992, published 1994): 49–68.

64. Robert C. Stacey in *The American Historical Review* 97 (1992): 836–37. See too such widely popular theory-driven works as Robert I. Moore's *The Formation of a Persecuting Society: Power and Deviance in Western Europe, 950–1250* (Cambridge, Mass., 1987) with ten reprintings to date.

65. See for example Barceló's *Sobre Mayūrqa* (Palma de Mallorca, 1984) in Quaderns de Ca la Gran cristiana 2. A sample of the Bazzana-Guichard cooperative work is "Du *hisn* musulman au *castrum* chrétien: le château de Perpunchent (Lorcha, province d'Alicante)," in *Mélanges de la Casa de Velázquez* 18 (1982): 449–65; and their "Recherche sur les habitats musulmans du Levant espagnole," *Colloquio internazionale di archeologia medievale*, 2 vols. (Palermo, 1976), 1.59–100. All these works have Mudejar implications.

66. Cambridge, 1994, again with implications for Mudejar history.

67. Charles Dufourcq, *L'Espagne catalane et le Maghrib aux XIIIe et XIVe siècles, de la bataille de Las Navas de Tolosa (1212) à l'avènement du sultan mérenide Abou-l-Hasan (1331)* (Paris, 1966). See also Àngels Masià de Ros, *Jaume II: Aragó, Granada i Marroc: aportació documental* (Barcelona, 1989); the conference acts *Relaciones de la península ibérica con el Magreb, siglos XII–XVI*, ed. Mercedes García-Arenal and María J. Viguera (Madrid, 1988); and especially María Dolores López Pérez, *La Corona de Aragón y el Magreb en el siglo XIV (1331–1410)* (Barcelona, 1995).

68. *Los judíos en la edad media hispana*, Cuadernos de investigación medieval 5 (Madrid, 1986).

69. Roth, *Conversos, Inquisition, and the Expulsion of the Jews from Spain* (Madison, 1995). See also his *Jews, Visigoths, and Muslims in Mediterranean Spain: Cooperation and Conflict* (Leiden: 1994). Assís, *The Jewish Economy in the Medieval Crown of Aragon* (Leiden, 1997) and *The Golden Age of Aragonese Jewry 1213–1327* (Oxford, 1997). See too Robert Chazan's remarkable *Barcelona and Beyond: The Disputation of 1263 and Its Aftermath* (Berkeley/Los Angeles, 1992). And see my *Jews in the Notarial Culture: Latinate Wills in Mediterranean Spain* (Berkeley/Los Angeles, 1996).

70. See above, note 44 and text, and below, note 90 and text. In this connection see Jerrilynn Dodds, "Mudejar Tradition and the Synagogues of Medieval Spain: Cultural Identity and Cultural Hegemony" in *Convivencia: Jews, Muslims, and Christians in Medieval Spain*, ed. Vivian Mann et al. (New York, 1992), 113–31.

71. *Under Crescent and Cross: The Jews in the Middle Ages* (Princeton, 1994).

72. "The Mozarabs: Interaction of Christians, Jews, and Muslims in Medieval Spain," under the direction of H. E. Kassis. See also the *I Congreso internacional de estudios mozárabes* (Toledo, 1979). *Indigenous Communities,* ed. Michael Gervers and Ramzi Jibran Bikhazi (Toronto, 1990), including a chapter on Valencian Mudejars by Mark Meyerson (pp. 365–80). For a radically revisionist view of the most notable Mozarabic episode in al-Andalus, see Kenneth Baxter Wolf, *Christian Martyrs in Muslim Spain* (Cambridge, 1988); cf. Jessica Coope, *The Martyrs of Córdoba: Community and Family Conflict in an Age of Mass Conversion* (Lincoln, 1995). For an overview currently see Míkel de Epalza, "Mozarabs: An Emblematic Christian Minority in Islamic al-Andalus," *Legacy of Muslim Spain,* 148–75. Most recently see Leopoldo Peñarroja Torrejón, *Cristianos bajo el Islam: Los mozarabes hasta la reconquista de Valencia* (Madrid, 1994), and such works of Thomas Burman as his *Religious Polemic and the Intellectual History of the Mozarabs, 1050 to 1200* (Leiden, 1994).

73. "The Missionary Syndrome: Crusader and Pacific Northwest Religious Expansionism," *Comparative Studies in Society and History* 30 (1988): 271–85.

74. See pp. 20–39.

75. See above, note 38 and text.

76. *Cartas pueblas de las morerías valencianas y documentos* (Zaragoza, 1991). See too the Valencian Mudejar *cartas* transcribed by Enric Guinot Rodríguez among his 320 *Cartes de poblament medievales valencianes* (Valencia, 1991), and the posthumous *Las cartas pueblas del reino de Valencia* by Miguel Gual Camarena, ed. Desamparados Pérez Pérez (Valencia, 1989), chapter 6 on Mudejars. Manual Febrer i Romaguera has also contributed two important archival studies: "Las morerías valencianas y la organización de sus aljamas," *Anales de la Real academia de cultura valenciana* 67 (1991): 117–67, and "Los tribunales de los alcadíes moros en las aljamas mudéjares valencianas," *Anuario de estudios medievales* 22 (1992): 45–78.

77. *Regesto de documentos del Archivo de protocolos de Sevilla referentes a judíos y moros* (Seville, 1978); since only "unos pocos documentos" survive from before 1450, the chronology primarily covers 1436 to 1500.

78. "Documentos mudéjares aragoneses," in *XIII Congresso européene dell'Union d'arabisants e d'islamisants,* Quaderni di studi arabi 5–6 (1987–88), 786–90.

79. Manfred Wolf in *American Scholar* 63 (1994): 146, citing Rob Kroes, *De leegte van Amerika: een massacultuur in de wereld* (Amsterdam, 1992).

80. See below, pp. 309–322.

81. Karl and Elis Butzer and Juan Mateu, "Medieval Muslim Communities of the Sierra de Espadán, Kingdom of Valencia," *Viator* 17 (1986): 339–420; and their "Una alquería islámica medieval en la Sierra de Espadán," *Boletín de la Sociedad castellonense de cultura* 61 (1985): 305–65.

82. See above, note 65.

83. Ana Labarta's *La onomastica de los moriscos valencianos* (Madrid, 1987), is a pioneering work at the juncture of macaronic scribal garbles for Muslim names and the reconstructed originals. Federico Corriente's *A Grammatical Sketch of the Spanish Arabic Dialect Bundle* (Madrid, 1977) is a landmark in the language of Mudejars as well as their predecessors and the Moriscos. See also his *Léxico árabe andalusí según el "Vocabulista in arábico"* (Madrid, 1990), a thirteenth-century word-list for converting Mudejars.

84. *Un tratado catalan medieval de derecho islámico: el Llibre de la Çuna e Xara dels moros,* ed. María Carmen Barceló Torres (Córdoba, 1989). The only similar surviving work is the well-known *Leyes de moros* in Castilian, much inferior, known only in an eighteenth-century copy published in 1853.

85. The Centro is housed in the Instituto de Estudios Turolenses, Plaza Pérez Prado 3, 44001 Teruel.

86. Leiden, 1995.

87. Manchester, 1995.

88. *Medieval Encounters* 1 (1995): 51–113.

89. Leiden, 1995–96.

90. Princeton, 1996. It won the Premio del Rey of the American Historical Association in 1997.

91. Aldershot, 1996.

92. Meyerson, in *Medieval Encounters* 1 (1995): 144–73 and 2 (1996): 286–343. Bensch, in *Viator* 25 (1994): 63–93. Cf. Robert I. Burns, "La manumisión de un musulmán: un documento doble de Valencia en 1300," *Sharq al-Andalus* 5 (1988): 141–45, and "Regalo para un madre: una muchacha esclava musulmana del nieto de Abū Zayd, el señor de Borriol (1301)," *Sharq al-Andalus* 6 (1989): 115–17.

93. "Almohad Prince and Mudejar Convert: New Documentation on Abū Zayd" in *Medieval Iberia: Essays on the History and Literature of Medieval Spain,* ed. Donald Kagay and Joseph Snow (New York, 1996), 170–88. "The Many Crusades of Valencia's Conquest (1225–1280): An Historiographical Labyrinth" in *On the Social Origins of Medieval Institutions: Essays in Honor of Joseph F. O'Callaghan,* ed. Teresa Vann (Leiden, 1996), 167–77; "Muslim Scribes" in *Jews in the Notarial Culture* (above in note 69), 33–38; and "Paper Comes to the West, 800–1400" in *Europäische Technik im Mittelalter, 800 bis 1400: Tradition und Innovation,* ed. Uta Lindgren (Berlin, 1996), 413–22.

94. Isabel Bonet O'Connor, "En busca d'una minoria perduda: notícies sobre els mudéjars de Xàtiva," *Sharq al-Andalus* 12 (1995): 67–84; and "In a Foreign Court: Mudejar Civil and Criminal Cases Judged by Christian Officials," *Sharq al-Andalus* 12 (1998): in press.

95. See her article "Medieval Patterns of Social Exclusion and Integration: The Regulation of Non-Christian Clothing in Thirteenth-Century Hungary," *Revue Mabillon* 69 (1997): 155–76.

96. See for example Pilar Pérez Viñuales, "Los protocolos notariales como fuente para el estudio de la historia local: la comunidad mudéjar en la vega baja del río Jalón (Zaragoza)" in *Fuentes y métodos de la historia local* (Zamora, 1991), 291–98.

97. Maria Teresa Ferrer i Mallol is directing, with the assistance of Blanca Basáñez and Maria Echaniz, covering all the Mudejar documents in the crown registers in the Arxiu de la Corona d'Aragó, beginning with the reign of James II (1292–1327), the first volume of which is in press at the Consejo Superior de Investigaciones Científicas. It will feature short abstracts or title-summaries. She and her staff plan further volumes on Mudejar history as part of their governmentally funded project "Cristianos y musulmanes en el Mediterráneo occidental en los siglos XIV–XV," as well as a "Colección documental" for the Mudejars of the upland Kingdom of Aragon proper.

6

Muslim-Jewish Relations in Crusader Majorca in the Thirteenth Century: An Inquiry Based on Patrimony Register 342

LARRY J. SIMON

THERE ARE TWO preliminary obstacles to understanding Muslim-Jewish relations in crusader Majorca in the thirteenth century. Any exploration of the nature of these relations must perforce rest on an assessment of the standing of the individual Muslim and Jewish communities vis-à-vis Majorca's Christian colonizers. There is broad agreement that Majorca's Jews, despite legal restrictions and Christian hostility, enjoyed considerable favor and royal protection, guarded themselves against the assimilationist pressures of an aggressive Christian society, and profited by their skills in artisanry and moneylending, medicine and trade. The royal charters copied in the celebrated fourteenth-century Códice Pueyo of Majorca, or registered in the Crown of Aragon Archives, a portion of which were indexed by Jean Régné, indicate that Majorca's Jews enjoyed a wide range of communal privileges; acquaintance with more prosaic archival materials allows one to reconstruct important families or to sketch the wide range of Jewish economic activities.[1]

There is, however, consensus neither on what happened to all of Majorca's Muslims immediately following the Catalan conquest of 1229–1232, nor on their status in the course of succeeding generations. If the battles are less pitched and the rhetoric less animated than debates on Mudejar society elsewhere, the range of recent opinion is enormous. Twenty-five years ago it was commonly accepted that the vast majority of Muslims who were not killed in the conquest fled to North Africa, and that of the few Muslims who remained most were enslaved. Not only was the Majorcan crusade a successful one, but it was followed by a very complete and, depending upon one's point of view, successful colonialism. This widely accepted thesis was altered in 1970 by Elena Lourie, who argued that post-conquest "colonization by Muslims was going on on a fairly large scale," and was built upon "a steady trickle of Muslims from the status of slaves, whether preconquest or imported, into the class of free tenant farmers, whose conditions were far from being uniformly harsh," and who discovered free Muslims practicing various trades in the towns. Lourie concluded that royal preoccupation with the Majorcan equivalent of the annual royal besant collected from Mudejars elsewhere "argues the existence of a considerable population of free Saracens," and accounted for the absence of judicial or religious officials as "a chance silence in the surviving documents."[2]

Ricard Soto i Company, by contrast, in three articles published in the early 1980s, catalogued 156 slave sales between 1239 and 1256, described Majorca as a major slave emporium, and argued that absent communal or religious officials, the few scattered free Muslims can scarcely be seen as forming any society whatsoever.[3] Surveying the Majorcan bibliography, Robert I. Burns has recently referred to the "murky history of Majorca's postconquest Muslims." David Abulafia, while acknowledging the existence of the free Muslims whom Lourie uncovered, has in a "friendly critique" turned some of Lourie's own evidence against her position, and has made good use of materials in a too little known study by Alvaro Santamaría, the dean of Majorcan historians, to point out that the "Muslim population appears to have withered away during the period of the autonomous Majorcan kingdom."[4] If free Muslims, many of them foreign residents on the island or newly emerged from servitude, formed a numerous or prosperous class on the island in the thirteenth century, they certainly left few documentary or other traces in subsequent centuries.

My own research has tended to emphasize the centrality of slavery, but also to further complicate an already obscure situation. Elsewhere I have argued that a substantial number of Majorcan Muslims, many of them while slaves, converted to Christianity and assimilated into Christian society.[5] By charting *baptizatus* as an adjectival second or proto-surname in notarial-like documentation (in a few cases the individuals appear with two names and *baptizatus* as adjectival explanation), I have found free landholding converts as early as 1236, a substantial number of converts in the years 1241 to 1245, a declining number of references to converts in the years 1245 to 1278, and only a negligible number thereafter. The largest number of references to converts on Majorca thus predates the Dominican preaching mandates of the 1250s, the Franciscan founding at Miramar of a school for the training of Christian missionaries in 1274, and the varied activities of the peripatetic and hyperkinetic Ramon Llull. Rather than Llull converting large numbers of Majorcan Muslims, it might well have been the existence of large number of conquest- and slave-produced *baptizati* in the Majorca of his youth which converted Llull to his illusive and lifelong dream of converting Muslims and Jews.[6] Neo-Christian-Jewish or neo-Christian-Muslim relations may well deserve inquiry, but the point for this present article is that the Muslims of Majorca formed no real community, or were a community in the process of disintegration. All historians of the subject do agree that Majorcan Muslims did not enjoy the status of their co-religionists in, for example, neighboring Valencia, and that the contrast in status accorded Majorca's Muslims and Majorca's Jews was great. After examining thousands of documents in the royal registers of Alfonso III of Aragon (1285–1291), Lourie pointed out that letters sent to all Muslim *aljamas* never mention, while letters sent to all Jewish *aljamas* in the lands of the Crown of Aragon never fail to mention, Majorca.

The second obstacle hindering exploration of this topic is the lamentable fact that there survives very little relevant documentation. Even in better documented times and places information on Jewish-Muslim relations is apparently scant. Burns's massive Mudejar books do contain important information on Muslim-Jewish interaction, especially on Jews "serving as secretaries or diplomats in Islamic affairs and looming prominently in revenue collection and finance."[7] And in sifting through thousands of documents for the years 1355–1366 in the Crown of Aragon Archives, the late John Boswell uncovered several compelling stories of Muslim-Jewish interaction, the most intriguing, because such actions were punishable by death, being the conversions of several Muslim women to the Judaism of their spouses.[8] Lourie has utilized documents indexed by Régné and other materials to make an important contribution to current understanding, and Eleazar Gutwirth has completed a fascinating study of Muslim-Jewish relations in the fifteenth century from the standpoint of high culture.[9] Several lines of the analysis in these last three studies have recently been extended further by David Nirenberg who, nonetheless, begins his study with the observation that "the study of minority interaction is undertaken in an historical vacuum; virtually no work has been done on Muslim-Jewish relations under Christian rule in the Iberian peninsula, so that we know little of the material infrastructure of these relations."[10]

For thirteenth-century Majorca there is no direct secondary bibliography, and the royal materials, utilized by historians of Mudejars elsewhere, are relatively disappointing, though still revealing. On May 6, 1250 Jaume I confirmed the right of Jews to purchase property and to possess Muslim slaves. Two years later, on May 8, 1252 a general list of privileges promulgated by Jaume included the order that Christians and Muslims, on penalty of 100 morabatins, were not to remove stones or earth, or otherwise quarry in the Jewish cemetery.[11] On July 21, 1269 Jaume decreed that Muslim slaves or captives would not be permitted to bear witness against Jews, and confirmed an earlier concession that in all legal cases between a Christian and a Jew in Majorca, evidence by the testimony of only a Christian or a Muslim would not suffice and must be supported by a Christian and a Jew, or a Muslim and a Jew.[12] On March 12, 1274, or perhaps 1275, he granted to the Christians of Majorca that Jews of the city might not, on penalty of losing the capital and being obliged to return the security to the slave's master, loan on security to Muslim slaves.[13] Jaume II of Majorca, the Conqueror's second eldest surviving son and inheritor of Majorca, Rousillon, and assorted other claims in southern France (Aragon, Valencia, and Catalonia went to his elder sibling), and Alfonso III of Aragon, Jaume I's grandson, who conquered Majorca from his uncle (and left it upon his death to his brother Jaume II of Aragon, who in 1298 would be forced to cede it back to Jaume II of Majorca)—the two subsequent thirteenth-century monarchs—both granted general privileges which included the Jewish right to purchase, possess, and sell Muslim slaves.[14] Alfonso furthermore, on January 9, 1286, the same date he confirmed these privileges, not only granted Majorcan Jewish merchants the right to export male and female Muslim slaves from the kingdom and island of Majorca, but exempted them from paying the exit tax on the slaves. Subsequently, on September 7, 1289, Alfonso wrote to his representative Pere de Libian and requested that Pere purchase, on his behalf, a Muslim Muḥammad Sedeno and Muḥammad's wife Soffra.[15]

There are at least three documents among the 1500 notarial parchments surviving in various archives for the thirteenth century which cast light on Muslim-Jewish interaction, and all three pertain to slavery. In 1266 Solomon Halabo, a Valencian Jew, sold a white female Muslim named Nexma for six and one-half Valencia pounds to Arnau Carbonell, a Majorcan citizen.[16] At the beginning of the fourteenth century Nina, a Jewess and wife of Jacob Didissi, identified as a Jew of Majorca, purchased a white Muslim woman named Mobarcha, known also as ʿAʾisha, from the notary Bernat Cunil for sixteen Majorcan pounds.[17] Also, in the last will and testament of the Majorcan Jew Salima ben Aaron Bernat, dated July 6, 1288, reference is made to his black female Muslim slave.[18]

The story of Muslim-Jewish interaction in thirteenth-century Majorca, if it can be told, can only be reconstructed from a unique, underutilized, imperfectly understood, and frequently frustrating source in the Archives of the Reign (or Kingdom) of Majorca—a source to which J. N. Hillgarth, in his address at a 1991 Sephardic history conference at the University of Maryland, has redirected attention.[19] There exist fifteen variously titled registers surviving in the royal patrimony section of the Arxiu del Regne de Mallorca in Palma; they begin in 1232, but appear with great regularity only in late 1239 and extend to the end of the thirteenth century and beyond. Some folios contain slave sales and commercial documents, a few contain testaments and dowry agreements, but most concern land transactions in the royal half of the island.[20] If the Aragonese royal registers contain a mixture of the prosaic and the profound, only the most prosaic of documents are usually to be found here. Jews can be found making loans to Muslims; free Muslim artisans can occasionally be seen, but interacting more with Christians than with Jews; and an occasional Jewish-Muslim land transaction can be found. By and large, however, the majority of documents concerning Muslim-Jewish relations, perhaps Muslim-Christian relations as well, relate to the institution of slavery. In a careful study of the first hundred folios, containing close to a thousand documents, of Register 342, a fairly coherent and the first complete register in the series, one finds numerous instances of Muslim-Jewish interaction.

In 1240, in the third slave sale in Register 342, Miquel Companys sold to a Majorcan Jew, for fifty-one Melgorian sous, a Muslim slave named Sayt.[21] Subsequently, Jacob ben Simon sold to Jaume Ferrer a Muslim named Hamet for eighty Melgorian sous, and in 1241 Abraham ben Alhorayef, a Jew of Sijilmāsa in North Africa, sold Maymona, a black Muslim woman, and her daughter Ahambar, "similiter nigra," to Pere Pintor for seven pounds less five sous.[22] In May 1241 Abraham ben Juçef sold to Miquel Nunis, a knight, a white Muslim slave Azmet for seventy Melgorian sous. In July 1242 Dominic Suger sold to Josef ben Salām of Peniscola an ʿAlī de Lorcha for thirty-three besants.[23] Later in the register, but earlier chronologically, in April 1242, Juçef ben Simon sold to Bernat de Mora, a layman of Tortosa, a white Muslim woman Miriam for a hundred Melgorian sous. Subsequently Juçef Tilimseni sold to Ambar, son of the Jew Solomon, half of the right he had to a mulatto slave Sayt for fifty sous.[24] The Christian Valentini de Turribus owns the other half of the slave, and, for his part, Sayt has paid ten of the eighty silver besant redemption price which has been established for him.

Of the thirty-five slave sales recorded in this first hundred folios, Jews are a party to the transaction seven times or 20 percent of the time. This is somewhat high in comparison to my overall tabulation of thirteenth-century Majorcan numbers, but since every slave sale involves two parties, and Jews do not appear in this run of documentation as both buyer and seller, that percentage can be reduced by half. This is still perhaps a rate double the Jewish percentage of the population, but given their wealth, industry, and scrupulousness in having their transactions with Christians recorded, the figure is unremarkable. The limited incentive for two Jewish parties to a transaction to seek out a Christian notary diminishes, and our lack of understanding of these registers obscures, the overall view of Jewish patterns of buying and selling slaves, but, empirically, of the seventy buyers and sellers in the first hundred folios of Register 342, Jews represent seven of the parties or precisely 10 percent.

I belabor this point because in January 1241 or 1242 Solomon of

Sijilmāsa, a Jew, provided for his slave ᶜAlī ibn Musa de Rif's redemption for fifty-one silver besants. Solomon ben Davech provided for his slave Halef ᶜAbd al-Raḥmān's redemption for twenty besants. In May 1242 Abraham ben Juçef permitted the redemption of his slave Safor ibn Mūsā for twenty-two besants.[25] In early June Abraham ben Horayef provided for the redemption within two years of Fatima and her daughter Maria upon payment of sixty besants; two days later Juçef ben Simon's slave ᶜAʾisha is to be freed upon payment of thirty-four besants; within the next month, ᶜAlī ibn Hamet is able to arrange for his redemption from his Jewish master, Abraham ben Horya of Sijilmāsa (most likely the same owner as that of Fatima and Maria) at a price of 103 sous.[26] In July 1242 a Jewish woman permitted her Muslim slave to be redeemed within two years for 115 Melgorian sous.[27] In September 1242 two separate documents detailed redemption arrangements granted by Solomon ben Juçef Tilimseni to, first of all, ᶜAlī ibn Sulayman for 150 Melgorian sous, and, second of all, a female Muslim named ᶜAzīza, who may well have been related to ᶜAlī, for forty-five Melgorian sous.[28] In all, the first hundred folios of Register 342 contain twenty-five slave redemption documents; Jews grant, curiously enough, the redemption in nine of the cases or precisely 36 percent.

Why would Jews free their Muslim slaves, or, rather, allow their Muslim slaves to redeem themselves, at a rate almost four to eight times greater, or even in this run of documentation, where Jews are liberally represented as buyers and sellers, at a rate almost two to four times greater, than their apparent rate of slaveholding? My initial impression was that Jews provided for the eventual freedom of their Muslim slaves most likely because they feared the conversion of the slaves, and doubted their ability to maintain ownership. From patristic times forward, almost all canonical and civil legislation forbade Jews from owning Christians. According to Ramon Penyafort's *Summa,* homeborn slaves and slaves purchased for service are to be set free upon their conversion; Jews owning slaves purchased for business are given three months in which to sell the converts.[29] In the earlier discussed charter of 1252, however, Jaume I had decreed that the Muslim slaves of Majorcan Jews baptized at any time other than Easter, Pentecost, and Christmas must pay twelve maravedís to the king's bailiff. Later, in 1269, the king had appended the following to a list of privileges to the Majorcan *aljama:* if any Muslim slave of a Jew enters a church of Majorca to have himself baptized, baptism was to be delayed for several days, and the convert was not to go free but to become the slave of the king (parenthetically it might be added that in the fourteenth century, at any rate, royal slaves who fell out of favor were known to be sold to work in the Ibizan salt mines). This decree is repeated in a letter from Valencia on August 25, 1273.[30]

Another explanation is the possibility that medieval Jews simply had a more highly developed sense of social charity about slavery than medieval Christians. Perhaps remembrance of their own biblical history made the freeing of one's slaves particularly meritorious; perhaps something in Jewish law, tinged with memories of Egyptian bondage, would provide a clue. Biblical law does mandate that Hebrew slaves be set free after six years, but provides, however, that Canaanite, or non-Hebrew, slaves were to serve in perpetuity and that it was a duty not to squander the inheritance owed one's progeny. Much of Maimonides' treatise on slavery in his *Mishneh Torah* was taken up with a discussion of Jewish slaves, for which there had long been no evidence of their continued existence. Maimonides further explains that "a heathen slave is acquired by five modes, and he acquires his freedom by three; he is acquired by money or by a deed or by an act of possession or by symbolic barter or by the act of drawing; he acquires his freedom by money or by a deed or by the loss of one of his projecting limbs." He argues that although it is permitted to emancipate a slave for a religious duty or when the slave is a stumbling block for a sinner, generally "it is forbidden for anyone to emancipate a heathen slave. Whoever does emancipate him transgresses a positive commandment, as it is said: *of them may ye take your bondmen forever* (Lev 25:46)." Conversely, the redemption of Jewish captives was absolutely obligatory. Although Maimonides concludes his treatise with scriptural quotes and by arguing that "it is the quality of piety and the way of wisdom that a man be merciful and pursue justice and not make his yoke heavy upon the slave," and that a master should not "heap upon the slave oral abuse and anger, but rather speak to him softly and listen to his claims," he begins the section by stating: "It is permitted to work a heathen slave with rigor."[31]

Despite the obligation to preserve one's inheritance, some rabbinic literature did sanction, for various reasons, manumission, and there is no doubt that a considerable number of manumissions took place. Shlomo Dov Goitein found only seven deeds of manumission in the Cairo *Geniza*—six for females, and one for a male—but from the number of references to freedmen in other documents concludes in his monumental *Mediterranean Society* that "the emancipation of slaves must have been extremely common."[32] The problem in comparing this to post-crusade Majorca, however, is that the emancipated individuals are apparently pagan or Christian converts to Judaism, and there is no analogy to Jews freeing their Muslim slaves: Muslim males and females would have to undergo ritual immersion before they could be employed in household tasks by Jews living in Christian lands, but Muslim males were already circumcised, and complete conversion to Judaism would thus be unnecessary. Although ecclesiastical and civil approbation of slavery was universal in the Middle Ages, Christianity likewise counseled fairness in the treatment of one's slaves and saw merit in the emancipation of slaves, especially Christian slaves; almost all Christian emancipations by last testament from thirteenth-century Majorca are of baptized slaves, however, and even a substantial number of the slaves being permitted in Register 342 to purchase their freedom from Christians are baptized. There might well be something in Jewish law or in medieval Jewish religious or ethical practice to account for this documentary evidence, but it is neither obvious nor easily located. Perhaps a *responsum* of Solomon ben Abraham Adret, c. 1235–c. 1310 and rabbi of Barcelona, or something preserved from an earlier time in a *responsum* of Simeon ben Ẓemah Duran, 1361–1444, rabbinic authority who fled Majorca for Algiers after the massacre of 1391, would shed further light on this situation.[33]

A third alternative does exist, though if historiography teaches anything on complex matters of ethno-religious relations, it is that of the making of alternative explanations, there is no end. Is it possible that perhaps the emancipations in question are really not dramatic changes from slavery to freedom, but smaller shifts from slave to *exaricus*, slave to sharecropper, or slave to one of the many forms of medieval servitude that did not consitute chattel slavery? The last will of the Christian Bernat d'Olzet, dating to the early 1240s, has the line: "Item dimito Berengario babtizato qui manet in alcheria mea decem solidos."[34] Was Berenguer, formerly a Muslim slave, freed or emancipated upon his conversion, and did he then choose to remain in Bernat's *alquería,* or were these terms of his emancipation? Bernat's testament does not indicate. Some redemption documents, however, are explicit about land and equipment being granted to help Muslim slaves earn their redemption money through years of service, usually five or six, and several of these actually mandate continued cultivation, even after emancipation, of the land in question. Although Majorcan Jews apparently owned land cultivated by sharecroppers, all of the charters with such clauses currently known to me concern the Muslim slaves of Christian landholders. Jewish law on emancipation would seem to unequivocally rule out this alternative as an explanation; unlike in Roman law or in Islamic law, where a freed slave either did or easily could retain close ties as a client of their former master, Jewish law forbade such an association if the emancipation were to be valid.[35] It is not clear, however, how rabbinic authorities would have interpreted these redemption documents, some of which nevertheless did provide for payment over time rather than the immediate and complete emancipation of the slave.

There does not have to be one univocal explanation for this observed phenomenon of Jews allowing their Muslim slaves to redeem themselves, but it seems to me that perhaps the initial explanation is the most promising. Jaume I's decrees were not issued until 1252 and 1269, and the latter had to be renewed in 1273. The Majorcan *aljama* would not have been petitioning the king had there been no problem with Jewish-held slaves attempting to convert; more detailed work with these royal patrimony registers in the future will undoubtedly shed more light on the issue. At the start of the 1240s there had persisted even among Christian-held slaves the impression that manumission would follow upon conversion, a policy which undoubtedly appealed more to Muslim slaves and perhaps some missionaries than landholding slave owners. Baptism may have increased the likelihood of eventual manumission, but it alone was not sufficient; on April 24, 1240 Pope Gregory IX had granted the Majorcan bishop the right to concede to Majorcans that they could continue to own and trade baptized slaves.[36] There exists in Register 342 evidence documenting the concern over possible conversion of Jewish-held slaves in the early 1240s, and this comes from loans made by Jews to Christians. In several instances Christians pledged their Muslim slaves as collateral, but mentioned, moreover, that should their collateral be seized for nonpayment of the loan and promptly die, flee, or convert the borrower would still be obligated in full for repayment of the loan. In this explanatory scenario, then, conflict and competition among all three ethno-religious groups is emphasized: Jews, forbidden to own Christian slaves, preferred to take redemption money rather than lose their investment; Majorcan Muslims, far more disadvantaged than Jews vis-à-vis Christians, contemplated apostasy, in numerous cases actually apostatized, and enjoyed the threat of apostasy when dealing with Jews; Christian legal discrimination against Jews, and their dramatic conquest and colonization of Islamic Majorca animated and was the driving force behind the entire process.

Even if Jews had not in fact provided for the redemptions of their slaves at a remarkable rate, much of the interaction between Muslims and Jews, it is safe to assume, concerned slavery, and the relative impoverishment and massive enslavement of Majorcan Muslims provided the backdrop to Muslim-Jewish relations. Rather than end on this depressing note, there is one interesting element in several of the Jewish emancipations. Only in one or two cases were the Christian-held soon-to-be-freedmen mentioned as leaving Majorca, either permanently or to raise the last of their redemption money, and many were, of course, still to be tied by law to the land or by poverty to the island. Solomon of Sijilmāsa's slave ʿAlī, Abraham ben Juçef's slave Safer, and Abraham ben Horayhaf's slave Fāṭima all would be heading, however, "in terram sarracenorum" to raise the remaining fraction of their ransoms; in the case of Fāṭima, her daughter Maria would remain behind as security for the full amount. Solomon ben Davech's slave would be headed to Minorca, after 1231 a Muslim tributary of the kings of Aragon until its conquest in 1287; and Juçef ben Simon's slave ʿAʾisha would be heading, after payment of twenty-four besants, quite specifically, to Bougie so she could raise her remaining ten besants of ransom money.[37] Majorca offered a fertile frontier for Jews and Christians, and many Jews in the thirteenth century immigrated from both Christian and Islamic lands; the possible ties of the Jewish slave owners in these specific documents to Sijilmāsa and Tlemcen is particularly noteworthy. Islamic Majorca, however, was shattered, and perhaps it may not be entirely fanciful to imagine that some Majorcan Jewish slaveholders were among those who recognized this, and, then, acted practically, if not also mercifully, upon the idea that the island no longer provided a healthy environment in which to remain a good Muslim.

NOTES

1. Régné's abstracts appeared serially between 1910 and 1923 in the *Revue des études juives* and have been collected and published as *History of the Jews in Aragon: Regesta and Documents 1213–1327,* ed. Yom Tov Assis (Jerusalem, 1978). While Régné's coverage was comprehensive if not complete for the registers of Jaume I (1257–1276), Pedro III (1276–1285), and Alfonso III (1285–1291), his index is neither complete nor comprehensive for the registers, some 260 total, extant for the reign of Jaume II of Aragon (1291–1327). For general works, utilizing especially royal charters, on Majorca's Jews see David Abulafia, "From Privilege to Persecution: Crown, Church, and Synagogue in the City of Majorca, 1229–1343," in *Church and City, 1000–1500: Essays in Honour of Christopher Brooke,* ed. David Abulafia, Michael J. Franklin, and Miri Rubin (Cambridge, 1992), 111–26; David Abulafia, *A Mediterranean Emporium: The Catalan Kingdom of Majorca* (Cambridge, 1994), 75–102; Fidel Fita and Gabriel Llabrés, "Privilegios de los Hebreos mallorquines en el Códice Pueyo," *Boletín de la Real academia de la historia* 36 (1900): 13–35, 122–48, 185–209, 273–306, 369–402, and 458–94 (unfortunately, only thirteen of the 113 documents predate 1300); A. Lionel Isaacs, *The Jews of Majorca* (London, 1936); and Antonio Pons, *Los Judíos del Reino de Mallorca durante los siglos XIII y XIV,* 2 vols. (Madrid, 1957–60; rpt. Palma de Mallorca, 1984). For an important initial study of families and economic life, see Ricardo Soto i Company, "La Aljama Judaica de Ciutat en el siglo XIII," *Bolletí de la Societat arqueològica lul·liana* 94 (1978): 145–84.

2. Elena Lourie, "Free Moslems in the Balearics under Christian Rule in the Thirteenth Century," *Speculum* 40 (1970): 624–49.

3. "La población musulmana de Mallorca bajo el dominio cristiano (1240–1276)," *Fontes rerum Balearium* 2, nos. 1, 3 (1978): 65–80, 549–64, an article which was to be, but apparently was not continued (likewise the journal was not); "El primer tràfic esclavista a Mallorca," *L'Avenç* 35 (1981): 60–65; and "Sobre mudeixars a Mallorca fins a finals del segle XIII," in *Estudis de prehistòria, d'història de Mayurqa i d'història de Mallorca dedicats a Guillem Rosselló i Bordoy* (Palma de Mallorca, 1982), 195–221.

4. Robert I. Burns, "Muslims in the Thirteenth-Century Realms of Aragon," in *Muslims under Latin Rule, 1100–1500,* ed. James M. Powell (Princeton, 1990), 67; Abulafia, *Mediterranean Emporium,* 57–64; and Alvaro Santamaría, *Ejecutoria del Reino de Mallorca* (Palma, 1990), 51–265.

5. Larry J. Simon, "Surnames among the Ruins: Charting Muslim Conversion to Christianity in Crusader Majorca," unpublished paper read at the 108th annual meeting of the American Historical Association in January 1994. I am in the process of completing a monograph on "The Muslims and Jews of Crusader Majorca in the Thirteenth Century: A Comparative Study." Though dealing with a very different milieu, the classic work on Muslim conversion in thirteenth-century Spain remains Robert I. Burns, "Journey from Islam: Incipient Cultural Transition in the Conquered Kingdom of Valencia," *Speculum* 35 (1960): 337–56.

6. For recent surveys of Llull's attitudes toward Europe's ethno-religious minorities and toward crusade and mission, see Mark D. Johnston, "Ramon Lull and the Compulsory Evangelization of Jews and Muslims," and Pamela Drost Beattie, "'*Pro exaltatione sanctae fidei catholicae*': Mission and Crusade in the Writings of Ramon Llull," in *Iberia and the Mediterranean World of the Middle Ages: Studies in Honor of Robert I. Burns, S.J.*, vol. I: *Proceedings from Kalamazoo,* ed. Larry J. Simon (Leiden, 1995), 3–37, 113–29. See also my article "The Church and Slavery in Ramon Llull's Majorca," 345–63, with citation of some of the burgeoning bibliography on Majorcan slavery in the late Middle Ages on p. 351 n. 18.

7. See Burns, *Medieval Colonialism: Postcrusade Exploitation of Islamic Valencia* (Princeton, 1975), 16, 270–91; *Islam under the Crusaders: Colonial Survival in the Thirteenth-Century Kingdom of Valencia* (Princeton, 1973).

8. John Boswell, *The Royal Treasure: Muslim Communities under the Crown of Aragon in the Fourteenth Century* (New Haven, 1977), 351–52, 379–81, 436–37.

9. See the index listings in Régné, *Regesta* under "Muslims" and "Muslims, Relations with Jews." For Lourie see "Anatomy of Ambivalence: Muslims under the Crown of Aragon in the Late Thirteenth Century," the only previously unpublished article in her collected studies volume *Crusade and Colonisation: Muslims, Christians, and Jews in Medieval Aragon* (London, 1990), VII, 51–68; and for Gutwirth see his "Hispano-Jewish Attitudes to the Moors in the Fifteenth Century," *Sefarad* 49 (1989): 237–62.

10. Nirenberg, "Muslim-Jewish Relations in the Fourteenth-Century Crown of Aragon," *Viator* 24 (1993): 249–68; and now in revised form as chapter 6 of *Communities of Violence: Persecution of Minorities in the Middle Ages* (Princeton, 1996), 166–99.

11. The documents are published in *Viage literario a las iglesias de España,* ed. Jaime Villanueva, 22 vols. (Madrid, 1803–52), 22.328–30 and 330–31; and indexed by Régné, *Regesta,* nos. 43 and 46.

12. The later document is published by Fita and Llabrés, "Privilegios de los Hebreos mallorquines," 23–25, no. 8, and indexed by Régné, *Regesta,* no. 433; the earlier document from June 24, 1269 is Fita and Llabrés, "Privilegios de los Hebreos mallorquines," 22–23, no. 7, and indexed by Régné, *Regesta,* no. 432.

13. Villanueva, *Viage literario,* 22.314; and Régné, *Regesta,* no. 617.

14. For Jaume II of Majorca, see Fita and Llabrés, "Privilegios de los Hebreos mallorquines," 29–30, no. 13; for Alfonso, see Régné, *Regesta,* no. 1478.

15. Barcelona, Arxiu de la Corona de Aragó [hereafter ACA], canc. reial, reg. 63, f. 30^{r}, indexed by Régné, *Regesta,* no. 1479 and published by him as no. XX, pp. 207–208; and ACA, canc. reial, reg. 80, f. 48^{r}, indexed by Régné, *Regesta,* no. 1996.

16. Madrid, Archivo Histórico Nacional [hereafter AHN], Clero, pergs., carp. 86, no. 3 (June 12, 1266). The Christian scribe records the name as "Suleyamo"; another common scribal variation on the same name is "Salamo."

17. Palma, Arxiu del Regne de Mallorca, pergs., audiencia, s.XIV, no. 10 (March 17, 1301).

18. AHN, Clero, pergs., carp. 89, no. 10.

19. Since the presentation of this paper in 1994, Hillgarth has published his talk as "Sources for the History of the Jews of Majorca," *Traditio* 50 (1995), 334–41. The Maryland Sephardic conference has now been recently published as *In Iberia and Beyond: Hispanic Jews between Cultures,* ed. Bernard Dov Cooperman (Newark: University of Delaware Press, 1998).

20. The registers are found in Palma, Arxiu del Regne de Mallorca, Reial Patrimoni, Escrivania de Cartes Reials [hereafter ARM, RP, ECR]; they are referred to as the ECR because they relate to the royal patrimony, although few royal charters are among the documents. On occasion they have been cited as "Civitatis et partis foraneae" or the "Protocolos de (o Contratos de) Civitatis et partis foraneae." They are not the registers of individual public notaries, and are in fact not orderly registers but represent a later binding together of diverse materials and fragments; it is impossible to date many of the documents and some folio sections follow no observable chronological order; paleographical difficulties abound. Registers 341–55 concern the thirteenth century.

21. ARM, RP, ECR, reg. 342, f. 4^{v}. Sayt is perhaps the Latinization of Saʿid.

22. ARM, RP, ECR, reg. 342, f. 15^{v}. ("Hamet" perhaps for Aḥmad); and for Abraham ben Alhorayef (f. 26^{r}).

23. Reg. 342, ff. 74^{r} and 84^{v}.

24. Reg. 342, ff. 91^{v} and 97^{r}.

25. Reg. 342, ff. 11^{v}, 21^{r}, 76^{r}.

26. Reg. 342, ff. 77^{r}–^{v}, 82^{r}.

27. Reg. 342, f. 82^{v}.

28. Reg. 342, f. 89^{v}, docs. 3 and 4.

29. See Walter Pakter, *Medieval Canon Law and the Jews* (Ebelsbach, 1988), 84–142. The title "Concerning Jews, Saracens, and Their Slaves" from Ramon de Penyafort's *Summa de poenitentia et matrimonio* (Rome, 1603) has been translated by Robert Chazan in his *Church, State, and Jew in the Middle Ages* (New York, 1980), 38–42.

30. Fita and Llabrés, "Privilegios de los Hebreos mallorquines," 23–25, no. 8, indexed by Régné, *Regesta,* no. 433; and for the renewal, Régné, *Regesta,* no. 562.

31. See *The Code of Maimonides,* Book Twelve: *The Book of Acquisition,* trans. Isaac Klein (New Haven, 1951), 245–82, with quotations at 264, 280, and 281; and the general discussion by Salo W. Baron, "The Economic Views of Maimonides," in *Essays on Maimonides: An Octocentennial Volume,* ed. Salo W. Baron (New York, 1941), 229–47. See in particular Simha Assaf, "Slavery and the Slave-Trade among the Jews during the Middle Ages (from the Jewish Sources) [in Hebrew with English abstract]," *Tsiyon* 4 (1938/39): 91–125 and 5 (1939/40), 271–80; and, more generally, the citations and entry written by Haim Herman Cohn on "Slavery" in *Encyclopaedia Judaica* (New York, 1971), 14.1655–60.

32. See Shlomo D. Goitein, *A Mediterranean Society: The Jewish Communities of the Arab World as Portrayed in the Documents of the Cairo Geniza,* vol. I: *Economic Foundations* (Berkeley, 1967), 130–47 and 431–37 (133). Concubinage and the emancipation of one's converted slave for the purpose of marriage (the latter forbidden by rabbinic law if the slave were already your concubine) were, of course, extremely common; see not only Goitein, but Louis M. Epstein, "The Institution of Concubinage among the Jews," *Proceedings of the American Academy for Jewish Research* 6 (1935): 184–86; Ben Zion Wacholder, "The Halakah and the Proselyting of Slaves during the Gaonic Era," *Historia judaica* 18 (1956): 89–106; and for Spain see Yom Tov Assis, "Sexual Behaviour in Mediaeval Hispano-Jewish Society," in *Jewish History: Essays in Honour of Chimen Abramsky,* ed. Ada Rapoport-Albert and Steven J. Zipperstein (London, 1988), 36–40 for concubinage. It may well have been the conversion of non-Jews to Judaism and the existence of concubinage which led some rabbinic authorities to take a dim view of emancipating one's slaves.

33. Or perhaps further study of these registers will indicate that there was something unique to the 1240s or to the first one hundred folios of this one register, one of the first, that will explain away or lessen the significance of the phenomenon.

34. *Diplomatari del Monestir de Santa Maria de la Real de Mallorca,* vol. I: *1232–1360,* ed. Pau Mora and Lorenzo Andrinal (Palma de Mallorca, 1982), 243–47, no. 31.

35. This can be seen in Maimonides' treatment of emancipation. For Islam see Paul G. Forand, "The Relation of the Slave and the Client to the

Master or Patron in Medieval Islam," *International Journal of Middle East Studies* 2 (1971): 59–66. For the status of the freedman in Roman law, the bibliography is enormous; see, for example, the citations in Joseph C. Miller, *Slavery: A Worldwide Bibliography, 1900–1982* (White Plains, N.Y., 1985), 276–302.

36. Palma, Arxiu de la Catedral de Mallorca, *Liber privilegiorum,* f. 2^r: "Gregorius nonus concessit episcopo Maioricensi ut possit concedere populo maioricensi quod baptizatos servos suos valeant vendere, prout sibi videbitur expedire." See also Benjamin Kedar, *Crusade and Mission: European Approaches toward the Muslims* (Princeton, 1984), 149, 214–15.

37. The specific citations are all available above in notes 25 through 29.

7

Religious and Sexual Boundaries in the Medieval Crown of Aragon

DAVID NIRENBERG

Convivencia is a central issue in the historiography of religious minorities in the Iberian Peninsula. The term, a Spanish word meaning "living together," was coined by the philologist Américo Castro in his discussion of the effects upon Spanish culture of the coexistence of Christianity, Islam, and Judaism in the Iberian Peninsula.[1] Narrowly defined the word is not controversial: Christians, Jews, and Muslims certainly "coexisted" in Iberia. The nature of this coexistence, however, is hotly debated along many lines. One of these is its harmony. Though there is no reason why *convivencia* need designate only peaceful coexistence, it has in fact acquired this meaning among many historians. These historians present the Christian kingdoms of the Iberian Peninsula as uniquely tolerant of religious minorities until the expulsion of 1492. They minimize periods of violence and persecution, stress cultural cooperation, and talk frequently of a "golden age" of minority culture.[2] At the opposite end of the spectrum are certain schools of Jewish historical interpretation, particularly the so-called "lachrymose" and Jerusalem schools.[3] The lachrymose school, which dates back to medieval chronicle traditions, sees the history of Judaism since the fall of Jerusalem in 70 C.E. as a vale of tears, a progression of violent tragedies. It is in part an eschatological vision, with each disaster increasing in magnitude until the last and greatest disaster precipitates the coming of the Messiah and redemption. The Jerusalem school is in some ways a post-holocaust, secularized version of the lachrymose school. Though its messianism is more muted, it shares with its predecessor a teleological vision in which each incident of persecution foreshadows greater persecutions to come. Within the field of Sefardic Jewish studies the Jerusalem school has been very influential, due in large part to the work of Yitzhak Baer, whose two volume *A History of the Jews in Christian Spain* remains the standard reference.[4]

These polarized interpretations, rose-tinted haven of tolerance or darkening valley of tears, parallel the central dichotomy in modern studies of the treatment of medieval minorities: that between peaceful tolerance and violent intolerance.[5] Thus opposed, violence, hostility, and competition can only be seen as destructive breakdowns of social relations, the antithesis of associative action. Strange as it may seem, accounts of sexual intercourse between minority men and Christian women (especially prostitutes) and the violence such accounts provoked provide a vantage point from which to argue against these polarized views of *convivencia* and to create new space for violence in models of coexistence. The following pages outline such an argument. They claim that violence, in this case violence about sex, was a central aspect of the coexistence of majority and minorities in medieval Spain, or at least the Crown of Aragon, and suggest that coexistence was in part predicated on such violence.[6]

For the sake of conceptual clarity and because of the brief compass of this essay, I will focus on just one subset of this violence: institutional, judicial violence against minority men on charges of sexual intercourse with Christian women.[7] The few previous treatments of this subject in the Iberian peninsula start with the law. Here is an example of such law from the city of Tortosa, in Catalonia:

> If Jew or Muslim males are found lying with a Christian woman, the Jew or Muslim should be drawn and quartered and the Christian woman should be burned, in such a manner that they should die. And this accusation can be brought by any inhabitant of the town, without the penalty of *talio* or any other [penalty].[8]

From law, they move to practice, focusing on those moments (and there were such moments) when Muslim or Jewish men, or Christian women, were executed on charges of miscegenation.[9] Finally, they invoke ecclesiastical legislation. At the Fourth Lateran Council in 1215, for example, the fear that minority men might sleep with Christian women was explicitly used to justify the most extensive attempts at segregation undertaken by the medieval church. It was decided that it was difficult to separate Christian, Jewish, and Muslim men by physical appearance, and since this difficulty could lead to sexual intercourse between Christians and non-Christians, Jews and Muslims would henceforth be required to dress differently from Christians.[10] Those infamous emblems of difference, the Jewish cape and badge of colored cloth and the Muslim haircut and dress, were enacted and justified as visual representations of a sexual boundary not to be transgressed.[11]

These legal and ecclesiastical texts, corroborated by occasional archival references to executions on such charges, are taken as signs of an immense collective anxiety about sexual mixing, an anxiety compared (wrongly, I think) by one historian to that over Black-White sexual intercourse in the post-bellum United States, and used to explain increasing violence and intolerance toward the minorities involved.[12]

The problem as I see it is that here analysis stops. I say "problem" because too many questions are left unasked: How "collective" was this "collective anxiety"? There are almost no examples of popular lynchings on such charges in the Crown of Aragon, for example, though there is evidence of Christian women engaging in long-term affairs with minority men.[13] And why should this anxiety focus on sex, and not on other types of interaction? How did this anxiety "function" in society? Why should we assume that it fomented intolerance and violence? How and to what effect did individuals invoke this type of anxiety, and the judicial violence it made possible, in their face-to-face interactions? These are all large issues. I would like to discuss just a few of them, namely, why such judicial violence should focus on sex, and not on other forms of interaction (for example, conversion, comensality, or economic cooperation) as it did in other times and places; and second, what functions such violence played in social interaction.

To a non-medievalist, the first question (why sex?) seems naive. Many multi-ethnic societies erect barriers to sexual activity across group boundaries, proclaiming as their intent the prevention of racial mixing, generally of self-styled "superior" with "inferior" races.

In the case of Jews, one need only think of the Nuremberg laws of 1935 and their prohibition of Jewish-German intermarriage under the rubric *Rassenschande* ("race pollution"); or of the early modern Spanish obsession with *limpieza de sangre* ("purity of blood") and restrictions on the descendants of Jewish converts to Christianity.[14] These anxieties focus on sex because they are concerned with the reproduction of racial categories, categories whose very existence seems threatened by miscegenation.

Such concerns are, however, very different from those of the fourteenth-century Crown of Aragon, though they share with them a certain sexual vocabulary. Prior to the mass conversions of Jews to Christianity in 1391, anxiety about the reproduction of racial categories, or even evidence for such categories, is difficult to find. It does not seem that descendants of converts were commonly stigmatized as "racially impure" or of dubious orthodoxy before the fifteenth century. Further, Christian (and Jewish) men were willing to marry converted Muslim women.[15] This was, of course, a calm predicated on a certain confidence in the efficacy of conversion, a confidence attested to by the numerous cases in which charges of miscegenation against Jewish or Muslim males were dropped once the defendant converted to Christianity.[16] It was predicated, too, on the arrogant conviction that any child with a Christian biological parent was by definition Christian if the parent cared to claim it.[17] The Christian officials who seized the Muslim Adambacaix's son Mahomet because the Christian Antoni Safàbrega had declared on his deathbed that the child was the product of his adulterous relationship with Adambacaix's deceased wife Axa, were not acting out of fear that boundaries of exclusion were necessary to maintain racial integrity.[18]

If race was not the issue, then what was? To this question the thirteenth-century king Alfonso the Wise of Castile provides something of an answer:

> Since Christians who commit adultery with married women deserve death, how much more so do Jews who lie with Christian women, for these are spiritually espoused to Our Lord Jesus Christ by virtue of the faith and baptism they received in His name. . . . And the Christian woman who commits such a transgression . . . shall receive the same punishment as the Christian woman who lies with a Muslim.[19]

Each Christian woman, wed or unwed, is the bride of Christ, just as the collective Christian church, the *ecclesia*, is traditionally represented as his bride. Through such synecdoche, miscegenation becomes the cuckolding of Christ.

Alfonso's focus on women as a site of dishonor seems to gesture toward the concept of "honor and shame," so beloved of Mediterranean anthropologists like Julian Pitt-Rivers, Julio Caro Baroja, and others.[20] Likewise, his raising of the individual woman's body to the level of the collective seems inspired by a careful reading of Mary Douglas. Consider her view of the ways in which group identity is expressed:

> the image of the human body [is used] to express both the exclusive nature of the allegiance and the confused social experience. The group is likened to the human body; the orifices are to be carefully guarded to prevent unlawful intrusions.[21]

The fears of pollution that arise when the boundaries of such groups come under pressure are expressed through metaphors of the body: the female body becomes the site of fears of penetration and corruption, the male of diffusion and enfeeblement.[22]

This "Alfonsine" model has the advantage of accounting for some of the rhetoric of castigation (not quite the same as corruption) which pervades contemporary discussions about the consequences of miscegenation. When the municipal council of Valencia agonized over the consequences of the many enormous sins, notably miscegenation, committed in their city, they wrote of the horrific divine punishment such sins would bring upon the community: "for which sins, so enormous and grave . . . our Lord God . . . gives great whippings, even canings" in the form of plagues and bad weather.[23] It seems that the transgression of boundaries was feared, not so much because it brought about corruption or enfeeblement, but because it was inevitably followed by harsh discipline. God and his lash hovered over those places where religions met and mingled.

And yet there were many such places. Despite repeated ecclesiastical condemnation, Christians, Muslims, and Jews drank together, gambled together, went to war together, lived in the same neighborhoods (sometimes in the same house!), established business partnerships, engaged in all forms of commercial exchange, even watched each other's religious ceremonies and processions. None of these forms of interaction and exchange were nearly as conflictive as miscegenation. Why should the "pressure" on group boundaries of which Douglas writes be experienced where sex occurred and nowhere else?

We might turn to the famous, though problematic, formulation of yet another anthropologist:

> a continuous transition exists from war to exchange, and from exchange to intermarriage, and the exchange of brides is merely the conclusion to an uninterrupted process of reciprocal gifts, which effects the transition from hostility to alliance, from anxiety to confidence, and from fear to friendship.[24]

Here the exchange of women appears as the culmination of processes of interaction which range from war to alliance and kinship, as the most precious and basic form of gift-giving. But it has its own particularities, although in the above passage they are elided. Like all forms of exchange, it "provides the means of binding men together." However, to "the artificial links . . . of alliance governed by rule" which other forms of exchange create are added "the natural links of kinship."[25]

The "exchange" of women is thus more dangerous than other forms of exchange because of this difference, because it has the potential to "naturalize" more "artificial" forms of exchange such as commercial relations. If this naturalizing exchange of women is the culmination of other forms of exchange, then it renders these other forms more dangerous, since they become one in an "uninterrupted" series of steps across boundaries. Conversely, the prohibition of this naturalizing form of interaction defuses other types of exchange, since they are by themselves incapable of achieving a transition from hostility to alliance.

Women's bodies thus become both the boundary between "natural" and "artificial," and the site at which the "self" (the collective group) recognizes and rejects the "other." The story of Alicsend de Tolba and Aytola the Sarracen may be a fitting allegorization of women's bounding role. Alicsend was a Christian prostitute who, together with one colleague, made her way to a shepherds' camp near

Xivert on the ninth kalends of December, 1304. After a time, the two prostitutes asked the shepherds if there were any other likely customers among them, but were told that only "un moro" ("a Moor") remained. It was then, according to witnesses, that Lorenç the Shepherd went to the Muslim called Aytola the Sarracen and asked him if he wouldn't like to sleep with Alicsend. Aytola objected, quite naturally, that he was a Muslim, and that he had no money. Lorenç not only offered to lend Aytola the money, but gave useful advice as well: "he told the said moor to say that his name was Johan, to speak in [. . . .], and to say that he was from the port."[26]

To this point the story seems an idyllic example of *convivencia:* an interfaith community of shepherds willing to obscure the religious differences which divided them. In any event the illusion was shattered by Alicsend's scream when she "recognized that he was a moor in his member."[27] Aytola fled, and Alicsend denounced both him and Lorenç for falsity and deviousness "in dishonor of God and of the Catholic faith."[28] In this case it is Aytola's expulsion from Alicsend that marks him as alien, an "otherness" which not coincidentally is physicalized and recognized in his sexual member.

I am suggesting that Christian women were the active agents of recognition of the "other" because their bodies had been constituted as the limits of legitimate and non-threatening exchange. It is important to stress here the historical specificity of this model. Though anthropologists like Lévi-Strauss would emphasize the universality of notions about the exchange of women, I would argue that these notions function in many different ways within and across societies. I can think of no better expression for this than the phrase repeated with ever-increasing stridency in the post-bellum United States South: "Where do we draw the color line?" The question reflects a concern about sexual access to a group's women, but this does not mean that the boundaries drawn as a response to it focus explicitly on women's bodies. In the United States South, for example, the color line was often drawn through more mundane social interactions like eating and drinking, or even at the act of voting [hence political slogans like the often reiterated threat that blacks would move "from the ballot box to the bedroom"]. The same is true of the medieval Crown of Aragon, where there were many different opinions as to what sorts of interactions were dangerous: interfaith wine-drinking is one example frequently mentioned in Jewish, Muslim, and Christian legislation.

What is interesting to me about the Aragonese model in the early fourteenth century, however, is that the "religious line" seems to have been drawn most clearly and consistently on women's bodies themselves, particularly on the bodies of prostitutes, and not on more mundane forms of interaction.[29] This "supercharging" of prostitutes' bodies drained a vast range of other forms of exchange of their potential for violent conflict. Consider as an example this picture of tavern life in the village of Paterna and its environs just outside Valencia. One witness, Tomas Marques, stopped at such a tavern in Benimahabet sometime in early 1307 and found there Christians, "baptized [Muslims] from Paterna," (i.e., converts to Christianity), and Muslims from Quart, all playing dice together and getting drunk. Tomas of course joined in. Present amid all this interfaith gambling, drinking, and money lending, he reports, was the prostitute Marieta de Murcia. When Jacme Camarido visited the same tavern there were three prostitutes present, who would be taken by winning gamblers to the neighboring vineyard. A similar picture of interfaith conviviality was reported in the tavern of Paterna, where a prostitute joined in the dice game. But the limits to this conviviality were always made clear by the women. Tomas tells us that Marieta made a trade "of her body in the said place to any man who wanted [it] who was a Christian."[30] The existence of this boundary rendered all the rest unthreatening, almost (but never quite) unremarkable.[31]

Thus far my analysis has focused on showing how what is traditionally seen as an "intolerant collective anxiety" about sexual interaction creates a boundary-maintaining taboo between groups so highly charged that it generates institutional violence; and how such a taboo might serve to render other types of interaction less conflictual, lessening their potential for violence. But this is only half the story. We still need to descend to the level of strategic action in order to see how individuals used these boundaries, and conversely how the boundaries structured individual action.

At first glance, the kinds of individual action preserved in archives seem to support the first part of the conclusions I just mentioned and rebut the second. It is clear that contemporaries were aware of the immense potential for violence that accrued in charges of miscegenation: so aware, in fact, that they resorted to such accusations constantly in attempts to tap into that violence.

We might start by returning to those very prostitutes whose bodies were constituted as boundaries, as sites for the recognition and rejection of the non-Christian. I say "were constituted," because individual women did not necessarily view themselves as boundary markers, though they were aware of the normativity of such roles and of the risks and possibilities inherent in them. Alicsend's scream in the shepherds' camp was motivated not only by the shock of difference, but also by a situational calculus. Had Lorenç conspired to entrap her as an opportunity for extortion? If so, her scream argued for her ignorance and innocence. Conversely, she was herself now in a position to extort: to this her scream staked public claim. As it was, she pressed charges only when Lorenç's promise to blackmail Aytola and share the proceeds with her became unfulfillable after the Muslim's flight.[32] Even here, then, in the cases of prostitutes who formed the front lines, so to speak, in the struggle of identity and difference, there was room for the strategic actions and choices of the individual.

The strategic nature of miscegenation anxiety is most evident at a slight remove from the prostitutes themselves, in those many moments when individuals tried to divert the violence accruing about the issue of miscegenation and channel it into conflicts arising from less heightened interactions via the medium of accusations. The accusation of miscegenation was commonly used against Jews and Muslims precisely because it was highly charged and therefore particularly effective at bringing the judicial apparatus unpleasantly to bear upon the accused. For example, when Jucef, a Jew of Calatayud, lost all his money and his clothes gambling in the house of the Christian Dominic del Gan and infuriated his fellow gamblers by refusing to go further into debt to continue gambling, the frustrated players made a choice about how to proceed. They did not beat him up. Instead, "as he waited, totally naked, for the shades of night to fall so that he could [discretely] leave the house . . . the said Dominic falsely accused him of entering into the house to commit adultery with his wife . . . so that he had to flee the town." Words, not deeds, but violent nonetheless in intent and effect.[33]

Individuals used such accusations to raise otherwise relatively mundane legal disputes to the level of defense of the faith. Thus, for example, a Christian debtor's complaint about a loan might begin with charges of usury, move to the unfair seizure of goods as security by the Jewish creditor, and end with the charge that the creditor tried to rape the debtor's daughter.[34] Though many of these charges were probably vague, made in the hopes that torture or character witnesses might uncover particulars, others went to great lengths to provide a suitable lightning rod in the form of a woman. A wife or daughter might serve as the alleged site of transgression, though sometimes more creativity was called for. Jahuda Avenbruch, a Jew of Lleida, complained in 1286 that while he had been visiting Albesa, some men of the place together with a Christian woman broke into the house where he was staying and claimed to have found him lying with their accomplice. They used this as a pretext to rob him, and the count of Urgell used their accusation to extort thousands of sous in fines. Jahuda was now worried that he might be accused of the crime by another Jew, an occurrence which the king's letter sought to prevent.[35]

Among other things, Jahuda's story makes clear that Christians were not the only ones to bring accusations of miscegenation against minorities. Members of minority communities themselves tried frequently to use the judicial apparatus against their enemies. Jewish communities complained constantly of lower-class Jews bringing such accusations against wealthy ones, and attempted to prohibit accusations by Jews against other Jews in Christian courts.[36] Mudejars came to echo this complaint, as accusations of miscegenation became a preferred tool of factions fighting for control over positions of authority in Muslim communities, with the enemies of incumbent officials accusing them in the hopes of getting them removed from office.[37] Minority officials, on the other hand, not only brought such accusations against their enemies, but also used them to raise revenue for themselves.[38]

These accusations are obviously attempts to generalize the violence normally reserved for very specific transgressions and apply it to a great variety of everyday conflicts. As such, they seem to challenge the argument that heightening sexual boundaries reduces tension in other forms of interaction, or at the very least to suggest a constant tension between delimiting and generalizing conflict. Such a tension does exist, but it is more complex than may at first appear. We tend to forget that accusations of miscegenation, like all accusations, were merely claims. Their truth value was established through negotiation and contextualization, never taken as apparent. These processes of negotiation tended to constrain the violent potential of any accusation. Hence, although the registers of the Crown are full of records of accusation, the execution of corporal punishment is a rare event. Some cases ended in acquittal, with the accusing official ordered to publicize the accused's innocence and good name; many others in an acquittal obtained for a fee; still others in the purchase of a remission from guilt or a pardon. A majority probably never made their way into the courts or the documentary record. The violence generated by sexual boundaries was not easy to exploit.[39]

This was in part due to the fact that the strategic nature of such charges was no mystery to contemporaries. Consider the case of Jaco Abutarda, Jew of Daroca. Jaco regularly flouted the authorities. When the community's tax collector came knocking on his door, Jaco punched him in the face. Such behavior made him enemies who had to be dealt with. Jaco seems to have been exquisitely aware that enmity against minorities often took the form of accusations and he took suitable precautions. Hence he always carried an amulet of "names, characters and precious stones," which he boasted protected him from the king's justice. The amulet must have worked, because Jaco was absolved of the charges of miscegenation against him, albeit at the cost of a considerable sum of money.[40]

The workings of this economy of accusation were relatively clear to everyone. Muslims and Jews could only be tried in the courts of their lords, who both passed judgment and executed it. Accusations thus became a form of extraordinary taxation in which lords convicted their own subjects in order to extract money from them. This system limited violence not only by monetizing it, but also by contextualizing it within interest groups. Lords, for example, might be eager for the bits of extraordinary revenue such accusations brought in, but they were also extremely sensitive to the fact that excessive arbitrariness would depopulate their minority communities through emigration and kill the goose that laid the golden egg.[41] And just as lords might be willing to expoliate or even execute someone else's Muslim or Jew, they wanted to protect their own.[42] The result of what one might call these "checks and balances" was that the violent charge inherent in accusations of miscegenation was diffused to the point where it was rarely lethal, though often a costly nuisance.[43] This is something of a circular equilibrium. The potential for conflict in everyday social relations between groups was concentrated onto charges of miscegenation centered about the bodies of prostitutes, while at the same time these very charges were drained of virulence by their constant invocation and contextualization within everyday relations.

Of course there were moments when the power of this boundary flashed out in full and horrific force. I think of the Avignonese Jew Pandonus, convicted of adultery with a Christian and castrated, his amputated flesh nailed to the doors of the palace of justice as a stark symbol of his transgression; of the Muslim ᶜAlī "Killer of Lions," burned to death on charges of sex with a Christian girl who proved on later examination to be a virgin; or of the Muslim grain trader, a vassal of the Templars, who was traveling through lands belonging to his lord's enemies when they seized his ship and cargo, injured and killed some of the friends who tried to save him, and burned him on charges of miscegenation when his distant seigneurs proved helpless to protect him.[44] In some ways such moments were exceptional. The victims were individuals stripped of the customary protections and social relations which tended to be mobilized by such accusations and attenuate their force. But these moments were also systemic. They were the product of a society whose stability depended in part on the display, only occasional but of terrifying clarity, of the violent consequences of difference.

NOTES

When read at Notre Dame in 1994, this paper represented an early attempt to work through part of a larger project on violence against and between minorities. It appears here unchanged, apart from the addition of notes. In the intervening time, however, my understanding of the problem and of the project has changed considerably. For a broader and much revised version of the argument given here, see chapter 5 of my *Communities of Violence: Per-*

secution of Minorities in the Middle Ages published by Princeton University Press in 1996. I am grateful to Princeton University Press for permission to provide this earlier version of that text here.

1. See his *España en su historia: cristianos, moros, y judíos,* 2nd ed. (Barcelona, 1983), 200–209. Castro's position was attacked by Claudio Sánchez-Albornoz in his *España: un enigma histórico,* 2 vols. (Buenos Aires, 1956), precipitating a bitter and long-running debate within Spanish historiography. For an analysis of the debate, see Thomas Glick, *Islamic and Christian Spain in the Early Middle Ages: Comparative Perspectives on Social and Cultural Formation* (Princeton, 1979), 6–13.

2. Perhaps the most extremely optimistic of these historians is Norman Roth, who does "not like to talk about a particular 'golden age' of Jewish culture in medieval Spain, for the whole history of that civilization was a golden age for the Jews." See his "The Jews in Spain at the Time of Maimonides," in *Moses Maimonides and His Times,* ed. Eric L. Ormsby, Studies in Philosophy and the History of Philosophy 19 (Washington D.C., 1989).

3. This school is specifically concerned with Jewish history, though it has influenced the way the history of Muslims in Christian Spain is periodized as well.

4. Yitzhak Baer, *A History of the Jews in Christian Spain* (Philadelphia, 1978). It is worth noting that the same polarization between "golden age" and vale of tears occurs in Italian Jewish historiography, on which see Robert Bonfil, *Jewish Life in Renaissance Italy* (Berkeley, 1994), 6–9. On the Jerusalem school in general, see David Myers, *"From Zion Will Go Forth Torah": Jewish Scholarship and the Zionist Return to History,* unpublished doctoral dissertation, Columbia University, 1991. For Myers's treatment of Baer, see pp. 219–58.

5. For more on this subject, see the introduction to my *Communities of Violence.*

6. Though not heretofore applied to *convivencia,* the role of conflict in the maintenance of stability is often posited in post-Enlightenment political philosophy. See for example Kant's "Idea for a Universal History with a Cosmopolitan Purpose," the seventh proposition in *Kant's Political Writings,* ed. Hans Reiss (Cambridge, 1970), 47: "Nature has thus again employed the unsociableness of men, and even of the large societies and states which human beings construct, as a means of arriving at a condition of calm and security through their inevitable *antagonism*" [emphasis in original]. See also his "On the Common Saying: 'This May Be True in Theory, But It Does Not Apply in Practice'" (91); and, for Kant's argument in "Perpetual Peace" that even wars, unless they are wars of obliteration, are forms of interaction which seek to establish relations and presuppose them, "Perpetual Peace: A Philosophical Sketch" (96). See also Georg Simmel: "In contrast to . . . pure negativity, conflict contains something positive. Its positive and negative aspects, however, are integrated; they can be separated conceptually, but not

empirically." The quotation is from his *"Conflict" and "The Web of Group Affiliation"*, trans. Kurt H. Wolff (London, 1955), 14.

7. For a broader treatment, see *Communities of Violence,* chapter 5.

8. *Costums de Tortosa* [*Código de las costumbres escritas de Tortosa,* ed. Ramon Goguet and Jose Foguet Marsal (Tortosa, 1912), IX.2.7. See also *Furs de València,* IX.2.8–9, where both parties are condemned to be burned; and the *Fuero de Teruel,* sec. 386: "Similarly if a [Christian] woman is surprised with a Muslim or a Jew, and they can be captured, let both be burned together." Many more texts could be added. These are chosen as examples of the law in three principal polities of the Crown. The crime of miscegenation was considered so horrible as to be excluded from standard royal pardons and safe-conducts. For one among countless such safe conducts, see Archive of the Crown of Aragon, Chancery section [henceforth ACA:C] register 880, folio 132^r [henceforth given as $880{:}132^r$], dated (1345/2/20). For a remission, see ACA:C $520{:}260^v$ (1329/2/6). Other crimes usually excluded from standard pardons included sodomy, abetting heretics, poisoning, false moneying, and lese majeste.

9. The word "miscegenation" is a nineteenth-century neologism whose first extensive use seems to have been in the United States immediately following the Civil War. Though it generally means "a mixture of races; esp.: marriage or cohabitation between a white person and a member of another race," I am using it here in an etymologicaly stricter sense, to indicate a mixing of categories (Latin *miscere* and *genus*), in this case defined primarily along religious lines. Some of the ways in which medieval notions of miscegenation differ from modern ones will be discussed more explicitly below. The definition cited above is from *Webster's Third New International Dictionary* (1961). The *Oxford English Dictionary* further specifies the races as "white" and "negro," though it gives instances of other usages (e.g., "Christian" and "pagan").

10. See Canon 68 of the 4th Lateran Council (1215), in *Constitutiones concilii quarti Lateranensis una cum commentariis glossatorum,* ed. A. García y García, Monumenta iuris canonici, Corpus glossatorum 2 (Vatican City, 1981), 107. Similar requirements had been instituted a century before in the Crusader Kingdoms, where Frank and Muslim lived in close proximity. See, for example, the Council of Nablus (1120), c. 12, 15, 17, in Giovanni Domenico Mansi, *Sacrorum conciliorum nova et amplissima collectio* (Paris, 1901–1927), 21.264, and the discussion by James Brundage in "Prostitution, Miscegenation, and Sexual Purity in the First Crusade," in *Crusade and Settlement,* ed. Peter W. Edbury (Cardiff, 1985), 60–61.

11. Alan Cutler, "Innocent III and the Distinctive Clothing of Jews and Muslims," *Studies in Medieval Culture* 3 (1970): 92–116, argued that the distinction was imposed not to prevent sexual intercourse but to humiliate minorities. In Aragon, however, the documentation repeatedly stresses sexual boundaries as the motivation behind distinctive clothing. See, for example,

ACA:C 384:48^{v}–49^{r}, concerning the Jews of Apiera; ACA:C 1090:10^{r-v} (1373/11/8), concerning the Muslims of Valencia. See also James Brundage, "Intermarriage between Christians and Jews in Medieval Canon Law," *Jewish History* 3 (1988): 30; Elena Lourie, "Anatomy of Ambivalence: Muslims under the Crown of Aragon in the Late Thirteenth Century," in her *Crusade and Colonisation: Muslims, Christians and Jews in Medieval Aragon,* Variorum Collected Studies 317 (Aldershot, 1990), 54. That distinctive clothing is meant to reinforce sexual boundaries is also evident in the Castilian *Siete Partidas,* 7.24.11. See D. Carpenter, *Alfonso X and the Jews: An Edition and Commentary on Siete Partidas 7.24 "De los judíos,"* Modern Philology 115 (Berkeley, 1986), 100–101.

12. John Boswell, *The Royal Treasure: Muslim Communities under the Crown of Aragon in the Fourteenth Century* (New Haven, 1977), 344 n. 60.

13. The few riots that are documented are complicated by jurisdictional quarrels. Thus the Justice of Daroca and his men attacked the house of the lieutenant of the Bailiff General when the latter proposed to free a Muslim accused of sex with a Christian woman, but doubtless alleging that the Muslim should be punished. I know of no such cases that do not involve competing officials. On this case, cf. ACA:C 239, 59^{r-v} (1311/4/16) and ACA:C 239, 62^{v}–63^{r} (1311/4/19); Maria Teresa Ferrer i Mallol, *Els sarraïns de la Corona Catalano-Aragonesa en el segle XIV: segregació i discriminació* (Barcelona, 1987), 28–29, 225–26.

14. See Yosef Hayim Yerushalmi, *Assimilation and Racial Anti-Semitism: The Iberian and the German Models,* Leo Baeck Memorial Lecture 26 (New York, 1982).

15. For example, Domingo Carbonell of Xàtiva married a converted Muslim woman about 1310. Such cases are rarely recorded because they were unremarkable. Domingo's is preserved in the archives only because his wife's brother tried to break into the Muslim quarter to retrieve some of her goods. The brother later converted as well. See Ferrer, *Els sarraïns,* 19, 76, and ACA:C 207, 176^{v} (transcribed on page 222). A similar but much later case is that of ACA:C 3653, 157^{r-v} (1498), discussed by Mark Meyerson, "Prostitution of Muslim Women in the Kingdom of Valencia: Religious and Sexual Discrimination in a Medieval Plural Society," in *The Medieval Mediterranean: Cross-Cultural Contacts,* ed. Marilyn J. Chiat and Kathryn L. Reyerson, Medieval Studies at Minnesota 3 (St. Cloud, Minn., 1988), 88.

16. Though we know distressingly little about Christian attitudes toward converts in the thirteenth- and fourteenth-century Crown, the problem is too large to approach here. For an example of remissions granted converts, see ACA:C 1152:159^{r-v} (1357/4/16), where a Muslim who has been condemned to execution by burning for having had sex with a Christian woman is absolved on the condition that he accept baptism and abandon Islam. See Josefa Mutgé Vives, *L'aljama sarraïna de Lleida a l'edat mitjana: aproximacó a la seva historia* (Barcelona, 1992), 321.

17. In the case of offspring produced by intercourse between a Christian and a Muslim slave, for example, the status of the child was carefully legislated. In all cases, however, the child was Christian. See for example *Costums de Tortosa,* 6.1, paragraphs 12, 14, 17, 18.

18. For a description of the case, see Ferrer, *Els sarraïns,* 27–28, citing ACA:C 2132, 114^{v}–15^{r}; 121^{r-v}; 139^{v}–40^{r}. The events occurred in 1401.

19. *Siete Partidas,* 7.24.9. The translation is by Carpenter (*Alfonso X and the Jews,* 35). For the punishment of Muslims, see *Siete Partidas,* 7.25.10, briefly discussed in Carpenter's "Minorities in Medieval Spain: The Legal Status of Jews and Muslims in the *Siete Partidas,*" *Romance Quarterly* 33 (1986): 283.

20. Because this model has already been applied to the medieval Mediterranean, I limit myself here to a few citations. For the Crown of Aragon, see Meyerson, "Prostitution," 90 and his *The Muslims of Valencia in the Age of Fernando and Isabel: Between Coexistence and Crusade* (Berkeley, 1991), chapter 6. For the anthropological literature, see, inter alia, the following essays collected in *Honour and Shame: The Values of a Mediterranean Society,* ed. John Peristiany (London, 1965): A. Abou-Zeid, "Honour and Shame among the Bedouins of Egypt," 245–59; Pierre Bourdieu, "The Sentiment of Honour in Kabyle Society," 191–243; Julio Caro Baroja, "Honour and Shame, a Historical Account of Several Conflicts," 79–139. See also Jane Schneider, "Of Vigilance and Virgins: Honor, Shame, and Access to Resources in Mediterranean Societies," *Ethnology* 10 (1971): 1–24; Julian Pitt-Rivers, *The Fate of Shechem, or the Politics of Sex: Six Essays in the Anthropology of the Mediterranean* (Cambridge, 1977).

21. Mary Douglas, *Natural Symbols: Explorations in Cosmology* (New York, 1982), viii.

22. Mary Douglas, *Purity and Danger: An Analysis of the Concepts of Pollution and Taboo* (Boston, 1966), 122–28.

23. This example is from Archivo Municipal de Valencia, Lletres Missives, g^{3}–1, f. 51^{v} (1335/11). For its text, see A. Rubio Vela, *Peste negra, crisis y comportamientos sociales en la España del siglo XIV: la ciudad de Valencia (1348–1401)* (Granada, 1979), 20–21, and his *Epistolari de la València medieval* (Valencia, 1985), 353–54. Punishment could, however, take the form of corruption, for example, corruption of the air or plague. This is, admittedly, a fine distinction.

24. Claude Lévi-Strauss, *The Elementary Structures of Kinship,* ed. Rodney Needham, trans. James Hale Bell, John Richard von Sturmer, and Rodney Needham (Boston, 1969), 67–68.

25. Ibid., 480. Though here my use of Lévi-Strauss's model is oversimplified, it is elaborated considerably in *Communities of Violence,* chapter 5.

26. ACA:C Procesos, new numeration 12/14 (1304), folio 2^{v}, testimony of Pedro, fil d'en Enegot Saragoça. Unfortunately the advice as to how Aytola should speak is illegible. "John" seems to be the name of preference among

Muslims seeking to pass as Christians. For another case, see ACA 528, 285^{r}–^{v} (1334/2/28).

27. ACA:C Procesos, new numeration 12/14 (1304), folio 2^{v}: "[ha]via conegut que ere moro en son menbre."

28. This is a notarial formula used often in cases of blasphemy or miscegenation (in this case see for example folio 9^{r}). Aytola fled town before the accusation was made. Lorenç was tried and defended himself on three counts: first, he was a good Christian and would never do such a thing. Second, he could not be tried for complicity in a crime in which the perpetrator was not available for trial. Third, Alicsend's testimony should not be believed, since as a prostitute she was of "mala fama." The document is in very poor condition, but it seems Lorenç was acquitted, despite the fact that the testimony of several shepherds supported Alicsend. Why this transcript from a seigneurial court is preserved in the royal archive is not clear.

29. The role of prostitutes in maintaining religious boundaries is more extensively developed in *Communities of Violence,* chapter 5.

30. The information presented here is a pastiche of testimony from ACA:C Proceso 515/10 [old numeration] (1307). See in particular folios 77^{v}–78^{r} (Tomas); 9^{v} (Jacme); 10^{v}–11^{r} (Bernat d'Oriola, ferrer); 11^{v} (Pere de Teragona, esparter). All of these witnesses mention the presence of numerous prostitutes, for example Marieta de Murcia and Marieta d'en Bayard (a.k.a. Marieta puta xica, "the small whore") [see folio 14^{r} for the nickname].

31. Such conviviality was, or soon would be, illegal, though this illegality was often overlooked. Decrees forbidding conversation between Christian prostitutes and Muslims in taverns throughout the kingdom of Valencia were issued in 1311 and 1312 by James II, though there may have been earlier ones as well. These are published in *Aureum opus,* L, p. 162, and LVI, p. 166.

32. Authorities often suspected that prostitutes only denounced their non-Christian clients when they feared that they themselves might otherwise face charges. For a detailed example in which Infant Martin himself instructs officials on how to carry out an interrogation in hopes of catching a prostitute in contradiction, see ACA:C 2077, 9^{v}–10^{r} (1389/1/20), discussed and transcribed in Ferrer, *Els Sarraïns,* 37, 329–30.

33. ACA:C 174, 153^{v} (1322/3/18): " . . . ibique remanens totaliter denudatus noctis tenebras ut inde exire posset expectando . . . idem Dominicus false diffamavit Jucefum predictum quod domum intraverat ut cum uxore sua adulterium comitteret." Physical violence did not, of course, exclude the concurrent use of accusations, as when a Christian beat up a Muslim and then, when the Muslim sued, accused him of having had sex with a Christian woman (ACA:C 175, 264^{v} [1322/7/21]).

34. ACA:C 365, 188^{v}–89^{r} (1320/12/13). Pedro Domingo of Ayneto made such complaints against his creditor, Jucef Abutarda of Daroca,

though Pedro claimed that Jucef's son Jaco, not Jucef himself, had tried to seduce his daughter and wrongfully seized some chickens. For more on Jaco's career, see below.

35. ACA:C 70, 23^{r}, number 1693 in Jean Régné, *History of the Jews in the Crown of Aragon,* ed. Yom Tov Assis and Adam Gruzman (Jerusalem, 1978), 439–40. Compare ACA:C 172, 263^{r}–^{v} (1322/1/20), where a Christian of Zaragoza and his concubine conspire to frame Samuel Alaçar.

36. One example of a complaint: ACA:C 519, 111^{r}–^{v} (1328/5/31), where Abraam, a.k.a. Recandell, is accused of theft and of extorting money from other Jews by threatening to denounce them "coram inquisitor heretice pravitatis" for sleeping with Christian women. On the issue of *malshins* ("informers," i.e., accusers in Christian courts) in Jewish communities, see Elena Lourie, "Mafiosi and Malsines"; Francisco de Bofarull, "Los judíos malsines," *Boletín de la Real academia de buenas letras de Barcelona* 6 (1911): 207–16.

37. The host of accusations made against members of a leading Muslim clan of Teruel, the Olleros, is typical. The accusations took as broad an aim as possible. The patriarch of the clan, Mahomat Ollero, and his sons Jucef and Galip (Galip was holding the office of *alamin* at the time the charges were made) were all accused of a variety of excesses, but sex crimes peppered the list. One of Mahomat's daughters was accused of sleeping with a Christian man, one of his sons of sleeping with a servant to whom he was related, and one of Jucef's sons of sleeping with a Christian woman (ACA:C 246, 190^{r} [1321/4/6]). Such accusations were common. Cf. ACA:C 121, 66^{v} (1301/6/30), where the Muslim *alfaqi* of Zaragoza is accused by municipal officials of magic and miscegenation (Ferrer, *Els sarraïns,* 33). On the Muslim adoption of laws about *malshins,* see ACA:C 1905, 233^{v}–34^{v} (1393/12/18), granting the Muslim *aljama* of Huesca the right to put to death "sarracenus aliquis . . . per vos repertus fuerit accusator, qui hebraice malsini et agarenice namem vulgariter nuncupatur." Each such execution would cost the *aljama* a fee of 1,000 sous of Jaca. The document is published in María Blanca Basañez, *La aljama sarracena de Huesca en el siglo XIV* (Barcelona, 1989), doc. number 96, pp. 235–37.

38. For an example of testimony against a Muslim on such charges, see the depositions against Jaale Abunacia of Miravet contained in ACA:C Procesos 502/11 (1309). In the furtherance of his extortions, Jaale is even said to have accused one man's daughter of being pregnant, despite the fact that she was "only a little girl." The document is in Catalan, with subscriptions in Arabic. See also Lourie, "Ambivalence," 45.

39. For a public proclamation of innocence, see Anchel Conte Cazcarro, *La aljama de Moros de Huesca* (Huesca, 1992), 40, citing ACA:CR 163, 155^{r} (1317). Elena Lourie points out that defendants could often buy pardons for such offences, but even innocence could prove expensive. See Lourie, "Anatomy," 54–55. For a sampling of accusations, fines, etc., against Jews, see Yom Tov Assis, "Sexual Behavior in Mediaeval Hispano-Jewish Society,"

in *Jewish History: Essays in Honour of Chimen Abramsky,* ed. Ada Rapaport-Albert and Steven J. Zipperstein (London, 1988), 42–44. Assis knows of only one case that ends with the death penalty imposed on both the Jewish male and the Christian female accused, and that case, in 1381, involved a nun (p. 44, citing Jaime Villanueva, *Viaje literario a las iglesias de España,* 22 vols. [Madrid, 1803–1852], 21.219); and Alfred Morel-Fatio, "Notes et documents pour servir à l'histoire des Juifs des Baléares sous la domination aragonaise du XIIIe au XVe siècle," *Revue des études juives* 4 (1882): 37.

40. ACA:C 488, 52^{v}–53^{v} (1334/8/16): "deferendo tecum nominas, caractaras ac lapides preciosas asserendo quod propter hoc nos vel aliquis nostro nomine contra te cum justicia procedere non possemus." The document, which constitutes Jaco's remission for these crimes, detailed other charges as well. See also ACA:C 529, 21^{r}–^{v} (1334/3/30). On Mediterranean Jewish amulets see the introduction to Lawrence H. Schiffman and Michael D. Schwartz, *Hebrew and Aramaic Incantation Texts from the Cairo Genizah* (Sheffield, 1992). On their decoration and use as jewelry see Shlomo Goitein, *A Mediterranean Society: The Jewish Communities of the Arab World as Portrayed in the Documents of the Cairo Geniza,* vol. 4: *Daily Life* (Berkeley, 1983), 218f.

41. Complaints that accusations are depopulating a given Muslim or Jewish *aljama* were frequent. For one example, a letter from the Infant Alfonso to King James II concerning Teruel's *aljamas,* see ACA:C 385bis, 145^{v} (1321/2/17).

42. A few of many examples: in ACA:C 534, 35^{v}–36^{r} (1331/11/22), the Countess of Terranova halts an accusation of theft against her Muslims by complaining to the king that it is depopulating her *alqueria.* The Viscountess of Cardona's complaint that one of Infant Peter's officials had arrested one of her Muslim women vassals on charges of adultery with a Christian prompted the king to ask the Archbishop of Zaragoza to investigate the case (ACA:C 534, 126^{r} [1333/4/18]). In ACA:C 886, 182^{r}–^{v}, Lope de Luna, seigneur of Sogorb, complains that people accuse his Muslims of, among other things, miscegenation, solely for purposes of extortion. For a case involving Jews, see ACA:C 533, 111^{v}, where the Master of Calatrava intervenes on behalf of his vassal Jucef Abinfalvo. Representative of the other point of view is the complaint of the city of Barbastro, which argued that the noble Guillem d'Entencia had interfered with its right to execute a Muslim condemned to burn because he had sex with two Christians. Guillem was insisting that since the Muslim was his vassal, he could only be tried in his courts.

43. These "checks and balances" were to some extent enshrined in the *furs nous,* the new "constitutions" issued to Valencia by Alfonso the Benign. These provided for a division of the revenue of justice between the Crown as judge and the lord of the person tried. For the *fur,* see *Furs de València,* ed. Germà Colon and Arcadi Garcia (Barcelona, 1978), III. V.78, III. V.81, III. V.85, 3.127–30, 133, 136–38; see also S. Romeu Alfaro, "Los fueros de Va-

lencia y los fueros de Aragón: jurisdicción Alfonsina," *Anuario de historia del derecho español* 42 (1972): 100f. For a case insisting on the principle, see ACA:C 456, 99^{v}.

44. For Pandonus, see Norman Zacour, *Jews and Muslims in the Consilia of Oldradus de Ponte,* Studies and Texts 100 (Toronto, 1990), 30–32, 68–70, 90. For ʿAlī and the grain trader, see Ferrer, *Els Sarraïns,* 29–30, ACA:C 118, 31^{v}–32^{r} (1301/3/14) transcribed on pp. 214–15; ACA:C 121, 27^{v} (1301/6/19).

8

History and Intertextuality in Late Medieval Spain

ELEAZAR GUTWIRTH

As is well known there is a model of approaching medieval Jewish historiography or medieval Jewish interest in history which has a tendency to underprivilege them. In practice such models appeal to a radical opposition between Jewish and Christian historiography of the period. This tendency is not a new product of the 1980s nor is it internally consistent. I deal elsewhere with the history of this old idea and its contradictions. One aspect of this current of thought is directly related to the Bible. Indeed, Baer in his *Galut* had maintained that "Die wahre Geschichte ist ihm ein fuer allemal in der heiligen Schrift niedergelegt. In ihr findet sich der Typus, das Urbild fuer alle spaetere Geschichte. Was einmal geschehen ist, kann sich nur in immer groeser werdenden Kreisen wiederholen." His impression is that "Darum verliert auch das spaetere Einzelgeschehen seinen eigenen Wert." Biblical influence on medieval Jewish writing is thus seen as a factor in Jewish undervaluing of non-biblical history.

The subject of the relation of biblical texts to the writing of medieval history is of course a large area. But here attention will be paid to a practice whose existence is well known and directly related to the Bible's influence on medieval Jewish historical writing: biblical allusion. In practice, historians who deal with late medieval Hebrew chronicles written in Christian Spain act as if the main value of these chronicles lies in the data which they offer. The historian's task as they see it is either to verify the data or correct it on the basis of comparisons with other sources. Biblical allusions, it would appear from this method, are at best ornamental, superfluous to the main business of the chronicle which is to inform on the events outside the text. At worst they are a negative factor: they obscure the "eigenen Wert" of the "spaetere Einzelgeschehen." Of course even Baer was not entirely consistent on this point. Years later he could emphasize the value of brief fragmentary narratives which belonged to an "ancient tradition" of history writing. Elsewhere he could argue that although "the centuries old tradition closed the doors to the development of secular historiography and autobiography Todros [the thirteenth-century Hebrew poet] left us in his poems a more complete autobiography than his Jewish predecessors." In this view, poetry takes the place of history and biography in medieval Jewish culture, even though poetry is at least as strongly marked by biblical allusion as historiography.[1]

It is clear that behind the negative assessments of Baer and his many followers and predecessors there is a certain negative attitude to citation which, it is undoubtedly felt, lacks the reliability and freshness of the direct unmediated reproduction of experience. The peculiar "centuries old tradition" of the Jews marks them apart in that theirs is a religious historiography modeled on the Bible. It is, however, difficult to think of textual non-Hebrew counterparts which do not rely on citations. Indeed twentieth-century views on citations and the relations of texts to previous models depart from different assumptions. Theories of intertextuality emphasize that "a text cannot exist as a hermetic or self-sufficient whole, and so does not function as a closed system," that "a text is available only through some process of reading: what is produced at the moment of reading is due to the cross-fertilization of the reader to it. A delicate allusion to a work unknown to the reader which therefore goes unnoticed, will have a dormant existence in the reading." Of course some form of "theories of intertextuality" may be found "wherever there has been discourse about texts" among other reasons because "thinkers were aware of intertextual relations." Judith Still and Michael Worton have noted such ideas in Plato's and Aristotle's theories of imitation, in Horace's notion of appropriateness, in Longinus' *On the Sublime,* in Cicero's

De oratore, or Quintilian's *Institutions.* I have pointed to the presence of such concerns in medieval Spain. The preceptive poetic notions of Arabs and Jews on allusion were congruent with the textual practice of Jews in Spain. Less known was the *oral* enactment of such assumptions in daily *verbal* exchanges in medieval Spain. The field of humor offered a number of noteworthy examples. The "average medieval Jewish reader" who remembers, quotes, and translates biblical verses need not be a mere supposition but has been documented on the basis of archival records. In any case from this perspective quotation is not a negative component of the text which renders it a "less interesting" marginal exercise but, quite on the contrary, makes these texts, if my readings are accepted, significant paradigms of cultural experience.[2]

I have chosen two texts to test these assumptions. One is Samuel Çarça's description of the attacks on the Jewish communities of Castile in 1366/8 and the other is the description of the pogroms of 1391 written by Hasdai Crescas in October 13, 1391.[3] My questions would be first, what is the role of biblical allusion in these chronicles and second, whether this influence of the Bible is indeed something which justifies the construction of the opposition between Jewish and Christian historiography in this area and period.

Biblical allusion is a well-known phenomenon of medieval Hebrew texts but its serious study seems to be restricted mainly to the context of medieval Hebrew poetics.[4] This holds true even if biblical influence on historiographic texts has occasionally been examined.[5] I would propose that attention to biblical citations be paid which is similar in kind to that which is the norm in poetic texts. The approach I propose which sees biblical allusion as one of the central features of the chronicles is long since due and amply justified, as I hope to show, by the methodology applied to other, non-Hebrew historiographic texts. Brian Tate, who has spent most of his career studying medieval Christian Hispanic historiography, and editing and establishing its critical texts, devoted his presidential address to the Association of British Hispanists, significantly titled "Narrationem expellas furca; tamen usque recurret," to arguing that the poetics of history should be seen as intrinsic to historical understanding.[6] For our project of applying to the historiographic text the kind of attention usually reserved for other genres it is relevant to recall that, albeit in a completely different context, Wansborough has recently maintained that

> What must however be said is that historiography like every other kind of literature does employ a new medium. That medium is language which evolves willy-nilly its own set of constraints. . . . Language is also constrained by semantic association: every unit evokes not merely itself but also its antithesis, and a penumbra of metaphorical and metonymical reference. Employment of . . . simple and apparently unambiguous epithets . . . must entail for every reader and more important for every writer a concatenation of acquired imagery . . . the historical record consists of nothing more or less than human utterance and ought to be assessed by reference to all the criteria now assembled for this very rewarding task.[7]

Both these writers are referring to non-Jewish histories. In the case of medieval Hebrew chronicles with their constant use of biblical allusion their statements apply much more strongly. A few examples might show the allusive technique in practice.

In his chronicle of the attacks on the Jews during the Castilian Civil War,[8] Samuel Çarça has to describe the entrance of the troops of Don Enrique into Castile in March 1366. He does not write "Enrique entered Castile with his men" but

> and the armies that came with him were a nation of impudent faces who had no respect for the elderly and no mercy for the young, a people of difficult language whose speech is unintelligible. (p. 200 1.4)

On a first reading, the passage is likely to be dismissed as an ornate elaboration on a very simple idea which could have been stated simply as "Enrique came with a company of evil men." Çarça is, of course, alluding to biblical passages. Thus Ezekiel 3:5 is devoted to Ezekiel's call to be a prophet and prophesy the impending ruin of Jerusalem:

> And he said unto me Son of man go . . . thou art not sent to *a people of a strange speech and of a hard language* but to the house of Israel. Not to *many people of a strange speech and of a hard language whose words thou canst*

> *not understand* surely had I sent thee to them they would have hearkened unto thee.

Deuteronomy 28:15–50 is the pericope in which we find listed the curses which will befall Israel if it does not keep the commandments. Among these curses is that in verse 50:

> The Lord shall bring a nation against thee from afar from the end of the earth as swift as the eagle flieth *a nation whose tongue thou shalt not understand. A nation of a fierce countenance which shall not regard the person of the old nor show favor to the young.*

By his subtle manipulation of allusion Çarça has managed to imply a number of concepts: the identification of each Castilian Jewish community to Jerusalem and the conventional theodicy of the martyrological histories. He has also opened the events to a theological interpretation of the invading armies to what in the analysis of Christian medieval chronicles is called "furor Deus." But his allusion served him well in the task of representation. He has managed to represent the particular impression of "foreigness" given by the armies of Enrique II who was accompanied, as the *Cronica Abreviada* of these events informs us, by the companies of Beltran Claquin of Brittany, later Constable of France, the count of Marches, the Sire of Veaju, the marshal Danovant "and other knights and squires and men of arms from England and Gascony." The impression of strangeness would have been reinforced by the new type of armor; the *Cronica Abreviada* of the Civil War describes the changes in dress and armor which were introduced precisely by the companies which Çarça has described so economically:

> ca ay comenzaron las armas de bacinetes e piezas e cotas e arnes de piernas e brazos e glaves e dagas e estoques ca antes otras usaban perpuntes e lanzas e capellinas e antes decian omes de caballo e de aqui comenzaron tantas lanzas.[9]

It would be difficult to dismiss as ornamental this impression of strangeness which left a mark on non-Jewish chronicles as well.

When Çarça describes the Northern Castilian popular reaction to Don Enrique after he entered Castile in the spring of 1366, he writes:

"and they said this is the day we have awaited," citing the words which were supposed to have been said by the enemies of Jerusalem in Lamentations 2:16,

> All thine enemies have opened their mouths against thee: they hiss and gnash their teeth: they say We have swallowed her up: certainly *this is the day that we looked for;* we have found, we have seen it.

Çarça is not merely conveying a favorable popular reception of the bastard count. He succeeds in evoking associations of anti-Jewish sentiment and in identifying the community with Jerusalem. Most significant of all, he reverses the process of marginalization of Jewish events operating in non-Jewish chronicles. In fact it is only by hindsight that Çarça can manage to give the impression of an anti-Jewish factor in the reception of Don Enrique by the Castilians, an event which at that stage did not necessarily have a direct connection to Jewish history.

When describing the destruction of the community of Briviesca, Çarça uses the words of the prophet Jeremiah: "their carcasses were meat for the fowls of heaven and for the beasts of the earth." Jeremiah utters the prophecy of the destruction of Jerusalem concerning

> the sons and . . . the daughters that are born in this place . . . they shall die of grievous deaths; they shall not be lamented, neither shall they be buried; but they shall be as dung upon the face of the earth; and they shall be consumed by the sword and by famine; and their carcasses shall be meat for the fowls of heaven and for the beasts of the earth. (16:4)

The allusion could also be to Deuteronomy 28:26: "And thy carcass shall be meat unto all fowls of the air and unto the beasts of the earth and no man shall fray them away." The quotation belongs to the same Deuteronomy chapter which served to describe the invading armies of Don Enrique. Both the entry of the armies into Castile and the destruction of the community of Briviesca can be described in terms which are theologically apt: both belong to the same semantic dimension of curses for abandoning the Lord and are within the chronicle's general tendency, the vindication of divine providence in view of the existence of evil. Çarça narrates that about half a year after Don Pedro's coming

> the community of Valladolid sinned against him and proclaimed long live the King don Enrique..and they robbed the Jews who lived amongst them and . . . nothing was left but the carcasses, naked and their lands were destroyed and they destroyed eight synagogues and they said: "rase it, rase it, even unto the foundation thereof."

Çarça is citing Psalm 137:7: "Remember oh Lord the children of Edom in the day of Jerusalem, who said *Rase it, rase it even unto the foundation thereof.*" Edom was of course traditionally identified by Jews with the Christians. Valladolid then is another Jerusalem, burning.

These allusions cannot be described as determined by the simple need to express destruction in Hebrew: when Çarça describes the entry of the King of Granada himself to punish those towns which had betrayed Don Pedro, he uses the following words:

> and he [the king of Granada with many armies] entered by force all the places that had sinned against him [that is, Don Pedro] and he *smote them with the stroke of the sword and slaughter and destruction* and he went into Jaen by force and killed innumerable men and king Pedro ordered that they should not raise their hands against the Jews for they were not guilty.

When describing an event which is seen as favorable to the Jews, the destruction of Jerusalem is not alluded to. Çarça can cite Esther 9:5 where the Jews are said to have killed those who tried to harm them: "Then the Jews *smote all their enemies with the stroke of the sword and slaughter and destruction* and did what they would unto those that hated them." There may be an unspoken implication of retribution here, coloring the citation as it is applied to the enemies of Pedro and the Jews. The allusion identifies the King of Granada, ally of Don Pedro, with the Jews. It serves, again, to "Judaize" events of the Civil War.

So far I have given some of many possible examples of the extraordinary expressive economy afforded by allusion and particularly allusions which serve to identify local fourteenth-century Castilian communities with biblical Jerusalem. But in some cases lack of attention to the context of allusion results in absurd readings. For example, the entry of the Prince of Wales, the Black Prince, with Don Pedro on February 20, 1367 appears to be welcomed rather than deplored by Çarça:

> and when a whole year had passed since the beginning of the reign of the king don Enrique, may the Lord protect him, the king don Pedro entered the kingdom of Castile and with him came a great prince, the prince of Wales, *a man who had courage and counsel.*

Çarça's description of the Black Prince as "a man who had courage and counsel" seems somewhat intriguing as the narrative continues with the description of the killings of the Jews in the community of Villadiego and Aguilar by the companies of the Black Prince, and indeed, in view of documents attesting to the English role in the destruction of the Aguilar community. Thus a document describes how on September 5, 1370

> the monastery of Aquilar demanded a tithe of 300 maravedies . . . and the Jews argued that the aljama was deserted and they had abandoned the town because of the many deaths and damage they had suffered from the English.[10]

It is all the more surprising as Aguilar was part of the region of Palencia where Çarça himself resided at the time of the Civil War. The first context of Çarça's allusion is the biblical narrative of Senacherib the king of Assyria who conquered the towns of Judah and sent Rab-shakeh to speak to Hezekiah the king. Rab-shakeh said to the messengers:

> Speak ye now to Hezekiah. . . . What confidence is this wherein thou trustest? Thou sayest *but they are but vain words I have counsel and strength for the war.* (2 Kings 18:20)

The reader of Çarça's chronicle could not help but reconstruct the original context where "counsel and strength for the war" are described as "vain words" and read the text ironically.

Similar visions of history underlie the description of events in Crescas's chronicle of the events of 1391 written in the autumn of the same year.[11] When describing the attack on the Jewish community of Seville, Crescas refers to the Christian Spanish attackers as the "bitter and hasty [i.e., impetuous] nation." His Bible-versed audience would identify the resonances of Habukkuk 1:6

> For, lo, I raise up the Chaldeans, *that bitter and hasty nation* which shall march through the breadth of the land, to possess the dwelling places that are not theirs.

In Lamentations 2:4 Jeremiah laments Jerusalem's misery and complains to God:

> *He hath bent his bow like an enemy:* he stood with his right hand as an adversary, and slew all that were pleasant to the eye in the tabernacle of the daughter of Zion: *He poured out his fury like fire.*

Crescas describes the attack on Seville with the same words: "The Lord hath bent his bow like an enemy." Barcelona is described as the community on which "the Lord poured his fury like fire." Nehemiah 1:3 is the lament for the afflicted state of Jerusalem:

> And they said unto me The remnant that are left of the captivity there in the province are in great affliction and reproach: the wall of Jerusalem also is broken down *and the gates thereof are burnt by fire.*

Crescas, speaking of the attack on Seville, writes "and its gates were burnt by fire" using the same words we find in Nehemiah. When describing the destruction of Toledo, Crescas writes that it occurred on the 17th of Tammuz, "the day when troubles were doubled," alluding to the day referred to in the Mishnah as a day of calamities for Jerusalem.[12] Speaking of Toledo he writes "for from there the Torah goes out and the word of the Lord." Crescas is, of course, quoting Isaiah's words about Jerusalem (2:3): "for out of Zion shall go forth the Law and the word of the Lord from Jerusalem."

The results of this research on the first contexts of biblical allusions in these two chronicles leave no doubt that the allusion is neither ornamental nor superfluous. It is an economic expressive tool, with theological as well as historiographic implications: the constant and consistent allusion to biblical passages which refer to Jerusalem give a historical depth to Crescas's vision of the 1391 pogroms which is lost in the other accounts such as the *Crónica de Pero Niño,* the chronicle of Ayala, or the account in the Escorial Codex, which by comparison appear not as more "neutral" or more informed but as lacking in a comprehensive view of Jewish events and in the final analysis as more superficial.[13]

The central and unifying metaphor of these chronicles is that which compares local Hispano-Jewish communities to Jerusalem. Melzetin, while studying the structure of the fifteenth-century *Crónica de los reyes de Navarra* of the Prince of Viana, emphasized the particular difficulties in writing such a text. He underlined the problem of cohesion in texts which, unlike the novel, cannot avoid contradictory or inexplicable elements. In this particular chronicle repetition is the main medium for establishing cohesion. This repetition strongly marks the text and opens it to a connotative interpretation.[14] In our case, both Çarça and Crescas solve the problem of cohesion and connotation by means of biblical allusion. Their solution to this basic problem in writing such texts is certainly no less effective than that of repetition in the Navarran *Crónica.*

If one asks why such a view could be maintained by realistic leaders who knew full well that Barcelona was not Jerusalem, we could draw on studies of other texts, even if such studies have not paid attention to the texts we are studying here. It could be argued that there is a Jewish tendency of reacting to catastrophe by placing individual events within a continuum of suffering. This is in fact a restatement of Baer's views in his *Galut.* Another explanation could point to the medieval historiographic adaptation and adoption of the exegetical principle which is termed *figura* among the Christians and which by this stage was part of Jewish exegesis in general and Hispano-Jewish exegesis in particular. On the other hand the significance of *figura* in the late medieval Hebrew chronicles themselves rather than in the philosophical texts of Maimonides or the exegesis of Nahmanides has not been consistently studied.[15] Indeed, Nancy Partner, who has studied rhetorical usage in medieval Christian chronicles, pours scorn on the idea that *figurae* were significant rhetorical models for such chroniclers as John of Salisbury who wrote on the papal curia 1148–1152.[16] Without entering into this problematic issue, it is nevertheless clear that if we are able to adapt these theories to our problem it is because the allusion to biblical prophecies and descriptions of the destruction of Jerusalem is not a mere ornamentation, nor a linguistic necessity by users of Hebrew who had no other source for their language apart from biblical allusion, but part of traits of a general Jewish mentality in its approach to catastrophe or to history.

One could offer some added explanations which are not necessarily exclusive or dismissive of these views. Indeed what we have in the chronicles are descriptions of events such as looting, extortion, destruction of buildings, killings, events which by themselves could be described in a number of ways. The allusion to Jerusalem offers a coherent explanation which exalts these events. And here we may draw on the studies of the imaginary in the Middle Ages. It may suffice to point to the studies on the imaginary recently published by the Caixa de Barcelona in Catalan and cite briefly from Jean-Claude Schmitt's remarks there on the imaginary of the Middle Ages:

> the collective imaginary by analogy with the individual imaginary appears in principle as a vast field divided by two opposing poles: the positive pole of desire and the negative pole of fear, death, and revulsion . . . the imaginary of death, suffering, and torture are exalted in the texts of the martyrs and described with horror in the macabre texts. [my translation][17]

Again, the feature of thinking of Jerusalem as a model for the town is present in Schmitt's analysis of the medieval European imaginary. According to him, when in the eleventh century the city appears in the essentially rural European landscape it would be understood and imagined by reference to biblical models: the positive model of Jerusalem and the negative one of Babylon. One may recall that Helen Rosenau saw this urban typology as a biblical contribution to thought on ideal towns.[18]

Now this imaginary is not merely an area which concerns poetry or belletristic. It pervades as yet uncharted but numerous aspects of medieval Jewish life including that in Christian Spain, only a few of which, from the field of liturgy, may be recalled here: the tribune at an Aragonese synagogue of the fourteenth century is made in the shape of a wooden tower which recalls the wooden tower on which Ezra stood in Jerusalem to read the Torah (Neh. 8:4). The Holy Ark was situated in the wall facing Jerusalem, the curtain suspended in front of the doors of the Ark was called "parokhet," the veil that separated the Holy of Holies where the Ark was kept from the rest of the Sanctuary in the Temple of Jerusalem. The prayers at the local synagogue replaced the sacrifices at the Temple of Jerusalem and the Bible was called "miqdash YH," the Temple of the Lord. These are only some well-known examples of this identification of medieval communities in Spain (and elsewhere) with Jerusalem which extend to fields other than the textual or even the historiographical. Are these also ornamental?

Biblical allusion provides a frame thanks to which data acquire relevance. It also serves to avoid the "parochial" nature of other chronicles and sets them by implication within a much larger context of older and more universal histories. By this time such "unparochial histories" were to be found among the Christians as well, as witnessed by the *General Historia.*[19]

This brings us to the next point to be considered, namely the relation between Jewish and Christian historiography on the issue of biblical allusion. The perception of such late medieval Hispano-Jewish chronicles as arising out of a medieval context both Jewish and Christian may seem surprising as it has been an underlying assumption of much writing on Jewish historiography that it is unique and incommensurate with its non-Jewish counterparts. And yet there seem to be ample grounds for such comparisons.

In general it should be pointed out that while students of Jewish historiography tend to restrictive definitions of historiography, students of medieval Christian historiography have tended to view the issue more broadly. It will readily be admitted that the problem of including, as we have done in our conception of chronicle, a text which, like Çarça's, is formally the colophon to a work of exegesis or homiletics and a text which, like Crescas's, is formally a letter, is far less complex than that posed by studies on hagiography and visual representation within the framework of historiographic research. In both these cases scholars have pointed to the use of biblical allusion and typology. In visual representation it may suffice to refer to Michelangelo Cagiano de Azevedo[20] who has studied early medieval visual arts as historiography and maintains that, for example, in the seventh-century Northumbrian Capsella of whalebone at the British Museum the depiction of the exile of the Jews from Jerusalem is an evident echo of the illustrations of the Exodus. According to him the Warmund sacramentary codex at Ivrea in its representation of the Martyrdom of the Innocents depicts one of the mothers as Rachel.

These may be described as examples of a symbology of Israel translated into image historiography, to use Cagiano de Azevedo's phrase, but their basic feature is that of biblical allusion. In hagiography there is a multitude of examples of biblical influence. One should remember that Erich Auerbach maintained that the Bible as written history formed the historical vision of the medieval European clerics and their aesthetic and moral presuppositions. Baudouin de Gaiffier, in his study of hagiography and historiography,[21] summarizes the various contacts between Bible and hagiographic writing by saying that "la pensee des hagiographes trouvera son expression preferée dans des citations de la Bible" to such an extent that some saints' lives are transformed into a collection of citations. Jacques Fontaine, when studying the life of St. Martin, has affirmed that it was written by applying a prophetic typology based on the Old Testament scenes of the life of Elijah at Mount Carmel.[22] Such studies do not seem to support a view of Jewish chronicles as incommensurate with their Christian counterparts on this issue.

Most of these studies refer not to Spain but to the rest of Europe. The obvious question would be whether we are able to adduce similar phenomena from within the context of Çarça's and Crescas's work. This may be of some methodological importance since it is not uncommon to find studies which try to re-create the non-Jewish context of Hispano-Jewish phenomena by adducing non-Hispanic analogues.

Here again the evidence is readily available. When we read the allusive texts of Çarça or Crescas we are reminded of texts such as the *Latin Chronicle of the Kings of Castile.* An example should suffice here: when relating the events of the year 1274 of the era when the Christians of Córdoba ask the king for reinforcements the chronicler writes, "the spirit of the Lord was upon the King and he hardened his ears so as not to hear those who like magicians with persuasive words tried to impede such a noble act."[23] Linehan has recently made extensive use of the Alfonsine historiographic texts to reconstruct contemporary mentality. He has often noted the centrality of biblical models and asserted that:

> The assistants of the king who had excluded theology from the Salamanca curriculum were historians, and the Bible was part of the *historical* record, though that did not mean that it was merely a source of

> information concerning the Kings and prophets of ancient Israel. Quite on the contrary. In common with all other sources of information regarding the distant past it contained signs and precepts for the present. Alfonso's chronicles were written in order to provide men with examples of virtue rewarded and evil chastised. . . . History for the ancients had taken the form of a dialogue between the ages.[24]

Mercedes Vaquero after reading fifteenth-century Vizcayan chronicles has remarked on the parallels between the biblical history of Joseph and Potiphar and that of Yñigo Esquerra in those chronicles.[25]

The pivotal feature is that of thinking of the past in terms of biblical structures which in the Hebrew texts are revealed through the study of its allusive language. That such biblical influences are not an exclusive feature of medieval Jewish historiography may be shown by paying attention to Aragonese sources. And here we may find that the same feature is revealed in the writings of that most "realistic" and authoritarian of kings (whom Crescas might have known), Pedro IV of Aragon, the Ceremonious, who saw himself in his chronicle as David and his enemies as Absalom.[26] But the history of this phenomenon goes back further. Karl D. Uitti has called attention to the fact that in the Alfonsine chronicles Moses is called "the historian" because he wrote the historical book of Genesis.[27] Deyermond has analyzed the biblical patterns which give coherence to the myth of the *Reconquista* in these chronicles:[28] Pelayo survives the Muslim invasion and is able to begin the *Reconquista;* he is seen as echoing the story of Noah, another survivor of an evil generation. In the lament for conquered Spain: "Spain weeps for its children and cannot be consoled for they are no more" there is a clear allusion to Rachel's lament (Jer. 31:15). Medieval Hispanic history is thus part of sacred history. The important point is that, as argued by Deyermond, we are dealing not merely with an occasional allusion but that some of the main ideological patterns are biblical.

The backbone of medieval historiography, the *translatio imperii* of the universal chronicles both Hispanic and non-Hispanic, is of biblical affiliation. Fraker commented on this ideological program of the *Primera crónica general.*[29] These results of recent historiographic research, generally unnoticed by the students of medieval Jewish chronicles, so many of which were written within a Hispanic context, have changed the terms of reference of the biblically oriented vision of history which we find in Çarça, Crescas, and others. A particularly apt example would be that of a chronicle written by a man who like Çarça had spent a long time in Castile, who had moved in the same social circles as Crescas, and who matured as Rabbi in Burgos—Solomon Ha-Levi. A recent study of his historiographic work in verse has concentrated on his conception of history.[30] The very structure of the work, divided into seven, influenced ultimately by Augustine, is tinged like the *Megilat Ha-Megaleh* with overtones of the biblical account of Creation, and Pablo de Santa María quotes Elijah and Daniel in the Introduction. The fusion of secular and sacred history in the universal histories "stimulates the application of a millenarian and messianic interpretation." The historian/poet prepares his analogy of the Castilian monarch (Juan II), to "the culmination of Biblical history (Jesus)" by a number of devices. One of these is the use of biblical genealogy: that of Adam and Eve and that of David. The "Fourth Monarchy" is, of course, that of the Castilian kings. The Jewish kingdoms and the Roman empire can be said to be *figurae* of the Castile of Juan II.

In the texts discussed here attention to the allusive pattern is particularly important because it is in this allusive texture that the singular "vision of history" lies, which at first sight would seem to be absent from these brief medieval Jewish narratives. It is this pattern which gives a certain generic coherence to medieval Jewish chronicles and makes unacceptable a view of them as isolated, unrelated writings. The function of allusion in the economy of representation varies: irony, cohesion, the placing of parochial events in much older patterns are some of the functions we have been able to identify here.[31] Attention to this issue brings to the fore the inadequacy and triviality of applying standards of length to the study of these dense and highly allusive texts. Finally, the preceding lines have tried to show that there is no particular merit in ignoring the context of Jewish history writing in the Middle Ages.

NOTES

1. Fritz Baer, *Galut* (Berlin, 1936), 8. Nevertheless, in his Introduction to *Shevet Judah* (Jerusalem, 1947), 12, he asserted: "One must not hold these modest writings in contempt. Their writers were the legitimate inheritors of

a great and ancient historical vision. Every story is a whole chapter in the long line of sufferings which are decreed on the Jews" (Fritz Baer, "Todros ben Yehudah Ha-Levi and His Time," *Zion* 2 [1937]: 55). Further bibliography on modern studies of medieval Jewish historiography may be found in the notes to my "The Expulsion of the Jews from Spain and Jewish Historiography," in *Jewish History: Essays in Honour of Chimen Abramsky,* ed. Ada Rapoport-Albert and Steven J. Zipperstein (London, 1988), 141–61; and my "History and Apologetics in Fifteenth-Century Hispano-Jewish Thought," *Helmantica* 35 (1984): 231–42.

2. Michael Worton and Judith Still, "Introduction," to their *Intertextuality: Theories and Practices* (Manchester, 1990), 1–44; I have dealt with allusion in non-poetic genres in "From Jewish to Converso Humour in Fifteenth-Century Spain," *Bulletin of Hispanic Studies* 67 (1990): 223–33. On evidence for documenting memorization and oral translations of the Bible among Jews of various classes in Christian Spain, see my "Religión, historia y las *Biblas romanceadas,*" *Revista catalana de teologia* 13 (1988): 115–34.

3. On Çarça see Yitzhak Baer, *A History of the Jews in Christian Spain* (Hebrew) (Tel-Aviv, 1987), 221 n. 5. On Crescas see the index, s.v. Hasdai Crescas.

4. David Yellin, *Introduction to the Hebrew Poetry of the Spanish Period* [Hebrew], 3rd ed. (Jerusalem, 1978), 102–103, 110. On allusion see also Alejandro Díez Macho, "La metafora y la alusion biblicas segun la Poetica Hebraica de Mose ibn Ezra," *Sefarad* 5 (1945): 49–81; Seeger Adrianus Bonebakker, "Aspects of the History of Literary, Rhetoric, and Poetics in Arabic Literature," *Viator* 1 (1970): 89; and my "From Jewish to Converso Humor," 223–33.

5. Biblical typology in a Hispanic-Jewish chronicle of an earlier period has been noticed by Gerson D. Cohen in his edition of Ibn Dawd's *The Book of Tradition: Sefer ha-qabbalah* (London, 1969). I pointed to biblical motifs and typology in the sections of Capsali's chronicle dealing with Abraham Seneor in my "Social Tensions within Fifteenth-Century Hispano-Jewish Communities," unpublished doctoral dissertation, University of London, 1978, "Appendix: The Reputation of Abraham Seneor in the Fifteenth and Sixteenth Centuries." See also "Abraham Seneor: Social Tensions and the Court-Jew," *Michael* 11 (1989): 169–229. There are references to biblical allusions, typology, and motifs in fifteenth-century Castilian Christian chronicles in my "The Jews in Fifteenth-Century Castilian Chronicles," *Jewish Quarterly Review* 84 (1984): 370–96.

6. The presidential address at the conference of the Association of Hispanists of Great Britain and Ireland at Leeds University in 1985 (*Abstracts,* 1–2).

7. John E. Wausborough, *Res ipsa loquitar: History and Mimesis* (Jerusalem, 1987), 14.

8. The manuscripts are Munich, Bayerische Staatsbibliothek, MS 51 (Italy, 16th century) and MS 7 (Germany, 16th century). The Mantua edition of 1559 omits it. I have used the text and valuable notes in Fritz Baer, *Die Juden im Christlichen Spanien* (Berlin, 1936), 2.200–201, number 209.

9. *Biblioteca de autores españoles,* 66.537, a. 1366.

10. Cf. Pilar Leon Tello, *Los judios de Palencia* (Palencia, n.d.), document number 57.

11. References to Crescas's chronicle are to the edition in M. Wiener, *Das Buch Schevet Judah* (Hannover, 1855), 129ff.

12. Taanith 4:6: "Five calamities befell our ancestors on the seventeenth of Tammuz . . . the tablets of the Law were broken, the daily burnt offerings ceased, the walls of Jerusalem were breached, wicked Apostomos burned the law and set up an idol in the Temple."

13. Gutwirth, "The Jews in Fifteenth-Century Castilian Chronicles," 379–96.

14. M. Melzetin, "Acerca de la estructura de *Crónica de los reyes de Navarra* del principe de Viana" in *Homenaje a Alvaro Galmés de Fuentes,* 3 vols. (Oviedo-Madrid, 1985–87), 2.383–93.

15. David G. Roskies, *Against the Apocalypse: Responses to Catastrophe in Modern Jewish Culture* (Cambridge, Mass., 1984). See also Ivan Marcus, "From Politics to Martyrdom: Shifting Paradigms in the Hebrew Narratives of the 1096 Crusade Riots," *Prooftexts* 2 (1982): 40–52; Haim Hillel Ben-Sasson, *A History of the Jewish People* (London, 1977), 504–10; Amos Funkenstein, *Perceptions of Jewish History* (Berkeley, 1993).

16. Nancy Partner, "The New Cornificius: Medieval History and the Artifice of Words," in *Classical Rhetoric and Medieval Historiography,* ed. Ernest Breisach (Kalamazoo, 1985), 5–60.

17. Jean-Claude Schmitt, "Introduccio a una historia de l'imaginari medieval," in *El mon imaginari i el mon meravellos a l'edat mitjana* (Barcelona, 1986), 15–33.

18. Helen Rosenau, *The Ideal City* (London, 1974).

19. Karl D. Uitti, "A Note on Historiographical Vernacularization in Thirteenth-Century France and Spain," in *Homenaje a Alvaro Galmés de Fuentes,* 2.573–92.

20. Michelangelo Cagiano de Azevedo, "Storiografia per immagini," in *La storiografia altomedievale,* Settimane di studio del Centro italiano di studi sull'alto medioevo 17 (Spoleto, 1970), 131, 133.

21. Erich Auerbach, "Figura," in *Neue Dantestudien* (Istanbul, 1944), 11–71; reprinted in his *Literatursprache und Publikum in der lateinischen Spaetantike und Mittelalter* (Bern, 1958); Baudouin de Gaiffier, "Hagiographie et historiographie," in *La storiografia altomedievale,* 139–66.

22. Jacques Fontaine, *Vie de St. Martin* (Paris, 1967), 127–28.

23. *Cronica latina de los reyes de Castilla,* ed. Luis Charlo Brea (Cadiz, 1984).

24. Peter Linehan, *History and the Historians of Medieval Spain* (Oxford, 1993).

25. Sabino Aguirre Gandarias, *Las dos Primeras crónicas de Vizcaya* (Bilbao, 1983), and Mercedes Vaquero's review in *Hispanic Review* 58 (1990): 113–14. See also Francis Gormly, *The Use of the Bible in Representative Works of Medieval Spanish Literature, 1250–1300* (Washington, D.C., 1962); A. A. Deyermond, "Uses of the Bible in the *Poema de Fernan Gonzalez,*" in *Cultures in Contact in Medieval Spain: Historical and Literary Essays Presented to L. P. Harvey,* ed. Alan D. Hook and Barry Taylor (London, 1990), 47–70.

26. Eleazar Gutwirth, "Profayt Duran on Ahitofel: The Practice of Jewish History in Late Medieval Spain," *Jewish History* 4 (1989): 59–74.

27. Uitti, "Note," 508.

28. Alan A. Deyermond, "The Death and Rebirth of Visigothic Spain in the *Estoria de Espana,*" *Rivista canadiense de estudios hispanicos* 9 (1985): 345–67.

29. Charles F. Fraker, "The *Fet des Romains* and the *Primera crónica general,*" *Hispanic Review* 46 (1978): 199–220; "Alfonso X, the Empire and the *Primera crónica,*" *Bulletin of Hispanic Studies* 55 (1978): 95–102.

30. Alan D. Deyermond, "Historia universal e ideología nacional en Pablo de Santa María," *Homenaje a Alvaro Galmés de Fuentes,* 2.313–24.

31. I deal with analogies between Jewish and Catalan history writing in "Profayt Duran"; for tendencies in writing of history at the time of Pedro IV, see Albert G. Hauf, "Mes sobre la intencionalitat dels textos historiografics catalans medievals," in *Medieval and Renaissance Studies in Honour of Robert Brian Tate,* ed. Ian Michael and Richard A. Cardwell (Oxford, 1986), 47–62.

9

Undermining the Jewish Sense of Future: Alfonso of Valladolid and the New Christian Missionizing

ROBERT CHAZAN

CHRISTIAN-JEWISH POLEMICS covered an extremely wide range of issues, with each side claiming accurate perception of truth, proper patterns of behavior, effective avenues to personal salvation, and the promise of corporate redemption.[1] By and large, early medieval Christian and Jewish polemical literature was intended for internal consumption, with Christian authors seeking to convince their Christian readers and Jewish authors addressing their Jewish constituency. During the twelfth century, this inward orientation of polemical thinking and writing began to shift, at least on the part of the Christian majority. An increasingly aggressive Christian society looked outward, seeking to convince its non-Christian neighbors and subjects of the incontrovertible truth of the Christian vision.[2] When this change took place, new styles of argumentation came to the fore. Claims based on Scripture could have no real impact on Muslim targets of the new missionizing ardor, and thus extensive efforts were made to develop argumentation that was based entirely on reason alone. Similarly, Christian readings of those biblical books which were shared with the Jews had, over the ages, been thoroughly repudiated by the Jews; there could be no serious hope of winning Jews to Christian truth through this medium. Thus, Christian efforts to convince Jews were likewise based on arguments from reason or—more strikingly—on a mining of authoritative post-biblical Jewish literature.[3] Just as the new missionizing proclivities of Christian society brought to the fore new styles of argumentation, so too did they alter the major claims advanced. The concern with convincing Christian audiences of Christian truth led to the highlighting of one set of issues; the desire to win over Jewish auditors and readers led in alternative directions. I am not suggesting that entirely new issues were created; what I am arguing is that the missionizing thrust of late twelfth-century and subsequent Christian polemical literature resulted in a neglect of certain age-old claims and a focus on others.

One of the most prominent, if not *the* most prominent, claim in the newly aggressive Christian polemical stance was the assertion that the Jews had no hope for future redemption. To be sure, this claim was an old one, fundamental to key Christian beliefs. If, as Christianity argued, Jesus of Nazareth was the promised messiah and if the Jews had spurned him, earning for themselves divine rejection in the process, and if the Jewish place in the covenantal relationship had been ceded to the Christian community, then it obviously follows that Jews have no future redemption toward which to long and for which to hope. Thus, in Christian eyes, the lengthy Jewish exile constituted a punishment which authenticated the messianic mission of Jesus and a morass from which the Jews would never escape. All this was noted in early medieval polemics, largely as further validation of Christian truth claims.[4] However, as the new missionizing aggressiveness developed, the same set of themes was increasingly turned directly against the Jews. The emphasis shifted from validating key truth claims for Christian believers to driving home to the Jews the hopelessness of their circumstances. Jews readily and repeatedly acknowledged the abject conditions in which they found themselves; they balanced this acknowledgment, however, with proud assertions of eventual redemption. The Christian side believed these assertions to be incorrect and perceived this issue as a point of considerable Jewish vulnerability. The assault on the Jewish future became one of the staples of the new missionizing argumentation. Clearly, the claim of Jewish hopelessness involved far more than a simple intellectual gambit. In choosing this issue as a focal point of the new outwardly directed polemics, the Christian side was well aware of the profound psychological significance of this issue. Neither individuals nor groups can long function effectively when stripped of all hope for a better future. The aggressive Christian missionizers well knew that; in attacking the Jewish sense of the future, they were both addressing key theological doctrines and piercing to the heart of Jewish capacity to struggle forward in the face of daunting circumstances. Present-day research has not attended sufficiently to this assault and to its cumulative impact on the Jews of the later Middle Ages, particularly in the southern areas of western Christendom.

Let us look briefly at some evidence of this new line of attack from Christian sources and a bit more fully at reflections of the same in Jewish sources. As I have indicated elsewhere, some of our best evidence for the new Christian missionizing sensibility comes from the efforts of Friar Paul Christian, culminating in his famous missionizing encounter with Rabbi Moses ben Nahman in Barcelona in 1263.[5] While the agenda spelled out for us with precision in the brief Latin account of the encounter notes four items for discussion, the first, the claim that the messiah has already come, is clearly the key.[6] Although this item was intended to form the foundation for proof of the messianic role of Jesus, the obvious implication of loss of any future redemption for the Jews was never far from the surface. As we will see shortly, the Jewish protagonist, Rabbi Moses ben Nahman, was exquisitely sensitive to this implication of the claim of prior messianic appearance. When the innovative missionizing arguments of Friar Paul were subjected to augmentation and refinement in Friar Raymond Martin's *Pugio fidei,* the claim of prior messianic advent and its corollary notion of Jewish hopelessness figured prominently. In fact, the first major thrust of the *Pugio fidei* with respect to the Jews involved the claim of a prior messianic advent, and, significantly, the closing issue raised in this massive missionizing compendium was the utter hopelessness of Jewish circumstances.[7]

While the evidence from the Christian side is in itself impressive enough, yet more important is Jewish awareness of the new Christian attacks. How did the Jews perceive the pressures to which they were increasingly subjected? Right from the earliest of the Jewish polemical responses, the issue of the Jewish future looms large in Jewish consciousness of the enhanced Christian aggressiveness. As widely noted, the first fullscale Jewish polemical works from western Christendom stem from the closing decades of the twelfth century. Both the *Milḥamot ha-Shem* and the *Sefer ha-Berit* were composed in the 1160s or 1170s, the former probably and the latter surely in southern

France. In both cases, the authors address a wide range of polemical concerns; in both cases, the issue of future redemption plays a special role. In the *Milḥamot ha-Shem,* the final chapter is devoted to a series of proofs that the messiah has not yet come, meaning of course that the messianic promises had not yet been fulfilled and remain therefore yet to be accomplished for the Jewish people.[8] Far more striking is the centrality of this issue in Joseph Kimhi's *Sefer ha-Berit.* That composition has unfortunately reached us in a lamentable state.[9] In a separate essay, I have attempted to reconstruct the work as it originally appeared from the pen of Joseph Kimhi and have suggested that the entire second half of the work was devoted to an explication of the prophetic promises of redemption. Throughout the first half of the work, which is couched in dialogue format, the Christian disputant is made to challenge the Jew on the grounds of the dolorous circumstances of present-day Jewish life. None of these challenges is taken up by the Jewish disputant. Rather, I have suggested, this issue is left for the second half of the work, now no longer available, in which the deficiencies of the Jewish present are seen in the light of eventual redemption, which was promised, has not yet dawned, and will unquestionably eventuate.[10] An interesting polemical letter of Alfonso of Valladolid, upon whom this essay will focus, provides us with a sense of a few of the passages of the lost second half of the *Sefer ha-Berit,* in particular a few Kimhian comments on the Book of Daniel, the key to much of Jewish doctrine concerning eventual redemption.[11] Thus, both pioneering Jewish polemical works show considerable Jewish sensitivity to the new Christian assault on the Jewish future.

One of the most interesting polemical works of the middle decades of the thirteenth century is the *Milḥemet Miẓvah* of Meir bar Simon of Narbonne.[12] Once again, southern France emerges as the locus of considerable Christian-Jewish give-and-take. The *Milḥemet Miẓvah* is a mélange made up of numerous compositions, most involving polemical concerns. The entire collection is distinguished by an unusually high level of sensitivity to current political, economic, social, and religious trends.[13] Throughout the polemical sections the issue of current Jewish circumstances and Jewish hopes for the future dominate. Let us note briefly examples of these tendencies.

The author's awareness of and concern with current Jewish circumstances are reflected in the longest of the polemical dialogues contained in the compilation.[14] Not very impressive as a literary composition, this dialogue begins with a brief statement by the Christian, which then introduces a lengthy Jewish rebuttal. The focus of the Christian statement is again the parlous situation of contemporary Jewry. The brief Christian statement is as follows:

> Why do you not abandon completely the faith of the Jews. For you see that they are in exile this lengthy time and day by day decline. You also see, with respect to the faith of the Christians, that they day by day increase, and their successes are great all this lengthy time. You would live among us with great honor and high status, instead of your current condition of exile and degradation and humiliation and accursedness.[15]

Included among the works that make up the *Milḥemet Miẓvah* are two sermons supposedly delivered by the author.[16] The more interesting of the two is purported to be a sermon delivered in the synagogue of Narbonne as a rebuttal to a Dominican missionizing address offered earlier the same day in the same place. Close reading of the rabbi's counter-sermon indicates a focus on reassurance with respect to eventual redemption for the Jew, with heavy emphasis on the rich rewards that will flow from Jewish faithfulness. This Jewish focus surely suggests that the Dominican address argued for the abrogation of divine promises of redemption for the Jews and the consequent hopelessness of Jewish circumstances.[17] Thus, throughout his work, the author of the *Milḥemet Miẓvah* shows a high level of sensitivity to the related issues of current Jewish suffering and eventual salvation of the Jews or lack thereof.

I have already noted indication of the issue of Jewish future in the Christian report on the Barcelona disputation. Sensitivity to this issue is far more clearly reflected in the Nahmanidean narrative and in the Ramban's further post-1263 writings.[18] Peppered throughout the Hebrew report of the Barcelona give-and-take are reassurances of eventual Jewish redemption. Nahmanides portrays himself recurrently speaking of some of the circumstances of that redemption, for instance, the appearance of the Jewish messiah at the papal court in Rome.[19]

The most revealing instance of this recurrent insistence on Jewish redemption comes in the Ramban's report of the second day's discussion.[20] Nahmanides has Friar Paul attempting to prove the prior advent of the messiah from the oft-cited Daniel 9:24–27. Friar Paul's use of these widely cited verses differs slightly from that normally reflected in earlier Jewish polemical works. What the friar is purported to have done is to argue simply that the seventy weeks of Daniel, which translate into a period of 490 years, must be understood by Jews against the backdrop of their own tradition, which posits a period of 490 years from the destruction of the First Temple to the destruction of the Second Temple. This allegedly Jewish reading of Daniel reinforces the rabbinic view cited prominently on the first day of the proceedings, according to which the messiah came at the time of the destruction of the Second Temple. Nahmanides blasts the friar's view of the Daniel verses, arguing that Paul does not begin to understand this difficult passage. Nahmanides insists that all intelligent readers of the Daniel passage must surely understand that it has nothing whatsoever to do with messianic advent; it only addresses itself to the historical realities of the Second Temple period. According to Nahmanides, only one section of the Book of Daniel foretells the messianic advent, and that is the closing section, which culminates in the messianic message of Daniel 12:11–12.

At this point, by any reasonable measure, the rabbi's statement on Daniel 9:24–27 should have come to a close. According to his own report, he had successfully rebutted the friar's effort to utilize these critical verses. Yet, in perhaps the most striking digression recorded in the entire Nahmanidean narrative, the author portrays himself proceeding far beyond the rules of the encounter and explicating the messianic message of the Book of Daniel. Nahmanides argues that the closing verses of the book indicate the onset of messianic redemption 1,290 years after the desecration and destruction of the Second Temple, with full redemption following forty-five years later. In order to drive home the precise meaning of his exegesis, the Ramban closes with the following:

> Behold, there have now elapsed from the time of the destruction [of the Second Temple] one thousand one hundred and ninety-five years. Thus, there are missing from the sum indicated by Daniel ninety-five

> years. We hope that the redeemer will come at that time, for this explication is correct and proper and it is fitting to believe in it.[21]

Such a precise messianic prediction in any public setting would be unusual; uttered allegedly in the remarkable circumstances of the Barcelona confrontation, it is all the more striking. Clearly, Rabbi Moses ben Nahman perceived the Christian assault as focusing heavily on the hopelessness of Jewish circumstances, necessitating his unusually assertive stance on the precise dating of the messianic advent. This perception lies at the root of his subsequent *Sefer ha-Geʾulah,* one of the most remarkable medieval efforts at reinforcing Jewish security in messianic redemption, with its confident closing assertion of the exact date of the onset of redemption.[22]

A contemporary of Nahmanides, Mordechai ben Jehosapha of Avignon, shared the Gerona rabbi's sense of the Christian onslaught on the Jewish sense of the future and likewise felt the need to reassure his co-religionists. His unpublished *Maḥazik Emunah* is perhaps the fullest medieval Jewish treatment of the issues of exile and redemption, with strong emphasis on the inevitability of the latter, although without the Ramban's inclination to offer a precise timetable for its onset.[23]

During the early decades of the fourteenth century, we continue to find Jewish leadership concerned with rebutting the Christian attack on the Jewish sense of the future. One of the most active of the Jewish apologists, Isaac Polgar, again highlights the issue of current Jewish circumstances and future Jewish hopes in the introductory remarks to the first section of his *ʿEzer ha-Dat.*[24] Polgar portrays his fellow Jews as crushed between the pressures of Christianity and Islam, with both of these formidable opponents taking every opportunity to do damage to a vulnerable Jewry. He pictures these powerful opponents as pressing the Jews with a series of damaging questions:

> Where is your God, who established his covenant with you? Let him stand forth and redeem you. On whom do you rely? Where is your king? Where is the place of your redeemer? No! He who dwells in terror[25] has pierced you repeatedly; he has destroyed you utterly. The Lord has abandoned you and forgotten you.[26] You have fallen and will never rise again.[27]

This is once more a striking perception of the new Christian assault.

Alfonso of Valladolid (Abner of Burgos) offers us important further insights into the new Christian attack on the Jewish sense of the future.[28] In the first place, Alfonso portrays himself as very much influenced by this new assault. In depicting his conversion to Christianity, he emphasizes the role of his own personal sense of hopelessness and despair. Let us recall Alfonso's vivid characterization of his conversion experience:

> I saw the poverty of the Jews, my people, from whom I am descended, who have been oppressed and broken and heavily burdened by taxes throughout their long captivity—this people that has lost its former honor and glory; and there is none to help or sustain them. One day when I had meditated much on the matter, I went to the synagogue, weeping sorely and sad at heart. And I prayed to the Lord, saying: "I beseech you, O Lord God, for compassion, that you may take note of these afflictions which beset us. Why are you so angered with your people these many days, your people and the sheep of your pasture? Why should the gentiles say: 'Where is their God?' Now, O Lord, hear my prayer and my supplication and cause the light to shine upon your desolate sanctuary and have mercy upon your people Israel."[29] After the great anxieties of my heart and all the toil I had taken upon myself, I rested and fell asleep. . . . In a dream, I saw the figure of a tall man who said to me: "Why do you slumber? Hearken to these words that I say to you and prepare yourself against the appointed season. I say to you that the Jews have remained so long in captivity for their folly and wickedness and because they have no teacher of righteousness through whom they may recognize the truth."[30]

Alfonso portrays himself as beset by precisely the kinds of questions specified by Isaac Polgar. Tormented by such queries, which were regularly addressed by the Christian majority against the Jewish minority, Alfonso sought relief and essentially found none. In fact, he encountered what he believed to be a divine message corroborating the claims of the attackers. His conversion, according to his own testimony, was triggered by the sense of hopelessness and futility which the aggressive Christian camp had been laboring for almost two centuries to plant in Jewish minds and hearts.

Given the backdrop of Christian argumentation and its successful impact on Alfonso/Abner, it is hardly surprising that, in taking up the missionizing effort after his conversion, he should choose to press the attack on just those areas which his own experience had shown him to be areas of Jewish vulnerability.[31] I would like to focus briefly on the fascinating set of epistolary exchanges between Alfonso and the Jew Joseph Shalom. These letters have come down to us in a format established by Alfonso. The exchange, as we have it, consists of three letters written by Alfonso to former Jewish associates, rebuttals penned by Joseph Shalom on behalf of the Jewish side, and Alfonso's rebuttal of the Shalom arguments.[32] For our purposes, the critical elements lie in the original attack mounted by Alfonso/Abner, as reflected in the first and third of his initial letters.

The third of Alfonso's three letters focuses on rabbinic materials that treat the messianic era. In a striking way, Alfonso works these disparate materials into a carefully ordered, rabbinically expressed case for the prior advent of the messianic age and for the rejection and damnation of the Jews. In an earlier study, I summarized Alfonso's argument under the following rubrics:

(1) The messiah has already come.
(2) Because of their sins, the coming of the messiah did not result in the salvation of the Jews.
(3) Another people took the place of the Jews and enjoyed redemption.
(4) Since the promised redemption was supposed to be inevitable, the Jewish sin was surely a unique one.
(5) This unique sin involved the willful failure to accept the divinely-revealed knowledge of the Divine Name and the related unwillingness to accept the divinely-promised spiritual messiah.[33]

From the perspective of traditional Christian theology, all this is hardly innovative. What is innovative of course is the establishment of this case on the grounds of rabbinic dicta. As emphasized throughout this essay, Alfonso no longer was making a case for Christian readers and auditors; he was anxious to make a case that would convince Jews committed to the rabbinic texts that he was explicating and manipulating. Alfonso argued to his Jewish audience the message of his own personal revelation: the Jews were doomed to an existence of hopelessness. In the face of the eternal rejection which their ancestors had brought about, there was surely no other reasonable course than to abandon the Jewish camp in favor of Christianity, which had been selected to fill the covenantal void created by alleged Jewish malfeasance.

Alfonso knew as well as any medieval Jew that the Jewish vision of a future redemption was profoundly rooted in an understanding of the opaque messages of the Book of Daniel. He was fully aware of the long Jewish tradition of exegesis of this crucial book and of the hope that Jews traditionally reposed in the secrets vouchsafed to Daniel. His familiarity with the corpus of medieval commentary on Daniel is reflected in the second of the letters in this collection, in which he attacks much of the medieval Jewish exegesis of this book. Aware of the details of this medieval exegesis, he obviously understood that, for medieval Jewry, this book constituted the cornerstone of all hope for a future redemption. Alfonso was clearly conversant, for example, with the exegesis of Nahmanides and therefore well knew that, for Rabbi Moses ben Nahman as for so many others, the Book of Daniel was the most important biblical source for the inevitability of redemption and for the clues that could lead to an unraveling of its mysteries. It is this understanding that led Alfonso, in the first and most significant of the three letters, to attempt to subvert all prior Jewish understanding of this critical biblical book.

Alfonso focuses his critique of Jewish understanding of the Book of Daniel on the traditional four-stage view of world history which had been erected upon the foundations of the Jewish reading of Daniel.[34] For Jews over the ages, the four kingdoms of Daniel were: Babylonia, Media-Persia, Greece, and Edom, which was generally taken by Jewish exegetes as a reference to Rome. Thus, the completion of the historical process foretold in the Book of Daniel and the messianic advent could only take place in conjunction with the destruction of the last of the four kingdoms, the kingdom of Edom-Rome. This destruction and the concomitant messianic advent, for Jews, of course lay yet in the future. While Jews occasionally disagreed over the identity of the fourth kingdom, substituting Islam for Rome, no one disputed the essential notion of Greece as the third of the kingdoms, of yet a further kingdom beyond Greece, of redemption dawning with the dissolution of this fourth and last empire, and of the twin process of destruction and redemption as yet to come. It is precisely this unanimously shared sense that Alfonso set out to undo, arguing to his Jewish readers that this entire traditional Jewish reading of Daniel and hence the resultant historical scheme was fundamentally in error. According to Alfonso, the four kingdoms of the book of Daniel are: Babylonia, Media, Persia, and Greece, with the messianic advent—which for Alfonso has already taken place—linked to the decline of this fourth and last kingdom. What is clearly crucial here is not the technical issue of identifying the elements in the Daniel scheme; what is crucial is the undermining of the Jewish sense of a redemption still to be realized.

Let us attend to a bit of the attack mounted by Alfonso on the traditional Jewish reading of the four kingdoms of Daniel. His first thrust is a simple one; he argues that nowhere is Edom projected as part of the four-part imperial scheme. The only specific nations identified in the Daniel scheme are Babylonia, Media, Persia, and Greece. Edom is mentioned explicitly in Daniel, Alfonso notes, but only in Daniel 11:41: "He [the king of the south] will invade the beautiful land, too, and many will fall, but these will escape his clutches: Edom, Moab, and the chief part of the Ammonites." Thus, for Alfonso, Edom clearly lies outside the sequence of empires; it is depicted only as one of the victims of the fourth empire; it can surely not be the fourth empire itself.[35]

According to Alfonso, the traditional Jewish error with respect to the fourth kingdom is rooted in a misreading of the prior kingdoms, specifically a misunderstanding of the middle of the sequence. Jews and Alfonso agree that the first kingdom is Babylonia; over that identification there is no dispute. The problem lies with kingdoms two and three. For the traditional Jewish view, kingdom two is Media-Persia and kingdom three is Greece. According to Alfonso, close reading of the Book of Daniel indicates that kingdom two is Media and kingdom three is Persia, meaning that the fourth and final kingdom must be Greece. For Alfonso, misunderstanding of kingdoms two and three lie at the root of Jewish error, and, as a result, he devotes considerable attention to this issue. Alfonso argues the following considerations:

(1) Nowhere in Scriptures is there reference to a king of Media-Persia or Persia-Media. That is to say, Media and Persia are treated in the biblical corpus as two separate and distinct entities. Thus the Jewish combination of the two is thoroughly unwarranted.
(2) Given the fact that the Book of Daniel itself notes four kings of Persia, then any combination of Median-Persian kings must include a minimum of at least five kings, contradicting traditional Jewish exegesis of Daniel 7:5 as referring to the second beast and its three kings. Once again, this suggests that the Media-Persia combination is erroneous.
(3) In fact, the account of the third beast in Daniel 7 mentions four wings and four heads, which, according to Alfonso, correspond precisely to the four known kings of Persia.[36]

Thus, there can be no Media-Persia combination; the third beast must be Persia; the second beast must surely be Media.

The clear implication of the tripartite Babylonia-Media-Persia succession is that only Greece can be the fourth and last of the four great empires. Indeed, argues Alfonso, the depiction of the fourth beast in Daniel 7 in fact corresponds precisely to what is said expressly of Greece in chapter 8 and chapters 10–12. Thus, the inference of Greece as the fourth empire, which derives from Alfonso's analysis of its three predecessors, is, according to him, corroborated incontrovertibly by the actual Daniel portrayal of the fourth and last kingdom.[37] From all this it follows that the traditional Jewish scheme is fatally flawed, that the actual pre-messianic succession stipulated in Daniel involves Babylonia, Media, Persia, with Greece the culminating empire. The destruction of Greek power by the Romans was then the herald of the onset of messianic times. The messianic figure foretold in the Book of Daniel was surely Jesus, who came on the scene at the predicted time of dissolution of the fourth empire. Dissolution of the fourth empire and advent of the messiah have both already taken place, leaving no room for Jewish assertions of future redemption. Alfonso has, on the one hand, buttressed traditional Christian doctrine; more important for his immediate purposes, he has delivered a harsh assault on Jewish hopes for the future.[38]

The attack on the Jewish sense of the future is a striking element in the aggressive Christian posture that began to develop in the twelfth century and that reached the stage of a well-financed and well-orchestrated missionizing campaign in the thirteenth. Alfonso affords us a useful sense of this assault on the Jewish future in his self-portrayal as a victim of that assault, on the one hand, and in his determined post-conversion effort to develop additional arguments that would further undermine Jewish confidence, on the other. The subsequent impact of these intense Christian pressures on late fourteenth- and fifteenth-century Iberian Jewry remains to be studied.

NOTES

1. There is, unfortunately, no fully satisfying overview available of either medieval Christian or medieval Jewish polemical literature. The situation is somewhat better on the Christian side. Useful are the surveys provided in A. Lukeyn Williams, *Adversus Judaeos* (Cambridge, 1935); Heinz Schreckenberg, *Die christlichen Adversus-Judaeos-Texte und ihr literarisches und historisches Umfeld* (Frankfort, 1982); *Die christlichen Adversus-Judaeos-Texte (11.–13. Jh)* (Frankfort, 1988). More analytic in focus are the two recent works by Gilbert Dahan: Part Four (L'Affrontement) of his *Les intellectuels chrétiens sur les juifs au Moyen Age* (Paris, 1990) and *La polémique chrétienne contre le Judaïsme au Moyen Age* (Paris, 1991). The most useful overview of the Jewish polemical attacks is provided by Salo W. Baron, *A Social and Religious History of the Jews*, 2nd ed., 18 vols. (New York, 1952–83) 9.97–134. A full bibliography of Jewish polemical writings was provided by Judah Rosenthal, "Anti-Christian Polemic from Its Beginnings to the End of the Eighteenth Century" [Hebrew], *Areshet* 2 (1960): 130–79, with additions in *Areshet* 3:433–39.

2. For an overview of this striking development, see the valuable analysis of Benjamin Z. Kedar, *Crusade and Mission: European Approaches to the Muslims* (Princeton, 1984), and the extensive literature cited therein.

3. For the first stages in the development of these new lines of argumentation, see the important study of Amos Funkenstein, "Changes in the Patterns of Christian Anti-Jewish Polemics in the Twelfth Century" (Hebrew), *Zion* 33 (1968): 124–44. I have studied in some detail the elaboration of this new argumentation into a formalized missionizing campaign in *Daggers of Faith: Thirteenth-Century Christian Missionizing and Jewish Response* (Berkeley, 1989) and *Barcelona and Beyond: The Disputation of 1263 and Its Aftermath* (Berkeley, 1992).

4. Among the early Church authorities to emphasize the rejection of the Jews and the hopelessness of their circumstances can be counted Cyprian, Origen, Chrysostom, and Augustine.

5. See my two publications noted above in note 3.

6. See my full analysis of the Christian attacks in *Barcelona and Beyond,* chapter 2.

7. *Pugio fidei* (Leipzig, 1687), Part 2, chapters 1–10; Part 3, chapters 21–23.

8. The text of the *Milḥamot ha-Shem* was published by Judah Rosenthal (Jerusalem, 1963) and is preceded by useful introductory comments by the editor. Much work remains to be done on this important and interesting polemical text. The closing chapter, in particular, merits considerable attention.

9. The *Sefer ha-Berit* was first published in the collection entitled *Milḥemet Ḥovah* (Constantinople, 1710), 18b–38a. It was republished with notes by Frank Talmage at Jerusalem in 1974 and in *The Book of the Covenant, and Other Writings* (Toronto, 1972).

10. Robert Chazan, "Joseph Kimhi's *Sefer ha-Berit:* Pathbreaking Medieval Jewish Apologetics," *Harvard Theological Review* 85 (1992): 417–32.

11. The text of this letter, the second in a series of three epistles addressed to former Jewish associates, was published by Judah Rosenthal in *The Abraham Weiss Jubilee Volume: Studies in His Honor Presented by His Colleagues and Disciples on the Occasion of His Completing Four Decades of Pioneering Scholarship* (New York, 1964) [Hebrew section], 483–510.

12. Important segments of the *Milḥemet Miẓvah* were published by William Herskowitz, "Judaeo-Christian Dialogue in Provence as Reflected in *Milḥemet Miẓvah* of R. Meir ha-Meili," unpublished doctoral dissertation, Yeshiva University, 1974, and by Moshe Yehudah Blau, *Shitat ha-Kadmonim ᶜal Masekhet Nazir* (New York, 1974), 305–57. The fullest description of this important text was provided by Siegfried Stein, *Jewish-Christian Disputations in Thirteenth-Century Narbonne* (London, 1969). I have analyzed some of the major polemical thrusts in this text in "Polemical Themes in the *Milḥemet Miẓvah,*" in *Les Juifs au regard de l'histoire: mélanges en l'honneur de Bernhard Blumenkranz,* ed. Gilbert Dahan (Paris, 1985), 169–84, and in *Daggers of Faith,* chapter 4.

13. For some of this material see Robert Chazan, "Archbishop Guy Fulcodi and His Jews," *Revue des études juives* 132 (1973): 587–94; "Anti-Usury Efforts in Thirteenth-Century Narbonne and the Jewish Response," *Proceedings of the American Academy for Jewish Research* 41 (1973–74): 45–67; "A Jewish Plaint to Saint Louis," *Hebrew Union College Annual* 45 (1974): 287–305.

14. Blau, *Shitat ha-Kadmonim,* 305–57.

15. Ibid., 305.

16. The first of the sermons can be found in Herskovitz, "Judaeo-Christian Dialogue," 25–31; the second can be found there on pages 61–75.

17. I have analyzed this sermon in "Confrontation in the Synagogue of Narbonne: A Christian Sermon and a Jewish Reply," *Harvard Theological Review* 67 (1974): 437–57.

18. Full analysis of this narrative and the Ramban's other post-1263 writings is provided in *Barcelona and Beyond,* chapters 4–7.

19. See for example Nahmanides' narrative as published in *Kitvei Rabbenu Moshe ben Nahman,* 4th printing, 2 vols. (Jerusalem, 1971), 1.309–310, 312, 316.

20. Ibid., 312–15.

21. Ibid., 314.

22. See *Barcelona and Beyond,* chapter 7, for a full discussion of the Ramban's *Sefer ha-Ge'ulah.*

23. For a preliminary discussion of this important text, see *Daggers of Faith,* 103–14.

24. A critical edition of *ʿEzer ha-Dat* was published by Jacob Levinger (Tel Aviv, 1984).

25. Job 30:6.

26. Literally the text reads: "The Lord has abandoned the earth and has forgotten all creation." Because the focus is so clearly upon the rupture of the relationship between God and Israel, I have chosen to translate freely.

27. *ʿEzer ha-Dat,* 29.

28. Yitzhak Baer was vitally interested in Alfonso throughout his long scholarly career. He wrote his first essay on Alfonso in the late 1920s—"Abner aus Burgos," *Korrespondenzblatt des Vereins zur Gründung und Erhaltung einer Akademie für die Wissenschaft des Judentums* 9 (1929): 20–37; his fullest treatment of Alfonso can be found in the English version of his broad history of Spanish Jewry, *A History of the Jews in Christian Spain,* trans. Louis Schoffman et al., 2 vols. (Philadelphia, 1961–1966), 1.327–54. For a full listing of the known writings of Alfonso and their availability in both manuscript and printed form, see Walter Mettmann, *Alfonso de Valladolid: Ofrenda de zelos und Libro de la ley* (Opladen, 1990), 8–9.

29. Note here the obvious impact of the imagery of Daniel.

30. The text was published by Isidore Loeb, "Polemistes chrétiens and juifs en France et en Espagne," *Revue des études juives* 18 (1889): 55–56. I have utilized the translation provided by Baer in *A History of the Jews in Christian Spain,* 1.328–29.

31. For the listing of Alfonso's post-conversion writings, see Mettmann, as indicated in note 28.

32. The texts were published by Judah Rosenthal in the following manner: (1) the first epistle with the rebuttal of Joseph Shalom, *Studies and Essays in Honor of Abraham A. Neuman,* ed. Meir Ben-Horin et al. (Philadelphia,

1962), 588–621; (2) the second epistle with the rebuttal of Joseph Shalom in *The Abraham Weiss Jubilee Volume* [Hebrew section], 483–510; (3) the third epistle with the rebuttal by Joseph Shalom (*Studies in Bibliography and Booklore* 5 [1961]: [Hebrew section], 42–51; (4) the responses of Alfonso to the rebuttals of Joseph Shalom—Judah Rosenthal, *Meḥkarim,* 2 vols. (Jerusalem, 1967), 1.324–267.

33. Robert Chazan, "Maestre Alfonso of Valladolid and the New Missionizing," *Revue des études juives* 143 (1984): 83–94.

34. For a penetrating discussion of the four kingdoms, see the important observations of Gerson D. Cohen in *Abraham ibn Daud, Sefer ha-Qabbalah,* ed. and trans. Gerson D. Cohen (Philadelphia, 1967), 223–62. On the identification of Edom and Rome, see Gerson D. Cohen, "Esau as Symbol in Early Medieval Thought," *Jewish Medieval and Renaissance Studies,* ed. Alexander Altmann (Cambridge, Mass., 1967), 19–48 (reprinted in Gerson D. Cohen, *Studies in the Variety of Rabbinic Cultures* [Philadelphia, 1991], 243–69).

35. See the text edited by Rosenthal in *Studies and Essays in Honor of Abraham A. Neuman,* 616.

36. Ibid., 615.

37. Ibid., 614–15.

38. The dashing of Jewish hopes for the future is a central theme in Alfonso's lengthy reply to the letter of Isaac Polgar, a text which has been edited by Jonathan Hecht as a doctoral dissertation at New York University. The material from Alfonso's *Mostrador* presented in the Loeb essay cited above in note 30, and by Walter Mettman, *Die volkssprachliche apologetische Literatur auf der Iberischen Halbinsel im Mittelalter* (Opladen, 1987), 41–75, similarly shows the centrality of this theme in Alfonso's *magnum opus.*

PART III

Conversos

IO

Crypto-Jewish Women Facing the Spanish Inquisition: Transmitting Religious Practices, Beliefs, and Attitudes

RENÉE LEVINE MELAMMED

WHEN ASSESSING crypto-Judaism, one cannot help but be duly impressed by the determination of the baptized Jews and their descendents in the face of adversity. How did they manage to continue their clandestine observance despite the ominous presence of the Inquisition? How did they obtain their knowledge of Judaism? And how did they maintain their religion or "marranism," as it is often called?[1]

Insight into these aspects of the lives of crypto-Jews can be gained through the study of Inquisition documents. These records are transcripts of legal proceedings that transpired in the courts of the Holy Tribunal. While not all are complete or even extant, those that are accessible often reveal information about the Judaizer's knowledge and activities. In certain cases, the defendants provided confessions and although some of these confessions were extracted under torture, the information obtained had to be subsequently confirmed under less extenuating circumstances.[2]

All trials required the testimonies of witnesses for the prosecution; these statements were necessary in order to begin the proceedings, for they served as the basis of the prosecutor's list of charges in the accusation.[3] In addition, part of the investigation involved questioning the defendant on the part of the Inquisitors; for example, by the beginning of the sixteenth century in Castile, questions regarding the nature or identity of the teacher of the Judaizer frequently appeared.[4] Thus one can sometimes easily trace the source of Judaizing and observe a clear transmission of crypto-Judaism.

In normative Judaism, the knowledge of laws and customs is transmitted in both formal and informal ways. Formally, there are institutions which provide for organized prayer and for the study of Jewish law. The male is required to train his son and is responsible for his education; the synagogue and educational systems provide the men with effective means of immersing themselves in Jewish law and tradition. The traditional interpretation of *halakha* has assumed that the female was not required to fulfill all of the obligations incumbent upon the male. As a result, little or no formal education was provided for Jewish girls. The training received was usually limited to the confines of the home; mothers acquired expertise in various realms of the law such as those dealing with the dietary laws, the laws of purity, and the Sabbath. While there is clear evidence that some Jewish women in medieval Spain were literate, they were rarely experts in the male-dominated world of Hebrew, Aramaic, or Judeo-Arabic literature.[5]

As a result, Jewish women adapted and created their own informal system of education; for them, the home was also a center for learning and their pedagogic techniques were a far cry from the methods used in the text-centered *sinagoga* or *Beit Midrash* (House of Study). Oral explanations were accompanied by "hands-on" learning which was by no means limited to the confines of the kitchen. While less formal in structure, this education was, however, no less exacting or precise in its teachings, for Jewish law was a serious matter for all concerned.

The situation that developed in crypto-Jewish society was clearly the result of a logical progression. In order to determine the nature of the conditions confronted by the potential Judaizer, it is necessary to consider the environment of the newly baptized Jews. At first, in 1391, the environment of the converso was quite similar, at least superficially, to the pre-1391 surroundings. Most lived in close proximity to a surviving Jewish community which could provide them with both spiritual and material aid. However, the converso was expected to attend church and to behave in a manner which behooved a Spanish Catholic. In reality, those converts who desired to maintain ties with the Jewish community were able to do so with relative ease. At the same time, however, internal organization was necessary for the Judaizers and the community-oriented aspect of traditional Jewish society would be imitated by the crypto-Jews. Thus attempts were made by clandestine groups of Judaizing conversos to organize themselves for prayers, holidays, and other observances. At first, the majority of the leaders of these groups appear to have been male, yet one can detect the presence of female leaders as well. In other words, the traditional framework of Jewish leadership began to break down as women occasionally took the lead. This was, perhaps, the first indication of the change that would occur, for re-creating a traditional framework in this society would prove to be an impossibility.

Two factors were extremely significant in the development of crypto-Judaism in Spain. The first was the presence of the Jewish community which would serve as a source of guidance and inspiration.[6] Once the Jews were expelled in 1492, more than the Jews themselves disappeared. No longer did the crypto-Jews have access to the literature and the texts, to the synagogues and the ritual baths, to the slaughterhouses and the suppliers of ritual objects and foods. All of the institutions that could have provided support for the Judaizers had vanished. The second factor working against the perpetuation of crypto-Judaism was time itself. As the memory of Judaism and Jewish life faded, observance became more and more difficult.[7] A text-based religion transmitted by males would be doomed to extinction once the texts and the memories of those texts were no longer available. Perpetuation of such a tradition would be a major challenge under these conditions.

In the long run, it appears that the crypto-Jewish women rose to the challenge of maintaining their religious tradition, frequently in spite of the most difficult circumstances. Crypto-Judaism would not be identical to the Judaism upon which it was based, and could not be expected to have been so; the very fact that it was clandestine would result in changes. Besides, a tradition transmitted almost entirely by word of mouth would suffer from distortions that would occur naturally and without being detected.

On the other hand, perhaps the results would not be as distorted as might be expected because some of the members of this community had considerable experience in the realm of oral transmission. As a matter of fact, these women were not only experienced thusly, but also quite accustomed to utilizing their homes as educational facilities. Consequently, when no other institutions were available, they were able to adapt relatively easily. However, the situation for the Jewish men stands out in strong contrast. They had always relied upon texts of both written and oral law for transmission of knowledge. In addition, the home had never been the center of their lives as observant Jews. When facing life as a clandestine Judaizer, the crypto-Jewish male was quite obviously at a distinct disadvantage.

Scholars have long contended that women were outstanding in their devotion to Judaism, and that the crypto-Jewish women were no exception to this rule.[8] They appear to have had a background that would allow them to adapt more easily to the exigencies of a secret religion; they were not changing the focus of their lives because the home remained, for them, as central as ever. Yet the fact remains that every act, be it of Judaizing or of teaching a ritual, if discovered, could incriminate the crypto-Jew. When the home became the center for religious observance, it did not offer the "privacy" one might associate with one's personal abode; it was not necessarily a safe place for Judaizing. Because the majority of the conversos were members of the middle class, their households, like those of the average middle and lower middle class, had numerous servants including those specifically assigned to work in the kitchen. Thus potential witnesses were built in to this society who were indispensable in two respects, because of the work they did and because an absence of servants would be as suspicious to the outsider as were the Judaizing activities themselves.

A look at some of these women's trials which transpired both before as well as after 1492 will shed light on their concern with observing as well as with perpetuating their traditions.[9] Conversas who had not been born as Jews eventually learned about their heritage because some person or persons exposed them to Judaism, essentially initiating them. It is interesting to discover that while the outstanding and most recurrent link between generations of Judaizers was the mother, there were often other crypto-Jews who perceived their responsibility in a similar way. Thus, in addition to mothers, there were sisters, in-laws, cousins, neighbors, and others who actively taught the younger generation to observe the Law of Moses.[10]

The trial of Juana Martínez uncovers the saga of a Castilian Judaizing family from Alcázar de Consuegra and the intricacies of maintaining the crypto-Jewish tradition in the late fifteenth and early sixteenth centuries. Juana's mother, Constanza Núñez, decided that her family should be reconciled to the Church in April 1486 during the Grace Period declared by the Inquisitorial Court of Toledo.

The proceedings contain numerous confessions which include those of Juana, her sister Marí, her brother Fernando, and two brothers-in-law, one of whom was already a widower.[11] While the information offered varied from individual to individual, certain patterns soon become apparent. The first confessions were received from the sons-in-law on April 10. García de Alcala, a cobbler, was married to Juana's older sister, Marí Núñez. This converso emphasized his wife's active Judaizing, to which he had consented for an eight- or nine-year period between 1475 and 1484. He had allowed her to light candles on Friday nights and despite his original objections, he eventually agreed to let Marí fast on Yom Kippur when she would prepare a special meal for breaking the fast. García permitted her to remove the fat from meat and admitted that after the birth of each child, there had been *hadas* or celebrations including music and a repast in their home. He had even eaten fish and eggs while sitting at low tables following the death of his wife's niece, and had bathed or aided in the bathing of deceased conversos. García explained that he had agreed to all of the above in order to co-exist peacefully with his wife.[12]

While peaceful co-existence was García's rationale, many conversos reporting Judaizing activities in their homes pointed out that they had simply consented to their wives' way of life, never providing a rationale for their stance. This emphasis on passive consent as opposed to active participation reflected the role played by many male Judaizers. Needless to say, not all males were passive in their actions; on the contrary, some were quite active at the same time that other men were oblivious to the activities of their wives. Nevertheless the Inquisitors themselves were aware of the general shift of power that had occurred. This was reflected in the precise wording of the charges presented by the prosecution; husbands were frequently accused of allowing or giving consent to the women's Judaizing while the women themselves were charged with carrying out the heretical acts.

Benito González was, like García, a cobbler married to one of Juana's older sisters, Elvira Núñez, who had passed away by 1486. The tone of this confession waivers between that of a fairly active Judaizer and that of a consenting husband. Benito had sometimes consented to the lighting of Sabbath candles by his wife, yet he himself had occasionally observed this day and donned clean clothes in its honor. He had eaten Sabbath stews prepared on Fridays which he had allowed his wife to prepare. This converso had occasionally fasted on Yom Kippur and asked forgiveness of others; he had even read or heard the contents of a Jewish book. Benito had allowed the fat to be removed from meat or had removed it himself, and had eaten meat slaughtered by Jews. He had given charity to Jews for the purchase of oil for their synagogue, had aided in the bathing of the dead, and when his own father had died, he placed a glass of water and a lit candle in the room.[13] In addition, he had eaten at some post-burial meals and there had been *hadas* in his home at the appropriate times. He had even abstained from eating certain foods forbidden by the Law of Moses; lastly, he reiterated that it was he who had consented to his wife's activities. The cobbler then added that he had seen his wife engaging in many Judaizing rituals such as observing the Sabbath, hearing Jewish prayers, removing the fat from meat, and fasting on Yom Kippur. On this solemn day, he witnessed his wife asking forgiveness of her mother, her sisters, her brothers, Pedro and Diego, and of María and Juana.[14] In both the body of his confession and in his addendum, he concluded with an emphasis on his deceased wife's Judaizing.[15]

Thus, while this brother-in-law was a far more active Judaizer than his counterpart, during the course of his confession, he repeatedly pointed to his wife's activities and to the fact that he had granted his permission. He revealed a life in which he had more contact with Jewish rites than did his brother-in-law; he also attributed more observances to his wife than did García. While Elvira was no longer alive in 1486, Marí, García's wife and Constanza's surviving married daughter, also sought reconciliation and on the following day, April 11, the court received her confession.

A comparison of the transgressions listed by Marí with those mentioned by her husband reveals a fuller and longer list supplied by the conversa. García stated that candle lighting took place in their home on Friday nights; Marí pointed out that at this time, she lit them earlier than the other nights of the week. She added that she had sometimes prepared and eaten Sabbath stews; perhaps García was not at home on these occasions, although his brother-in-law had eaten them in his home. The cobbler referred to allowing Marí to remove the fat from meat, but his wife, as did her brother-in-law Benito, admitted to eating meat slaughtered by Jews. Both husband and wife referred to the fact that she fasted on Yom Kippur, however Marí added that she had asked forgiveness of others on that day too. Interestingly enough, her sister's husband not only confessed to observing likewise, but listed the names of the family members from whom his wife had requested forgiveness. García did not seem to know that his wife had also observed some holidays such as Passover when she ate *matsah.*

Since the *hadas* took place in their home in the company of relatives, both husband and wife mentioned this celebration as did Benito. Both had aided in bathing the dead as did Benito; Marí had also prepared shrouds. Both referred to eating at *cohuerzos* as did Marí's brother-in-law. Only Marí mentioned that her mother had shown her how to bless her children by placing her hand on their heads (in the Jewish manner) without crossing herself. In addition, García apparently was not aware of the fact that his wife separated a piece of dough which she then threw in the fire as required by Jewish law.[16] While the cobbler was involved minimally in a few of the observances, he only seemed to be aware of some, but by no means all, of those maintained by his wife. It seems that in order to keep peace in the house, she preferred to keep certain aspects of her Judaizing hidden from her spouse as well. There is no doubt that the Inquisitors' appetites were whet after hearing García's confession with his emphasis on his wife's betrayal of the Church in conjunction with his shameful and passive consent. On the very next day, their suspicions that more information would be unearthed were proven to be justified, for Marí's confession revealed that she had indeed succeeded in hiding from her own husband additional observances such as the aforementioned Sabbath and Passover celebrations.

Juana's half-brother Fernando testified for the first time on the fourteenth of April. He explained that as a young boy in his mother's house, he had been ordered to observe Jewish laws because these actions would lead to salvation. As a result, he had observed the Sabbath, wearing clean clothes in its honor and eating Sabbath stews. On Yom Kippur, he had fasted, he had eaten meat during Lent, and the meat he had eaten had sometimes been prepared by Jews. In June 1530, Fernando again emphasized the fact that his mother was the motivating force behind his Judaizing; he had become accustomed to this way of life while living in her house and had continued when he later lived with his brother Pedro. The training his mother had provided was not restricted to the confines of her home; he then noted that the lifestyle of all his sisters was similar to his.[17]

Constanza had indoctrinated her children well. Her daughters as well as one or more of her sons were Judaizing, individually as well as in a family unit. One daughter married a Judaizer with whom she shared her religion; another convinced her husband to let her go her own way and at times he joined her, although more often she was observing on her own. Fernando specifically stated that his mother's home was the center and headquarters of Judaizing for the family; his father or step-father might have joined Constanza, but this was not emphasized, for the crypto-Jewess provided the mainstay of the family's observances.

This contention is supported by the testimony of the defendant Juana Martínez, the youngest member of the family seeking reconciliation and the last to testify during the Grace Period of 1486. On April 24, a short confession was provided by the fourteen-year-old conversa, who appears to already have been married for about a year. When she was approximately eight years old, Juana's mother Constanza began to instruct her and to explain to her the importance of observing the Law of Moses which would bring about her salvation. Thus she observed the Sabbath, wearing clean clothes on this day, lighting candles on Friday nights, and preparing food in advance on Friday for consumption on the Sabbath day. Holiday observance was included as well, such as the festival of Passover when unleavened bread was eaten and the solemn day of Yom Kippur when one fasted and asked forgiveness of others. Fat was removed from meat, a piece of dough was thrown into the fire, meat slaughtered by Jews was eaten while pork and other forbidden meats and fishes were not. Essentially, these were Juana's Judaizing activities, which, she repeated, she had learned from her mother, especially by watching her in action.[18]

Because she was younger and still living with her mother during the first years of her marriage, Juana's frame of reference, as compared to that of her married sister(s), was bound to be her mother. Yet even her older brother emphasized the fact that Constanza was the center of the family's Judaizing. The two older and more mature daughters had moved out of their mother's home, had been married for a longer period of time, and were already mothers themselves. The fact that they celebrated *hadas,* were taught how to bless their children in the Jewish manner, and had experienced death and mourning ceremonies attests to this fact. Although ostensibly independent from their mother as they Judaized in their respective homes, they had frequently Judaized with Constanza in her home as well.

Since Juana was recalled by the Inquisition in 1530, additional information is available concerning the role of the various members of this Judaizing family. Constanza, the matriarch of the family, had died about twenty years earlier, and by this time, Juana had also lost her second sister, Marí. Her brother Fernando was simultaneously being detained by the Holy Tribunal. Juana was almost sixty years old, and did not remember the details of the reconciliation of her youth. However, once her own confession was read to her, she was able to recall certain details as well as to reply to some of the questions posed to her at the interrogation.

The role of Constanza again emerges as dominant and essential in preserving the Judaizing traditions in this family. Juana explained that she had Judaized following her mother's advice and teachings. Most of the activities were done together with her, for example, Sabbath observance when she would watch her mother light candles.[19] During the Passover holiday, her sisters came to join their mother and sister in observance, eating the required *matsah;* these women fasted together on Yom Kippur as well.[20] At first, Juana stated that her brothers-in-law did not Judaize, although she later admitted that the two had observed certain ceremonies.[21] Ritually slaughtered meat had been eaten together with her mother and sisters; the women also would gather together in Constanza's home on the

Sabbath. Her sisters had lit Sabbath candles in their own abodes as well as at their mother's, and all had adorned their homes in honor of the day of rest. This mother had not neglected any of her daughters and had, said Juana, taught them everything they knew.[22] When the Inquisitors sought to verify these claims, the defendant told them that the women in the family had talked about why they observed the Law of Moses.[23]

Juana was adamant about the fact that her husband never Judaized nor saw her Judaizing.[24] On the other hand, she eventually included her brother and finally her father, Rodrigo de Villarreal, in her list of Judaizers who had observed together with the women of the family.[25] There is no doubt that some of the men had indeed Judaized; the 1486 confessions of Fernando and his two brothers-in-law speak for themselves. Yet what is particularly clear in this case, and this family was by no means unique among Judaizers, is the leading role taken by the women. Whether or not these women married Judaizing men, they continued observing and teaching their children. Some of the men admitted to Judaizing, some tried to shift the focus to their wives' dominant role, and others categorically declared themselves or were declared to be non-Judaizers. Constanza, however, was consistent and passed on her knowledge of Jewish life, teaching her offspring to observe the Sabbath, Yom Kippur, and Passover. Some of the dietary laws were taught along with the proper way to prepare *hallah.* Older daughters were initiated into the rites of mourning and death as well as birth and shown how to bless their children. This conversa introduced her children to their heritage when they were as young as eight years old; she consistently continued to guide them both by instruction as well as by example. The very fact that her married daughters often chose to Judaize together with their mother attests to the success of Constanza as a teacher of crypto-Judaism.

Crypto-Judaism is most often defined as the observance of Jewish laws and rites which, due to its clandestine nature, might have included certain atrophied or distorted rituals as well as others that had been created by the crypto-Jews.[26] However, there was another aspect of this religion that played an important role in the psychological maintenance of such a dualistic life. Clearly, in order to live outwardly as a Christian, yet remain inwardly faithful to Judaism, a defense mechanism had to be developed in which the denial of Christianity would play an important part.[27] In other words, attitudes as well as methods of denial were being transmitted by the crypto-Jews. Attitudes, unlike rituals, do not need to be formally taught, for in a receptive environment, they, willy-nilly, infiltrate the consciousness of others present.

Concrete examples of anti-Christian statements as well as specific actions of this nature can be found in the dossiers of many conversas. Some Judaizing women would defiantly wash or sew on Sunday, the Christian day of rest, rather than on Saturday, the Jewish Sabbath.[28] Marina González tried to justify her Sunday activities by claiming that she had to work on this day in order to compensate for her frail husband's meagre earnings and because she was anticipating the eventual marriage of her daughter.[29] Some defendants were accused of eating meat and eggs during Lent and on other days when such foods were specifically forbidden by the Church.[30]

Conversas were also accused of not making the sign of the cross at appropriate times,[31] of not attending church or of not hearing the Divine offices,[32] or if attending, of not praying while in attendance. While praying, some conversas neglected to mention the name of Jesus Christ or the Virgin Mary; they might have preferred to allude only to the "Creator of the World."[33] Others were bolder and spoke irreverently of Christianity or of its beliefs. Some mocked the mass,[34] others belittled the religion,[35] and still others seriously insulted the faith and its dogmas.

While there were conversas who chose not to have any images of saints in their homes, others opted to denigrate those that were in their possession. María Alvarez bemoaned the very day she had converted, having abandoned her Jewish husband and children. She wondered how she had forsaken the superior Law of Moses "for those wooden saints."[36] An image of the Virgin Mary was found in the home of Leonor Gutierrez of Hita, but she had intentionally turned it around so that it faced the wall.[37] Catalina de Zamora quite vehemently rejected the notion of the Virgin Mary. A witness heard her say that Mary was a common woman who had not encountered any miracle; on the contrary, she had been stained with blood (i.e., lost her virginity) and had been a whore as well. In addition, when Catalina passed by churches erected in honor of the Virgin, she made vulgar motions at them with her hand.[38] María González was even more defiant; she had taken a board which had the image of Mary painted on it, threw it into a filthy drain near the doorway leading out of her kitchen and brazenly spit on it.[39]

Another method of defiance was to denigrate Old Christian society as well as to belittle the effectiveness of the Inquisition's campaign, especially the efficaciousness of such bombastic events as the *autos-da-fé.* The midwife Beatriz Rodríguez claimed that the Old Christians simply wanted to harm the New Christians due to their jealousy of the conversos' prosperity; after all, the Jews were the "apple of God's eye."[40] More than one witness heard the aforementioned Catalina de Zamora comment on the fate of those Judaizers burned at the stake. She apparently said that while the flesh and body cannot endure martyrization, the heart will nevertheless remain with the Creator.[41] The conversos frequently referred to those who perished at the *autos* as martyrs, for their deaths would then have been in sanctification of the name of God, a traditionally meritorious death in traditional Jewish society. Here, however, the defiance was double; not only was the salvation of the Judaizer's soul involved, but the Jewish Creator was at the "heart" of the matter. María González of Casarrubios del Monte said that while the Inquisitors might burn the parents, the children survive them (to continue the traditions).[42] In the trial of María González of Ciudad Real, one finds assorted witness testimonies for the prosecution which point in this direction. The husband of this conversa had been burned at the stake in 1484. Not only did his widow insist that he had died as a martyr, but she related that he had appeared to her in a dream in the form of an (infant) angel. One witness reported that María even had the audacity to ask a friar in a monastery to recite two masses for the soul of her deceased husband![43] Defiance was again the dominant motif in the above statements and actions by these conversas striving, on whatever level they could, to maintain a sense of value and dignity in their lives.

Essentially, any act of Judaizing was an act of defiance; the crypto-Jews were rejecting Catholicism, the Church, and its teachings, when they belittled the Virgin Mary as well as when they observed the Sabbath. The crypto-Jewish women who faced the Inquisition of Castile in the fifteenth and sixteenth centuries were not concerned with Catholic dogma, but rather with the religion of their ancestors and with successfully transmitting these values. The traditional framework had disintegrated, but the concern with educating the younger generation was intact. Crypto-Judaism survived because there was concern for survival and continuity; the Inquisition's goal was, on the other hand, to interrupt and, if possible, destroy the continuity in its campaign to extirpate heresy.

The records of the trials of the Inquisition provide an entrée into the secret lives of these Judaizers. A shift of power within the family can be perceived as the home became the only feasible locale for clandestine observance. This new center of Judaizing was the woman's domain; in addition, she was equally at home in the art of oral transmission in this now textless society. Ultimately, the crypto-Jewish women had a significant advantage over the men which they utilized to enable them to perpetuate their traditions.

The men were not powerless per se, but rather working with new and difficult conditions. Some were active Judaizers and also made efforts to transmit their religion. At the same time, those who explained to the Tribunal that they had consented and allowed their wives to Judaize might have construed their declarations as still according them power; after all, what would these women have done without their consent? The truth is that these women did not necessarily need their permission. While there were cases of Judaizing women who desisted in observing because they had married Old Christians, such a decision might even have been expected, for why should these Old Christian husbands have tolerated such inexcusable heresy in their homes? Yet some of the converso men, being of the same Jewish ancestry as the women, might have been making one last attempt to retain a semblance of control by intimating that their consent was essential. However, there are sufficient examples of conversas who Judaized without their husbands' knowledge, and yet others who did so despite their spouses' objections, to seriously undermine the strength of this contention.

The façade of male power implicit in such statements was little more than that; these women, such as Constanza Núñez the matriarch, her daughter Juana, or any of numerous others, were, by and large, the guardians of crypto-Judaism. Whether they transmitted actual observances or contrived rebellious acts against the Church and its symbols, they were making a statement to all involved. Through such statements, their families were being exposed to the heritage of their forefathers, although the possibility that the Inquisition might learn of their proclivities had to be considered as well.

In the long run, many of the crypto-Jewish women opted to adapt to the realities of Spanish life; numerous female teachers remained active and devoted to successfully transmitting their heritage and, as can been seen, more often than not, ultimately had to face the Inquisition. But, as the Judaizing women themselves explained, the Inquisitors might have burned the parents, however their children survived and continued the tradition. Transmission of crypto-Judaism was indeed a life and death matter for these Judaizing women, yet they continued while they could, in bold defiance of both the Church and the Inquisition.

NOTES

1. There is a detailed discussion of "marranism" in the magnificent introduction of *From Spanish Court to Italian Ghetto, Isaac Cardoso: A Study in Seventeenth-Century Marranism and Jewish Apologetics* (New York, 1971) by Yosef Hayim Yerushalmi (in particular, 21–42).

2. Recent studies have drawn interesting conclusions about torture. For example, William Monter writes:

> Among the hoary myths surrounding the history of Spain's Holy Office, none is more difficult to eradicate than the fables about its refined and ferocious tortures. . . . The truth is that the Spanish Inquisition, like any self-respecting legal system in continental Europe, employed torture and sometimes wrung important confessions from prisoners under torture. But Lea long ago pointed out that the Spanish Inquisition used torture less frequently and less severely than secular courts. And it did not obtain many confessions this way; as he noted, Spain's Holy Office had more scientific methods for extracting admissions of guilt from its prisoners than such crude ordeals. Although most of the people whom the Spanish Inquisition tortured withstood it successfully, most of its prisoners either confessed without torture or were convicted by accumulated testimony. (*Frontiers of Heresy: The Spanish Inquisition from the Basque Lands to Sicily* [Cambridge, 1990], 74)

3. Haim Beinart provides valuable details concerning the inner workings of the court in his book, *Conversos on Trial: The Inquisition in Ciudad Real* (Jerusalem, 1981), 105–202.

4. See Renée Levine Melammed, "The Ultimate Challenge: Safeguarding the Crypto-Judaic Heritage," *Proceedings of the American Academy for Jewish Research* 53 (1986): 95.

5. See Joel L. Kraemer, "Spanish Ladies from the Cairo Geniza," *Mediterranean Historical Review* 6 (1991): 237–67. Kraemer has examples of letters, mostly from the sixteenth century, which were written in Hebrew and Judeo-Spanish by exiled women of Spain. Eleazer Gutwirth refers to Judeo-Spanish letters involving women in "The Family in Judeo-Spanish Genizah Letters of Cairo," *Vierteljahrschrift für Sozial-und Wirtschaftgeschichte* 73 (1986): 210–15. See David Nirenberg, "A Female Rabbi in Fourteenth-Century Zaragoza," *Sefarad* 51:1 (1991): 179–82, for a reference to a Spanish woman with an unusual role in the community.

6. Concrete examples of support provided by the Jewish community are discussed in a chapter in my forthcoming book.

7. The situation was far more complex than this. Unlike Portugal, Spain witnessed various waves of conversion of its Jews. The first in the series were the forced conversions of 1391. Jane Gerber estimates that as many as 100,000 converted at this time. See *The Jews of Spain* (New York, 1992), 113. On page 117 Gerber also claims that perhaps another 50,000 converted by 1415. Finally, there were those Jews who chose not to leave their homeland; Gerber on page 140 estimates this final wave of converts at 100,000. While some of these attempted to become devout Catholics, others never made the attempt. Yet others were discouraged by the very hostile reception that the "Old Christians" displayed toward all of their efforts to assimilate. In terms of crypto-Judaism, this meant that the converso population was quite diverse, acquiring new members both during the first twenty-five years of its existence and in 1492, after an entire century. These new members could be of great potential value for the Judaizer whose acquaintance with Judaism was apt to lose its grip.

8. Israël Salvator Révah stated that these women often observed without the knowledge of their husbands and children ("La religion d'Uriel da Costa, Marrane de Porto," *Revue de l'histoire des religion* 161 [1962]: 59). Brian S. Pullan contended that the data he found supports "the suggestion that secret Judaism was generally passed on by wives and mothers rather than husbands and fathers" ("The Inquisition and the Jews of Venice: The Case of Gaspare Ribeiro, 1580–1591," *Bulletin of the John Rylands Library* 62 [1979]: 230). Seymour Leibman wrote that "these women were stalwart defenders of their faith and bulwarks of strength to their husbands. If one were to measure degrees of orthodox observances, unquestionably the females would scale the highest" (*New World Jewry, 1493–1825: Requiem for the Forgotten* [New York, 1982], 71). See also Arnold Witznitzer, "Crypto-Jews in Mexico during the Seventeenth Century," in *The Jewish Experience in Latin America: Selected Studies from the Publications of the American Jewish Historical Society,* ed. Martin

Cohen, 2 vols. (Waltham, Mass., 1972), 1.177. The above is only a partial list of comments of this nature.

9. The reader should keep in mind the fact that many of the trials do not reveal information pertaining to transmission of tradition. Some defendants automatically included a description as to how they were indoctrinated when they confessed to having Judaized; others chose to protect their sources as some of these individuals were still alive at the time of the trial and obviously would be subject to arrest as well. Occasionally, interrogation provided this information, and sometimes witnesses included descriptions of learning processes.

10. For details including statistics for the years 1492–1520, see my "The Ultimate Challenge."

11. The trial, recorded and classified by file numbers as Legajo 165, no. 2, took place during the years 1530–1532, some forty-four years after these family members were reconciled. Among the collection of confessions found there are two that seem to be misplaced; one of them was given by a man with the same name as Juana's father, Rodrigo de Villarreal, which would explain the confusion. This might account for the fact that the confession of Juana's mother was not retrieved from the book of confessions from Alcázar. The scribes themselves noted that the aforementioned two confessants were not Juana's parents. The actual family situation is somewhat complicated, if only because the various testimonies did not provide information which would clarify matters. Constanza was married twice, the first time to Juan Núñez, *el mozo,* and the second time to Rodrigo de Villarreal, Juana's father. The female siblings mentioned are all named Núñez, which was also Constanza's surname. On the basis of the age differences involved, one assumes that they were Juana's half-sisters; on f. 12^r, Juana is also referred to as Núñez rather than Martínez, which actually makes more sense. The notarial script for these names are quite similar paleographically. The one brother is Fernando or Hernando de Villarreal, who specifically stated that Rodrigo de Villarreal was his step-father and that Juan Núñez was his father, f. 11^v. Perhaps his father died when he was an infant, explaining the fact that he took his step-father's name. Juana never provided the order of the siblings, which would have clarified matters considerably.

12. The sins of García de Alcala appear in the above order. He admitted that "algunas vezes consenti encender candiles a mi muger el viernes en la noche . . . que algunas vezes consenti a mi muger ayunar los ayunos de los judios y defendiselo algunas vezes y por no tener mala vida en my casa lo consenti . . . consenti a mi muger quytar el sevo a las carne e por no dar mala vida lo consentia . . . algunas vezes quando mi muger paria venia a mi casa la setena noche y dava las fruta agora dizen que son fadas . . . una vez fallesçio vna sobrina de my muger e fuemos alla e comimos en mesas baxas pescado e huevos. Peque que ayude avañar algunos muertos" (ff. 8^v–9^r. For discussions of *hadas,* see Renée Levine Melammed, "Noticias Sobre Los Ritos

de Los Nacimientos y de la Pureza de las Judeo-Conversas del Siglo XVI," *El Olivo* 13 (1989): 29–30. Regarding mourning, see my "Some Death and Mourning Customs of Castilian Conversas," in *Exile and Diaspora: Studies in the History of the Jewish People Presented to Professor Haim Beinart*, ed. Aaron Mirsky, Avraham Grossman, and Yosepf Kaplan (Jerusalem, 1991).

13. See my "Some Death and Mourning Customs" for explanations of this activity.

14. The wording is odd here: "Yten dixo que vido a su muger yr a demandar perdon el dia del ayuno mayor a su madre e a sus hermanas e a Pero Nunez zapatero e Diego Nunez sus hermanos e a la de Garcia de Alcala zapatero e a Juana Martinez muger de Alvar Gracia zapatero vecinos de Alcaçar" (fol. 10^{v}). Since the last two mentioned, Juan and la de Garcia or María, were his wife's sisters, perhaps there were additional sisters in the family who were not mentioned in the trial.

15. Benito admitted to sinning "en consentir a mi muger ençender candiles los viernes en las noches algunas vezes . . . en que guarde algunos sabados y en el dia vesti ropas linpias. Digo mi culpa en que peque que comi guisado del viernes para el sabado e lo consenti a mi muger de todo pido penitencia . . . ayune ayunos de judios espeçial el ayuno mayor e pedi perdon en este dia e otros a mi algunas vezes . . . en que consenti quitar el sevo a la carne y lo quite e comi carne degollada de mano de judios algunas vezes . . . algunas vezes di limosnas a judios espeçial que di para azeite a sus sinogas . . . me halle adonde avia algund finado e lo vañavan lo ayude avañar . . . quando my padre fallesçio que ponia mesa linpia en las noches e una taça de agua demando penitencia dello ençendia vn candil . . . algunas vezes comi adonde avia finados e mesas baxas pescado e huevos . . . dizen que es coguerço . . . quando mi muger paria la setenta noche venian a mi casa parientas e parientes e comian fruta e çenavan siguiente dizen que son fadas . . . dexe de comer cosas vedadas por la ley de moysen . . . Peque en que en todo lo susodicho fue consentidor a mi muger la qual es defunta. Peque en que todas estas cosas fize por cerimonia de la ley de moysen" (ff. 9^{v}–10^{r}). The addition included statements such as "dixo que en su confesion que vido a su muger fazer muchas cerimonyas de la ley de Moysen lo qual es muerta especialmente guysar el viernes para el sabado ençender candiles guardar los sabados oyr oraciones judaycas quytar el sevo a la carne ayunar el ayuno mayor e otras cosas" (fol. 10^{v}).

16. Mari confessed: "Peque en que algunos viernes ençendi candiles mas temprano que otras noches. Peque en que algunas vezes guise el viernes para el sabado e comi dello. Peque en que algunos sabados folgue mas por la voluntad que no por la obra e vesti ropas limpias e di limosna a judios. Peque en que algunas vezes comy carne degollada de mano de judios e quite el sevo a la carne. Peque en que ayune algunos ayunos de los judios espeçial el ayuno mayor e en tal dia pedi perdon . . . folgue algunas pascuas de los judios espeçial la pascua del pan çençeno e lo comi . . . que quando paria a

la setena noche fazia fadas . . . comi en mortuorios en mesas baxas pescado e huevos e me dezian que hera coguerço. Digo mi culpa que quando mi madre me tenia en su casa me amostrava que si tuviese algunas criaturas que les pusiese la mano en la cabeça e no las santiguase . . . Peque que quando amasava echava un pedaço de masa en el fuego e ayude avañar e amortajar algunos muertos los quales cosas hazia en la ley de moysen pensando que por hazer ellas me avia de salvar" (ff. 7^v–8^r).

17. Pero (Pedro) is referred to as Núñez, so his father was Juan. Hernando pointed out (f. 12^r) that Pedro was "su hermano de parte de los parientes de su madre y padre" and that Rodrigo de Villarreal was his stepfather. Marí and Elvira and Juana are also listed as sisters, but Diego is not mentioned by name. On April 14, 1486, Fernando specified "que seyendo moço e de poca hedad en casa de la dicha mi madre me mando que guardase las cosas de la ley de Moysen y que por aquello me avia de salvar" (f. 11^v). In 1530, he said "que hizo las dichas cosas de la ley de moysen que tiene confesadas desde el principio que la dicha su madre se las avezo en casa de la dicha su madre que entonçes bivia en vna tienda de Rodrigo de Villa Real su marido . . . asimesmo las hizo en casa de Pero Nunes su hermano . . . Dixo que en casa de su madre deste declarante que hizieron juntamente las dichas cosas que tiene confesadas de la ley de moysen este declarante y la dicha su madre y Rodrigo de Villa Real su padrasto deste declarante y todas sus hermanas Marí Nuñes y Elvira Nuñes y Juana Nuñez" (f. 12^r). Again, this Juana is apparently the defendant.

18. Because she was the defendant, her confession appeared first in this dossier. Juana stated that "desde seyendo nyña en casa de la dicha my madre donde agora estoy la dicha my madre me ynpuso e fixo entender que guardase la ley de moysen haziendome entender que aquello hera la verdad e por aquello me avia de salvar e yo pensando ser ansi erre e peque. Digo my culpa. Peque en que guarde algunos sabados e vesti ropas linpias en algunos dellos e ençendi candil linpio viernes en la noche e guyse de comer el viernes para el sabado e comi. Peque que guarde algunas pascuas de judios espeçial la del pan çençeno e lo comi e ayune algunos ayunos de judios espeçial el ayuno mayor e pedi pardon a otros e quite el sevo a la carne e la pella de la masa e la eche en el fuego e comi carne degollada por mano de judio e dexe de comer toçino e carnes e pescados defendidos en la ley de moysen algunas veses e quebrante domyngos e fiestas mandados guardar por la Santa Yglesia e en quaresmas e en otros dias vedados por ella comy carne e queso y leche y huevos algunos vezes. . . . Las quales cosas yo hecho vi años a este parte poco mas o menos hasta que el edicto se leyo en Alcaçar e todo por la ley de moysen no creyendo la ley de Ihesu Christo. . . . Vi a mi madre hazer todas las cosas por my fechas" (f. 3^r–3^v). Juana listed the Catholic precepts that she had abrogated as well, also taught to her by her mother.

19. Juana explained "que ansi lo hizo esta declarante por consejo de su madre . . . todas las cosas que confiesa aver fecho de la qual la dicha su

madre la ynpuso. . . . Preguntada con que personas holgava e guardava los dichos sabados dixo que con la dicha su madre e que no se acuerda holgarlos con otra persona alguna e que los holgava en casa de la dicha su madre. . . . Dixo que lo comia con la dicha su madre . . . e que esta declarante ençenderia por mandado de la dicha su madre los dichos candiles e que tambien se los vio ençender a la dicha su madre" (f. 14^r–14^v).

20. Juana did not recall many of the specifics of her observance nor did she know the reasons for them. Nevertheless, concerning Passover, she stated: "Dixo que con su madre e con sus hermanas las guardo en casa de la dicha su madre que se venian las dichas sus hermanas alli a holgar . . . Fue preguntada con que personas comio el dicho pan çençeno juntamente. Dixo que con la dicha su madre e con sus hermanas e siendo preguntada dixo que no se acuerda si su hermano comio del dicho pan çençeno. . . . Preguntada con que personas hizo el dicho ayuno mayor. Dixo que con las dichas sus hermanas Mari Nuñez y Elvira Nuñez y con la dicha su madre e que las dichas sus hermanas se venyan aquel dia del dicho ayuno a casa de la dicha su madre y se estavan todo el dia alli y comian juntas" (ff. 14^v–15^r).

21. After being warned for the third time, Juana mentioned Benito and García (f. 19^v).

22. In this interrogation, Juana was asked "si los maridos de las dichas sus hermanas si comian aquel dia juntamente con las dichas sus mugeres e con esta declarante e con su madre. Dixo que no comian" (f. 15^r). "Preguntada con que personas comio aquella carne degollada de mano de judios. Dixo que con sus hermanas e con su madre la comio y que la comieron en casa de la dicha su madre" (f. 15^v). "Dixo que su madre e las dichas sus hermanas que se venian a casa de la dicha su madre los holgavan juntamente e no los vio holgar a otras personas algunas. . . . Dixo que les (a Mari Nunez y Elvira Nunez) vido ençender los dichos candiles de la manera que le ha sydo preguntado los dichos viernes en las noches ansi en sus casas como en casa de la dicha su madre. . . . Dixo que si holgavan ansi en sus casas como en casa de la dicha su madre e aderesçavan sus casas aquellas dichas noches e los mesmo hazia en casa de la dicha su madre los dichos viernes en las noches . . . si sabe que las ynpuso en ellas la dicha su madre como ynpuso esta declarante. Dixo que si" (f. 16^r–16^v).

23. This too was of interest to the Inquisitors. "Preguntada como lo sabe. Dixo que porque todas platicavan como lo hazian por la ley de Moysen" (f. 16^v).

24. Since he was still very much alive, one cannot be certain if she was protecting him or not, yet she was adamant that he was not a Judaizer. "Dixo que nunca ella vido hazer ny dezir el dicho su marido cosa nynguna juntamente contra la fee . . . el dicho su marido nunca le vido fazer cosa nynguna juntamente con esta declarante ni con las otras personas" (ff. 17^v–18^r). There is a notation on the top of f. 17^v that indicates that this was a copy of a statement made in the trial of Juana's father; in addition, the heading of

the page states that this entry was intended for the proceedings of Alvar García. As it turns out, there are no extant records of the trial of Fernando, but there are records of the trial from 1530–1531 of a converso named Alvar García de Alcazar who was condemned. He too was a cobbler, but his residence was listed as Madridejos rather than Alcázar de Consuegra which seems rather odd since all the other data corresponds to that of Juana's husband; whether or not this defendant was from Juana's family has yet to be ascertained. Later in Juana's trial, the Inquisitors tried to discern if Alvar had prompted her or her brother prior to their court appearances: "Preguntada sy le dixo el dicho su marido e la mando que si la llamasen los Ynquisidores e la preguntasen alguna cosa que dixese e respondiese que no se acordava de nada e que se refierese a su reconciliaçion. Dixo que si dixo a esta declarante e a su hermano Hernando de Villarreal diziendoles que se remitiesen a sus confesiones e que dixesen que no se acordavan de nada y que quando se lo dixo estavan solos" (f. 19^{v}).

25. On July 3, 1530, Juana stated that she "se acuerda que Rodrigo de Villarreal su padre y el dicho Hernando de Villarreal su hermano hazian juntamente con la dicha su madre y hermanas y con esta declarante todas las cosas que tiene declarados en su confesion" (f. 19^{r}). On September 15, Juana contradicted herself: "Dixo que nunca vido hazer el dicho su padre cosa que fuese contra Santa Fe Catholic" (f. 21^{r}). But on September 17, she returned to her earlier contention: "es verdad lo que primero tenia dicho de como su padre e su hermano Fernando de Villarreal hazian juntamente con la dicha su madre e hermanas e con esta declarante las cosas que tiene confesadas en su reconçiliacion y que esta es la verdad y que en ello se afirma" (f. 21^{r}). As has been ascertained, Rodrigo de Villarreal was being tried posthumously at the same time that Juana and Fernando were on trial. Surprisingly enough, Rodrigo was absolved; see Leg. 188, (old) no. 85.

26. An example of this was washing off the infant by conversos, their debaptizing ceremony, which followed the ceremony of baptism required by the Catholic Church.

27. Haim Beinart included a chapter in *Conversos,* 286–99, entitled "The Attitude of the Conversos of Ciudad Real to Christianity and Their Outlook on Life and Death." Although I have used as examples the stances of two conversas that he already discussed here, (Catalina de Zamora and María González), our emphases differ enough to merit additional analysis.

28. In the arraignment of Juan de Fez and his wife Catalina Gómez, the latter, a seamstress, was charged with sewing "algunos domingos fasta ora de comer e que tanbien xabonaua sus tocas e lauaua camisas a sus fijos los que criaua." See Haim Beinart, *Records of the Trials of the Spanish Inquisition in Ciudad Real,* 4 vols. (Jerusalem, 1974), 1.184. María Alonso was also charged with working on Sundays and holidays (227). Leonor de la Higuera was seen resting on the Jewish Sabbath, but sewing and engaging in light chores on Sundays (*Records,* 2.142).

29. The conversation was recorded in *Records,* 2.24. The witness and her husband stayed at this home and questioned the hostess about her actions. Marina replied: "Ay, señora prima, que sy no fuese por mi trabajo, segund Francisco es floxo y no sabe ganar, no me podra valer ni tenia para casar mi hija."

30. The standard formulation for being charged with such rebellious activity can be found in the trial of María Alonso (*Records,* 1.227) as follows: "Yten, que comio carne e huevos en Quaresma e en otros dias vedados por la Santa Madre Yglesia syn neçesidad ni cabsa para ello, en menospreçio de nuestra Fe e siguiendo la dicha Ley de Moysen."

31. The sentence of Marina González included "que non se santiguava ni sinaua ni fasia ningun señal de christiana" (*Records,* 1.312).

32. The sentence of Isabel, wife of Lope de la Higuera, began similarly but expanded upon her sins, for she did not "se santiguaua ni fasia señales de christiana ni yva a Misa ni a oyr otros Ofiçios Divinos" (*Records,* 1.360).

33. See, for example, the witness testimony in *Records,* 2.164, in which the González sisters were reported to have prayed "e que nunca les oyo nonbrar en aquellas oraçiones el Nonbre de Ihesus ni de Santa Maria, syne a Señor del mundo." In the trial of María Alvarez of Guadalajara, a similar statement appeared: "Non creyendo (en) la santa Yglesia nin fee Christiana; non nonbrava el nonbre de Ihesus nin de Santa Maria, creyendo como judio que por ello pecava" (Leg. 134, no. 5 [1492–93]). A third example of a conversa with such a stance is Isabel de los Olivos y López. One prosecution witness testified as follows: "E que nunca los oyo nonbrar Ihesu Christo ni Santa Maria ni Nonbre de Ihesus ni nonbre de ningund santo ni santa, ni tenian ymagen de Nuestro Señor ni de Nuestra Señora ni de otro santo ni santa en el dicho palaçio, ni los oyo dezir palabra de las que los christianos dizen quando rezan o leen cosas de nuestra Santa Fe" (*Records,* 2.552).

34. See the witness testimony in the trial of María González: "E que algunas vezes hablavan en las cosas de la Yglesia e de la Fe, e hazian burla de la Misa. E que sabe que las susodichas no creyan en la Misa, no yban syno por conplir, que no por yr a Misa, y asy lo hazia este confesante y este confesante a ellas, y lo comunicavan con otras, teniendolo por burla las cosas de la Misa y de la Fe. E que sabe que todas las susodichas se hazian muchas vezes malas por no yr a Misa" (*Records,* 2.389).

35. For example, Juana Núñez was reported to have chatted with a fellow conversa "sy platicaban algunas cosas que fuesen contra la fee, diziendo que la ley de Muysen hera la buena, escarneçiendo e burlando de la Fee" (*Records,* 2.494–95). Likewise, María Díaz was said to have "faser ningund abto ny solepnidad a las cosas de nuestra Santisima Fe ny a lo que somos obligados a la Santa Madre Yglesia, mas antes faser burla e echarnio [*sic*] de todo, demandando vengança a Dios de sus enemigos los christianos." This term should be escarnio, or ridicule (*Records,* 1.58).

36. "Dexé mi casa e mis fijos e mi honra por la honra que he ganado con este mal honbre por aquellos santos de palo que estan en aquella yglesia." For further details, see Francisco Cantera Burgos and Carlos Carrete Parrondo, "Las Juderías Medievales en la Provincia de Guadalajara," *Sefarad* 34 (1974): 316–17.

37. This is reported by Francisco Cantera Burgos and Carlos Carrete Parrondo, "La Judería de Hita," *Sefarad* 32 (1972): 264; her trial (Legajo 156, no. 9) took place between 1538 to 1539. Interestingly enough, there are precedents from earlier periods for this type of behavior on the part of the Jewish community. For attitudes towards pagan statues, images, and gods, see the *Mishnah,* Tractate Avoda Zara, chapters 3–4, especially the story of Rabban Gamliel and Aphrodite in the bathhouse, chap. 3:4. See too Saul Lieberman, *Hellenism in Jewish Palestine* (New York, 1962), 115–27.

38. In the arraignment of this trial transcribed in *Records,* 1.369, the following appears: "Que judayso, heretico e apostato yendo contra los articulos de nuestra Santa Fe en grand desonra e menospreçio della, espeçialmente, disiendo e negando la virginidad de Nuestra Señora la Virgen Maria, e disiendo della ave seydo ensangrentada; yten, llamandola e disiendola que era vna puta; yten, quando pasaua por las yglesias hedificadas en honra e veneraçion de Nuestra Señora la Gloriosa Virgen Maria, daua pugeres e higas contra ellas por se llamara e ser hedificadas en Su Nonbre." The witness testimonies describing the details of her comments appear later (1.388–89). See also Beinart, *Conversos,* 287 and 295, for references to Catalina.

39. This act was done in the presence of a number of people (*Records,* 2.253). The charge of the prosecutor (248) stated: "Iten, que la dicha Mari Gonsales, como infiel e no creyendo nuestra Santa Fe Catholica e en vituperio della, vna vez, dandole vna tabla en que estaua pintada la ymagen de Nuestra Señora la Virgen Maria, ella la tomo, e como la ovo tornada, con burla y escarnio que de la hizo, la arrojo en vn albañar muy suzio que estaua cabe la cozina, e despues de asi echada la dicha ymagen, la escopio."

40. Beatriz had this conversation in 1514, although the proceedings against her did not begin until 1536. In Leg. 177, no. 4 (1536–1563), the following testimony was recorded: "La dicha comadre dixo, 'Quieren nos mal los cristianos viejos por que mediamos pues no les quitamos los suyo; mas el dio lo fablo por su boca que quiso mucho a esta ley e dixo judio ojo mio.'"

41. One testimony appears in *Records,* 1.394: "Estas carnes y el cuerpo bien puede ser que padescan marterisado, mas el coraçon esta con el Señor que lo crio." The Old Christian–New Christian tensions also emerged in these testimonies. Another witness reported that when a group of well-dressed conversas had walked by, an Old Christian neighbor commented, "Vistos estos diablos de conversas, que luçidas y que galanas que van?" Catalina did not let the comment pass, but returned, put her hand on the

speaker's shoulder and said to her, "Callad, que bendita es esta simiente de Muysen" (1.391); see also *Conversos,* 298.

42. In Leg. 154, no. 33 (1486, 1500), the statement appeared "que aunque quemasen los Inquisidores a los padres ay quedavan los hijos."

43. The fullest description was given in 1511 by Maria Ruyz who stated that about twenty years earlier, the defendant said that "su marido, e otros que con el fueron quemados por la Ynquisiçion aquella sazon, auian muerto martires, e que el dicho Pero Dias de Villaruuia, su marido, despues de quemado auia venido vna noche a la cama donde estaua acostada e que se le auia hechado en el braço como vn niño de dos años hermoso . . . e que vio e oyo este testigo como la dicha muger de Pero Dias dixo a vn frayle del dicho monasterio que dixese dos misas por el anima del dicho Pero Dias, su marido, diziendo que avia muerto martir" (*Records,* 2.208). Pedro Díaz was condemned to death seven years earlier. Another witness referred to the dream as well "e que le avia pareșçido como vn angel, e que como se puso a miralle, que se desapareșçio, e que lo que este testigo pudo conprehender de sus palabras fue que quiso hazer entender a este testigo que el dicho su marido auia sydo martir" (2.206). This witness estimated that the dream had taken place in 1509, two years prior to this court appearance. In 1484, Diego Ruíz stated that the defendant had claimed that her husband was not a heretic "mas que le auian muerto a sin razon con testigos falsos que juraron la mentira e no dixeron la verdad" (2.212); see also *Conversos,* 297–98. Beinart claims that she was naive, particularly because she requested that masses be recited for the soul of her husband, who had been declared to be a heretic, but that "this in no way minimizes the general trend of her outlook and her dreams." He then presents additional examples of others who viewed the victims of the Inquisition as martyrs (see *Conversos,* 298 n. 49. While María might have lacked cunning, her attitude was not unique and was part of a psychological mechanism created within converso society for dealing with the fate of the Judaizers.

11

Relations between Conversos and Old Christians in Early Modern Toledo: Some Different Perspectives

LINDA MARTZ

THROUGHOUT THE FIFTEENTH and sixteenth centuries, the most familiar aspects of relations between conversos and the majority Old Christian community in the city of Toledo are all negative, with near constant hostility directed against the new converts from Judaism. In the fifteenth century two attempts were made to remove conversos from their municipal offices and their church benefices by the enactment of pure blood statutes, first in 1449 and again in 1467.[1] Prompted in part by indignation over converso success in attaining positions of influence and power, many conversos were also accused of crypto-Judaism.[2] Neither of these statutes succeeded in permanently removing conversos from their posts or, apparently, in encouraging them to become more faithful believers in Christianity. These tasks were left to the last and most brutal blow of the fifteenth century, the Inquisition, far more effective in convincing most conversos that they would have to become sincere practitioners of Christianity if they planned to stay in the Crown of Castile. Installed in the city of Toledo in 1485, the Inquisition was not, of course, unique to any one city or place, but rather a nationwide institution.

Even the Inquisition did not permanently remove conversos from positions of authority, nor was its ominous presence adequate to dispel the distrust and resentment harbored by many toward a minority of overachievers. Evidence for these conclusions is provided by the two pure blood statutes imposed in the sixteenth century. One was foisted upon the Toledo cathedral chapter in 1547 by cardinal-archbishop Juan Martínez Silíceo, and in 1566 the crown attempted to impose a statute on the citizen's bench of the Toledo city council.[3] These statutes were no more effective than those of the fifteenth century in removing conversos from their posts, but some changes are evident in the sixteenth-century edicts. One is that the 1547 statute gained approval from both the crown and the papacy, a dramatic reversal of the policy adopted in 1449. Another notable change is that no one accused the conversos of Judaizing, a charge the rabid anti-converso Cardinal Silíceo surely would have leveled had it been applicable. Justification for their exclusion was based upon undesirable personality traits, occupations, lineage, and other sins inherited from ancestors.

Based upon all these exclusionary actions, it might be concluded that contacts between conversos and Old Christians were characterized by unremitting animosity, polarization, and distrust. But the relationship between the two groups is complex and not subject to easy analysis or simple generalizations. Conclusions vary, depending upon what documents are used and what sphere of life is being discussed. By focusing exclusively on Inquisition documents, one can construct a world of continued Judaizing and isolation, but in other areas contacts and interaction between the two groups are numerous. This is true in the world of finance, manufacturing, and commerce, dominated in large part by conversos. It is also true of the local ecclesiastical and political institutions, where conversos were abundantly represented as parish priests, chaplains, and cathedral canons or, in politics, as *regidores* (city councilors) or *jurados,* members of a nonvoting auxiliary governing council.

Another factor that affects conclusions about contacts between the two groups is the social status, occupation, and marriage patterns of the individuals included in the discussion. Despite all the pure blood statutes, and surely one of the factors contributing to them, in fifteenth-century Toledo there was a fair amount of intermarriage between conversos and Old Christians, at least among the upper levels of society, as wealthy conversos prominent in the royal bureaucracy married into the Castilian aristocracy.[4] Among the Toledo elites, in addition to the traditional division between conversos and Old Christians, it is useful to add yet another category to encompass those of mixed origin. Most of the men who appear here are upwardly mobile merchants, tax-farmers, and entrepreneurs who attained prominence only in the sixteenth century. Some invested a portion of their considerable fortunes in purchasing an office of *regidor* in Toledo, but a few were prominent in the church. While some of their ancestors had been punished by the Inquisition, they managed to escape contact with the Holy Office, at least for charges of Judaizing. As far as such matters can be determined, they are not of mixed origin but unadulterated conversos.

To delve a bit more deeply into the muddy waters of relations between conversos and the majority population, I would like to depart from the pure blood statutes of the cathedral and the city council and focus on some different facets of life, primarily in the post-Inquisition period. Loosely connected with the ecclesiastical sphere, these are matters not usually considered in the question of contacts between the two ethnic groups: parishes, burial chapels, and female religious institutions.

PARISHES AND BURIAL CHAPELS

Certain geographic areas of the city, delimited in this period by parishes, were favored by conversos. These preferred parishes can be determined on the basis of a document compiled by the Inquisition in 1495–97, when some conversos who had been punished in earlier years paid to have certain penalties commuted.[5] It should be emphasized that not all Toledo conversos appear in this document, but the number of those who did and the parishes where they lived are given in Table 1. As the table demonstrates, conversos lived in all the parishes of the city but were more heavily concentrated in some parishes than others. The figures for the ten parishes with the heaviest converso concentration are included in a map of the city, which graphically illustrates the preferred converso living area.[6] Stretching from the parishes of Santo Tomé and San Martín in the southwestern edge of the city northward to the parishes of Santa Leocadia, San Vicente, and San Nicolás, it appears that conversos avoided the southeastern area and the northern parish of Santiago.

Some areas of converso concentration in 1495–97 are a reflection of the location of the old Jewish quarters, also indicated in the map. The Judería Mayor, surrounded by walls and gates, was located in the

Table 1: Parish Distribution of Some Toledo Conversos and Amount Paid to the Inquisition, 1495–97[1]

Number of Persons Listed		Total Amount Collected (mrs)	
1. Tomé	310	1. Juan Bautista	792,500
2. Román	235	2. Vicente	518,600
3. Vicente	191	3. Tomé	446,100
4. Pedro	168	4. Nicolás	389,900
5. Nicolás	147	5. Román	345,700
6. Leocadia	132	6. Pedro	338,200
7. Juan Bautista	122	7. Ginés	201,000
8. M. Magdalena	77	8. Leocadia	190,100
9. Ginés	58	9. M. Magdalena	77,600
10. Salvador	53	10. Salvador	63,900
11. Justa	26	11. Miguel	50,200
12. Justo	23	12. Justa	42,000
13. Antolín y Soles	21	13. Justo	32,300
14. Miguel	19	14. Antolín y Soles	26,200
15. Andrés	10	15. Cristóbal	17,100
16. Cristóbal	9	16. Olalla	9,000
17. Olalla	6	17. Andrés	6,200
18. Santiago	4	18. Cebrián	5,500
19. Cebrián	4	19. Marcos	500
20. Lorenzo	2	20. Lorenzo	300
21. Marcos	2	21. Santiago	300
Total	1,619	Total	3,553,200

[1]The figures are taken from the F. Cantera Burgos, "Prólogo", *JAT,* xxvi, xxxi–ii. The numbers given on this chart do not total the 1,640 people given by the author on page xxx, and I have not arrived at the same figures for some of the parishes with the greatest number of conversos. However, it is extremely difficult to arrive at accurate totals since the names of some individuals appear to be repeated and in some cases the number of children are not specified (sus hijos or hijos de). The figures in the first column are best seen as close estimates, a generalization that applies to most of the figures of this period. At this time, the parish of San Juan Bautista was known as San Juan de la Leche.

THE CITY OF TOLEDO

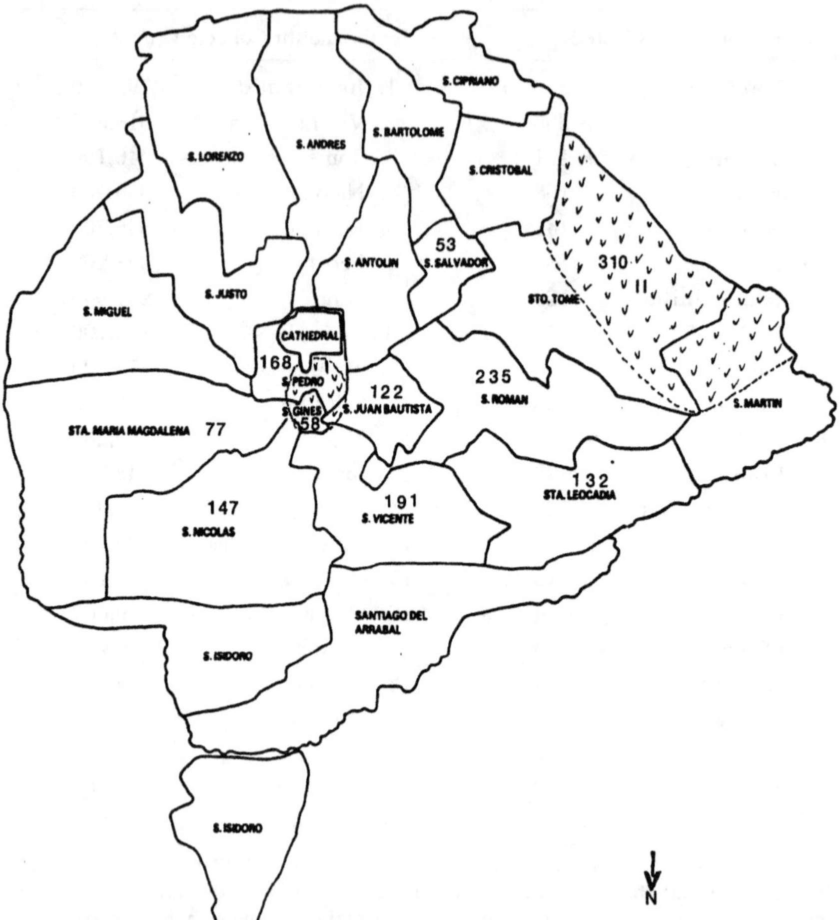

Ten parishes preferred by conversos, 1495–97
I = Judería Menor II = Judería Mayor

parishes of Santo Tomé and San Martín.[7] After the expulsion of the Jews in 1492, this area was renamed Barrio Nuevo or the new neighborhood, but it still conserves the remnants of two synagogues, Santa María la Blanca, converted to a Christian church in 1411 when St. Vicent Ferrer visited the city, and El Tránsito, built by the treasurer of Pedro the Cruel, Samuel Levi, and given by the Catholic monarchs to the military order of Calatrava. While Santo Tomé was the most heavily populated of the city parishes, unfortunately, since the parish population is unknown until 1561, it is impossible to say how many people resided there in earlier years.[8] It housed a heterogenous population, ranging from the Count of Fuensalida, one of the aristocrats who controlled the city's politics, to more humble tailors, spinners, and weavers. A smaller area that housed many Jews as well as other citizens, the Judería Menor, was located in the center of the city, to the north of the cathedral, overlapping into the small parishes of San Pedro, San Ginés, and San Juan Bautista.[9] In 1495–97, this area registered a sizeable number of conversos. The Judería Menor was not enclosed by walls, and in 1355 and again in 1391, many Jews who lived here were massacred or forcibly baptized, while those in the Judería Mayor were able to keep out the attackers and save their lives thanks to the protection afforded by gates and walls.

Another factor that may have contributed to the preference of some parishes over others was a desire to be near the city's business, commercial, and financial centers, since conversos played an active role in these activities. The main plaza of the city, known as Zocodover, in the parish of Santa María Magdalena, was a hub of commerce, exchange, and small businesses, as were most of the streets leading from this area to the southwest. However, accessibility to commerce and trade is not the only explanation, as some popular converso parishes such as Santa Leocadia and San Román were quieter, largely residential areas. The most important consideration in determining the living quarters of the vast majority of the converso population was probably a simple matter of money, as it was obviously cheaper to remain in an ancestral home than to move to a new house or parish.

Since the Inquisition document of 1495–97 also includes the amount of money paid by adults, children, groups of children, or grandchildren, an estimate of the comparative wealth of the converso community in each parish can be calculated. (See Table 1). The parochial ranking based on wealth is distinct from that based on density of population. The returns from the four parishes that yielded the greatest amount of money, San Juan Bautista, San Vicente, Santo Tomé, and San Nicolás, suggest that they harbored the greatest number of wealthy conversos. I want to focus on three of these parishes, San Juan Bautista, San Nicolás and San Vicente, for many years favored by prosperous merchants. In the interests of simplification, they are called here the three converso parishes, which is not to say that they are the only parishes that housed conversos, or that only conversos lived in these three parishes.

The later years of the fifteenth century witnessed the beginnings of a religious reform in many areas of the Crown of Castile. A portion of this reform centered upon strengthening the parish, to be achieved in part by expanding the duties and responsibilities of the parish priests. In Toledo, this is evident in the 1497 and 1498 diocesan legislation of Archbishop Francisco Jiménez de Cisneros, which exhorted parish priests to undertake a variety of tasks.[10] They were to keep records of their parishioners' confessions and to inform their superiors of any public or secret crimes worthy of correction; to keep parish baptismal records, as well as a list of all their parishioners and the names of those who lived in each household; and to indoctrinate the children in their charge in the Christian faith. To assist them in this latter task, a new catechism, "Table of what must be taught to the children," was published in 1498. As envisioned by Cisneros, the parish priests were to serve as a network of informers, catechizers, and spiritual and secular supervisors. Much of the Cisnerian reform program was implemented in the Toledo parish of San Vicente, where baptismal records survive from this period,[11] and the parish priest, Lope Fernández de Angulo, reported in 1507 that one of his parishioners, the merchant Francisco de Santo Domingo, gave alms to the needy, confessed and took the sacrament on a yearly basis, and that his children and slaves had been baptized and catechized in the parish school.[12] It is doubtful that the parish priests of the city of Toledo, or those of any area where Cisneros spent much time, such as Madrid or Alcalá de Henares, could ignore the dictates of so forceful a prelate, although in the suffragan bishopric of Cuenca the reforms of this period appear to be minimal at best.[13]

If the parish took on added significance in the daily lives of most citizens, for those punished by the Inquisition it was surely even more pronounced. For any converso who chose to stay on in the city, performance of Christian duties—attendance at mass, confession, and communion—was mandatory. For those of substance, other obligations included the giving of alms to the church and the poor, membership in a parochial confraternity, and the endowment of masses and chapels. Parish priests frequently appeared as character witnesses when Inquisitors were judging a case of dubious converso activity, and their judgments carried some weight. The testimony of Lope Fernández de Angulo cited above was given at an Inquisition hearing, and there are many other examples of parish priests testifying for or against an individual being prosecuted by the Inquisition.[14]

To insinuate that conversos performed parochial duties merely to maintain appearances for vigilant parish priests or Inquisitors is inaccurate. After the family and household, the parish where one lived was vital in providing a sense of identity, place, and community in a frequently fragmented society. Here one's children were baptized and confirmed, a suitable spouse might be found, daughters were officially married by the church, and many were buried. Membership in parish confraternities also contributed to communal involvement, although most men of means also belonged to one of the larger brotherhoods that offered charitable assistance on a citywide basis. In the three converso parishes, identity was enhanced by daily contact with relatives and others of similar ethnic origin, customs, and occupations. In the parish of San Vicente from 1500 to 1589, three parish priests appear to have been conversos: Lope Fernández de Angulo, Juan Farinas, and the best-known, Luis Hurtado, who wrote an extremely valuable chronicle of the city in 1576.[15] It is likely that the parish priests of all three parishes were conversos since who would be better qualified to judge the orthodoxy of converso parishioners?

Most churches of the city were constantly remodeled throughout the sixteenth century, in part to accommodate the numerous burial chapels founded in these years.[16] The unavailability of church records deters efforts to determine exactly how many burial chapels existed in Toledo at any one date, but by the end of the sixteenth century they numbered in the hundreds and could be found in all the city's many churches, including those of the regular orders, the parishes, the cathedral, and other pious places such as hospitals. The proliferation of burial chapels in parish churches might be explained in part by feelings of pride and identity with a neighborhood institution, not to mention the challenge of keeping up with, or surpassing, other parish churches. In addition, keeping a chapel close to home conferred a certain amount of control and oversight to the founder and his family, and familiarity with the parish priest and fellow parishioners offered some degree of hope that one's wishes would be respected and that the foundation would indeed last into perpetuity. Yet another enticement was that in some cases a chapel in a parish church was less expensive than one founded in a church of a regular religious order.

The enthusiasm for founding burial chapels may be explained by the many purposes they served. Most obviously they were built as a tribute to the glory of God and the Catholic faith, and as a means of assisting the donor's soul to reach his or her final resting place as quickly and as comfortably as possible. Burial chapels were as well visible symbols of the founder's prestige and social status: in addition to works of art, coats-of-arms usually adorned the chapel, in some cases iron screens kept out unwanted visitors, and frequently plaques recorded the deeds of the founder, and at times his ancestors, and the amount of money left for the celebration of masses and other spiritual obligations. Chapels were also a means of promoting and preserving the family name, lineage, and achievements, and they provided a focus for family unity and continuity. Aside from enjoying a special burial place, future generations could enjoy the much admired privilege of patronage by appointing a family member as chaplain and the eldest son as patron.

Among the parishes, the three converso parishes certainly ranked among the highest in terms of the number of burial chapels that embellished the churches, a reflection of the number of wealthy parishioners who could afford such a luxury. By the end of the sixteenth century, little space remained in any of the three churches for the construction of new chapels. The number of burial chapels in each of these churches in the late sixteenth century, as well as the names of either the founders or patrons and, where available, the advocation, are given in Table 2. The parishes of San Nicolás and San Vicente each boasted eleven family burial chapels. The parish church of San Juan Bautista was smaller than the other two, but the scantiness of information about this parish raises doubts as to whether the

Table 2: Burial Chapels in Three Toledo Parishes, 1576–1585[1]

San Juan Bautista: 1576 (Names of Founders)

1. Sancho de Toledo	5. Hernández
2. Ortiz	6. Herrera
3. Palma	7. Vaca de Herrera
4. San Pedro	8. López de Sevilla

San Nicolás: 1585 (Advocation and Patrons)

1. Reyes—Dr. Arroyo
2. Santiago—Juan Sánchez de Canales
3. Nra. Sra. Concepción—Sancho de Moncada, El Viejo & jurado Sancho de Moncada
4. Nra. Sra. Encarnación—ex-patron Bartolomé de Alarcón, and patrons Diego y Gonzalo de la Palma y consortes
5. Nra. Sra. Ascención—Licenciado Pabón, cleric
6. Descendimiento de la Cruz—Alonso de Montalbán
7. Crucifijo, in front of the high altar—Luis Hurtado
8. Crucifijo, under the tribune—Matia Romano, Gaspar de San Martín, García de Ruyloba, Tristán Sánchez Cota, Juan de Herrera, Fernando Alvarez de Toledo.
9. Trinidad—Francisco Ramírez de Montalbán
10. Unknown—Juan Pérez de Villareal
11. S. Bernardo—Tomás Gaitán de Ribera

(2 chapels of confraternities: La Concepción and Las Animas)

San Vicente: 1576 (Advocation, Patrons, Some Founders)

1. Santiago—Juan Torre de la Fuente
2. Espíritu Santo—Regidor Francisco Sánchez de Toledo
3. Nra. Sra. Asunción—Jurado Alonso de Cisneros
4. Piedad—Lorenzo Suárez de Robles
5. S. Ildefonso—Juan de la Fuente Hurtado
6. Nra. Sra. Visitación—Garcí Sánchez de las Cuentas
7. Tránsito—Alonso Díaz de la Cruz & Francisco de Villamayor
8. S. Antón—Luis de Fuensalida
9. Nra. Sra. Esperanza—Vayllos
10. Dos San Juanes—Lope Fernández de Angulo

Table 2 continued on next page

Table 2 *continued*

San Vicente: 1576 (Advocation, Patrons, Some Founders) *continued*
11. Unknown—Luis Hurtado, parish priest and author
(1 chapel of confraternity: Las Animas)

1. Sources: San Juan Bautista, Hurtado, "Memorial," 532. San Nicolás, Archivo de la Parroquia de San Nicolás, leg. 13, doc. 5, in Mario Arellano García, "La Iglesia de San Nicolás de Bari, II parte," *Toletum* 24 (1990): 117–18. San Vicente: Hurtado, "Memorial," 530, and Antolín Abad Pérez, "Un obituario del siglo XVIII: el almocraz de San Vicente Mártir, de Toledo, 1734–1804," *Toletum* 22 (1988): 67–114.

mere eight chapels is an underestimate. However, a floor plan made before the church was demolished in the eighteenth century includes only seven chapels within the church building and another large, free-standing chapel, indicating that the 1576 estimate is accurate.[17] For those with familarity with the names of Toledo's converso families, it is obvious that the majority, if not all, of the chapels in these three parishes were converso foundations.[18]

Within these three parishes, conversos are the most visible parishioners, whether as officers, members or financial supporters of parochial confraternities, parish priests, or founders of burial chapels.[19] In the context of significant parochial activities, contacts with the majority population appear to be limited, and one could argue a fair degree of isolation between the two ethnic groups on this level. However, it should be recalled that conversos lived in all the city parishes, and in other parishes their presence was not so preponderant. Even in some parishes where conversos were numerous, there are visible remains of contacts between the two groups. For example, in the parish church of Santo Tomé, the counts of Fuensalida shared burial space with the converso tax-farmer of the Bull of Crusade, Bernardo Núñez de Toledo, and his wife, Catalina Suárez, one example of postmortem contact and coexistence.[20]

The prevalence of conversos in the parish of San Vicente and this general area may explain why the Inquisition, after occupying several other sites, finally established its large and ever-expanding headquarters right next to the parish church of San Vicente.[21] One of the chapels in the parish church served as a place where the inquisitors might hear mass if they so desired,[22] although the sprawling Inquisition complex had its own sizable chapel. Possibly the inquisitors were prompted to set up their tribunal in the parish of San Vicente because they found desirable property at a reasonable price, but given their influence and authority it is likely they could have found this in any parish of the city. The space occupied by the Inquisition was continually expanded through the purchase and incorporation of what had formerly been private residences, and by 1598 the complex literally engulfed the parish church of San Vicente.[23] This development symbolized in mortar and stone what was occurring in actual practice, as many wealthy conversos sought social acceptability and a pedigree of pure blood by becoming lay officials, or *familiares,* of the Holy Office.

NUNNERIES

The religious revival of the late fifteenth and early sixteenth centuries also inspired the foundation of many new religious groups, especially for women. Of the twenty-two regular religious foundations for women that existed in Toledo in 1650, ten were founded between 1477 and 1520. (See Table 3.) In this same period, men gained only one new foundation, the Franciscan monastery of San Juan de los Reyes, a large foundation, it is true, but no larger than Cardinal Cisneros's nunnery of San Juan de la Penitencia.[24] It may be that women were favored in the renaissance of new religious foundations because single and widowed females formed a sizeable portion of the population as a whole, but it is doubtful that this imbalance was any more pronounced at the time of Cisneros than it was in 1561, when widows and single women accounted for 19 percent of the Toledo population, and the decade of the 1560s witnessed no surge of female religious foundations.[25] Another possibility is that religious foundations for women had been neglected in earlier years, leaving females with a lack of places, affordable or otherwise, in regular religious orders. But the most likely explanation is that women were encouraged to involve themselves in the religious revival of the period by the support of Cardinal Cisneros, archbishop of Toledo from 1495 to 1517, aided and abetted until 1504 by the influence and example of a popular queen. That Cardinal Cisneros was concerned about the plight of women, many of whom "because of pov-

Table 3: Nunneries and *Beaterios* Founded in Toledo, 1477–1520

Name	Foundation date	Order
Nunneries		
Santa Isabel de los Reyes	1477	Franciscan
La Concepción Franciscana	1501	Franciscan
San Juan de la Penitencia	1514	Franciscan
Beaterios		Order Later Adopted
San Miguel de los Angeles	1492	Franciscan
San Antonio de Padua	pre-1512	Franciscan
Santa Ana	pre-1513	Franciscan
Madre de Dios	1482	Dominican
Vida Pobre	1493	Hieronymite
Santa Mónica	pre-1520	Augustinian
Beatas de San Pedro	1487	Benedictine (Benitas de la Purísima Concepción, 17th c.)

erty and hunger were degraded to living a life of sin and dishonor,"[26] is certainly an important explanation for the expansion of the female religious orders in much of Castile.[27]

In Toledo, many of the early foundations for women started as small, loosely structured communities of *beatas*. Living communally and dedicating themselves to spiritual and charitable ends, many of these women gained support from Cisneros as well as King Ferdinand and highly placed aristocrats.[28] From 1477 until 1520, at least seven *beaterios* emerged in Toledo, and there were probably more since history records only those that survived and became absorbed into the mainstream. Of these seven foundations, at least four were founded and subsidized by conversos: San Miguel de los Angeles, founded in 1492 by María de Santa Cruz, the widow of a royal treasurer and a Toledo *regidor*, Diego López de Toledo;[29] the *beatas* of San Pedro, founded in 1487 by the parish priest of San Pedro, Diego Hernández de Ubeda;[30] San Antonio de Padua, founded in the early 1500s by a branch of the Jarada or the Fuente family;[31] and Santa Ana, located in the old Jewish quarter in Santo Tomé and founded by María González in the early 1500s but underwritten in the early years by members of a family that used the name Herrera and made their fortune in the Canary Islands.[32] Added to these early foundations is the later nunnery of Teresa of Avila, first tentatively established in Toledo in the late 1550s,[33] making a total of five converso establishments for women.

The early *beaterios* were tiny; San Miguel de los Angeles, for example, housed only twelve *beatas* when it was officially founded. But as time passed, many grew into larger cloistered nunneries. It is likely that the women in all four of these foundations (five if St. Teresa's convent is included) were exclusively conversas. In some cases this was dictated by the foundation statutes, which gave preference to family members in the selection of applicants, as is the case of San Miguel de los Angeles. Even if not stated in any documents, the acceptance of new members or novices was in most cases controlled by the *beatas,* or nuns, and their leader, who voted on accepting a new applicant. Conclusions about the ethnic origin of women in one nunnery, San Antonio de Padua, controlled by the Fuente family, are possible thanks to the survival and publication of documents that include the names of the nuns and their parents,[34] and the clientele of this convent was almost exclusively converso. Based on this information, one could conclude that conversos met the needs of their community by founding their own nunneries.

However, this apparent exclusivity is not the whole story, for conversas could be found in nearly all the nunneries of the city. As one example of many, from 1556 to 1572, the wealthy *regidor* Juan de Herrera placed three of his daughters in the prestigious Dominican convent of Santo Domingo el Real, a nunnery that included conversas, Old Christians, and those of mixed origin. The price of entering this nunnery was substantially higher than that of San Antonio de Padua. In 1556, Juan de Herrera paid a total of 276,250 mrs. to the nuns of Santo Domingo el Real for his daughter, María de Herrera, and in the same year Juan Vázquez de Dueñas paid 175,000 mrs. for his daughter, Yomar [Guiomar] de San Francisco, to enter San Antonio de Padua.[35] The discrepancy was even greater two decades later, with Juan de Herrera paying 537,500 mrs. in 1572 for his daughter Mariana de Herrera, while another converso *regidor,* Antonio Alvarez de Alcocer, paid 229,500 mrs. in 1573–75 for his daughter, Micaela Eugenia, to enter San Antonio de Padua.[36] The substantial increase in the entrance fees of both convents from the 1550s to the 1570s illustrates the inflation of the period and the ever higher cost of placing daughters. The figures also demonstrate that membership in an ethnically diverse nunnery like Santo Domingo el Real cost more than one that was exclusively converso, and that subtle differentiations based on ethnicity existed in many local institutions.

Many wealthy conversos left sizable testamentary gifts to the converso nunneries. The merchant *regidor* Diego de San Pedro left 12,000 ducats to endow a large burial chapel that formed the main altar of the church in the nunnery of San Miguel de los Angeles.[37] Much of the wealth of another merchant *regidor,* Hernán Franco (d. 1571), was spent by his widow, Catalina de la Fuente, to build a large burial chapel in the church of San Antonio de Padua where she and her spouse were buried and their tombs can still be seen today.[38] Saint Teresa's numerous foundations in Toledo were underwritten by conversos, with varying degrees of success. One of the more successful supporters was Hernán Franco del Aguila, in earlier years a treasurer-general of the city, who ended his days as a secular cleric and in 1625 was patron of the Discalced Carmelites. His wealth contributed to the building of a new church and the remodeling of a large house the nuns had acquired in 1607.[39]

In addition to giving donations to already extant nunneries, conversos continued to found new ones. When the licentiate of canon law, Hernán Pérez de la Fuente, died in 1598, he left his fortune to found a Cistercian nunnery where he was to be buried.[40] The two stipulations he made for the new foundation, that twelve of his female relatives had to be admitted without a dowry and that the abbess had to be related to him, suggest that one of the founder's goals was to provide for his female relatives. The new nunnery, Nuestra Señora de la Asunción de Bernardas Recoletas, was officially founded in 1605, although the stipulation that the abbess had to be a relative of the founder was rejected by Pope Paul V in 1608.

While building monuments to the Christian faith, some conversos attempted to maintain a degree of ethnic identity not just in choosing the place where they founded them but also in selecting the people who were to inhabit them. This tendency to exclusivity was not unique to conversos, who were, after all, excluded from many religious institutions and secular corporations by the pure blood statutes. Even if the pure blood statutes were unsuccessful in physically eliminating conversos from their offices and benefices, they must surely have exacerbated hard feelings between the two groups, leaving conversos with feelings of resentment or rejection that further emphasized an innate preference of staying within the confines of one's own ethnic group. The well-known *arbitrista,* Jerónimo de Ceballos,[41] after retiring from an active secular life to become a royal chaplain in the Toledo cathedral, finally revealed his ideas in 1635 and when he wrote a discourse against the pure blood statutes, "stating my sentiments clearly and without fear, at 75 years of age and full of so many positive acts [proofs] of pure blood."[42] He argued that the many endowments previously given to the cathedral by the canons and prebendaries, especially useful to the poor, had ceased after a pure blood statute had been imposed in the cathedral: "since it has been in effect, scarcely anyone has given anything worthy of memory." Ceballos's observation suggests that the pure blood statutes encouraged wealthy conversos to make donations to institutions where they were accepted and wanted, not where they were at least theoretically excluded.

The topics addressed in this essay are in one sense testimony to interaction and contacts between conversos and the majority population, since the numerous nunneries and burial chapels founded by conversos indicate that they had abandoned the beliefs of their ancestors and embraced Christianity. Yet another testimony of interaction is that conversos and members of the majority culture could be found together in the same nunnery or buried in the same parish church. But for all the examples of interaction and apparent assimilation, there existed another world of isolation. Even while observing the outward forms of Christianity, many conversos at the same time preserved ethnic solidarity in choosing the parish where they lived, building their burial chapels, placing their convent-bound daughters, or investing large sums of money for religious foundations. Doctrinally, unity had been achieved in religion, but a degree of pluralism still existed in the separate-but-equal parish churches and nunneries. In their own ways, conversos contributed to the abundant (or overabundant, according to some seventeenth-century *arbitristas*) religious foundations of their native city. Their contribution is all the more remarkable in view of the many prejudices developed against conversos in the name of this same religion.

NOTES

1. Eloy Benito Ruano, *Toledo en el siglo XV. Vida Política* (Madrid, 1961) provides the most detailed coverage for the fifteenth century, but the Toledo events appear in most general histories, including those of the Spanish Inquisition. For a study of the pure blood statutes, Albert A. Sicroff, *Los estatutos de limpieza de sangre. Controversias entre los siglos XV y XVII,* trans. Mauro Armiño (Madrid, 1985); Antonio Domínguez Ortiz, *Los Judeoconversos en España y América* (Madrid, 1971).

2. See Francisco Márquez Villanueva, "Conversos y cargos concejiles en el siglo XV," *Revista de archivos, bibliotecas y museos* 63 (1957): 503–40, for converso office-holders in the fifteenth century.

3. See Linda Martz, "Pure Blood Statutes in Sixteenth-Century Toledo: Implementation as Opposed to Adoption," *Sefarad* 54 (1994): 83–107 for details and bibliography for the 1566 statute.

4. For some idea of the intermarriage in fifteenth-century Castile, see the 1449 "Instrucción del Relator para el obispo de Cuenca, a favor de la nación Hebrea," 250–52 in the copy reprinted by Fermín Caballero, *Noticias de la vida, cargos y escritos del doctor Alonso Díaz de Montalvo* (Madrid, 1873), 243–54. Two important Toledo conversos mentioned by the Relator as marrying daughters to Old Christians are Alfonso Alvarez de Toledo (d. 1456–1457), contador mayor of Henry IV, a royal councilor of John II, and one of the Relator's many cousins; the other is Dr. Diego González Franco or De Toledo (d. 1460–1462) contador mayor de cuentas and a royal councilor of John II. His name is incorrectly transcribed as Dr. Fónico in the reprint of Caballero; see Juan Bautista Avalle-Arce, *Temas hispánicos medievales* (Madrid, 1974), 291 n. 18.

5. See Francisco Cantera Burgos and Pilar León Tello, *Judaizantes del arzobispado de Toledo habilitados por la Inquisición en 1495 y 1497* (Madrid, 1969) (hereafter *JAT*) for a transcription of the parish-by-parish list of the names and the amount paid.

6. The map is based on a plan drawn by El Greco or his son in the first decades of the seventeenth century. It includes the twenty-one Latin parishes of this period, but it appears that some changes in parishes had occurred since 1495–97; for example, neither San Martín nor San Isidoro, one of the largest parishes in El Greco's map, appear in the early lists.

7. The outlines for the Jewish quarters included in the map are meant to give only a general idea of their location. They are based on Julio Porres

Martín-Cleto, *Planos de Toledo* (Toledo, 1989), Plano 7, "Recinto de la Judería Mayor"; and his "Algunas precisiones sobre las juderías toledanas," *Anales toledanos* 16 (1983): 37–61. Also useful for reconstructing the area are the many documents in Pilar León Tello, *Judios de Toledo,* 2 vols. (Madrid, 1979).

8. See Linda Martz, *Poverty and Welfare in Habsburg Spain: The Example of Toledo* (Cambridge, 1983), 101, for the parish population in 1561. The parish of Santo Tomé registered 1,727 *vecinos,* or 8,635 inhabitants using a multiplier of 5.

9. For information about the Judería Menor, see Julio Porres, *Historia de las Calles de Toledo,* 2nd ed., 3 vols. (Toledo 1982), 1.93–98, 2.751–57.

10. Marcel Bataillon, *Erasmo y España: estudios sobre la historia espiritual del siglo XVI,* trans. Antonio Alatorre, 2nd ed. (Mexico City, 1966), 3; José García Oro, *Cisneros y la reforma del clero español en tiempo de los Reyes Católicos,* (Madrid, 1971), 334–39; Alvar Gómez de Castro, *De las hazañas de Francisco Jiménez de Cisneros,* trans. José Oroz Reta (Madrid, 1984), 75–79, 87. The legislation of the Talavera synod, which included the catechism, "Tabla de lo que han de enseñar a los niños," has been reprinted by Andrés de Ocerín-Jáuregui, "El Cardenal Cisneros y el sínodo de Talavera en 1498," *Estudios franciscanos* 16 (1916): 210–19, 304–12.

11. Archivo de la parroquia de San Nicolás, Libro 1, baptisms in the parish of San Vicente, 1499–1509.

12. Archivo Histórico Nacional (AHN), Inquisición (Inq.), leg. 143, exp. 21, ff. 18^r–19^r.

13. For the dismal conditions in the diocese of Cuenca, see Sara T. Nalle, *God in La Mancha. Religious Reform and the People of Cuenca, 1500–1650* (Baltimore, 1992), 8–13, 20–31, but this diocese may be the exception rather than the rule. According to a visit carried out in 1505 in a portion of the vast Toledo archdiocese (the archdeanery of Madrid), twenty-four of the priests interviewed knew how to read very well, three only moderately, and the remaining three knew little or nothing, figures that suggest ignorance did not prevail in this area. See Antonio de la Torre y del Cerro, "Una visita al arcedianzgo de Madrid por orden de Cisneros," *Revista de la biblioteca, archivo y museo del Ayuntamiento de Madrid* 13 (1944): 347–78. For some tentative conclusions about the training of priests at the end of the sixteenth century in the city and archdiocese of Toledo, see Ricardo Sáez, "Le Clergé des paroisses de Tolede a la fin du XVIe siecle," in *Tolede et l'expansion urbaine en Espagne (1450–1650)* (Madrid, 1991), 222–24.

14. AHN, Inq., leg. 183, exp. 18, Juan Sánchez de San Pedro, no foliation [nf]., Diego Alonso, parish priest of San Juan de la Leche, (i.e., San Juan Bautista); leg. 183, exp. 14, nf, Diego Sánchez de San Pedro, El Mozo, parish priests of San Juan de la Leche and San Nicolás (1509); leg. 149, exp. 10, Martín de San Francisco, alias Cota, f. 9^r, Juan Blázquez, parish priest of San Cristóbal (1526), who testified against the prisoner.

15. Archivo Histórico Provincial de Toledo (AHPT), prot. 1657, ff. 71^r–73^r, will of Juan Farinas (9 Mar. 1545) whose relatives suggest he was a converso; they include a licentiate Falcón; a sister, Elvira de la Cruz; an in-law, Alexo de la Fuente; his heir was Francisco Samilla, a chaplain of Reyes Viejos in the cathedral. Juan Farinas was as well a member of the predominantly converso confraternity, La Virgen y Madre de Dios. For the origin of Luis Hurtado, who was in fact a descendent of the vast San Pedro clan, see Linda Martz, "Converso Families in Fifteenth- and Sixteenth-Century Toledo: The Significance of Lineage," *Sefarad* 48 (1988): 145–47, chart 13. For his chronicle, see Luis Hurtado, "Memorial de algunas cosas notables que tiene la imperial ciudad de Toledo, [1576]," in *Relaciones de los pueblos de España ordenadas por Felipe II. Reino de Toledo, tercera parte* (Madrid, 1963), 481–576.

16. While some of the city's burial chapels, generally the largest, the best endowed and those containing important art works, have been studied on an individual basis, no one has undertaken a general study of the city's numerous chapels. For one regional study, see Ramón Sánchez González, "Las capellanías en el antiguo régimen (siglos XVI–XVIII): estudio de la zona de La Sagra," *Anales toledanos* 23 (1985): 101–147.

17. Julio Porres, *Historia de las calles de Toledo,* 1st ed., 2 vols. (Toledo, 1971), 2.496–97 for the 1771 floor plan of the church and the names of the chapel founders, from the Archive of the Escuela de Christo, leg. 1, No. 29.

18. For the names of many converso families of the city, see Francisco Cantera Burgos and Pilar León Tello (*JAT*); José Carlos Gómez Menor, *Cristianos nuevos y mercedares de Toledo* (Toledo, 1970); and Martz, "Families."

19. Archivo Diocesano de Toledo, Sala IV, Cofradías, No. 760, "Cuentas de la cofradía de las ánimas de la parroquia de San Vicente, 1571–1636." The number given for this document may have been changed as cataloguing in the archive continues.

20. Real Academia de la Historia, Colección Salazar y Castro, cod. 9/200, P. Salazar de Mendoza, "Chronico de la casa de Aiala," for the burial places of the counts of Fuensalida I through III. For the chapel of Bernardo Núñez and Catalina Suárez, see Matilde Revuelta et al., *Inventario artístico de Toledo capital* (Madrid, 1983), 324.

21. Fernando Marías, *La arquitectura del renacimiento en Toledo (1541–1631),* 4 vols. (Toledo-Madrid, 1983–1986) 3.32–34, 4.134–36; Porres, *Calles,* 2nd ed., 1.341–43.

22. Hurtado, "Memorial," 530; this was the chapel of the Villamayor.

23. See the diagram reproduced by Marías, *Arquitectura,* vol. 3, plate XCIII, from AHN, Inq., carpeta 1, no. 36.

24. Pedro de Alcocer, *Historia o descripción de la Imperial cibdad de Toledo* (1554, rept. Toledo, 1973), ff. CII–CXVIII, has much valuable information about the earliest years of these foundations. Much material is given by

Fernando Marías, *Arquitectura,* 3.117–79 for nunneries. See also Balbina Martínez Caviró, *Conventos de Toledo* (Madrid, 1990).

25. Martz, *Poverty and welfare,* 104–105.

26. Antolín Abad Pérez, "San Juan de la Penitencia, Obra Social del Cardenal Cisneros en Toledo," *Anales toledanos* 2 (1968): 1.

27. José García Oro, *El Cardenal Cisneros,* 2 vols. (Madrid, 1992–93), 1.297.

28. Bataillon, *Erasmo en España,* 51–71; García Oro, *Cisneros,* 1.239–54; William A. Christian, Jr., *Local Religion in Sixteenth-Century Spain* (Princeton, 1981), 15–17 for *beatas.*

29. AHN, Clero, libro 15,660, which includes the endowment of María de Santa Cruz (16 May 1492). The will of Diego López de Toledo and the foundation document of the *beaterio* were written and witnessed by a brother of Diego López, the *maestrescuela* Francisco Alvarez de Toledo (16 September 1495).

30. Marías, *Arquitectura,* 3.117; de Alcocer, *Historia,* f. CXVIII.

31. Antolín Abad Pérez, *Soledad Sonora: Monasterio de San Antonio* (Toledo, 1980).

32. De Alcocer, *Historia,* f. CX^{v} and Hurtado, "Memorial," 548 for details about Santa Ana; AHPT, prot. 7: "Mayorazgo of Licenciado Alonso de Herrera and Elvira Nieto, 11 July 1536," ff. 113^{v}–114^{v}, for the burial chapel this childless couple endowed in the main choir of the nunnery of Santa Ana.

33. See Efrén de la Madre de Dios and Otger Steggink, *Tiempo y vida de Santa Teresa,* 2nd ed. (Madrid, 1977) for some details about the Toledo foundations. Agustín Rodríguez Rodríguez, "Santa Teresa de Jesús en Toledo," *Boletín de la Real academia de bellas artes y ciencias históricas de Toledo* (1923): 5–73.

34. Abad Pérez, *Soledad Sonora.*

35. For María de Herrera, AHPT, prot. 1494, ff. 1306^{r}–1309^{r}, 1418^{v}–21^{v} (6 July 1556); total costs in prot. 1595, ff. 176^{r}, 191^{v}. For Yomar de San Francisco, Abad Pérez, *Soledad Sonora,* 117.

36. For Mariana de Herrera, AHPT, prot. 1871, ff. 988^{v}–93, 27 October 1572. Micaela Eugenia (Abad Pérez, *Soledad Sonora,* 120).

37. AHN, Clero, libro 15,688, ff. 56^{r}–61^{r}; AHPT, prot. 1580, ff. 2720^{r}–2740^{r}, will of María de Vargas (11 February 1580).

38. See Abad Pérez, *Soledad Sonora,* 148–53 for a transcription of the endowments of Catalina de la Fuente.

39. Hernán Franco, a son of Pedro Franco and his first wife, Juana de Robles, also used the name Hernán Franco(s) Cepeda del Aguila. For his role as patron, see Archivo General de Simancas, Contaduría de Mercedes,

leg. 457, f. 22[r], "Concierto entre Fernán Francos Cepeda del Aguila and Juan Suárez de Cárcoma; and Marías," *Arquitectura,* 3.142–46.

40. Carmen Torroja Menéndez, *Catálogo del Archivo de San Clemente* (Toledo, 1973), which also includes a catalogue for the Archive of the Monastery of Nuestra Señora de la Asunción (275–306).

41. John H. Elliott, *The Count-Duke of Olivares: The Statesman in an Age of Decline* (New Haven, 1986), 121–22, 149, 183, 189 for a discussion of the reforms recommended by Ceballos in his treatise, printed in 1623, *Arte Real.*

42. In Antonio Domínguez Ortiz, *La clase social de los conversos en Castilla en la edad moderna* (Madrid, 1955; rpt. Granada, 1991), 246, from AHN, Ordenes militares, libro 1320 C, 59–66.

12

Conversion and Subversion: Converso Texts in Fifteenth-Century Spain

DAYLE SEIDENSPINNER-NÚÑEZ

In the late Spanish Middle Ages, widespread pogroms, anti-Judaic policies, theological disputations, and an aggressive proselytizing movement by the mendicant orders combined to produce a new minority in an already tricultural population—the conversos—whose problematic presence would dismantle the last vestiges of *convivencia* and usher in inquisition and ultimately expulsion. The surprisingly rapid assimilation of early generations of conversos into Christian society has been attributed to the social structure of late medieval Christian Spain.[1] With the growth of cities in the fifteenth century, the medieval polarization between arms and agriculture (nobility *vs.* labor force) created a large vacuum, an intermediate space of services—economic, bureaucratic, administrative—immediately occupied by conversos. This rapid assimilation was paralleled by an intentioned effacement, for clearly it was in the interests of the newly converted to blend completely with Christian society and not to stand out.

By mid-century, however, the Jewish problem had become the converso problem, as the first statutes of *limpieza de sangre* were promulgated and violence was directed toward the new converts, most notably in the first Toledan rebellion of 1449.[2] Despite isolated reactions—Alonso de Cartagena's *Defensorium Unitatis Christianae* and Fernán Díaz de Toledo's *Instrucción del relator*—throughout the fifteenth century the conversos never defined themselves as a group nor aligned with a particular political band. Indeed, not even the Inquisition managed to mobilize conversos into any collective front. Nevertheless, converso authors intervened actively and decisively in fifteenth-century politics and culture, following established alignments and often confronting other conversos who took an opposite line.

The difficulties attendant to defining a converso literary presence should not blind us to the desirability of reconstructing the full spectrum of converso responses in the late Middle Ages. This essay examines two opposing converso discourses: the *letrado* rewriting of Spanish history and political theory in the fifteenth century and the subsequent subversion of *letrado* discourse in the sentimental romances.[3]

Throughout the Trastámara period, Castilian intellectuals sought to legitimize and define a dynasty that had seized the throne through civil war and fratricide. The ultimately dominant approach to Spanish history and political theory was formulated by the *letrados* (university graduates with advanced degrees in canon or civil law), heavily comprised of conversos.[4] The earliest formulator of *letrado* theory was Pablo de Santa María (ca. 1350–1435), bishop of Burgos.[5] Born Selomó ha-Levi, he was named *rabino mayor* of Burgos before the age of thirty where he presided over Spain's largest community of Jews and established the foremost school of rabbinical studies in Europe. After his conversion to Christianity in 1390/91, Santa María undertook religious studies at the universities at Salamanca and Paris; after receiving a doctorate in theology from the University of Paris, he served in the court of Benedict XIII at Avignon and later returned to Spain in 1399 to the court of Enrique III where he was appointed royal chancellor of Castile and tutor for Juan II (b. 1406). In 1412, Santa María wrote a summary of previous medieval chronicles of Spain and in 1418 he composed *Siete edades del mundo,* an *arte mayor* poem of 338 octaves comprising a compendium of universal and national history that was written for the instruction of Castile's future monarch. In the first 252 stanzas, universal history is divided into seven *edades*—from creation to the papal schism of 1380—reflecting history structured according to a divine scheme. The second part of the poem (st. 253–338), the "Población de España" or "De los reyes de España," traces the initial settlement of the peninsula by Tubal and the lineage of the Visigothic and Christian kings and concludes with an homage to Juan II whose birth is celebrated with messianic overtones.[6] In his rhymed chronicle, Santa María adapted early Spanish history to Old Testament names and chronology: he retained the tradition that Hercules was the first Spanish king, but he changed the name of Geryon to Gideon, claimed that Gideon had ruled a Castilian nation rather than a province that later formed part of the Roman Empire, and abbreviated the Carthaginian and Roman periods to emphasize instead the Goths and the Reconquest. This shift of emphases from classical myth to Old Testament history, from the Romans to the Goths, and from Roman province to Castilian nation would distinguish the *letrado* rewriting of Spain's past.

Santa María's son, Alonso de Cartagena (1384–1456), also studied at Salamanca, became bishop of Burgos, and revised Spanish history. He had an enormous influence on Castilian historiography because he took into his household and educated a number of clerics who later became officials of the Castilian monarchs. His most famous work was his speech in 1434 before the Council of Basel in which he argued that Castile's representatives should take precedence over those of England because of the greater antiquity of the Castilian monarch (this according to his father's own rewriting of early Spanish history) and because of the Castilian king's war against the infidel which reflected his superior obedience to divine will.

Towards the end of his life, Cartagena wrote the *Anacephaleosis* or *Epitome,* a brief compendium that both initiated and defined Latin historiography in fifteenth-century Spain and one of the first explicit testimonies of Castile's awareness of her own past and the national and international role she would claim for herself during the late Middle Ages.[7] The central theme of the *Anacephaleosis* is the Gothic ancestry of the Castilian royal line. Cartagena summarizes Gothic history before the colonization of Spain; the founding of their reigning house preceded Hercules and the Goths are glorified as the conquerors of Asia and Africa and as the captors of Rome. The devastation of Italy coupled with a dissociation of Spain from the Roman Empire are recurrent topics that became an integral part of subsequent Castilian historiography and served to establish the superiority of the Goths whose military victories, personal virtues, and civilization are celebrated. Cartagena expounds the accepted theory that the

Arabic invasion was in retribution for a decadent kingdom but he insists on the maintenance of the royal line. By divine dispensation, Pelayo succeeds Rodrigo and continues the Gothic line of descent which Cartagena traces from Pelayo to the kings of Asturias, León, and Castile, demonstrating, as he had previously argued at Basel, that the king of Castile "non solamente desçiende de los reyes de los godos e de las cassas de castilla e de leon, mas avn de linage de todos los reyes de España. E antes mas propiamente fablando, los reyes de España desçienden de ssu casa."[8]

This neo-Gothic thesis is hardly original to Cartagena, but its particular configuration does respond to the political and historical contingencies—international and national—of his writing. Cartagena constructed an alternate non-classical genealogy for the Castilian monarchy that transcended the antiquity of other European monarchies and deliberately devalued the impact of the Graeco-Roman tradition in Spain, a tradition identified by fifteenth-century Italian humanists with the cultural and intellectual supremacy of Italy. Moreover, the *Anacephaleosis* is a defense of Castilian hegemony in the peninsula based on Cartagena's rewriting of the earlier *Historia Gothica.* In the author's view, Castilian political supremacy was both historical fact and divinely ordained and would ultimately forge the future destiny of Spain because of Castile's special historical obligations and her contribution to the Reconquest. The compendium concludes with a prayer that God favor the expansion of Castile under the banner of the Holy Cross.

Alonso de Cartagena, his father, and his students introduced a political theory, a literary style, and a theological approach that were new to Castile and exercised a profound influence on the political, literary, and religious attitudes of the royal court and on the subsequent historiographical development of Castile.[9] One of Cartagena's students, the converso Rodrigo Sánchez de Arévalo, bishop of Palencia and Castile's representative to the papal court, was the most prolific and extreme theorist of *letrado* monarchism. His *Compendiosa Historia Hispanica* (Rome, 1470) implements the plan sketched out in the *Anacephaleosis,* developing and expanding upon the idearium of his mentor.[10] Ostensibly an updated continuation of El Toledano's *Historia Gothica,* Arévalo incorporates historical sources, legends, and glosses to expound the theological, moral, and political principles that inform his more theoretical tracts: his unflagging advocacy of militant monarchical authority, both papal and secular; his "messianic" commitment to holy war and belligerent promotion of Castilian expansion and imperialism; his providentialist interpretation of history and politics; his propagandizing of the antiquity and vigor of the Castilian cultural tradition of Gothic Christianity and its superiority over the Roman Catholic tradition of Italy. In his only two Castilian works (*Vergel de príncipes* and *Suma de política,* written in the 1450s) and in his Latin tracts (*De monarchia orbis, De regno dividendo*), Sánchez de Arévalo had expatiated on the origin and inviolate nature of Christian monarchy, the antiquity of monarchy as a political institution, and the divine protection accorded to it: no subject can interfere with the laws of succession nor depose a legitimate monarch; to do so would be sacrilege.[11] The monarch is divinely appointed and responsible to God alone as protector of the commonweal and active defender of the faith; his most important role is that of military leader, and in the *Compendiosa Historia Hispanica* Castilian monarchs are judged primarily as Christian warrior kings. The Reconquest is not only a divine obligation but a means of forging supreme Christian virtues indispensable for good government. Arévalo's reconstruction of the Visigothic origins and *imperium* of Peninsular monarchies serves not only to legitimize and exalt the Trastámara dynasty nationally and internationally but functions as a territorial imperative for the Castilian monarch, heir to the Visigoths by direct descent, to recuperate Moorish-occupied territory, to exercise Castile's historical claim to the Canary Islands, and to implement a policy of aggrandisement in northern Africa, thus restoring the historical (mythical) integrity of *Hispania* under the Goths. The preeminence of Castile is not only based on historical fact and the superior moral virtues of its inhabitants, but also on divine providence.[12]

The *letrado* theory of monarchy, history, and Castilian hegemony is perpetuated in the vernacular histories of Alonso de Palencia (*Crónica de Enrique IV, Décadas, La corónica de España*), Hernando del Pulgar (*Crónica de los Reyes Católicos*), and Andrés Bernáldez (*Memorias del reinado de los Reyes Católicos*): the monarch is God-appointed as guardian of a divinely ordained hierarchy; history is providential and fulfills God's plan; Castile is the heart of a unified peninsula which it had dominated in antiquity and which it would again dominate by force of its moral and political superiority. Thus, as Nader notes, the final object of the state for *letrado* writers became Hispania, the moral, political, and geographical recuperation of Spain under the leadership of the divinely inspired and appointed Castilian monarch. The Catholic monarchs' subsequent program of reform and centralization must have appeared to the *letrado* theorists as the first stage in the fulfillment of their hopes for a strong, moral monarchy and a unified Spain under the hegemony of Castile; the extreme monarchism—bordering on messianism—in the royal chronicles after 1480 reflects the exuberance of theorists whose theories are suddenly made credible by contemporary events.[13] While Fernando and Isabel surrounded themselves with tract-writers and historiographers deeply conscious of the ideologies disseminated by Alonso de Cartagena and his disciples, the *letrado* presence in the court of the Catholic kings was neither merely literary nor theoretical. An important change in the political and intellectual leadership of Castile became apparent in 1480 at the Cortes de Toledo when Fernando and Isabel formally changed the composition and scope of the *consejo real* so that seven of the twelve counselors were *letrados;* the dominance previously exercised by the military aristocracy was now in the hands of the legal profession.[14] Moreover, the duties and prerogatives of the *consejo* were expanded to include important decisions traditionally handled directly by the monarchy; thus the *letrados* became the principal formulators of Castilian political and religious policy:

> The letrados in the royal council of Fernando and Isabel brought to their positions a coherent and rational concept of the goals of the government and of their role in it, the concept developed by don Alfonso de Cartagena and his students long before the reign of the Catholic Monarchs. This letrado concept of the history and nature of the Spanish monarchy, based on medieval scholastic political theory and Roman law, formed a sharp contrast to the assumptions of previous royal councils. The consequences of this change in the consejo's ideals were all-encompassing for . . . the letrados started from the assumption of a rational universal order.[15]

For example, it was no coincidence, Nader notes, that the Inquisition—a judicial solution applied to a religious problem—was established just when the *letrados,* with their views of an all-powerful state, their legal training, and their concern for correct religious beliefs and practices, had replaced the aristocracy as the principal advisors to the crown.[16]

Márquez Villanueva has remarked that the political need of the Trastámara to consolidate and legitimize royal power found its complement in the converso commitment to the imperialistic enterprise and messianic ideal of a powerful antifeudal monarchy that would be its best ally and protection in an increasingly hostile Christian society.[17] This mutually beneficial alliance between the Judeo-conversos and the crown follows a pattern established during the Middle Ages whereby the Jews flourished under the direct protection of the king. This adhesion to central authority—advantageous to both monarchy and Jews—was characteristic of medieval Jewish policy and a status Spanish Jews continually sought to preserve.[18] Certainly the 1449 Toledan rebellion and popular unrest subsequently directed toward the conversos would only heighten the militant promonarchism of the two leading *letrado* theorists, the conversos Alonso de Cartagena and Rodrigo Sánchez de Arévalo.

The *letrados'* program, then, theorized divine-right monarchy, effected a providentialist mixture of religion and history, and fostered millennarian fantasies about the Catholic monarchs, propagandized Castilian reconquest and imperialism, assumed a rational universal order and the efficacy of formalist law to determine truth, advocated a rationalist adjudication of religious orthodoxy by examining outer works rather than inner piety, and fulfilled the political, social, and religious dreams of the Trastámara. The implementation of this program, once the *letrados* became the uncontested formulators of royal policy, became a tragic nightmare for the conversos.

In the historiography of medieval Spain, no century rivals the fifteenth in the production of propagandistic chronicles, biographies, general histories, memorials, theoretical tracts, and translations which sought to define and shape the historical past and political present and future of Castile. The preceding reconstruction of the ultimately dominant *letrado* political program and theory of history can uncover the political implications of late fifteenth-century (converso) texts that in their fictions obliquely express opposition to the dominant *letrado* ideology. For example, in Fernando de Rojas's *Celestina,* Sempronio's famous disquisition on the discontinuity, disorder, and nonsense of history can be read politically as an indictment of the *letrado* idearium:

> El mal y el bien, la prosperidad y la adversidad, la gloria y pena, todo pierde con el tiempo la fuerza de su acelerado principio. Pues los casos de admiración, y venidos con gran deseo, tan presto como pasados, olvidados. Cada día vemos novedades y las oímos y las pasamos y dejamos atrás. Disminúyelas el tiempo, hácelas contingibles. ¿Qué tanto te maravillarías si dijesen: la tierra tembló o otra semejante cosa que no olvidases luego? Así como: helado esté el río, el ciego ve ya, muerto es tu padre, un rayo cayó, ganada es Granada, el rey entra hoy, el turco es vencido, eclipse hay mañana, la puente es llevada, aquél es ya obispo, a Pedro robaron, Inés se ahorcó, Cristóbal fue borracho. ¿Qué me dirás, sino que a tres días pasados o a la segunda vista, no hay quien de ello se maraville? Todo es así, todo pasa de esta manera, todo se olvida, todo queda atrás.[19]

Here Sempronio views history as nonprovidential ("El mal y el bien, la prosperidad y la adversidad, la gloria y pena, todo pierde con el tiempo la fuerza de su acelerado principio"), comments on the futility of historiographic endeavor ("Pues los casos de admiración, y venidos con gran deseo, tan presto como pasados, olvidamos"), and presents the past as a jumbled confusion of disconnected trivia ("helado está el río, el ciego ve ya, muerto es tu padre, un rayo cayó . . . ") and as ultimately irrelevant ("Todo es así, todo pasa de esta manera, todo se olvida, todo queda atrás"). Furthermore, the sandwiching of the reconquest of Granada—centerpiece of the Catholic monarchs' political program—between the freezing of the river and the drunkenness of Cristóbal undermines the theoretical foundations—the providential design and assumption of a rational universal order—of *letrado* political theory and historiography.

Sempronio's tirade, nevertheless, does not appear in a vacuum. Recent *Celestina* criticism has explored precedents for Rojas's masterwork not in Roman or humanistic comedy but in the literary production of the late fifteenth century, most notably in the sentimental romances which, in turn, have recently been theorized as converso texts.[20] What I propose to do in the remainder of this essay is to examine three sentimental romances—*Siervo libre de amor* by Juan Rodríguez del Padrón, *Grisel y Mirabella* by Juan de Flores, and *Cárcel de amor* by Diego de San Pedro—as precursors of Sempronio's devastating dismissal of *letrado* theory.[21]

Almost thirty years ago, Francisco Márquez Villanueva analyzed the presence of a "political romance" embedded in Diego de San Pedro's "sentimental romance," *Cárcel de amor.*[22] For Márquez, in the substantial central segment of *Cárcel* that recounts Persio's calumny, the king's resultant persecution of his daughter, and the liberation of Laureola through armed insurrection, San Pedro intentionally departs from the love narrative to offer a critique of unrestrained monarchic power, to problematize the moral limitations of human authority, and to explore the legitimacy of armed resistance.[23] When Persio first denounces the love between Laureola and Leriano, King Gaulo imprisons his daughter and asks Persio to challenge Leriano to a judicial duel. Just as Leriano is at the point of winning the duel, the king is persuaded by Persio's family to suspend their combat. Subsequently, Persio bribes three false witnesses to denounce Laureola and on the force of their perjury, Gaulo sentences his daughter to die. Despite interventions by the cardinal of Gausa, accompanied by the prelates and knights of his court, who admonishes Gaulo to listen to right counsel, by the queen who pleads for moderation, and by Laureola herself who protests her innocence and seeks clemency, the king refuses to commute his daughter's execution. Having exhausted all diplomatic channels, Leriano has no alternative but to rebel against the tyrant king, free Laureola, and place her in the custody of her uncle.

Márquez attributes San Pedro's attack on monarchic despotism to his position as a converso at a time when the Catholic monarchs were consolidating their power, in part at the expense of the conversos: "Es la amarga decepción de la conciencia política de los conversos tras su entusiasmo con la 'monarquía prepotente' que soñaba Juan de Mena, pero que después no opta por aliarse con ellos, sino contra ellos, en liga con el pueblo pechero y con la nobleza cortesana."[24] In this interpretation, Persio's self-interested denouncement, the unchallenged credibility of false witnesses, the formalist application of law and penalty, the imprisonment and torture of Laureola are fictional correlates of the equally despicable operations of the recently established Inquisition.

Other sentimental romances also present a profoundly subversive critique of *letrado* theory which, as we have seen, provided the theoretical framework for the Catholic monarchs' policies of reform and centralization. In *Cárcel del amor,* Diego de San Pedro thematizes the potential abuse inherent in *letrado* theories of absolute monarchy and the attendant violence unrestrained royal power can engender. A similar treatment can be observed in another political romance, Juan de Flores's *Grisel y Mirabella.*[25] Here, as in *Cárcel,* the princess Mirabella is accused—accurately—of having an affair with Grisel. The king invokes the Ley d'Scocia whereby "el que más causa o principio fuesse al otro de hauer amado mereciesse muerte: y el que menos destierro" (342). When cross-examination and torture of the two lovers fail to assign guilt—both Grisel and Mirabella steadfastly implicate themselves and exonerate their partner—the king seeks counsel from his advisors, "demandó consejo a sus letrados." He convokes a judicial debate between the misogynist Pero Torrellas and the feminist Braçayda to determine the relative guilt of the two lovers.[26] After the debate has been decided in favor of Torrellas and the princess Mirabella sentenced to death, a series of unexpected and violent events ensues, beginning with the double suicide of the two lovers and climaxing in the torture and murder of Torrellas.

Insofar as the dominant culture of fictive Scocia resembles the dominant culture of Flores's time, the political events in *Grisel y Mirabella* may be read as a commentary on prevailing official attitudes toward law, authority, justice, and difference in late fifteenth-century Spain. Certainly Mirabella's father epitomizes fifteenth-century theories of kingship: "En el reyno de Scocia huvo vn excelente Rey de todas virtudes amigo. y principalmente en ser iusticiero. y era tanto iusto: como la misma iusticia" (344). The efficacy of his system of justice—dramatized in the judicial debate between Torrellas and Braçayda—is predicated on the power of language and reason to discover truth ("Y aquellos letrados o oydores del conseio real determinadamente concluyeron diziendo: que no auía otra mayor razón para saber la verdad," 342), the ability of the judges to hierarchically resolve difference by determining right and wrong, and the effective exercise of justice. These are, of course, the same premises underlying fifteenth-century secular and ecclesiastical juridical practice, for example, the theological disputations regarding religious difference or inquisitorial procedure to determine guilt or innocence.

The discrepancy between theory and practice and the exclusive hermeticism of Scocia's legal system do not go unnoticed by a disgruntled Braçayda who referring to the all-male court protests the "ellos son iuezes y partes y avocados del mismo pleyto [que Torrellas]" and that their verdict was, in fact, preordained, "conocida staua la sentençia." There are parallels here with medieval religious disputations like that of Tortosa where Jews and Christians argued before a panel of all Christian judges and public repression of difference was directed toward religious conversion and parallels as well with inquisitorial practice where public repression of difference was directed toward the imposition of religious orthodoxy. Moreover, instead of imposing social order, the judges' verdict initiates a chain of escalating social violence: Grisel countermands Mirabella's death sentence by hurling himself in her stead into the flames. On her last night, a grief-stricken Mirabella, dressed in a shift, approaches a window overlooking a courtyard where the king keeps his lions and casts herself down to the royal beasts: "los quales no usar con ella de aquella obediencia que ala sangre real deuian: segun en tal caso los suelen loar, mas antes miraron a su fambre: que ala realeza de Mirabella, a quien ninguna mesura cataron. y muy presto fue dellos spedaçada. y delas delicadas carnes cada uno contento el apetito."[27]

The repressive authority of the king and his council is overthrown, however, in the spectacular murder of Torrellas at the romance's conclusion, a grotesque inversion of the highly ritualized trial and conviction of Mirabella, planned and executed by the offended women of the royal court. The queen's opportunity to seek revenge on Torrellas materializes when he falls in love with his former adversary, Braçayda, and sends her a written declaration of love and service. The women are not deceived by his courtly rhetoric and continue to regard him as their enemy (their accurate decoding of his courtly clichés is ratified to us as readers when the misogynist brags to his male friends about his imminent seduction of Braçayda). The women's skillful reading of Torrellas's courtly text allows them to literalize his metaphorical desire to die for Braçayda's love by sacrificially killing him when he shows up for a love tryst with Braçayda.

Barbara Weissberger has identified the carnivalesque elements of Torrellas's torture-murder: the physical and verbal abuse the women heap on their victim; their own degradation into predators, recalling the hungry royal lions, as the women "con vnyas y dientes raviosamente le despedaçaron;" the sexual overtones of Torrellas's punishment; the references to food and feasting when the women take a break from torture to dine in full view of their moribund victim. Also characteristically carnivalesque is the scene's parodic religious character, the blasphemous allusions to the Last Supper in the "amarga cena" prepared for Torrellas and the sacrilegious reliquaries the women fashion from his ashes: "después que no dexaron ninguna carne en sus huessos: fueron quemados. y de su ceniza guardando cadaqual una buxeta por reliquias de su enemigo. y alguno houo que por cultre en el cuello la trahían. porque trayendo más a memoria su venganza mayor plazer hoviessen" (370). Weissberger interprets the bizarre ritual murder of Torrellas as a carnivalesque elaboration of the woman-on-top topos and concludes that Flores uses sexual inversion as a comic transgression of the patriarchal authority of courtly love and clerical misogyny, an inversion that would have appealed especially to Flores's female audience. She cogently analyzes the comic role of carnival in *Grisel* and effectively counters the traditional view of sentimental romances as highly serious, often tragic, representations of the conflictive demands of love and honor. However, there is a flip side to this celebration of the world-upside-down; insofar as the *mundus inversus* is a comic reflection or inversion of *de jure* structures of dependency, power, authority, and social discipline, the world-right-side-up can appear as arbitrary and absurd as its carnivalesque obverse.[28] Thus the festive misrule of the vengeful women and the arbitrary system of justice they impose on their victim Torrellas calls into question the pretensions of rational objectivity and detachment of those *letrados* who had condemned Mirabella; consequently both systems come to represent abusive extremes of mock justice. Here I disagree with Patricia Grieve's assertion that the complete breakdown of social laws, family bonds, and love relationships in the final scene culminates the destructive process of desire unleashed at the onset of the romance by Mirabella's extraordinary beauty.[29] This is a more traditional interpretation confined to the "sentimental romance" in *Grisel y Mirabella,* but if we address the political romance as well, we note there are several indications earlier in the text that this breakdown is inherent in the dominant culture itself. When the judges ceremoniously exit to deliver their verdict after the debate between Torrellas and Braçayda, they carry unsheathed bloodstained swords in their right hands, ominously symbolizing both the phallic nature of their authority and the repressed violence behind its exercise. The unnatural behavior of the royal lions that devour Mirabella symbolizes the violent irrationality and moral blindness of the royal court. Since their frenzy is also verbally associated with the vengeful women, a symbiotic link is suggested between the repressive violence of the royal court and the expressive violence of its vengeful victims.

Finally, the third text, "Estoria de dos amadores," is an interpolated romance within the frame of *Siervo libre de amor* by Juan Rodríguez del Padrón.[30] King Croes of Mondoya disapproves of the love of his son Ardanlier for Liessa. The lovers flee his wrath with Lamidoras (Ardanlier's tutor) and Bandyn (Liessa's slave) and travel to foreign courts throughout Europe where people marvel at his prowess and her beauty. At the French court, Princess Yrena falls in love with Ardanlier, but he declares his loyalty to Liessa, and Yrena gives him a key. Ultimately the lovers travel to Galicia and dwell in a subterranean palace for seven years. King Croes, in pursuit of the ill-fated lovers, recognizes Ardanlier's hunting dogs, follows them to the palace, and finds and kills Liessa (pregnant with Ardanlier's child) while her lover is away hunting. When Ardanlier returns he sends Lamidoras to Yrena with the key and an explanatory note and then to the Emperor of Hungary with another note; grief-stricken, he impales himself on his father's sword. Lamidoras completes both missions: the Emperor of Hungary declares war on Croes, and Yrena transforms the subterranean palace into a shrine. On her death, the shrine becomes enchanted, and the spell is broken only by Macías, the perfect lover; henceforth the shrine is open to the public on May 1st, June 24th (Día de San Juan), and July 25th (Feast Day of Santiago Apóstol).

Like the other sentimental romances, *Siervo libre de amor* again explores the violence of unrestrained monarchical authority. Moreover, the story of Ardanlier and Liessa, including the veneration of and pilgrimage to their tombs by other lovers, is presented as an overt, profane subversion of the cult of Santiago de Compostela. Thus the romance both parodies the distinctive *letrado* fusion of religion and history and by setting up its own alternative landmarks comments on the constructedness of official memory.

These sentimental romances, then, offer us an important politically charged commentary on the tyranny of absolute monarchs and on an inflexible system of justice that produces social violence rather than social order, a commentary often charged with a strong component of religious parody. They reflect a growing disenchantment with the anti-converso policies of the Catholic monarchs. These texts are deeply subversive, not because of any profeminist resolution or unmasking of courtly love conventions in *cancionero* poetry but because of their celebration of resistance to the repressive violence, arbitrary justice, and intolerant authority of a fictive society that offers disconcerting parallels to the dominant culture of late fifteenth-century Spain.

NOTES

1. See Francisco Márquez Villanueva, "El problema de los conversos: cuatro puntos cardinales," in *Hispania Judaica, I: History,* ed. Josep M. Solà-Solé, Samuel G. Armistead, and Joseph H. Silverman (Barcelona, 1980), 49–75.

2. See Eloy Benito Ruano, "Del problema judío al problema converso," *Los orígenes del problema converso* (Barcelona, 1976), 13–37; *Toledo en el siglo XV: vida política* (Madrid, 1961). For the texts by Alonso de Cartagena and Fernán Díaz de Toledo, see *Defensorium Unitatis Christianiae (Tratado en favor de los judíos conversos),* ed. Manuel Alonso (Madrid, 1943); the *Instrucción del relator* is included on pages 343–56. Albert A. Sicroff analyzes the *Defensorium* in *Les controverses des statuts de pureté de sang en Espagne du XVe au XVIIe siècle* (Paris, 1960), 41–62; see also Nicholas G. Round, "Politics, Style, and Group Attitudes in the *Instrucción del relator,*" *Bulletin of Hispanic Studies* 46 (1969): 289–319.

3. The issues compressed in this essay are explored in greater depth in two chapters, "Re-Inventing Spain: Conversos and the Writing of History in 15th-Century Castile" and "The World Upside Down: Sentimental Romances as Politically Symbolic Acts," for a book I am writing on the conversos in late medieval Spain.

4. My initial consideration of *letrado* historiography and political theory is heavily indebted to Helen Nader's remarkably informative presentation in *The Mendoza Family in the Spanish Renaissance* (New Brunswick, N.J., 1979), and the invaluable studies of Robert B. Tate on fifteenth-century historiog-

raphy cited in subsequent notes; Tate's studies have been collected and translated into Spanish in *Ensayos sobre la historiografía peninsular del siglo XV* (Madrid, 1970).

5. See Francisco Cantera Burgos, *Alvar García de Santa María y su familia de conversos* (Madrid, 1952); Alan Deyermond, "Historia universal e ideología nacional en Pablo de Santa María," in *Homenaje a Alvaro Galmes de Fuentes,* 3 vols. (Madrid, 1985), 2.313–24; M. Jean Sconza, "A Reevaluation of the *Siete edades del mundo,*" *La corónica* 16 (1987): 94–112, and *History and Literature in Fifteenth-Century Spain: An Edition and Study of Pablo de Santa María's "Siete edades del mundo"* (Madison, 1991); and Luciano Serrano, *Don Pablo de Santa María: gran rabino y obispo de Burgos* (Madrid, 1940) and *Los conversos Don Pablo de Santa María y Don Alfonso de Cartagena* (Madrid, 1942). For the text of *Siete edades,* see the critical edition by Sconza.

6. "Ilustre prosapia de reyes pasados / es éste por todas las partes del mundo / de donde desçiende don Juan el segundo / delante quien somos todos inclinados / e commo fuemos del tribo librados / por nuestro Señor en su avenimiento / asý somos deste por su nasçimiento / después en Castilla todos librados" (st. 338).

7. See Robert B. Tate, "The *Anacephaleosis* of Alfonso García de Santa María, Bishop of Burgos, 1435–1456," in *Hispanic Studies in Honour of I. González Llubera* (Oxford, 1959), 387–401. As Tate notes, had Cartagena had the opportunity to complete the work as originally planned, it would hold the same significance for the fifteenth century as Ximénez de Rada's *Historia Gothica* for the thirteenth. Tate examines the *Anacephaleosis* with regard to the political circumstances and the ideological and theoretical assumptions that inform its writing.

8. Cited by Tate, "*Anacephaleosis,*" 398.

9. *Letrado* theology is inseparable from *letrado* politics and historiography and, for Nader, constitutes one of the most significant innovations in Castilian intellectual life in the fifteenth century: "[A concern for theology] appears in Castile for the first time in don Pablo's work; and until 1500, it was peculiar to the Cartagena household and a handful of Castilians who had studied theology at Paris" (*The Mendoza Family,* 131). Breaking with the Castilian tradition of a pietist, eclectic, and nonintellectual approach to religion, Cartagena and his students advocated a theology based on the rationalism of Aristotle as central to the Christian faith; moreover, Nader proposes that, as both *letrados* and converso clerics, Cartagena, his family, and students may have had a special affinity with the religious attitudes of medieval works, their educational and religious background making them more receptive to the method and substance of scholastic theology than to the Renaissance humanism they encountered at Basel (133). During the reign of the Catholic monarchs, the *letrados,* precursors of the theological legalism that would flourish at Salamanca in the sixteenth century, became the formulators of Castilian religious policy and sought to reform, unify, and

regulate religious practices through the legal structures of the government, the church hierarchy, and the Inquisition. Inquisitional procedure involves a formalist application of standards of correctness ("laws") to religious practice and is grounded on the rationalist assumption that determination of faith can be resolved by an external examination of works rather than an inner examination of piety, devotion, motive, or conscience.

10. Tate documents Sánchez de Arévalo's extensive ideological debt to Cartagena in "Rodrigo Sánchez de Arévalo (1404–1470) and His *Compendiosa Historia Hispanica*," *Nottingham Mediaeval Studies* 4 (1960): 58–88, and "An Apology for Monarchy: A Study of an Unpublished 15th-Century Castilian Historical Pamphlet," *Romance Philology* 15 (1961–62): 111–23.

11. This is a politically delicate position since the murder of Pedro I at Montiel had assured Trastámara ascendancy to the throne of Castile; in the *Compendiosa historia hispanica* Sánchez de Arévalo maintains that both Pedro and Enrique were punished by Providence and that the crimes of their generation were expiated by the disasters that plagued the reign of Juan I. Tate suggests that Sánchez de Arévalo's unconventionally critical interpretation of the regicide and insistence on the inviolate nature of a legitimate monarch responds to the crisis of 1465 when the nobles challenged Enrique IV's power by proclaiming Alfonso king ("An Apology for Monarchy," 119). For a historical instance of *letrado* arguments against usurpation of monarchical authority, see the account of Alvaro de Luna's trial in Nicholas G. Round, *The Greatest Man Uncrowned: A Study of the Fall of Don Alvaro de Luna* (London, 1986).

12. "This belief that the nation had been chosen by God to fulfill some part of a providential design gathers momentum as the fifteenth century unfolds. Just before and immediately after the beginning of the reign of the Catholic Monarchs the air is heavy with prophecies of an undefined future grandeur for Castile. She is identified with the power that is to forge the future destiny of Spain by virtue of the role ascribed to her in the *Reconquista* from earliest times by historians and political pamphleteer" (Tate, "*Compendiosa historia hispanica*," 76–77).

13. See Nader, *The Mendoza Family*, 24; Tate, "An Apology for Monarchy," 122.

14. On the importance of the *consejo* as an advisory and policy-making council, see Nader, *The Mendoza Family*, 15 and 20. Nader disputes the conventional view that this change from government by the aristocracy to government by a meritocracy was a watershed in the political and intellectual history of Castile, marking the beginning of the modern state. The change in political leadership, formalized in the Cortes de Toledo, had already occurred during the reigns of Juan II and Enrique IV, and the reforms of 1480 confirmed and perpetuated the patterns of pre-Isabelline Castile (128–29).

15. Nader, *The Mendoza Family*, 130.

16. Ibid., 135. Nader adds that the *letrados* directly benefitted from the Inquisition: "The establishment of the Inquisition is the first issue on which letrados and caballeros displayed overt opposition. Clearly there was a conflict of interest, since seigneurial lands would now be subject to a judiciary responsible to the crown instead of the señor and to a written law instead of the customary justice typical of the seigneurial jurisdictions. It was not the nobles but the letrados—especially the graduates of the Colegio de San Bartolomé at the University of Salamanca—who would profit from the Inquisition."

17. Márquez Villanueva, "El problema de los conversos," 54.

18. See Dwayne E. Carpenter, *Alfonso X and the Jews: An Edition and Commentary on "Siete Partidas" 7.24, 'De los judíos'* (Berkeley, 1986). Tate also notes: "If the Jews and *conversos* of fifteenth-century Spain shared any set of views, it is certainly on the subject of kingship that they were most coherent. From Sem Tob through the pamphlets and histories of Alonso de Cartagena and his disciples down to Pulgar's, there flowed a strong current of opinion favouring a monarch with Old Testament attributes, directly responsible to God and the Pope who alone may depose him. In the chequered period preceding the acceptance of Ferdinand and Isabella as sovereigns of Aragon and Castile, Jews and *conversos* placed their abilities and their capital at the disposal of Spain's Catholic Monarchs. It is their interpretation of the providential plan guiding the royal pair to the throne that was accepted, glossed, and circulated throughout the 16th century by New and Old Christians alike" ("Four Notes on Gonzalo García de Santa María," *Romance Philology* 17 [1963–64]: 362–72).

19. Text from Fernando de Rojas, *Celestina,* ed. Dorothy S. Severin (Madrid, 1969); on this passage, see Stephen Gilman, "A Generation of *Conversos,*" *Romance Philology* 33 (1979–80): 87–101.

20. See Regula Rohland de Langbehn, "El problema de los conversos y la novela sentimental," *The Age of the Catholic Monarchs, 1476–1516: Literary Studies in Memory of Keith Whinnon,* ed. Alan Deyermond and Ian Macpherson, *Bulletin of Hispanic Studies,* Special Issue (Liverpool, 1989), 134–43. Rohland examines *Triste deleytaçión* (anonymous), the romances of Juan de Flores (*Triunfo de amor, Grisel y Mirabella, Grimalte y Gradissa*), and those of Diego de San Pedro (*Arnalte y Lucenda, Cárcel de amor*) as reflective of converso interests in the period before 1492 and concludes that the invariably tragic destiny of the characters "representa la honda desesperación a que la realización de sus intereses vitales reducía a ese grupo [i.e., los conversos] en la sociedad española del siglo XV" (141). She does not confront, however, the unresolved issue of converso authorship; this issue is, in most cases, predictably unresolvable since in the aftermath of the Toledo rebellions and, in particular, after the establishment of the Inquisition, few authors advertised themselves as card-carrying conversos. The identification of many converso texts in late fifteenth-century Spain is, therefore, necessarily reconstructive

and must be based on external historical documents when available (as in the case of Fernando de Rojas and Diego de San Pedro), hypothesis, and the evidence of the text. In this reconstruction, literary history can benefit from the methodology of historical linguistics that assigns asterisks to unattested forms for the purposes of defining certain principles of linguistic evolution. In this study, *Grisel y Mirabella* and *Cárcel de amor* are asterisked as converso texts.

21. In my chapter on sentimental romances, I theorize the genre as an aristocratic response to *letrado* theory with *Grisel y Mirabella* and *Cárcel de amor* as specifically converso texts within the genre; by converso text, I mean one that acquires added significance when read within the context of the converso problematic (see notes 22 and 25 below). While I do not regard *Siervo libre de amor,* one of the earliest sentimental romances, as a converso text, it is a precursor of *Celestina* insofar as it represents a critique of *letrado* theory.

22. Francisco Márquez Villanueva, "*Cárcel de amor,* novela política," *Revista de occidente* 14 (1966): 185–200; an important restatement of his interpretation, refuting the counterarguments of Keith Whinnom, is presented in "Historia cultural e historia literaria: el caso de *Cárcel de amor,*" in *The Analysis of Hispanic Texts: Current Trends in Methodology,* ed. Lisa E. Davis and Isabel Tarán (Jamaica, N.Y., 1976), 144–57. Whinnom presents his opposition in "Was Diego de San Pedro a *Converso?* A Re-Examination of Cotarelo's Documentary Evidence," *Bulletin of Hispanic Studies* 34 (1957): 187–200; "Two San Pedros," *Bulletin of Hispanic Studies* 42 (1965): 255–58; and "Introducción biográfica y crítica," *Diego de San Pedro: obras completas,* vol. 1, ed. Keith Whinnom (Madrid, 1973), especially 17–21. Both Whinnom and Márquez overlap on the following: the author Diego de San Pedro was in the service of Juan Téllez-Girón, Conde de Urueña, and lived in Peñafiel, a village and fortress that belonged to the Girón family; there were numerous San Pedros associated with Peñafiel (a 1467 list of members of the Cofradía de Hidalgos de Peñafiel includes a Diego de San Pedro, a comendador San Pedro, Juan de San Pedro, Alonso de San Pedro, a Diego de San Pedro *bachiller* and *teniente* to Pedro Girón); San Pedro was a typical converso surname and there is evidence of Inquisitional proceedings against "Constanza muger de Diego de San Pedro mercader" (not our author) who was condemned as a Judaizer in 1494. There is no incontrovertible evidence that Diego de San Pedro was—or was not—a converso, for *pruebas de linaje* are notorious for mustering conflicting witnesses to obfuscate or manufacture *limpieza;* however, in comparing the two critics, Márquez is the more masterful in negotiating the intentioned prevarications of these proceedings (see especially "Historia cultural," 150) and in interpreting evidence (see "*Cárcel de amor,* 199 n. 6). In the absence of documentary proof, one must look to circumstance ("hay que tomar en cuenta otros hechos que se orientan en ese sentido, como su típico apellido y su oficio de administrador y burócrata concejil al servicio de los Girones"), gossip ("el origen judío de 'el que trobó la Pasión' era, en

realidad, conocido y casi autonomástico en el siglo XVI"), and, in particular, the evidence of the text, as even Whinnom admits: "no es imposible que el autor Diego de San Pedro fuese converso y tal vez tengan razón Márquez y Bataillon al percibir en su obra actitudes y preocupaciones típicas de los neocristianos" ("Introducción," 20–21). For these reasons, I have asterisked *Cárcel de amor* as a converso text.

23. Márquez sees this right to resistance as fundamental to medieval Castilian political theory; see "Historia cultural e historia literaria," 154 n. 6.

24. "Historia cultural e historia literaria," 150–51.

25. Recent biographical studies of Juan de Flores include Carmen Parrilla, "Un cronista olvidado: Juan de Flores, autor de la *Crónica incompleta de los Reyes Católicos,*" in *The Age of the Catholic Monarchs, 1474–1516,* 123–33; and Joseph J. Gwara, "The Identity of Juan de Flores: The Evidence of the *Crónica incompleta de los Reyes Católicos,*" *Journal of Hispanic Philology* 11 (1987 [1988]): 103–130, 205–222. Published almost simultaneously, both studies examine much the same material; Parrilla offers the more cautious interpretation of the data while the creative composite Gwara reconstructs on page 221 is riddled with arbitrary assumptions and internal contradictions. Both authors conclude that Juan de Flores, the author of sentimental romances, is the same "Juan de Flores, fijo de Fernando de Flores, vesino de la çibdad de Salamanca" who was appointed chronicler to the Catholic monarchs on May 20, 1476, with an annual salary of 40,000 maravedíes for life. Parrilla's discovery of an additional legal document provides crucial information about Juan de Flores's background, a contract dated May 10, 1469, between Fernand Alfonso de Flores, "mercadero vezino de la noble y leal çibdad de Salamanca" and "su hijo Johan de Flores's and García Lopes, a silversmith" (126). As Parrilla notes, Juan de Flores's middle-class provenance would not deny him the university education desirable for a royal chronicler, "pues es sabido que las universidades contribuyeron a consolidar la burocracia con la aceptación en las aulas de personas procedentes del grupo medio de mercaderes y comerciantes" (127). It does, however, demolish a cornerstone of Gwara's construct which situates Flores within one of the wealthiest and most influential noble families of late fifteenth-century Spain as the nephew of the Conde de Lemos (116). Furthermore, Parrilla's findings suggest several parallels between Juan de Flores and Diego de San Pedro: both served in the employ of a powerful nobleman (Juan Téllez Girón in the case of San Pedro, the Duque de Alba in that of Juan de Flores) primarily as an administrator or bureaucrat rather than as a knight, and both were writers who represented the position of the caballeros not because they were born into wealth or power but because they professionally served the interests of the first estate. Finally, Juan de Flores's upbringing within the middle class of Salamanca would have exposed him either directly as a victim or indirectly as an observer to the increasingly marginalized existence of the conversos after the Toledan rebellions and to the injustices of exclusion (the statutes

of *limpieza de sangre*) and persecution (the Inquisition). These themes have been explored in Flores's work by Jorge Checa ("*Grisel y Mirabella* de Juan de Flores: rebeldía y violencia como síntomas de crisis," *Revista canadiense de estudios hispánicos* 12 [1988]: 369–82) and Barbara F. Weissberger ("Role-Reversal and Festivity in the Romances of Juan de Flores," *Journal of Hispanic Philology* 13 [1989]: 197–213) and acquire political dimensions when interpreted as a critique of *letrado* legal theory and policy, particularly as applied to conversos. While we have no evidence for or against the possibility of converso authorship here, given the documents uncovered by Parrilla, this consideration should not be dismissed and requires further investigation. Quotes from the text of *Grisel y Mirabella* are from the edition in Barbara Matulka, *The Novels of Juan de Flores and Their European Diffusion* (New York, 1931); I have added accents to the text edited by Matulka.

26. In the romance, the king's *consejo real* is comprised of twelve *letrados* who serve as his legal and political advisors. The initial *pesquisa* with an opportunity for confession and the application of torture to the accused conform to fifteenth-century inquisitional and juridical practice; see Stephen Haliczer, *Inquisition and Society in the Kingdom of Valencia, 1478–1834* (Berkeley, 1990). The scholastic disputation between Torrellas and Braçayda does not attend to the concrete problem of whether Grisel or Mirabella is more guilty of their specific crime but involves the more universal question concerning the greater culpability of Man or Woman: "Es necesario, además, hacer hincapié en que la parcialidad o imparcialidad de la sentencia ha de referirse exclusivamente a los términos internos del debate, no a su adecuación—inexistente—al caso de Grisel y Mirabella. Pues el debate no supone únicamente, como he dicho, una generalización equivocada; conlleva tambien el uso de argumentos racionales, y en ocasiones sofísticos, para explicar lo que es una pasión básica, irreductible a conceptos" (Checa, "Rebeldía y violencia," 373). The formalist and generic application of law, the abstract scholastic nature of the debate, and the theological overtones of legal procedures are all reminiscent of fifteenth-century legal practices.

Checa concludes "que el mundo ficticio de *Grisel* se distingue primordialmente por la discordancia entre la ley y la teoría, de un lado, y la realidad y la práctica, de otro" (373), a realization applicable to *letrado* theory and policy that was becoming increasingly apparent—particularly to the conversos—after the establishment of the Inquisition.

27. Both Checa and Weissberger examine the narrator's ironic commentary on the indecorous behavior of the royal lions that violates the bestiary tradition concerning the respect the king of beasts conventionally accords to his human counterpart. Given the traditionally metonymic relationship of the lions to the king, their unnatural behavior may imply criticism of the king's own extreme "hunger" for justice that compromises the life of his only child as Weissberger remarks ("Role-Reversal," 202) or may symbolize the king's own unnatural incest for his daughter as Matulka proposes (*The*

Novels of Juan de Flores, 69); as emblems of the royal court, the violence, unrestrained appetite, and lack of moderation of the lions are suggestive indeed.

28. This is clearly exemplified in the ending of Flores's *Triunfo de amor* where the women pursue the men: the women comb the streets ogling the men who coyly peer out from behind closed windows; they send love poetry to the men; the overly compliant men who give in to their suitors bemoan the loss of their virginity. The comic role reversal ridicules and subverts certain forms of behavior characteristic of the courtly code of love; see Weissberger, "Role-Reversal," 207.

29. Patricia E. Grieve, "Innovation within Tradition: The Interplay of Love and Justice in Juan de Flores' *Grisel y Mirabella,*" in *Desire and Death in the Spanish Sentimental Romance (1440–1550)* (Newark, 1987), 55–73.

30. For the text, see Juan Rodríguez del Padrón, *Siervo libre de amor,* ed. Antonio Prieto (Madrid, 1976).

PART IV

Moriscos

13

The Moriscos: Loyal Subjects of His Catholic Majesty Philip III

STEPHEN HALICZER

In the political thought of sixteenth- and seventeenth-century Europe, which was shaped by medieval notions of the ruler as God's representative on earth, religious conformity and political loyalty were closely linked. The danger posed by religious minorities was perceived as especially serious when the religious non-conformist was believed to have either military power or potential foreign allies or both. Thus while the decree expelling the Jews from Spain merely alleges their religious non-conformity and persistent efforts to "convert" Christians as the principal reasons for their removal from the community, since they were not seen as a security risk, the several decrees and proclamations expelling the Moriscos between 1609 and 1610 accuse them of "treason both human and divine." Specifically, in the edict expelling the Moriscos of Valencia which was published on August 22, 1609, they were described as having attempted through their envoys (presumably to other powers) and other means to "harm and disrupt our possessions."[1]

In the proclamation by Viceroy Gaston de Moncada, Marquis of Aytona, expelling the Moriscos of Aragon, the charge of treason is picked up from a royal letter of April 17, 1610, and explicitly linked to their obdurate refusal to take advantage of the many sincere efforts to convert them so that "swollen with obstinacy and stubbornness they have conspired against the royal crown and these Kingdoms of Spain."[2] Finally, the order expelling the Moriscos of Castile,

La Mancha, and Extremadura issued on July 10, 1610, specifically accused the Moriscos of having "sought the assistance of the Turk and other princes, offering them their persons and property" to further a conspiracy against "my royal crown and these Spanish Kingdoms."[3] One can almost feel the sense of relief of Spaniards like Jaime Bleda at the departure of a people he described as "barbarous and ungrateful," so that after 900 years of suffering their presence the kingdom was at last free of the "infinite spiritual and temporal harm" that they had caused.[4]

Anyone who is familiar with the long debate over the Morisco problem carried on at the highest levels of the Spanish government for more than fifty years is forced to conclude that the royal edicts linking the Moriscos' refusal to sincerely embrace Catholicism to their political unreliability and potential as a fifth column in the service of Spain's enemies reflected the views of the majority of the Spanish political leadership and was a key element in the decision to carry out the expulsion. Quite apart from Jaime Bleda himself, a Dominican who was so embittered by his failure to convert the Moriscos of the village of Corbera in Valencia that he carried on a personal campaign to bring about their expulsion, two of the intellectual leaders of the early seventeenth century also saw the Moriscos as a potential danger to the state. San Juan de Ribera, archbishop and later viceroy of Valencia, had a decisive influence on the debate within the Council of State with two memorials. In the first of these, dated at the end of 1601, he stressed the religious obduracy of the Moriscos and the danger that they represented to Spanish security, even going so far as to affirm that if they were not removed, Spain would be irretrievably lost. In the second memorial issued shortly thereafter, in January 1602, Ribera went even further, demanding the expulsion of the Moriscos because they were "obstinate heretics and traitors to the crown."[5]

Another significant memorial, which carried considerable weight because it was especially commissioned for the Council of State by the influential royal confessor Fray Diego de Mardones, was written by Pedro de Valencia. This brilliant and prolific Extremaduran intellectual, whose memorial about the judicial aspects of witchcraft trials was crucial to forming moderate opinion within the Holy Office about the validity of witchcraft accusations, revealed himself as a harsh critic of the Moriscos and their continued presence in Spain. In reading this document, it is extremely difficult to accept the view taken by Bernard Vincent and Antonio Domínguez Ortiz that it represented a moderate position simply because it advocated dispersion of the Morisco population rather than outright expulsion, since for Pedro de Valencia dispersion meant forced removal of the Moriscos from their homes at their own expense and resettlement not only in Spain but in other parts of the Empire.[6]

Beginning with a sweeping survey of the international scene, Pedro de Valencia sought to place the Morisco issue in historical perspective by demonstrating that it was one chapter in the long and continuing struggle between Christianity and Islam for world supremacy. The recent victories of the Christian powers, the impact of conversion efforts in Asia, and the conquest of America had stirred the enmity of the entire Islamic world. Islam was especially hostile to the king of Spain because of his leadership of the Catholic world and his possessions in North Africa. The Moriscos of Spain were a part of that hostile Islamic world and still thought of Spain itself as theirs by right of conquest.[7]

In spite of Spain's military power, however, its population had declined recently because of incessant warfare, immigration, and recruitment to the Church, so that it could easily be overwhelmed by an attack from the African Moors and the Turks. Pedro de Valencia was certain that this attack would be assisted by a rising of the Moriscos who constituted an armed fifth column 100,000 men strong.[8] Because of their refusal to accept Christianity or reconcile themselves to their status as second-class citizens in a country they once possessed, Spanish rulers should adopt an attitude of "prudent mistrust" toward the Moriscos and attempt to weaken them by any means necessary since, according to the text, "Nations and Republics have learned that peace and harmony cannot prevail among people of different religious beliefs."[9] It was in the hope that dispersion would force assimilation and weaken the military potential of the Moriscos that Pedro de Valencia recommended it and not because he was in any way a moderate on the Morisco issue.[10] He justified this draconian measure by pointing to their continued "perfidy and heresy" and declared that dispersion should be accompanied by a campaign of forced assimilation, which should include legal prohibitions against the use of Arabic, Islamic dress, and other traditional Islamic customs.[11]

Pedro de Valencia's memorial is notable even among the hardliners of the period for his refusal to accept any differences among the Moriscos in terms of their degree of assimilation or loyalty to the crown. For him, the Moriscos, whether they lived individually or in small groups among Old Christians or in large numbers in specific areas, were part of the same "nation" who communicated among themselves and shared the same visceral hatred of Christian Spain.[12]

Even though the close identification of political disloyalty and religious dissidence reflected in the decrees of expulsion of the Moriscos and in the memorials by hardliners like San Juan de Ribera or Pedro de Valencia may appear typical of the internal policies of the Catholic and specifically Habsburg rulers of the Counter-Reformation, in fact there existed many degrees of liberalism or illiberalism in Catholic state policies. During the sixteenth century, France, Poland under Stephen Báthory (1575–1586), Austria, and Hungary undertook important experiments in government-sponsored toleration, while in the early seventeenth century, during the reigns of Philip III and Philip IV, Spain played host to a significant and quasi-tolerated influx of Portuguese New Christians fleeing the rigors of the Portuguese Inquisition. Among intellectuals and clergy, the French politiques argued for religious toleration and the Polish hierarchy declared that Protestants should not be excluded from general church councils.[13]

So far as the potential political loyalty of religious dissidents was concerned, Catholic rulers and political thinkers could be equally flexible. The Emperor Charles V welcomed the help of his Protestant subjects during his conflicts with the Ottomans and eventually accepted the Peace of Augsburg (1555) which legalized the existence of Protestant states in Germany. In France, the Huguenots were characterized by a conspicuous degree of loyalty to the monarchy after 1624, which was only brought to an end by Louis XIV's insensate persecution.

The long argument over the Moriscos, with its frequent and abrupt shifts of policy which continued up until the time of the expulsion, is itself an example of the flexible response of a great Catholic state faced with the existence of a religious minority. Within the context of this argument, a significant number of political thinkers were quite capable of accepting the fact of the religious dissidence of the Moriscos and still seeing them as loyal subjects. The Count of Miranda, one of the members of the *Junta de Tres,* which deliberated in January and October 1607, pointed out that the Moriscos of Aragon had proven their loyalty during the political troubles in that kingdom and recommended that the king make known to them his satisfaction with their attitude. The *Junta* unanimously recommended a policy of increased missionary efforts employing the friars of the mendicant orders and retention of the Moriscos, and its *consulta* was approved by the king.[14]

The theme of the loyal subject was stressed even more strongly by Pedro Vaca de Castro, archbishop of Seville in a caustic letter to Philip III dated January 24, 1610. Protesting the indiscriminate nature of the edict of expulsion from Andalucía, which was published on January 10th, the archbishop noted that the edict was so general that it punished the innocent along with the guilty, and then proceeded to enumerate the various categories of Moriscos included in the decree, arguing that they either were of no danger whatever (women, old people, or children) or came from families who had already demonstrated conspicuous loyalty to the crown during the recent Morisco uprisings in Seville in the 1580s, "deserting their own kinsmen in order to serve your majesty in an outstanding manner . . . and it was because of this that your majesty allowed them to stay in this realm; these men have always served, they were loyal when the entire kingdom rebelled and it is impossible to believe that they would rebel now when they are alone among us."[15]

For its part, the Valencia tribunal of the Inquisition already learned to be dubious about so-called Morisco plots after its hard experience in the 1580s. At the *auto-de-fé* of April 19, 1587, nine Moriscos were punished for having perjured themselves in testimony about a rising in support of an Ottoman invasion. Alarmed by the kingdom's vulnerability to attack and all too eager to see the Moriscos as a security threat, the tribunal had moved swiftly to arrest the supposed plotters only to find that the entire scheme existed only in their imagination.[16] In 1589, the Holy Office punished Lic. Juan Alonso alias Diego de Morales, alias Lic. Gutierrez, a confidence man who was going through Morisco-dominated areas pretending to be a Holy Office commissioner. As soon as he arrived at a Morisco village he would present some counterfeit titles to the local authorities and order the arrest of wealthy local Moriscos on charges of carrying on a treasonous correspondence with the Porte. He would then demand 200 reales from the sequestered property for his expenses and repeat the same thing in another village. Even though the Holy Office interrogated him thoroughly it was never able to establish his true identity "since he has called himself by so many names."[17]

As for the Moriscos themselves, they were certainly level-headed enough to evaluate fantastic yarns about foreign intervention in their favor at their true value and avoid any serious involvement. On August 18, 1609, just before the first decree of expulsion was announced, Gaspar Soler, *notario real* in the village of Seros (Catalonia), testified before a Holy Office commissioner that Pedro de Amos had told village Moriscos that the Turk had put to sea with 30,000 sail "and some of those present started laughing saying that was impossible since neither the Turk nor the king had ever launched so many ships so it was just a laughing matter" ("y riendose algunos de los presentes dixieron que era imposible por que ni el turco ni el rey jamas se ubiesse echado tantos vaxales a la mar y asi era cosa de risa").[18]

We are fortunate in being provided with a kind of litmus test of the relative political loyalty of Philip III's Morisco subjects on the eve of the expulsion in a collection of documents entitled: "Papeles para los señores del concejo de la general inquisición en raçon del levantamiento de los moriscos de Aragón." These documents contain the replies of witnesses to a series of hearings held by Holy Office commissioners in the Morisco-dominated area between Zaragoza and Calatayud. They are all the more valuable to us because the testimony was taken between August and October 1609, just before and just after the promulgation of the edict expelling the Moriscos of Valencia. Naturally enough, the Moriscos of Aragon feared that they would be the next to be expelled while, at the same time, rumors abounded of a possible French invasion of the kingdom. The questionnaire prepared by the Zaragoza tribunal for the use of its commissioners was designed specifically to test the loyalty of the Moriscos and find out if they were preparing for revolt. It included such questions as whether the newly converted of the district were holding secret meetings and planning to rebel, and if they were collecting weapons and gunpowder for that purpose. The authorities' concern with possible Morisco support for a French or Turkish invasion of Aragon is reflected in questions six and seven, in which the commissioners were told to ask witnesses if, as a result of the news from France, the Moriscos showed signs of rejoicing and if any messages had come from France or Turkey instigating them to revolt.

Of course, the Old Christians who lived in Morisco-dominated communities automatically assumed that they were conspiring with Spain's enemies. For example, Mosen Jaime Pérez, the vicar of Sabiñan, testified before commissioner Mosen Miguel Ibañez on August 17, 1609 that "he was sure that they would rise if the Turk or the French were to show any intention of invading these kingdoms."[19] However, there is no reason to accept uncritically the opinions of these Old Christians who were greatly distrusted by their Morisco neighbors for whom they were little more than spies for the Holy Office. In this case, moreover, none of the Old Christian witnesses could confirm any Morisco preparations for revolt. It seems at least possible, for example, that the Moriscos of Telsa who told their Old Christian neighbor Miguel López, that the "the Turk was coming with a hundred galleys" may have simply been out to intimidate him.

A careful reading of the evidence contained in these documents regarding Morisco attitudes toward a possible French invasion would seem to indicate that they reacted much the way ordinary Aragonese Christians might have reacted—with anger and indignation. This is strongly suggested by a conversation reported by the vicar of Figueras between Joan Ricardo, a native of France who served as guard of boundaries, and Miguel de Oyud, one of the Moriscos, who on hearing the news of a possible French invasion said, "So Ricardo they say that your king is coming—is he coming to kill us? . . . and the Frenchman replied 'By God I don't know' . . . and the other said to him 'why don't you go to your king of France', and Ricardo replied 'this is good land here', and Miguel de Oyud declared that 'as long as we have blood in our arms we will defend ourselves.' "[20]

Another dialogue, this time reported by Mosen Joan Foyas, the vicar of Noella de Alpartel, speaks volumes about the political position of the Moriscos around the time of the expulsion. During a discussion of the possible invasion, Geronimo el Corambero, one of the Moriscos, declared that he wanted to volunteer to fight for the king, and the vicar replied that "the king does not trust you so you would not be able to enlist." Corambero then told the vicar that "We know that they don't count on us," but "we would not go over to the French side leaving our wives, families, and property."[21]

The Moriscos, loyal subjects of His Catholic Majesty Philip III? The question is an uncomfortable one because it brings up the issue of loyalty to what and to whom. In the Spain of the seventeenth century, loyalty and patriotism were felt most intensely for the village or town, then for the region, and only then, if at all, for the monarchy. Moriscos like Geronimo el Corambero were not unlike other Spaniards in that respect—they would fight for the king not to protect the monarchy but to save their homes and families. As subsequent events were to demonstrate, the real danger to the Spanish monarchy was to come not from the Moriscos but from its politically dissatisfied Christian subjects seeking to save regional autonomy from Castilian "imperialism." As for the Moriscos, their expulsion made Spain more and not less insecure, as they founded pirate colonies on the shores of Morocco and were joined by Dutch and English privateers in making war on Spanish shipping. From this perspective, therefore, the expulsion looks even more like a tragic mistake but one that was consistent with the increasing rigidity and growing intolerance of the Catholic world during the seventeenth century. In Austria and Bohemia the liberal policies of the early sixteenth century were modified under Rudolf II and reversed under Ferdinand II (1619–1637). In the Catholic states of Germany the prince bishops were still expelling their Protestant subjects in the eighteenth century.[22]

In France, the toleration of the Huguenots after 1624 gave way to persecution and forced conversion during the reign of Louis XIV. In Spain itself the favorable reception accorded the Portuguese New Christians was replaced by repression and persecution after the fall of Olivares in 1643. By the end of the seventeenth century, the experiment in toleration had come to an end and religious conformity had become synonymous with political loyalty in the Catholic states of Europe. In this process, the Moriscos were the earliest but by no means the only victims.

NOTES

1. Jaime Bleda, *Defensio fidei in causa neophytorum sive Morischorum regni Valentiae totiusque Hispaniae* (Valencia, 1610), 598.

2. Ibid., 602.

3. Ibid., 608.

4. Ibid., 595.

5. Antonio Domínguez Ortiz and Bernard Vincent, *Historia de los moriscos: vida y tragedia de una minoría* (Madrid, 1978), 167.

6. Madrid, Biblioteca Nacional, MS 8888, ff. 85^{r}–87^{v}: "Acerca de los moriscos de España."

7. Ibid., ff. 6^{v}–10^{r}, 22^{r}–23^{r}.

8. Ibid., f. 12^{r}.

9. Ibid.

10. Ibid., ff. 87^{r}–88^{r}.

11. Ibid., ff. 110^{r}–111^{r}.

12. Ibid., f. 13^{r}.

13. Arthur Geoffrey Dickens, *The Counter Reformation* (New York, 1968), 59.

14. Domínguez Ortiz and Vincent, *Historia,* 170–71.

15. Ibid., 281–82, 173–74.

16. Madrid, Archivio Histórico Nacional (hereafter AHN), Inquisition, lib. 937 (April 19, 1587).

17. AHN, Inquisition, lib. 937 (March 19, 1587).

18. AHN, Inquisition, leg. 1808, exp. 10 (August 18, 1609).

19. AHN, Inquisition, leg. 1808, exp. 10 (August 17, 1609).

20. AHN, Inquisition, leg. 1808, exp. 10 (August 13, 1609).

21. AHN, Inquisition, leg. 1808, exp. 10 (August 17, 1609).

22. Dickens, *Counter Reformation,* 152–54.

14

Moriscas and the Limits of Assimilation

MARY ELIZABETH PERRY

In the debate over "the Morisco question" that spilled from the sixteenth into the early seventeenth century, the most damning argument against Moriscos was that they refused to become like Christians. In Valencia, wrote Fray Nicolás del Río in 1606, Moriscos "say that there has been no one to teach them, but their obstinacy and hardness of heart has caused the teaching to have no effect."[1] Moreover, in resisting attempts to Christianize them, their women were the most "obstinate," according to another report.[2] They hid their children from Christian teachers and spoke the prohibited Arabic language longer than the men. In their homes they continued to clean, cook, and celebrate life and death in the Muslim manner. Moriscas played significant roles in the struggle over assimilation, and their experiences provide important insights into the complexities of this struggle.

Before considering the lives of these women, a working definition of the term 'assimilation' is in order. Although the term can be used in many different ways, it refers in this essay to the process by which a subordinate group of people is absorbed into a dominant group, becoming indistinguishable, at least culturally. It assumes the superiority and acceptability of the dominant culture, and it uses strategies that range from intermarriage to forced acculturation. Assimilation should be distinguished from acculturation, which is not necessarily forced and is usually a long-term, two-way process in which some cultural traits of the subordinate group may become integrated into the dominant culture.[3] In medieval Spain, for example, subject Mudejars influenced the ruling Christian culture in many ways, most notably in science, agriculture, music, architecture, and language.[4]

Conflict, however, eclipsed both acculturation and assimilation as a literate Christian elite in the kingdoms of late medieval Spain developed governments more responsive to its needs and interests.[5] During the first half of the fifteenth century, for example, the policy of Juan II of Castile (1406–1454) required Christians and Muslims to live separately, imposed special sumptuary laws against Muslims, prohibited male Muslims from cutting their hair or beards, and required them to wear a blue crescent on their right shoulder.[6] In the middle of the fifteenth century, officials in Toledo passed the first *limpieza de sangre* statutes that made assimilation more difficult by formally defining loyalty through an examination of lineage.[7] By 1480, the Cortes of Toledo agreed to a "complete separation of both races within the Spanish nation," and the goal appeared to be less acculturation than the subjection of Muslims.[8]

After the fall of Granada in 1492, some Christians emphasized the need to make Muslims into Christians, but they assumed that the difficulties of assimilation would require some time in which certain aspects of Muslim culture would continue. Many clerics called for converting Muslims, and most realized that this would require teaching them about the Christian religion, sometimes in the Arabic language.[9] For a time, some Christian liturgy incorporated the Arabic language and Muslim traditions such as the *zambra,* a dance of celebration.[10] Intermarriage could even be considered as a way to make Muslims into Christians, some Christians proposed, although most leaders of both religions opposed it. Christians who supported intermarriage believed that it was best to marry Old Christian men to Muslim women because husbands should dominate marriage and subject wives to their religion.[11] This arrangement, it should be noted, would preserve the existing gender order and protect the privilege of Old Christian men.

The significance of gender roles changed as Christian oppression increased against all Muslim practices during the sixteenth century. When they could no longer meet in mosques, possess books written in Arabic, speak in Arabic dialect, and carry out their cultural practices publicly, Moriscos withdrew into their private homes or small kinship groups where they might more safely continue their traditions. Here the sexual division of labor directed to Moriscas the tasks of child-rearing, cleanliness, and food preparation—cultural practices which Inquisitors regarded as evidence of apostasy. As their husbands and religious leaders disappeared into death or exile, Moriscas increasingly bore the responsibility of teaching their children the basic beliefs and practices of Islam.[12]

Despite their significant participation in struggles over assimilation, Moriscas rarely appear in traditional historical studies.[13] One explanation is that it is often difficult to uncover the experiences of women in the past. Only the exceptional woman appears in documents as an active participant in historical events, and most women have been subsumed into categories under male authority, such as *señoríos,* towns, parishes, and households. Women can be described as a "muted" group, not heard in most written records because they have been excluded from participating in public discourse, or the dominant system of communication.[14] Yet Moriscas do appear in reports of Christian clerics, Inquisition documents, chronicles, literature, and city records, primarily as the object of complaint or as a petitioner. Recorded by another person, who often prompted the information given, these documents nevertheless provide valuable evidence.

Two twentieth-century thinkers—an Italian communist and a Vietnamese film-maker and critic—help in analyzing the evidence of Moriscas' experiences. Antonio Gramsci emphasizes the significance of culture in struggles for political domination and, in particular, the active roles of popular culture and civil society.[15] The state, according to Gramsci, can use force, but it is even more effective in establishing hegemony through the institutions and "organisms" of civil society, such as churches, schools, and courts of law.[16]

Hegemony acts as a constant dynamic that attempts to level difference or to attain domination over others, even though, as Trinh Minh-ha points out, difference always exists—both within a culture and between cultures.[17] Protesting both the suppression of difference in the name of theory, as well as its definition by the dominant culture, Trinh suggests a gendered approach that recognizes "a politics of everyday life," and "the ethnic female subject as site of differences."[18]

In sixteenth-century Spain, Christian officials attempted to extend power and erase difference through assimilation. Their hegemony functioned through the smallest details of daily life, those tasks of cleaning, cooking, and childcare that are so often left to women. The focus of the struggle to make Moriscos become more like Christians turned very quickly from the male-dominated public arenas of battleground, court, and church to the private and often woman-centered homes of Moriscos.

It would be a gross over-simplification, however, to assume that all Moriscas resisted assimilation or even entered the struggle against Christians. Two Moriscas of very different experience can demonstrate the range of difference. Leonor de Jesús exemplifies those Moriscas who made only the minimum gestures of assimilation essential to survival and attempted to escape from Spain to go to North Africa.[19] In contrast, Beatriz de Robles represents those Moriscas so well assimilated that they intermarried with Old Christians, became fervent Catholics, and escaped the order to expel Moriscos decreed by Philip III in 1609–1611.[20] We know about these women because each of them got into trouble with the Inquisition, ironically one of the very few institutions that gave names and faces to Moriscas. Their stories provide significant insights not only into assimilation, but also into political imperatives for a developing Spanish state and the intimate relationship of politics, culture, and religion.

A CASE OF RESISTANCE AGAINST ASSIMILATION

Born in the kingdom of Granada in 1568, Leonor de Jesús had little reason to assimilate. When Granada capitulated in 1492, the Catholic monarchs had promised Muslims freedom to practice their own religion, but within ten years pressure to convert had exploded into a Muslim revolt that Christians defeated and then the monarchs decreed that Muslims of Granada had to convert to Christianity or leave the Spanish kingdoms.[21] Thousands went into exile, but many others remained in Spain, ostensibly Christians, but always suspect. Now subject to the Inquisition, which was directed to assist in the Christianization of these converts, their tributes to the Spanish crown bought only a few years of grace. By 1526 a *junta* meeting in Granada concluded that all Morisco "particularism" must be prohibited, including not merely religion, but all cultural practices, such as the Arabic language, Muslim songs and dances, modes of dressing, washing, and preparing food.[22]

Although regulations would later direct local authorities to enter Morisco homes in order to uncover hidden Muslim practices, most Moriscos in small villages and mountainous areas had little interference from Christians attempting to uproot their customary practices. Living in enclaves with only a few Old Christians present, these Moriscos were supposed to baptize their children, but they chose as godparents for their children Old Christian neighbors who would not intrude into their homes and traditions, and they warned one another when an outsider appeared who might be too inquisitive.[23] Even though they had to accept Christian names, they kept and often used Muslim names and clearly identified themselves as people of Muslim descent.

In 1568, the year of Leonor de Jesús's birth, a rebellion broke out among Moriscos of Granada and a nearby mountainous area, the Alpujarras. It quickly spread through much of southern Spain, frightening Christians who expected Turkish and North African invaders to come to the aid of the rebels. Atrocities escalated on both sides as Christian forces attempted to quell the insurrection. Moriscas fought alongside the men of their communities, sometimes armed with only stones and roasting spits.[24]

When Christians had finally defeated the rebels in 1570, Philip II decreed the dispersal of all Moriscos of Granada throughout his kingdom. Some 50,000 Moriscos left their homes in Granada, directed to leave in groups of 1,500, each group accompanied by 200 Christian soldiers.[25] At least one-quarter of these Moriscos died during their journey of exile, many from typhus. The women and children suffered many forms of violence, especially vulnerable without the protection of their homes.[26] As a very small child, Leonor de Jesús must have made this journey with some adults or surviving family members who could carry her, for it would have been very difficult for such a young child to walk the twenty kilometers that each group was to cover every day.

Leonor's journey ended finally in the city of Seville, which had been directed to accept 4,000 of the Granadan Moriscos. Here the Christian population regarded the newcomers with great suspicion, and the archbishop ordered his clergy to establish a strict vigilance over them.[27] All Moriscos were required to attend religious instruction on Sundays and feast days and to pay a fine for any absence. Parish priests were made responsible for knowing how Moriscos lived in their homes, to prevent them from speaking Arabic or teaching Arabic to their children, from living together with other Moriscos, and even from coming together with them in any place. No longer could these Moriscos continue their Muslim traditions in the privacy of their homes. Sheriffs could now enter at unexpected times to look for evidence that they prepared food with oil rather than with lard, as the Christians did, or that they ate seated on the ground in the Muslim manner. Such increased Christian vigilance threatened not only Morisco traditions, but their very identity—an identity that they had inherited with the blood in their veins. To assimilate meant they must deny their blood, their parentage, their self-identity, their community.[28]

Yet survival required at least an external assimilation, and many Moriscos turned to the Muslim tradition of *taqiyya,* or outward conformity while preserving inwardly their faith of Islam.[29] "God is not concerned with your exterior attitude, but with the intention of your hearts," the *muftī* of Oran had advised Moriscos in 1563. "And if they tell you to denounce Muḥammad, denounce him by word and love him at the same time in your heart."[30]

As a child, Leonor probably received some of the required religious instruction from a priest. It must have been difficult for her to learn the principles of Islam, however, for most leaders of Islam had been exiled and Moriscos were not even supposed to meet together. Most likely her mother or another older woman taught her the rudiments of Islam and Muslim culture in the shelter of their home.[31] While she learned the Christian observances necessary for survival, Leonor must have also learned her difference from Christians and to resist inwardly the Christian attempts to make her be like them.

Undoubtedly, Leonor had to earn some money even as a child, for the crown had confiscated goods and property of the Granadan Moriscos when they were resettled, and local regulations restricted their economic opportunities.[32] Many Moriscos became muleteers, some using their profits to become small merchants, buying goods that they would transport and resell.[33] Moriscas often sold food on the streets. Young girls like Leonor were frequently apprenticed to households where they worked as domestic servants, earning only their board and room and perhaps a small sum at the end of their service that was to help provide a dowry.[34]

Historical records tell us nothing of when Leonor married, but she was a widow by 1604, the year when she literally risked her life as she tried to escape to North Africa on a boat in the company of some other Moriscos. Caught by the Inquisition, she tried to defend herself from the accusation that she wanted to go to North Africa so that she could return to Islam. Under examination, however, she confessed in order to save herself from the bonfire, was reconciled to the Church, and received a sentence of a hundred lashes, the *sanbenito,* and perpetual prison. It seems very likely that her reconciliation was more fervent than sincere, and that her punishment discouraged further resistance more than it promoted assimilation. In this case, and many like it, assimilation appears to be intertwined with oppression and limited by it, as well.

A CASE OF UNACCEPTABLE ASSIMILATION

Yet Leonor de Jesús does not typify all Moriscas and, in fact, some became very well assimilated. Those who had lived for generations intermixed among Christians in the large urban centers no longer spoke Arabic or followed Islam. Some Moriscas became sincere, "even fervent," Christians, marrying Old Christian men and producing sons who became members of the lower clergy.[35] Many of them escaped Philip III's order that expelled Moriscos in the early seventeenth century.[36]

Beatriz de Robles, a Morisca who lived in the village of Fuentes near Seville, became so well assimilated that she married Juan de Baestra, an Old Christian, and remained in Spain following the expulsion of Moriscos. Little is known of her family or birth, except that she was born in 1576, six years after the 4,000 Granadan Moriscos were sent to Seville. It is possible that her family had lived in the area of Seville for several generations, perhaps among those few

Mudejar families that had earlier prospered and lived more easily with Christians. A report of 1588 from Seville described Moriscos there with "great riches," who bought and sold food, controlling "the greater part" of the bread market.[37] Their economic success had a double edge: it could promote assimilation through more formal education and intermarriage, but it could also discourage it, exacerbating tensions that resulted not simply from religious hatred, but from the resentment of Christian consumers against Morisco producers and sellers.[38]

A class difference distinguishes Leonor de Jesús from Beatriz de Robles, for the family of the latter had enough wealth to provide a dowry that would attract an Old Christian husband, an amount that probably had to be even greater following the abortive Morisco rebellion put down in Seville in 1580.[39] By the time that she was of marriageable age, in the last decade of the sixteenth century when Christian oppression against anything Morisco had reached a peak, Beatriz would have needed not only a substantial dowry, but the appearance of being very well assimilated in order to attract an Old Christian husband.

In fact, Beatriz became so well assimilated that she was later charged by the Inquisition not for following Islam, but for embracing illuminism, a Christian heresy that had found fertile ground in the region of Seville. In her testimony, she spoke of meeting with *beatas,* those irregular holy women who devoted their lives to God and worried church authorities with their independence from any rule or direction. As she described her visions and experiences to Inquisitors, she used the same language of many *beatas,* saying that she was "very beloved and favored by God," and that he came to her in the corners of her house to tell her "a thousand tender compliments."[40] After communion, she said, she was "full of the love of God," and sometimes she fainted and at other times she gave "many fearsome roars."

Whether Beatriz actually had these experiences is not clear. What we do know, however, is that her language and visions parallel very closely those of many other *beatas* prosecuted as *alumbradas,* or illuminists, by the Inquisition.[41] It is very possible that mysticism for these women became a language of the self and the body that became an alternative rhetoric and that Inquisitors used a formula for questioning *alumbrados* that elicited this language.[42] Clerics in the case of Beatriz de Robles may have been especially sensitive to illuminist rhetoric because they had uncovered a "congregation" of hundreds of people in Seville and nearby villages who were "infected" by this heresy.[43]

Mystical movements such as illuminism attracted New Christians, both Judeo-converso and Morisco, because they bypassed the authority of clerics who insisted on strict adherence to Church teachings. Perhaps the mystical tradition of Islam facilitated the assimilation into Christianity of women such as Beatriz de Robles. For example, both the Sufi sect of Muslim tradition and Christian illuminism emphasized emotion and personal experience rather than intellectual knowledge and external observance of religious formalism. Both sought union with God through turning inward, away from the world, and both engaged in individual trances and collective experiences that could become extravagantly emotional in dancing, weeping, and shouting.[44]

Clerical authorities said nothing about the imperfection of her assimilation when they sentenced her in 1624. Like other *alumbrados* penanced in this year, Beatriz de Robles was sentenced to appear in an *auto-de-fé,* to swear to no longer commit offenses against the Church, and to two years of reclusion in a hospital for women where she would work to earn her food. A "prudent confessor" would be assigned to hear her confessions and to "direct her in what is appropriate for the salvation of her soul." Assimilation for this woman had been limited by her attraction to a popular form of mysticism considered heretical by the Church. More precisely, the assimilation of Beatriz de Robles was "off-target." She embraced not the official Christianity of the Church, but one of many popular versions of this religion condemned by the Church. In the eyes of Inquisitors, she was neither Morisca nor acceptable Christian.

SIGNIFICANCE

What, then, are the insights that we can gain from the stories of these two Moriscas? First, they demonstrate the great diversity in the Morisco experience. Their generation, economic status, place of birth, and residence directly influenced their degree of assimilation. Second, the home became a focal point for testing assimilation—in the one case, to ensure the end of any vestiges of Morisco culture and, in the other, to learn about irregular religious experiences or meetings not directed by the Church. Third, their stories show that a history of oppression can harden resistance against assimilation. Finally, they show that assimilation to the "wrong kind" of Christianity was not enough and suggest that many Christians who followed various popular religious movements also had to be assimilated. The assimilation sought by authorities in early modern Spain meant acceptance of a control established over beliefs, behavior, and every aspect of culture.

We have come full circle, then, for we are back to hegemony. During the sixteenth century when the Spanish Crown was moving towards establishing a centralized state, the Church acted as its most important ally. Attempting to root out heresy and apostasy, the Church had to inquire into the everyday cultural practices that exposed the heretic and apostate, from offhand remarks to a neighbor to forms of preparing and consuming food. Even more importantly, the Church provided the one identity and institutional loyalty that all members of the nascent state of Spain could share, regardless of their local identifications.[45] Moreover, the Church also helped to identify common internal enemies—most notably, Judeo-conversos and Moriscos—that were essential as a "counter-identity," a means to unify all the diverse peoples of the Spanish kingdoms.[46] Here, as elsewhere, religion became a "pervasive daily marker of difference"; for Christians it served as a rationale for expelling Jews, Muslims, and finally Moriscos.[47]

Church and Crown did not always agree, however, and sometimes they competed for authority. Before the expulsion of the Moriscos, the Spanish Crown depended on the Inquisition, a major arm of the Church, to uncover and punish Moriscos who retained their differences from Christians. In deciding to expel them, the Crown used the language of religion, but it effectively neutralized some of the power that the Church had developed through prosecutions by the Inquisition. Announcement of the royal decree of expulsion followed by measures to enforce it became a secular ritual throughout the kingdoms of Spain that at least for a time overshadowed the religious ritual of the edict of grace and *auto-de-fé.* Following the expulsion, Spain could continue to evolve into a church-supported monarchical state rather than a theocracy.[48]

For both Crown and Church, Moriscos' failure to assimilate became an argument for expelling them. Yet assimilation did not work in the same way for all Moriscos. In the range of differences, Leonor de Jesús and Beatriz de Robles represent two extremes. Poles apart, they demonstrate the complexity of Morisco experiences; together, they reveal the dimensions of tragedy whenever any group attempts to obliterate the culture and identity of another.

NOTES

1. Memorial to Philip III, published in Mercedes García Arenal, *Los moriscos* (Madrid, 1975), 125–33; the quotation is on page 126. Unless otherwise noted, this and other texts have been translated from Spanish by the author of this essay.

2. "Informe de Madrid a Valencia sobre instrucción de los moriscos," included in García Arenal, *Los moriscos,* 116–25, especially 122.

3. For discussions of assimilation and acculturation, see Charlotte Seymour-Smith, *Dictionary of Anthropology* (Boston, 1986), especially 18; and *Encyclopedia of Anthropology,* ed. David E. Hunter and Phillip Whitten (New York, 1976), 2 and 46. A very helpful discussion of acculturation, particularly in Spanish history, is in Thomas F. Glick and Oriol Pi-Sunyer, "Acculturation as an Explanatory Concept in Spanish History," *Comparative Studies in Society and History* 2, no. 2 (1969): 136–54. An interesting use of assimilation as a social model is Alice S. Rossi, "Sex Equality: The Beginnings of Ideology," *The Humanist* 29, no. 5 (1969): 6; I wish to thank Judith Bennett, who suggested this article to me.

4. José Jiménez Lozano, *Judíos, moriscos y conversos* (Valladolid, 1982), 86–87, points out that medieval Spanish society became "Islamized" and Mudejars became more assimilated into Christian society. Robert I. Burns, *Muslims, Christians, and Jews in the Crusader Kingdom of Valencia: Societies in Symbiosis* (Cambridge, 1984) emphasizes the mutual benefits that the three major religious groups shared in living together peacefully. However, Leonard P. Harvey, *Islamic Spain, 1250 to 1500* (Chicago, 1990), 14–15, argues that by the thirteenth century, earlier coexistence between Muslims and Christians became less possible in Islamic Spain as tensions increased with the Reconquest.

5. See Robert I. Moore, *The Formation of a Persecuting Society* (Oxford, 1987), but note that the "twelfth-century revolution in government" and "tremendous extension of the power and influence of the literate" that he

describes for all of medieval Europe probably did not take place in the Spanish kingdoms until the later thirteenth, fourteenth, and fifteenth centuries.

6. For further discussion, see Celestino López Martínez, *Mudéjares y moriscos sevillanos* (Seville, 1935), 47–48; and Glick and Pi-Sunyer, "Acculturation," 143.

7. Andrew C. Hess, *The Forgotten Frontier: A History of the Sixteenth-Century Ibero-African Frontier* (Chicago, 1978), 129. For a broader discussion of these statutes, see Albert A. Sicroff, *Los estatutos de limpieza de sangre: controversias entre los siglos XV y XVII* (Madrid, 1985).

8. Pascual Boronat y Barrachina, *Los moriscos españoles y su expulsión: estudio histórico-crítico,* 2 vols. (Valencia, 1901), 1.96–97. Harvey points out that these policies went back at least to the Lateran Council of 1215 (*Islamic Spain,* 65–66); it should also be noted that persecution was not limited to Muslims and indeed increased against Jews, who became the targets of pogroms, forced conversions, and *limpieza de sangre* statutes.

9. The language differences between Muslims and Christians have a long history, of course, and did not begin in the sixteenth century. For a more complete discussion of this issue, see Robert I. Burns, "The Language Barrier: The Problem of Bilingualism and Muslim-Christian Interchange in the Medieval Kingdom of Valencia," in *Contributions to Mediterranean Studies,* ed. Mario Vassallo (Valletta, Malta, 1977), 116–36; and Robert I. Burns, "Christian-Islamic Confrontation in the West: The Thirteenth-Century Dream of Conversion," *American Historical Review* 76 (1971): 1386–1434.

10. For Christian concerns with using Arabic to Christianize Muslims, see Francisco Borja de Medina, "La Compañía de Jesús y la minoría morisca (1545–1614)," *Archivum historicum Societatis Iesu* 57 (1988): 69–73. Francisco Nuñez Muley in "Memoria al presidente" (MS 6176 of the Biblioteca Nacional [hereafter BN]), discussed the clerics who adapted Christian liturgy to include Arabic and Muslim dance and music (318^{r}–19^{r}).

11. Damian Fonseca, *Justa expulsión de los moriscos de España: con la instrvcion, apostasia, y traycion dellos: y respuesta á las dudas que se ofrecieron acerca desta materia* (Rome, 1612), 461. Note that Fonseca, himself, did not call for intermarriage and, in fact, believed it could be "against natural law" and would require "pure" people to marry the impure. Officially, both Christians and Muslims opposed intermarriage as diluting the faith; see Bernard Vincent, *Minorías y marginados en la España del siglo XVI* (Granada, 1987), 25–27.

12. Many Moriscos testified to Inquisitors that they learned Islam from women; for three examples, see the cases of Leonor Hernández, Lucia de la Cruz, and Ludia de León and María de León, found in Madrid, Archivo Histórico Nacional (hereafter AHN), Inquisición, legajo 2075, nos. 8, 11, and 19, respectively. Note, however, that this testimony was given under considerable duress, and it may also indicate attempts by these women to protect men in their families, who usually received more severe penalties (Mary

Elizabeth Perry, "Behind the Veil: Moriscas and the Politics of Resistance and Survival," in *Spanish Women in the Golden Age: Images and Realities,* ed. Alain Saint-Saëns and Magdalena S. Sánchez [Westport, Conn., 1996], 37–53).

13. Recently historians are breaking with this pattern. Three excellent examples are Vincent, *Minorías y marginados;* Ricardo García Cárcel, *Herejía y sociedad en el siglo XVI: la inquisición en Valencia 1530–1609* (Barcelona, 1980); and Jacqueline Fournel Guérin, "La femme morisque en Aragon," in *Les Morisques et leur temps: table ronde internationale 4–7 juillet 1981, Montpellier* (Paris, 1983).

14. This concept is discussed in David Sibley, *Outsiders in Urban Societies* (New York, 1981), 16.

15. Antonio Gramsci, *Letters from Prison* (New York, 1973), 204; and *Selections from the Prison Notebooks of Antonio Gramsci* (New York, 1972), 169–70, 238, 258, and 260.

16. Gramsci, *Selections,* 12.

17. Trinh T. Minh-ha, "Not You/Like You: Post-Colonial Women and the Interlocking Questions of Identity and Difference," *Inscriptions* 3–4 (1988): 72.

18. Trinh T. Minh-ha, *Woman, Native, Other: Writing Postcoloniality and Feminism* (Bloomington, 1989), 43–44; and *When the Moon Waxes Red: Representation, Gender, and Cultural Politics* (New York, 1991), especially 151.

19. AHN, Inquisición, legajo 2075, no. 14. This case is discussed in my essay, "Religión, género, y poder: las moriscas en la España de los siglos XVI y XVII," in *Retratos de mujeres en España, desde la época medieval hasta la época contemporánea,* ed. Alain Saint-Saëns (Madrid, 1994).

20. AHN, Inquisición, legajo 2075, no. 31; also, Libro 1259, "Relación sumaria del autho de fee celebrado en 30 de diciembre día de San Andres en Sevilla año de 1624 en la Plaza de San Francisco, 160. For the heresy of illuminism, or *alumbradismo,* see Antonio Márquez, *Los Alumbrados, orígines, y filosofía, 1525–1559* (Madrid, 1972). For more on the case of Beatriz de Robles, see my unpublished "Delusions, Assimilation, and Survival: A Christianized Muslim Holy Woman in Seventeenth-Century Spain," presented to the American Historical Association in Washington, D.C., December 1992.

21. The terms of capitulation and other documents relating to the fall of Granada are in *Colección de documentos inéditos para la historia de España,* 112 vols. (Madrid, 1846), 8.399–482. See Mark Meyerson, *The Muslims of Valencia in the Age of Fernando and Isabel: Between Coexistence and Crusade* (Berkeley, 1991), 54–58, for more discussion of the expulsion and conversion policies of the Catholic monarchs. Note that Charles V extended this decree to Muslims in other parts of his kingdoms in 1525.

22. Antonio Domínguez Ortiz and Bernard Vincent, *Historia de los moriscos: vida y tragedia de una minoría* (Madrid, 1978), 21–24; and Henry Charles

Lea, *The Moriscos of Spain: Their Conversion and Expulsion* (Philadelphia, 1901; rpt. New York, 1968), 142–48.

23. For godparents, see Vincent, *Minorías y marginados,* especially 82. For their warnings about outsiders, see Fonseca, *Justa expulsión,* 127.

24. *Relación muy verdadera sacada de vna carta que al Illustre Cabildo y regimiento desta ciudad* (Seville, 1569), n.p.

25. Estimates vary on the number of Moriscos expelled from Granada. Hess, for example, believes 70,000 to 80,000 Moriscos were expelled at this time (*The Forgotten Frontier,* 147).

26. Domínguez Ortiz and Vincent, *Historia de los moriscos,* 50–52. For the special vulnerability of women travelers, see María Milagros Rivera Garretas, *Textos y espacios de mujeres* (Barcelona, 1990), 39–50.

27. *Constituciones del Arcobispado de Sevilla* (Seville, 1609), 19–20; and Antonio Domínguez Ortiz, *Orto y ocaso de Sevilla: estudio sobre la prosperidad y decadencia de la ciudad durante los siglos XVI y XVII* (Seville, 1946), 57.

28. Meyerson, *The Muslims of Valencia,* 255–69, provides a thorough and thoughtful discussion of those qualities of Mudejar society that promoted its solidarity.

29. For more on this tradition, see Henri Lammens, *Islam: Beliefs and Institutions,* trans. Edward Deison Ross (London, 1968), 168–75.

30. "Respuesta que hizo el mufti de Oran a ciertas preguntas que le hicieron desde la Andalucía," May 3, 1563 (García Arenal, *Los moriscos,* 44–45).

31. Juan Aranda Doncel, "Las prácticas musulmanas de los moriscos andaluces a través de las relacioes de causas del tribunal de la inquisición de Córdoba," in *Las prácticas musulmanas de los moriscos andaluces (1492–1609),* ed. Abdejelil Temini (Zoghouan, 1989), 20–21; and Vincent, *Minorías y marginados,* 139.

32. Madrid, Biblioteca nacional, MS 8987 (*Papeles referentes a los bienes que dejaron los moriscos en las Alpujarras*).

33. Domínguez Ortiz and Vincent, *Historia de los moriscos,* 120.

34. Blanca Morell Peguero, *Mercaderes y artesanos en la Sevilla del descubrimiento* (Seville, 1986), 63–73.

35. Domínguez Ortiz and Vincent, *Historia de los moriscos,* 150–51.

36. Vincent, *Minorías y marginados,* 229–30.

37. "Informe" of Don Alonso Gutiérrez, reprinted in Boronat y Barrachina, *Los moriscos españoles,* 1.635.

38. Lea, *The Moriscos of Spain,* 208–211, discusses this point.

39. For the 1580 rebellion, see López Martínez, *Mudéjares y moriscos,* 58–59; Vincent, *Minorías y marginados,* discusses intermarriage, which neither Christians nor Moriscos favored (25–27); and Fonseca, *Justa expulsión,*

pointed out the difficulties of persuading people of "pure" blood to marry those with Jewish or Muslim forebears (461).

40. All quotations here and below about her case are from AHN, Inquisición, legajo 2075, no. 31. Jean Franco, *Plotting Women: Gender and Representation in Mexico* (New York, 1989), shows that women mystics in New Spain made similar claims and probably received comfort from believing they had been singled out by God (18).

41. Mary Elizabeth Perry, "Beatas and the Inquisition in Early Modern Seville," in *Inquisition and Society in Early Modern Europe,* ed. Stephen Haliczer (London, 1986), 147–68.

42. Franco, *Plotting Women,* 4.

43. "Memorial de la secta de los alumbrados de Sevilla y de sus doctinas y delictos y de la complicidad que en ella se ha descubierto 1625," published in Bernardino Llorca, "Documentos inéditos interesantes sobre los alumbrados de Sevilla de 1623–1628," *Estudios eclesiásticos* 2 (1932): 268–84, and 404–418; Antonio Domínguez Ortiz, "La Congregación de la Granada y la Inquisición de Sevilla (un episodio de la lucha contra los alumbrados)," in *La inquisición española: nueva visión, nuevos horizontes,* ed. Joaquin Pérez Villanueva (Madrid, 1980), 636–46.

44. For Muslim mysticism and Sufism, see Lammens, *Islam,* 117–126; and Ibn Khaldun, *The Muqaddimah: An Introduction to History,* 3 vols., trans. Franz Rosenthal (New York, 1958), especially 3.76. Juan A. Souto, "Los siete cielos planetarios: una imagen cósmica de tradición musulmana en un salero mudéjar de Teruel," in Temini, *Las prácticas,* argues that Saint Teresa's seven castles of the soul in her *Moradas del castillo interior* are images derived from Muslim mysticism (172). Common religious practices do not necessarily lead to conversion and may simply facilitate harmonious contact; Harvey Goldberg, "The Mellahs of Southern Morocco: Report of a Survey," *The Maghreb Review* 9 (1983): 61–69, suggests that the tradition of saints common to both Moroccan Jews and Moroccan Muslims served as a conceptual bridge that facilitated communication between them.

45. David I. Kertzer, "The Role of Ritual in State Formation," in *Religious Regimes and State Formation,* ed. Erik R. Wolf (Albany, 1991), 93, discusses a similar role for the Church in the making of modern Italy.

46. Emile Durkheim saw this as a way to emphasize the "collective conscience" of a community; his views are discussed in Kai Erikson, *Wayward Puritans: A Study in the Sociology of Deviance* (New York, 1966), 4; for the importance of counter-identities in formation of national identities, see Peter Sahlins, *Boundaries: The Making of France and Spain in the Pyrenees* (Berkeley, 1989), 9.

47. The phrase is from Manning Nash, *The Cauldron of Ethnicity in the Modern World* (Chicago, 1989), 38.

48. Mart Bax, "Religious Regimes and State-Formation: Toward a Research Perspective," in Wolf, *Religious Regimes,* 11, proposes that the relationship of secular and religious regimes is one of "anatagonistically interdependent configurations." Kertzer, "The Role of Ritual," in the same volume emphasizes the important role of ritual in bringing about solidarity in the absence of consensus, especially because ritual involves emotions more than clear-cut beliefs and thus helps to establish allegiance to a new state (89–90).

15

The Moriscos and Christian Doctrine

CONSUELO LÓPEZ-MORILLAS

THE ASPECTS OF Christian doctrine that I will examine in this essay, in spite of the sweeping implications of its title, are in fact only two, and those closely linked: the nature of Christ and the nature of the Trinity. Further, my exploration begins with a single *aljamiado* text, although as I hope to show, that text has taken me far from my starting point. The passage that gave rise to this study occurs in an *aljamiado* manuscript, copied by Moriscos and found in Aragon,[1] and reads in translation as follows:

> Qatāda said: It was told to us that when God, may He be exalted, raised Jesus up into Heaven, the Banū Içrā'īl chose four from among their wise men. And they said to the first, "What do you say about Jesus?" He replied, "That He is God, who has descended to earth and has created what He created and revealed what is revealed, and then has ascended to Heaven." And [some] people agreed with that, and they were the Jacobite Christians. And the other three wise men said, "We declare that you lie." Then they said to the second wise man, "What do you say about Jesus?" And he replied, "He is the son of God." And [some] people agreed with that, and these were the Nestorian Christians. Then the last two wise men said, "We declare that you are a liar." And they said to the third wise man, "What do you say about Jesus?" And he replied, "He is Lord and His mother is Lord and God is Lord." And [some] people agreed with that, and they were the Israelite Christians. Then the fourth wise man said, "I declare that you are a liar; for he was

merely God's servant and messenger, and God's word and spirit." And the peoples were in disagreement about it.[2]

When I encountered this passage, the two questions that sprang readily to mind were, first, Where did it come from? and second, Did the Moriscos really care how the Nestorians differed from the Jacobites? And it is what I have found on my way to answering these questions that forms the basis of this study.

The text is a commentary on the Quranic verse *fa-khtalafa l-aḥzābu min baynihim,* "But the parties have fallen into variance among themselves,"[3] which occurs in identical form at two points in the sacred book, *sūras* 19:37 and 43:65. The first of these Quranic passages, in *Sūrat Maryam,* recounts how Mary, as a virgin, gave birth to Jesus; the second, in *Sūrat al-Zukhruf* "The Ornaments," denies the divinity of Jesus while affirming his enjoyment of God's favor. In both verses the mention of the quarreling factions is a veiled reference to internal dissensions among Christian sects during the early centuries of the Church. The inability of Christians to agree on points of doctrine was a continuing motive for scorn among Muslims.

Our *aljamiado* manuscript is a translation into Spanish of the *Mukhtaṣar* or abridgment by Ibn Abī Zamānīn of Elvira (died 1008)[4] of the *Tafsīr* or Quranic commentary of Yaḥyā ibn Salām al-Taymī of Basra (died 815).[5] One should observe that this version places the Quʾrān verse actually being glossed, "and the peoples were in disagreement about it" in my rendering of the Spanish, only as the final sentence in an extended anecdote about four wise men and their opinions on the nature of Jesus. The wise men themselves do not figure in the Qurʾān, and the story about them must have come into this and other Quranic commentaries, as we shall see, by another route.

Although *aljamiado* literature abounds in translations of, and commentaries on, the Qurʾān, all are anonymous except this one by Ibn Abī Zamānīn; and both he and the scholar whose work he is summarizing, al-Taymī, are very minor figures among Quranic exegetes.[6] Perhaps this one name was still remembered in sixteenth-century Spain because Ibn Abī Zamānīn hailed from Elvira.[7] I assume, however, that the bulk of the *tafsīrs* or commentaries that the Mudejars and Moriscos preserved and translated must have come ultimately, though without attribution, from the pens of the great Arab exegetes whose writings are virtually canonical. These are the authorities to whom pious Muslims have always turned for clarification of difficult passages of scripture. As yet, little has been done to identify particular *aljamiado* commentaries with any of these Arabic originals,[8] but I have undertaken a search for more sources of our passage on the nature of Christ. It seemed so unlikely to find Moriscos concerned with early Christian sectarian disputes that I hoped to discover if our text was unique, or if it simply repeated the received wisdom of much Arabic Quranic scholarship.

I have examined the explication of the Qur'ān verse about "the parties falling into variance" in seven major commentaries written between the tenth and the fifteenth centuries.[9] The *aljamiado* anecdote contains five essential elements: 1) the attribution to Qatāda, a religious authority from the first century of Islam;[10] 2) the presence of the four wise men of the Banū Isrā'īl; 3) the belief, attributed to the Jacobites, that Jesus is the same as God the Father; 4) the belief, attributed to the Nestorians, that Jesus is the Son of God; and 5) the belief, attributed to the Israelite Christians, that the Trinity consists of God the Father, Jesus, and the Virgin Mary. I looked, therefore, for all five of these elements in the Quranic commentaries.

Only two of the Arabic texts, those of al-Ṭabarī and Ibn Kathīr, of the tenth and fourteenth centuries respectively, match the *aljamiado* version almost exactly.[11] Al-Zamakhsharī and al-Rāzī, for example, mention neither Qatāda nor the four wise men; al-Qurṭubī cites the former but not the latter. All the commentators other than al-Ṭabarī and Ibn Kathīr call the third Christian sect the "Melkites" (*al-malkāniyya*) rather than the "Israelites," and some change the order in which the sects are named. Al-Qurṭubī fails to include the Mother of Jesus in the supposed Trinity, and so on.[12] From this juxtaposition of accounts we can conclude, I think, two things. First, that stories about different early Christian sects and their beliefs, varying in accuracy and in detail, circulated widely in Arabic, and were pressed into service by commentators to elucidate verses in the Qur'ān that alluded to sectarian dissension.[13] This was good propaganda for Islam, which, although it had its share of politico-religious factionalism, at least had no doubts about the nature of the One God. Second, and more specific, our *aljamiado* anecdote does *not* stand alone, but finds its parallel in two of the most important Quranic commentaries, and shares with them an authoritative source, Qatāda.

The story of the wise men and the sects clearly contains a kernel of truth about the accusations of heresy and anti-orthodoxy that the Eastern Christians of the early centuries so often flung at each other. It will be helpful to review what were the actual doctrines involved in these disputes. The early Church convoked ecumenical councils every generation or two—thirteen such councils by Muḥammad's time—to castigate heresies and to decide and promulgate points of dogma. In the fourth and fifth centuries, a series of especially historic convocations addressed the Incarnation and the Trinity. The Council of Nicaea was called by the Emperor Constantine himself in 325,[14] after a doctrinal dispute within the Church at Alexandria had escalated into a potential schism. Arius, a parish priest, had challenged his bishop by preaching that God the Father and God the Son were not co-eternal; since only the Godhead is unoriginate, the Son must have had a beginning ("There was when He was not") and been created by the Father. In the orthodox view, this formulation reduced the Son to the status of a demigod. The Nicene council resulted in the crafting of the eponymous Creed, though its now familiar language, declaring the Son to be "begotten not made, being of one substance with the Father," was not fixed for some decades.[15] The council also excommunicated Arius and declared his teachings heretical. Arianism continued strong, however, until newly condemned at the Council of Constantinople (381), which established the relationship of the third member of the Trinity, the Holy Spirit, to the Father and the Son. The Council of Chalcedon,[16] held in 451, came to terms with the even more subtle mystery of the Incarnation. As at Nicaea, it was convoked in response to an unorthodox local prelate, in this case Bishop Nestorius of Constantinople, who began by objecting to the term *Theotokos* "Bearer of God" as applied to the Virgin Mary. How could God have a mother? Mary must have borne Christ the Man, even though his divinity and his humanity existed side by side: "Christ is indivisible in His being Christ, but He is twofold in His being God and Man." Nestorius's enemies accused him of preaching a Jesus who was merely human, linked to the Word by divine favor alone. (When the Quranic commentators attribute to the Nestorians the credo that Jesus was the Son of God, we should supply, "*only* the Son of God.") Cyril of Alexandria, Nestorius's chief opponent, asserted the single, incarnate nature of the divine Word. The Council of Chalcedon hammered out a definition that attempted to embrace both the unity and the duality of the God-Man: "one and the same Christ . . . [in] two natures [that exist] without confusion, without change, without division, without separation."[17]

This dogma, now become the orthodoxy of the established Church, was the basis for most of the ecclesiastical disputes of the succeeding centuries. After Chalcedon the greatest danger became Monophysitism, the belief that Christ had only one essential nature or *physis,* his divinity.[18] Since the Chalcedonian party held virtually total sway in the Eastern Empire, Monophysitism was repressed and in disarray until the time of Bishop Jacob ben Baradai (553–78).[19] His far-flung but clandestine missionary activity spread the Monophysite faith, which came to be called Jacobite after him, into many areas of the Near East where it had been unknown before. The Jacobites clung to the formulation of Cyril of Alexandria, "one nature of the divine Word"; to them, asserting the dual nature of Christ privileged Jesus's humanity over his divinity. This is why the *aljamiado* commentary claims for the Jacobites the belief that Jesus is God.

The Eastern Christians who accepted the definition of Chalcedon were known as Melkites (*al-malkāniyya*), meaning "monarchists."[20] It is by no means clear why this group is identified in our *aljamiado* text, and in the commentaries of al-Ṭabarī and Ibn Kathīr, as "Israelite Christians."[21] Nor can I determine why the Arab exegetes identify the Melkites so consistently with the notion that the Trinity is made up of God the Father, God the Mother, and God the Son. Both Ibn Abī Zamānīn and al-Ṭabarī voice this belief; the other commentators employ the Quranic phrase that Jesus was "the Third of Three" (*sūra* 5:77). And yet I find no reference in Church history to any particular Melkite belief about the Trinity; what defined this sect in principle was its adherence to the doctrine of two natures in the one person of Christ.

These are the real doctrinal differences that underlie our *aljamiado* parable about the Nestorians and the Jacobites. But the story incorporates folkloric elements as well, for example in its sequence of four speeches by four wise men, each of which is rejected until the final formulation, the one acceptable to Islam, is reached. In Ibn

Kathīr's *tafsīr,* the tale is followed immediately by this delightful amplification:

> Constantine called them together in one of their three famous councils, in a great meeting place; and the total number of their bishops was 2,170. And they disagreed mightily about Jesus, son of Mary (may peace be upon him): each faction gave its opinion, and one hundred said one thing, and seventy said another, and fifty still another, and 160 something different; and no more than three hundred agreed on any single proposition. Then eight of them insisted upon a certain statement, and the king, being a philosopher, inclined to them; so he put them forward, and gave them the victory, and banished those who opposed them. And they gave to that [statement] their utmost faith, although it was the most tremendous perfidy.[22]

Both the presence of Constantine and the number of three hundred bishops mark this anecdote unmistakably as a garbled memory, filtered through Islamic consciousness, of the Council of Nicaea;[23] and it is probably no accident, in the light of the Church history just recalled, that its transmitter Ibn Kathīr juxtaposed the wrangling bishops to the four disputatious wise men of the Banū Isrāʾīl. I see in these two closely linked accounts of Christian disputations a current of anti-Christian polemical folklore that probably dates to the earliest days of Islam. In Muḥammad's time the Nestorians were tolerated only in Persia, while the Jacobites predominated in Egypt, Syria, Abyssinia, and South Arabia. Most of the Christian communities with which early Islam had contact, including the Arab Ghassānid kingdom on the borders of Persia, were Monophysite.[24] Both the beliefs and the contentiousness of these sects were familiar to, or at least half understood by, the Prophet and his successors. This knowledge, adorned with the embroidery of popular narrative, was subsumed by commentators on the Qurʾān as early as the time of Qatāda, and it is through the authority of *tafsīr* that it arrived in Spain and was still being repeated in sixteenth-century Aragon.

And here I take up the second question that I posed earlier: Did the Moriscos really care about the arcana of early Christian doctrinal disputes? Does their preservation of the manuscript that contains the wise men's disputation imply a particular concern for the subject? The easy answer is that the survival of *aljamiado* manuscripts was so erratic that no particular weight can be assigned to the existence of this one.[25] The Moriscos' access to this fragment of Quranic commentary may result from mere chance. But a differently focused answer is also possible. Anti-Christian polemic had a long and active history in Muslim Spain: we possess polemical texts dating from the eleventh to the seventeenth centuries, by Andalusi Arabs, Mudejars, and Moriscos, written in Arabic, *aljamiado,* and Spanish, from both Spain and North Africa. Anti-Christian disputation became, in fact, increasingly compelling as the Reconquest and the forced conversions isolated Mudejars and Moriscos in a sea of Christianity. And I think that we can place the passage at issue into the wider context of this ongoing theological confrontation.

Ibn Ḥazm of Córdoba, the eleventh-century philosopher and theologian, laid the groundwork for Muslim Spain's anti-Christian literature in his *Kitāb al-Fiṣal,* the first critical and comparative history of religions.[26] His bibliographic sources include the proceedings of the six great ecumenical councils and a number of minor ones, and he even inserts into his text at one point a variant of the Nicene Creed. Ibn Ḥazm classes Christianity as a polytheist religion on the basis of its belief in the Trinity, and is fairly accurate in his division of Christian sects into Trinitarian and anti-Trinitarian; he places among the latter the Melkites, Nestorians, and Jacobites, whose doctrines he describes in some detail.[27] Generations of devotees in al-Andalus and North Africa transmitted Ibn Ḥazm's works; Asín Palacios traces the line of his intellectual disciples as far as one Abū ʿAbdallah Muḥammad al-Andalusī, a Moroccan of the sixteenth century.

An important polemical work of the Mudejar period was *Kitāb Miftāḥ al-dīn* of Muḥammad al-Qaysī, a Tunisian war captive who spent many years in Catalonia and southern France in the early fourteenth century.[28] He took part, probably against his will, in a public disputation with a Christian monk, and recalls in his work all the details of his own and his opponent's arguments. The *Miftāḥ* was very soon adapted and rendered into *aljamiado* by a Mudejar scholar; portions of it survive in four *aljamiado* manuscripts, proof that it enjoyed a wide Morisco readership into the sixteenth century.[29]

The first section of the *Miftāḥ* includes a remarkable parallel to the account of the sectarian disputation with which we are here concerned. It is contained in "a long passage in which the historical causes of the splitting up of the Christians are discussed":[30]

> [Pablos el Judí.o] dixo: "... ke salgan todos, salvo ku.atro: el p.rimero Yaᶜqûb, i Nasṭur, i Malqûn, i.-el Mûmin." Así ke salli.eron todos, sino akellos ku.atro. I díxoles ... : "Yo digo k-este onb.re ᶜÎçâ, k-es Allah. I se di.o a pareçer a nosotros, i depu.és s-enkub.ri.ó." ... I.-el p.rimero ke k.reyó en-lo-ke Pawlos dixo era Yaᶜqûb i Naxṭur, i ke dix k-era fijo de Di.os por ví.a de g.raçi.a. I Malqún dixo k-eran t.res según dizen agora estos goímes.[31] I díxole el k.reyente: "¡Mentíç! ... Ermanos, ¿no sabedes ke Almaçîḥ k-era onb.re karnal, i.-era si.ervo i mesajero del-K.ri.ador?"

The Yaᶜqûb of this version is clearly meant to be the Apostle James (the Arabic text goes on to say that he "was killed in Galicia which is adjacent to al-Andalus"), not the Jacob ben Baradai after whom the Jacobite Christians are historically named. Nastûr does recall Nestorius, while "Malqûn" is presumably an anthroponym inspired by the root *m-l-k,* cf. *al-malkāniyya* "the Melkites." At the same time the division into four, the order in which the three heads of sects are named, and the Believer (Ar. *muʾmin*) who presents the Islamic view of Jesus, all reproduce in essence the tale that we have traced back to the first century of Islam.

The next great anti-Christian polemicist in Western Islam was, perhaps not surprisingly, a renegade: the Franciscan Fray Anselmo Turmeda, a native of Majorca, known as ᶜAbdallah al-Tarjūmān after his conversion.[32] He composed the *Tuḥfa,* his attack on "the people of the Cross," in 1420, and among its many sources is Ibn Ḥazm's *al-Fiṣal.* Turmeda condemns the fragmentation of the Christians into sects, not naming any of them but claiming their total number as seventy-two.[33] Like the Qurʾān and its commentators, he believes that at least some Christians hold the Trinity to consist of God, Jesus, and the Virgin Mary, and he castigates the very notion as "a festering, inane, feeble, and contemptible lie."[34] The history of the *Tuḥfa* during its first two centuries of existence is obscure, though it gained wide appeal after a Turkish translation appeared in Constantinople in 1603. Its original Arabic version, however, was already being quoted by Maghrebi scholars as well as by exiled Spanish Moriscos.

Miguel de Epalza has observed that for the Moriscos in Spain all religious writing was a form of polemic, as it constituted a challenge flung in the face of the dominant creed.[35] But the Moriscos did preserve texts that were explicitly and intentionally polemical. What has survived in *aljamiado* from the pre-Expulsion period is limited, because of the danger of indulging in such expression within Spain, but manuscript Biblioteca Nacional 4944, already mentioned in relation to Muḥammad al-Qaysī, also contains other brief anti-Christian texts. One of its chapters, "Deskonkordami.ento de los k.risti.anos,"[36] refutes with a variety of arguments the belief that Jesus is God. While the chapter does not deal with the Christian sects we have been examining, but rather with inconsistencies among the Gospels, it reveals in its very title the Muslim disdain for *ikhtilāf.*

After the Morisco exodus to North Africa, polemical works in Spanish, now written in Latin letters, begin to proliferate as their authors shook off the yokes of the Inquisition and censorship. The genre has been so magisterially studied by Louis Cardaillac (see note 33) that I wish to single out here only a few observations that are particularly relevant to our topic. First, among the many Christian beliefs and practices that Morisco polemicists attack were the Crucifixion and Redemption, Jesus's miracles, clerical corruption, and so on. The Trinity and the Incarnation provoke the harshest censure and never fail to appear in any of the surviving texts. One reason may be that the authors have easy recourse to certain overtly anti-Trinitarian passages of the Qurʾān, like *sūra* 5:77: "They are unbelievers who say, 'God is the Third of Three.' No god is there but One God." The same verses are brandished in treatise after treatise; their use has clearly become traditional, and like all Quranic quotations, they afford divine sanction to the Muslims' argument. Second, the doctrines of the Trinity and the nature of Jesus are enormously difficult to comprehend; perhaps no other religion requires its adherents to believe in something so ineffable. How accurately Moriscos perceived the Trinity is well illustrated by the Morisca from Daimiel who described it to her Inquisitors as "Mahoma, Allah y Vizmillah."[37] The almost obsessive concern with these two dogmas out of so many reflects the age-old bafflement of Muslims in their presence.

Other elements of these late Morisco polemical works also recall our original *aljamiado* anecdote. The following account structures in a similar way the attribution of different opinions to separate groups:

> Desto que hablo salieron las gentes en diferentes opiniones, los muminin diciendo que es criatura de Dios y los Judíos que fue hijo de pecado y los christianos que era hijo de Dios.[38]

Nor is the Council of Nicaea forgotten; as late as the seventeenth century, it is condemned in verse in the Morisco Juan Alonso's *Romance hecho por Juan Alonso Aragonés a la religión y España:*

> Este fue el papa Silvestre
> con sus obispos trezientos
> en la gran Constantinopla
> en el conzilio nizeno.[39]

Folklore has here transformed the site of the council into Constantinople, probably by inference from the name of its convoker, Constantine.[40]

In conclusion, the survival in sixteenth-century Aragon of a Spanish translation of a Quranic commentary on early Christian doctrinal disputes was *not* fortuitous. The Moriscos did care about the Nestorians and the Jacobites, not only while they lived in Spain but into their North African exile. But obviously they cared for reasons conditioned by their culture and situation. For Muslims, the religious bases of these sectarian differences are less compelling than the simple fact that they exist, and thus cast doubt on Christian possession of the truth. The Moriscos repeat the traditional arguments against the sects because they *are* traditional; their reverence is more for the book than for its content. Still, Nestorians and Jacobites fight on in Morisco literature as part of a current of anti-Christian polemic that appears to have been a genuinely popular phenomenon up to the eclipse of Spanish Islam.

NOTES

I wish to thank participants in the Notre Dame conference, and particularly Thomas Burman and Steven Wasserstrom, for valuable suggestions for the expansion and revision of this essay.

1. MS J18, now in the Departamento de Arabe, Instituto de Filología, Consejo Superior de Investigaciones Científicas, Madrid. It was discovered, with dozens of others, in Almonacid de la Sierra (Zaragoza) in 1884, and is described in Julián Ribera and Miguel Asín, *Manuscritos árabes y aljamiados de la Biblioteca de la Junta* (Madrid, 1912), 90. While Ribera and Asín date it

in the sixteenth century, it may well be older; although earlier scholarship assumed that virtually all MSS once owned by Moriscos were the product of that century, more recent opinion ascribes many of them to the Mudejar period. The manuscript, written in the Arabic alphabet, was transliterated, edited, and published by Juan Vernet and C. López Lillo, "Un manuscrito morisco del Corán," *Boletín de la Real Academia de Buenas Letras de Barcelona* 35 (1973–74): 185–255. I have re-edited this passage from a microfilm of the original manuscript because the published version contains numerous inaccuracies.

2. Dīxo Qatādah: "Fue nombrado a nos quello es cuando alçó Allah (*ᶜazza wa-jalla*) a ᶜÎçā al çielo. Escogeron los de Banī Içrāʾīl cuatro de sus sabios dellos, y dixéronle al primero, "¿Qué es lo que dizes en ᶜĪçā?" Dīxo, "Que es Allah que a baxado a la tierra y a khaleqado lo que a khaleqado y a revelado lo ques revelado y depués ase subido al çielo." Y siguieron sobre aquello las gentes, y fueron los Yaᶜaqobianos de los cristianos. Y dixeron los otros tres de aquellos sabios, "Femos testigo que tú mientes." Y dixeron al segundo de los sabios, "¿Qué es lo que dizes en ᶜĪçā?" Y dīxo, "Es fijo de Allah." Y siguiéronlo sobre aquello las gentes, y éstos fueron los a-Naçṭōres de los cristianos. Y dixeron los dos çagueros de los sabios, "Fazemos testigo que tú eres mentiroso." Y dixeron al terçero de los sabios, "¿Qué es lo que dizes en ᶜĪçā?" Y dixo, "Es señor y su madre es señor y Allah es señor." Y siguiéronlo sobre aquello las gentes, y fueron los Irraelitas de los cristianos. Y dixo el cuatrén sabio, "Fago testigo que tú eres mentiroso; que no fue sino siervo de Allah y su mensajero, y palabra de Allah y su arrūḥ." Y ubieron pleito las gentes sobre aquello.

3. In the translation of Arthur John Arberry, *The Koran Interpreted* (London, 1955).

4. All dates in this essay are A.D. or C.E. unless otherwise noted.

5. The first scholar to observe that the *Mukhtaṣar* existed in an *aljamiado* translation was Leonard P. Harvey, "The Literary Culture of the Moriscos 1492–1609: A Study Based on the Extant Manuscripts in Arabic and Aljamía," unpublished doctoral dissertation, Oxford University, 1958, 145. Subsequent research in Spain has established that portions of the work are found in three *aljamiado* MSS: J18 (our present version), J47, and J51 (all catalogued by Ribera and Asín, see note 1). Teresa Losada Campo, "Estudios sobre coranes aljamiados," unpublished doctoral dissertation, University of Barcelona, 1975, edited J51 and the two extant Arabic MSS of the *Mukhtaṣar,* al-Qarawiyyīn 34 (Fez) and British Library 820. I have been unable to consult this dissertation, but it is cited in several of the following: five articles by María José Hermosilla: "Dos glosarios de Corán aljamiado," *Anuario de filología* (University of Barcelona) 9 (1983): 117–49; "Una versión aljamiada de Corán, 58, 1–3," *Al-Qanṭara* 4 (1983): 423–27; "Una versión aljamiada de Corán, 89, 6–8, sobre Iram, la de las columnas," *Al-Qanṭara* 5 (1985): 33–62; "Corán 102, según el MS 47 J," *Anuario de filología* 12 (1986): 37–43;

"Otra versión aljamiada de Corán, 90 (Ms 47 J)," in *Homenaje al Profesor Darío Cabanelas Rodríguez,* 2 vols. (Granada, 1987), 1:19–27; and three pieces by Juan Vernet: "Traducciones moriscas de El Corán," in *Der Orient in der Forschung. Festschrift für Otto Spies,* ed. Wilhelm Hoernerbach (Wiesbaden, 1967), 686–705; "La exégesis musulmana tradicional en los Coranes aljamiados," in *Actas del Coloquio Internacional Sobre Literatura Aljamiada y Morisca,* Colección de Literatura Española Aljamiado-Morisca 3, ed. Alvaro Galmés de Fuentes (Madrid, 1978), 123–45; "Apostillas a las traducciones moriscas de El Corán," in *Studi in onore di Francesco Gabrieli,* ed. Renato Traini (Rome, 1984), 843–46.

6. On the former see Carl Brockelmann, *Geschichte der arabischen Literatur,* 2nd ed., 3 vols. (Leiden, 1937–49), 1.205, and Supplement, 1:335; and Fuat Sezgin, *Geschichte des arabischen Schrifttums* (Leiden, 1967), 1.46. On the latter see Brockelmann, *Geschichte,* Suppl. 1.332, and Sezgin, *Geschichte,* 1.39.

7. "It is . . . very probable that the commentary of Ibn Abī Zamānīn was widely read among the Moriscos, and that there survived in sixteenth-century Spain an ancient tradition of *tafsīr* which relied heavily on Qatāda" (Harvey, *Literary Culture,* 145).

8. For an attempt to locate sources of *aljamiado* commentaries on *Sūrat al-Nāzi*ᶜ*āt,* see the chapter "Tafsīr" in Consuelo López-Morillas, *The Qur*ʾ*ān in Sixteenth-Century Spain: Six Morisco Versions of Sūra 79* (London, 1982), 47–55. Divergent views are to be found in the review by P. SS. van Koningsveld, *Al-*ᶜ*Arabiyya* 14 (1985): 135–41, and in Gerard Wiegers, *Islamic Literature in Spanish and Aljamiado: Yça of Segovia (fl. 1450), His Antecedents and Successors* (Leiden, 1994), 108–110.

9. Volume and page numbers refer to the authors' commentaries on *Sūrat Maryam* and *Sūrat al-Zukhruf,* respectively:

Abū Jaᶜfar Muḥammad ibn Jarīr al-Ṭabarī (d. 923), *Jāmi*ᶜ *al-bayān fī tafsīr al-Qur*ʾ*ān,* 30 vols. (Būlāq, 1323–30 A.H. [=1905–11], 16.64, 25.56.

Maḥmūd ibn ᶜUmar al-Zamakhsharī (d. 1144), *Al-Kashshāf* ᶜ*an ḥaqā*ʾ*iq al-tanzīl,* 3 vols. (Cairo, 1948–51), 2.509, 3.495.

Fakhr al-Dīn Muḥammad ibn ᶜUmar al-Rāzī (d. 1210), *Mafātīḥ al-ghayb ["Al-tafsīr al-kabīr"],* 32 vols. (Cairo, 1934–62), 21.220, 27.223.

Muḥammad ibn Aḥmad al-Qurṭubī (d. 1273), *Al-Jāmi*ᶜ *li-aḥkām al-Qur*ʾ*ān,* 3rd ed., 19 vols. (Cairo, 1967), 11.108, 16.109.

ᶜAbd Allah ibn ᶜUmar al-Bayḍāwī (d. 1286 or 1293), *Anwār al-tanzīl wa-asrār al-ta*ʾ*wīl,* 4 vols. (Cairo, 1330 A.H. [= 1911–12]), 2.7, 2.63.

Ismāʿīl ibn ᶜUmar Ibn Kathīr (d. 1373), *Tafsīr al-Qur*ʾ*ān al-*ᶜ*aẓīm,* 7 vols. (Beirut, 1966), 4.456, 6.236.

Jalāl al-Dīn Muhammad ibn Aḥmad al-Maḥallī (d. 1459) and Jalāl al-

Dīn ʿAbd al-Raḥmān ibn Abī Bakr al-Suyūtī (d. 1505) (known collectively as "al-Jalālayn" 'the two Jalāls'), *Tafsīr al-Qurʾān al-karīm ["Tafsīr al-Jalālayn"]* (Cairo, 1966), 283, 452.

10. Sezgin, *Geschichte,* 1:31–32, describes him as "Qurʾānkommentator, *faqīh* und ein grosser Kenner der Poesie, Genealogie und Geschichte." He lived from 679 to 736.

11. Al-Ṭabarī, *Jāmiʿ al-bayān* 16:64–65: Bashīr told us on the authority of Yazīd on the authority of Saʿīd on the authority of Qatādah . . . that when the son of Mary had been taken up, the Banū Isrāʾīl chose four of their theologians and said to the first one, "What do you say about Jesus?" He said, "He is God who descended to earth and created what He created and brought to life what He brought to life; then He arose into Heaven." Some of the people followed him in that, and they were the Jacobite Christians. And the other three said, "We bear witness that you are a liar." So they said to the second one, "What do you say about Jesus?" He said, "He is the son of God." Then some of the people followed him in that, and they were the Nestorian Christians. And the other two said, "We bear witness that you are a liar." So they said to the third one, "What do you say about Jesus?" He said, "He is a god and His mother is a god and Allah is a god." Then some of the people followed him in that, and they were the Israelite Christians. Then the fourth one said, "I bear witness that you are a liar, for he is the servant of God and His messenger, he is the word of God and His spirit." So the people quarreled with each other. [My translation]

Ibn Kathīr (*Tafsīr* 4.456): ʿAbd al-Razzāq said: Muʿammar told us on the authority of Qatāda . . . : The Banū Isrāʾīl gathered and brought forth from among them four persons, each tribe choosing its wise man. And they disagreed about Jesus after he was taken up, and some of them said, "He is God who came down to earth, and brought to life those whom He brought to life, and brought death to those to whom He brought death, then ascended to heaven"; and they are the Jacobites. Then the [other] three said, "You have lied." Then two of them said to the third, "You speak about him." He said, "He is the son of God"; and they are the Nestorians. Then the [other] two said, "You have lied." Then one of the two said to the other, "You speak about him"; so he said, "He is a third of Three: Allah is a god, and He is a god, and His mother is a god." And they were the Israelites, rulers of the Christians (God's curses be upon them!). The fourth one said, "You have lied, for he is the servant of God and His messenger, His spirit and His word"; and they were the Muslims. And each man among them had followers of what he had said; and so they fought with each other. [My translation]

12. Since the same verse occurs in two places in the Qurʾān in different contexts, each commentator discusses it twice, in accounts that may vary somewhat.

13. Citation of the "Banū Isrāʾīl" in our *aljamiado* and Arabic accounts suggests that the source of the story may ultimately go back to the *isrāʾīliyyāt*. These were traditions brought into Islam, especially in the first century or so, by Jewish and Christian converts and their descendants; many of these tales were of a folkloric or fantastic nature and found their way into *ḥadīth* and *tafsīr.* See Georges Vajda, "Isrāʾīliyyāt," in *Encyclopedia of Islam,* new ed. (Leiden, 1960–), 4.211–12, and Gordon D. Newby, "*Tafsīr Isrāʾīliyyāt:* The Development of Qurʾan Commentary in Early Islam in Its Relationship to Judeo-Christian Traditions of Scriptural Commentary," *Studies in Qurʾan and Tafsir: Journal of the American Academy of Religion Thematic Issue* 47 (1980): 685–97.

14. On Nicaea see Ignacio Ortiz de Urbina, *Nicée et Constantinople* (Paris, 1963), especially 20–48, and J. N. D. Kelly, *Early Christian Doctrines,* 5th ed. (London, 1977), 225–38.

15. The phrase first appeared in Epiphanius of Salamis's treatise *Ancoratus,* written in 374, and was confirmed at the Council of Constantinople in 381. See A. E. Burn, *The Council of Nicaea* (London, 1925), 83–89.

16. Kelly, *Early Christians,* 339–43; Pierre Camelot, *Éphèse et Chalcédoine* (Paris, 1962), 7–28.

17. The complete text is provided in Aloys Grillmeier, *Christ in Christian Tradition,* trans. J. S. Bowden (New York, 1965), 481.

18. Grillmeier, *Christ,* 482–85.

19. Ernest Honigmann, *Évêques et évêchés monophysites d'Asie antérieure au VIe siècle* (Louvain, 1951), 157–77. See also W. H. C. Frend, *The Rise of the Monophysite Movement* (Cambridge, 1972), and Reinhold Seeberg, *Text-Book of the History of Doctrines,* 2 vols., trans. Charles E. Hay (Grand Rapids, Mich., 1958), 1:273–79.

20. Confusingly, the present-day Syrian Melkites are distinguished for a different reason; they are the only Eastern Christian sect that accepts the authority of the pope of Rome.

21. Abdelmajid Charfi finds the designation "uncommon and rather surprising" in "Christianity in the Qurʾan Commentary of Ṭabarī," *Islamochristiana* 6 (1980): 140. "Israelite" or "Jewish" Christians were Jewish converts to a belief in Jesus as Christ, who nonetheless clung for some centuries to elements of Judaism such as the Hebrew language and the Mosaic Law. See Shlomo Pines, *The Jewish Christians of the Early Centuries of Christianity According to a New Source* (Jerusalem, 1966).

22. Commentary on *Sūrat Maryam, Tafsīr* 4:456–57.

23. The number of bishops that attended Nicaea varies in the ancient sources: Constantine recorded it as three hundred, Eusebius of Caesarea as about 250, Eustathius of Antioch as 270. We owe the definitive figure to Athanasius, who first gave it as about three hundred, and later, in *Ad Afros,* as 318. "From this time on the number 318 was almost universally accepted,

theological reflection connecting it with Genesis 14:14 which records that Abraham led 318 slaves forth to battle. If this connection was made at a time when the loyal Nicene party was being hard pressed, the eschatological motive may have been primary: as the 318 slaves of Abraham were victorious, so will the faith of the fathers at Nicaea triumph" (Ralph E. Person, *The Mode of Theological Decision Making at the Early Ecumenical Councils* [Basel, 1978], 54–55). Furthermore, the number three hundred is significant in folklore; see, for example, Stith Thompson, *Motif-Index of Folk Literature,* 2nd ed., 6 vols. (Bloomington, 1966), 6:793.

24. Richard Bell, *The Origin of Islam in Its Christian Environment* (London, 1968), 158.

25. Many Morisco manuscripts, in Arabic and *aljamiado,* have come to light in the last century when village houses in which they had been concealed were torn down; on the last such discovery, in 1984, see María Jesús Viguera's introduction to Federico Corriente Córdoba, *Relatos píos y profanos del ms. aljamiado de Urrea de Jalón* (Zaragoza, 1990), 9–16. The catalogues of the principal library holdings are Francisco Guillén Robles, *Catálogo de los manuscritos árabes existentes en la Biblioteca Nacional de Madrid* (Madrid, 1889); Ribera and Asín, *Manuscritos* (see note 1); and Eduardo Saavedra, "Indice general de la literatura aljamiada," Appendix to *Discursos leídos ante la Real Academia Española* (Madrid, 1878), reprinted in *Memorias de la Real Academia Española* 6 (1889): 140–328.

26. ʿAlī ibn Aḥmad ibn Ḥazm, *Kitāb al-Fiṣal fī-l-milal wa-l-ahwāʾ wa-l-naḥl,* 5 vols. (Cairo, 1317–20 A.H. [= 1899–1903]). I have used the Spanish translation contained in Miguel Asín Palacios, *Abenházam de Córdoba y su historia crítica de las ideas religiosas,* 2 vols. (Madrid, 1927), 2:83–392.

27. Asín Palacios, *Abenházam,* 2:151–53, 157–58, 172.

28. P. S. van Koningsveld and Gerard Albert Wiegers, "The Polemical Works of Muhammad al-Qaysî (fl. 1309) and Their Circulation in Arabic and Aljamiado among the Mudejars in the Fourteenth Century," *Al-Qanṭara* 15 (1994): 163–99. I am grateful to Dr. Wiegers for supplying me with a preprint of this article, from which this section of my essay is adapted (page number references are to the preprint).

29. Denise Cardaillac has edited these in "La Polémique anti-chrétienne du manuscrit Aljamiado No. 4944 de la Bibliothèque Nationale de Madrid," 2 vols., unpublished doctoral dissertation, Montpellier, 1972. She did not, however, recognize that she was dealing with a Mudejar (rather than a Morisco) text (van Koningsveld and Wiegers, "Polemical works," 15).

30. Van Koningsveld and Wiegers, "Polemical works," 4–5. The authors provide only a summary of the contents of the *Miftāḥ,* with a transcription in notes of selected passages from the Arabic original. I quote Denise Cardaillac's edition of the *aljamiado* adaptation from BN 4944, in *Polémique* 2.19–23;

the chapter is entitled "Desputa de los K.risti.anos," and the account is attributed not to Qatāda but to Ibn ʿAbbās.

31. *Sic!* Van Koningsveld and Wiegers, "Polemical works," assume from this use of *goímes* that the adaptor/translator of al-Qaysī's text was a Jewish convert to Islam.

32. Miguel de Epalza, *La Tuḥfa, autobiografía y polémica islámica contra el Cristianismo de ʿAbdallah al-Taryūmān (fray Anselmo Turmeda)* (Rome, 1971).

33. Epalza, *Tuḥfa,* 296–97. Seventy-two, like three hundred (see note 23), is a number with roots in folklore; in Jewish tradition, Adam mastered seventy-two kinds of wisdom (Thompson, *Motif-Index,* 2:323). Sources within Islam have held it to represent the existing number of *Muslim* sects (Epalza, *Tuḥfa,* 296 n. 2). A Morisco legend recounts, "Estando Mahoma en el vientre de su madre, habló y a la voz de Mahoma la cruz se hizo sesenta [*sic;* error for 'setenta'?] y dos pedaços" (Louis Cardaillac, *Moriscos y cristianos, un efrentamiento polémico,* trans. Mercedes García-Arenal [Mexico City, 1979], 237).

34. Epalza, *Tuḥfa,* 320–21 (my translation).

35. Ibid., 75.

36. Cardaillac, *Polémique,* 1.154–63, 2.29–97.

37. Cardaillac, *Moriscos,* 210.

38. Ibid., 335; MS, Biblioteca Nacional 9654, f. 12r. Cardaillac assumes that a single anonymous author, an Andalusian Muslim in North African exile, composed both this manuscript and Biblioteca Nacional 9653.

39. Ibid., 165. The text appears in two manuscripts, Biblioteca Nacional 9067 and 9655, both in Latin letters and probably by the same author.

40. Juan Alonso may have been misled by the fact that the Council of Constantinople, actually held in that city in 381, reaffirmed the Nicene creed and recast it in its present form. Sylvester I was pope at the time of Nicaea, though he did not attend the gathering.

PART V

Epilogue

After 1492: Spain as Seen by Non-Spaniards

J. N. HILLGARTH

AFTER THE EXPULSION OF 1492 from Castile and Aragon, the forced baptisms of 1497 in Portugal, and the expulsion from Navarre in 1498, there were officially no Jews and, after the forced conversions between 1500 and 1525, no Muslims in the Iberian Peninsula. Yet, throughout the sixteenth and seventeenth centuries, to non-Spaniards Spain and Portugal seemed Islamic and Jewish countries. With regard to Islam, there was some foundation for this view; it was widely known that the "conversion" of the Moriscos amounted to no more than forced baptism. But this does not explain the widespread identification of Spaniards and Portuguese, not only as Muslims, but as Jews. In the blurred, often distorted, mirror held up by foreigners to Spain in the sixteenth and seventeenth centuries, this perception of the Iberian Peninsula as Moorish and Jewish played a central part. Well after 1800 the views established in these centuries were to continue to influence the image of Spain prevalent in Europe.[1]

In 1517, when the regent of Spain, Cardinal Cisneros invited the greatest scholar of the age to come to Spain, Erasmus's reply was resoundingly clear. "Non placet Hispania," he wrote to More. And, later, "I have no desire to become Spanish." To Erasmus Spain, was, in Marcel Bataillon's words, "une autre humanité." It was a land in which traces of Islamic rule were still visible. It was, above all, a land of Jews. This statement may seem surprising. Erasmus presumably knew that the Jews had been expelled from Spain twenty-five years before 1517. But Erasmus was sure that there were more Jews in Spain than in Bohemia, Italy, and Germany combined. In Spain, he wrote in 1518, "there are scarcely any Christians."[2] Had he wished to do so, Erasmus could have cited the fact that Cardinal Cisneros also held the office of Grand Inquisitor. In the sixteenth century most Europeans thought that they knew why the Spanish Inquisition had been founded. It had been founded to deal with secret Jews masquerading as Christians. But many Europeans doubted whether it had proved effective in doing so.

Virtually all foreign visitors to Spain included an account of the Inquisition in their description of the country. Their views were generally connected with their perception of the role of Jews and Muslims in Spain. Some of these foreigners were not very intelligent but perhaps all the more valuable to us, because typical, for that reason. For the Polish-German knight, Nicolaus von Popplau, who was in Spain in 1484–85, the country was dominated by "pagans [i.e., Muslims], Jews, and peasants"; in Valencia a quarter of the population consisted of converted Jews, only one in a hundred of whom were true Christians. Popplau's exaggerations reappear when Judaism had officially disappeared from Spain. In 1512 one of the most intelligent of contemporary observers, the Florentine humanist, Francesco Guicciardini, had no doubt that before 1492 Spain was "full of Jews and heretics, and the greater part of the people stained with this depravity. They [the Jews, etc.] held all the main offices and were so powerful and numerous that in a few years Spain might have abandoned the Catholic Faith." The Inquisition was the only remedy. But "it is thought that if fear [of it] ceases many would return to their vomit." After referring to the "conversion" of the Mudejars of Granada, Guicciardini remarked "today in [almost] all Spain there are only Christians," the only exception was Aragon, where many "Moors" were tolerated because of the taxes they paid.[3] A few years later a Milanese traveler (probably a merchant) commented both on the conversos and the Moriscos; like Guicciardini, he correctly saw the Inquisition as originally directed against secret Jews. Visiting Toledo, he estimated the number of conversos there at 4,000, "of whom the majority are secret Jews." Elsewhere he notes that "many" condemned by the Inquisition prefer to be "roasted alive" rather than obtain license to be strangled first by saying that they are Christians. He quotes one converso as saying, when about to die, "I am only sorry that I die because I cannot teach my children the Faith of Moses" (no doubt a "Christianization" of the normal "Law of Moses").[4]

Although the Muslims of Granada had been officially converted to Christianity in 1502 and were now known as Moriscos, they were not as yet subject to the Inquisition. The Milanese traveler was more interested in the dress of the Morisco women in Granada—draped from head to knees in white, with only their eyes visible—than he was in their religion. The city, still unchanged in character, with its narrow streets and small houses, pleased him less. He noted that it was not a safe place to walk in at night; travelers could be seized by the Moriscos and reappear as slaves in North Africa. He preferred Valencia, where, he was told, "a quarter of the inhabitants are Moors," whereas (he was incorrectly informed) there were none in Catalonia or Aragon. The archbishop of Armagh, who passed through Aragon in 1518 as ambassador from Henry VIII, knew better. There, he wrote to Wolsey, most people "be Agarenes [Muslims] and in mine opinion finally shall be so all and sundry"; the nobility preferred them as tenants.[5]

Similar complaints about Granada as a city coupled with praise of "Moorish" agriculture as unique in Spain are found in the Venetian Zuan Negro, who was there in 1526 as part of a mission to Charles V. Negro was more struck, however, by the Jewish character of Spain as a whole. As he left Spain he exclaimed: "Praise be to God that we have escaped from the hands of the Jews!"[6]

Whereas Islamic influence was only perceptible in a few regions of Spain, the Inquisition did not allow anyone visiting the country to forget its Jews. In 1526 the German Johannes Lange noted, "almost all churches display twenty, forty, or seventy *sanbenitos.*" In 1532 the French Cistercian Bronseval went further and declared, rather as the Jewish exile Orobio de Castro was to do a century later, that the monasteries of Castile were filled with converts from Judaism. The introduction in 1534, only two years later, of a statute of pure blood for would-be entrants to the Cistercian Order shows that this was not pure fantasy on Bronseval's part.

Bronseval was no more favorably inclined towards the Moriscos than he was to conversos from Judaism. Speaking of the Moriscos subject to the Cistercian monastery of Valldigna, he calls them "enemies of the truth, horrid in aspect . . . complete infidels." He admitted that the Moriscos paid their dues regularly and that their love of their children was such that "if you buy one for two ducats, the parents are ready to pay four to get him back." In Aragon, when visiting a village of Moriscos, who had been "converted" only seven years before, he censured them as "mainly concerned with taking their ease and with carnal pleasures," though he added "we found them very serviceable and were well entertained"—an unusually favorable testimony from any contemporary traveler in Spain.[7]

The rebellion of Granada in 1568–1570 and the expulsion of the Moriscos that followed provoked a range of comments from foreigners in Spain at the time. While Brantôme celebrated the Christian victory and the dispersion of the Moriscos as "a very fine thing for the religion of Spain," as it lessened the risk to Spanish Catholics of religious contamination, a letter of 1571 in the Fugger correspondence was less optimistic. Describing the arrival at Seville of twenty-four galleys laden with Moors who were to be distributed all over Spain, the writer continues: "in this way Spaniards become more tainted and intermixed with Moors than heretofore. The [Moors] and the Jews will be the noblest and strongest races, for they multiply like royal rabbits."

Outside Spain, and especially in Holland, Germany, and England, the numbers of Spanish Protestants were greatly exaggerated and their fate was of much greater concern to popular opinion than that of the far more numerous Jews and Muslims persecuted by the Inquisition.[8]

In contrast, for most Spanish royal officials and clerics, and equally for foreign diplomats, the danger supposedly represented by native or foreign Protestants was incomparably less serious than that presented by secret Muslims and more especially by Jews. The situation was considered particularly serious in Portugal (ruled by Spain from 1580 to 1640). There, according to a report submitted to a conference in 1625, "the evil has succeeded in infecting the nobility, universities and cathedral churches . . . knights, commanders [of military orders], canons, the holders of university chairs in canon and civil law, monks and nuns. . . . Teachers in our universities sustain that Judaism is true and necessary to salvation."[9] But in Spain, too, the problem was thought to need desperate remedies. It was a very exceptional foreign diplomat who criticized the Inquisition, as two Venetians did in the 1520s, Contarini seeing it as "a true tyranny over the poor New Christians," while Navagiero dreaded its imposition on the Moriscos of Granada, as being "easily able to destroy the city." It was much more usual to lavish praise on the Catholic monarchs for having created the institution.[10]

In 1524 the Polish ambassador and future bishop remarked: "Here one is not allowed to speak of Luther. Vulcan [the Inquisition] is always at hand to shut their mouths." Much pleased at this firm attitude (the ambassador had met Luther a year before and thoroughly detested him), Dantiscus was less delighted when his servants were seized by the Inquisition and he found himself in need of a safe-conduct from Charles V. Yet Dantiscus, who had experienced the treatment the Inquisition could inflict on a Catholic ambassador and his suite (due, he unkindly suggests, to the anger of the Dominican confessor of the emperor at being caught out in an affair with the daughters of a Jewish family), still claimed that religion in Spain depended entirely on this institution—for the usual reason, the large number of only nominally "converted" Muslims and Jews in the country. Without it, he declared, Catholicism would be in as much danger in Spain as it was in Germany.[11]

Venetian reports also do not tend to underestimate the importance of the Inquisition, "without comparison," as one ambassador stated in 1563, "more reverenced and feared than the king himself," or (in 1565), "the true master (*padrone*) of Spain." The problem which had originally brought about the Inquisition continued to exist. Cavalli's statement in 1570, "the land is full of Jews, Marranos and Moors," sums up the general view. The superficial nature of the Christianity of the "New Christians" is reflected in Donato's ironical remark, in 1573, "[After 1492] Spain [became] completely Christian, *that is* distinguished by the water of holy baptism," and by his complementary observation that the behavior of descendants of converts was observed with so much attention that if they made the slightest mistake in ritual in church, they would be pounced on as heretics. For Donato the Inquisition was still indispensable. Its sentences were just and no real opposition to it existed. In 1602 Soranzo insists on the same theme. In contrast to the horrible disorder prevailing in France, Germany, Flanders, and England, Spain was secure because there the State could rely on the Inquisition; "its great rigour maintains true religion, for without it one could greatly fear serious trouble because of the great number of Moriscos and Marranos dispersed throughout the land."[12]

Jehan Lhermite of Antwerp, who had spent fifteen years (1587–1602) in Spain in royal service, shared the pessimistic outlook of the Venetians. For him, "the old root of Mohammedans, Jews, and Barbarians, enemies of our Holy Catholic and Roman Faith, I fear cannot be easily extirpated but only repressed and kept under." The Flemish soldier and humanist Henri Cock had come to Spain earlier than Lhermite. His approach is more subtle and his attitudes to secret Jews and Muslims differ. In 1586 he noted that "in many parts of Spain there is great suspicion that merchants are of very low birth or are descended from parents who may not be good Christians." In contrast he writes: "I have seen that in many parts of Spain this people [Moriscos] is more inclined to cultivate and plant than any other." His admiration went beyond the standard appreciation of Morisco agriculture to the Aragonese Moriscos' loyalty to their lords and to their insistence on preserving their laws and customs. He had no illusions, however, as to their religion. In one small town in Aragon, apart from the priest, the notary, and the innkeeper, "the rest would prefer the pilgrimage to Mecca to that to Santiago in Galicia."[13]

Already by the early sixteenth century Spanish suspicion of the outside world was becoming prevalent. One may cite the treatment received by the suite of the future Elector Palatine, when he visited Spain in 1538. Although the prince was in great favor with Charles V, it was fortunate for him that he had been warned in advance of what might happen. The Inquisition had planted spies in his lodgings to see if anything was said which sounded Lutheran. A mob, stirred up by a priest, assembled outside. When some of the Germans left a church during a sermon (although returning later), and because they did not kneel throughout the Mass, they were denounced to the Inquisition. When they replied that Spaniards behaved in the same way, the answer was that those from heretical lands should be more careful.[14]

The Inquisition's surveillance covered foreign merchants as well as ambassadors and visiting princes. Persecution of English merchants trading with Spain began in the 1530s; in a less severe form friction continued after the Peace Treaty of 1604. In 1604 the French Catholic Joly noted the crowd of inquisitorial spies capable of tracking suspects as far as Flanders or Italy. While Joly approved of the Inquisition in general, he warned travelers to be careful of what they said in public while they were in Spain.[15]

In the late seventeenth century foreign visitors continue to comment on the Inquisition. In 1690–91 we have the dispassionate views of the Moroccan ambassador. Himself an adherent of a religion fully as exclusive in its claims as Spanish Catholicism, the ambassador did not see the Inquisition's proceedings as exceptionally harsh. For him the institution was directed against judaizing Christians, who were mainly of Portuguese descent.[16]

The same view had been taken in the 1660s by Lady Fanshawe, the wife of a man who was successively ambassador to Portugal and Spain. She saw the Portuguese as "in religion divided between Papists and Jews." In both countries the foreign diplomatic view was that there were "very few Traders beside the New Christians." The belief that this group's orthodoxy was still questionable was reinforced by the repeated appearances in *autos-de-fé* of rich Madrid merchants. So, in 1683, a correspondent of Samuel Pepys, who was about to leave for Spain, wrote: "We hear that a great number of Jews are clapped up in the Inquisition: so you may see how these Holy Inquisitors propagate the Gospel by carbonading Jews."[17]

Contemporary French accounts of the great *auto-de-fé* of 1680, from the official *Gazette* to the romantic inventions of Madame d'Aulnoy—which were to inspire Victor Hugo in the nineteenth century—also link the Inquisition to Jews. The French ambassadress in Madrid at the time distinguished: "On y brûle beaucoup de Juifs et il y a d'autres supplices pour des hérétiques et des athées." But the *auto* seemed ineffective. A member of the embassy staff wrote: "These punishments do not much diminish the number of Jews in Spain and especially at Madrid, where, while some are punished so rigorously, others are in the finances, considered and respected." On a minor scale the situation in Majorca was not dissimilar. James Stanhope, visiting the island in 1691, informed his father that the impending execution of "Jews and heretics" was the cause of the "very ill accommodations" which were all he could find. With some exaggeration he continued: "The greater part of the criminals that . . . will be put to death, were the richest men of the island."[18]

It is interesting to compare the impression made in 1559 by an *auto* held at Valladolid on a devout Flemish follower of Philip II with that recorded by another Flemish Catholic who was present in Madrid in 1680. Vandenesse, who saw three Spanish Lutherans burnt alive and nine others burnt after first having been garrotted, was greatly moved. In contrast, for Moretus in 1680, as for the French diplomats who were also present, the Inquisition was a spectacle, like the procession of Corpus. It was impressive to see twenty-five grandees of Spain acting as officials of the Inquisition, and the Inquisitor General seated above the king and administering to him an oath (two hundred years after the expulsion of 1492) to exterminate Judaism in Spain. Moretus's description of the condemnation of suspected Judaizers contains no trace of emotion, still less of horror. He was more excited by the bull fight, celebrated a little earlier in the year, when thirty bulls, four bull fighters, and a great number of horses and dogs were killed in less than three hours.[19]

To foreign visitors to Spain the statutes of "Purity of Blood" were an established, if tedious, norm of Spanish life. "To become a member [of a military order] one has," wrote Bertaut in 1659, "to prove that one is an 'Old' Christian, and this *costs* a great deal as one has to buy witnesses for large sums."[20] These methods did not, of course, deceive many people. As late as 1798 everyone in Seville was aware of who descended from condemned Judaizers. Down to the French invasion of 1808 the concepts of "Old" and "New" Christians were still in use. Byron perfectly mirrored these views when he wrote (in 1818) of Don Juan's father (of Seville):

> His father's name was José—Don, of course,
> A true Hidalgo, free from every stain
> Of Moor or Hebrew blood, he traced *his* source
> Through the most Gothic gentlemen of Spain.

In Majorca the account of the great *auto* of 1691 was deliberately republished in 1931, at the beginning of the Second Republic; the intention was to embarrass the descendants of the conversos (whose names were listed) condemned 240 years earlier.

The sixteenth and seventeenth centuries were ages when art was employed as religious propaganda by Catholics and Protestants alike. Anti-Spanish propaganda benefited particularly from the horrifying illustrations published in 1688 that accompanied Dellon's account of the Portuguese Inquisition of Goa. It is on Dellon's work and on a pseudonymous publication of 1567 that Van Limborch's *Historia inquisitionis* of 1692 and many later authors largely rely.

So far this essay has been almost entirely confined to the impressions recorded by those who had visited Spain. Views expressed from outside were not very different. Whether the writers who commented on the Inquisition from outside Spain were Protestant like Van Limborch or Catholic, they were usually agreed on two main points. The first was that the Inquisition had originally been founded to deal with what a Dutch pamphleteer of 1571 called "the most hateful enemies of Spain and of the Christian Religion, namely the Moors, Mohammedans, and Jews." As used against the "Jewish and Muslim plague" (to quote De Thou) it seemed to the Englishman Peter Heylin (in 1621) "wondrous tolerable and laudable." The Inquisition, then, was indispensable *to Spain.* In 1612 the Frenchman André Favyn considered that "it cannot be too rigorous; without the terror it inspires there would be more Marranos in Spain than Lutherans in France."[21]

Favyn and an anonymous French traveler to Spain, also writing in 1612, were agreed that the Inquisition, "while insupportable to *free* peoples, such as the French, Flemish, and Germans, is suited to Spaniards, Italians, and other southerners." This view was close to that of the English Protestant, Richard Dugdale, who, in *A Narrative of Unheard of Popish Cruelties* (1680) and despite his hatred for the Inquisition, considered it "at first not only necessary but exceedingly laudable," when it was directed against secret Jews.[22]

The second point of general agreement was that while the Inquisition began well, it turned out ill when it began to persecute Protestants, and that (to quote Heylin again) "with such violence and extremitie of torture that it is counted the greatest tyranny . . . under heaven." Treatment which seemed to De Thou perfectly suitable to "Moors" was lamentable when it ruined the flourishing trade of the Low Countries.[23]

In 1715 the author of a popular illustrated work, *Les délices de l'Espagne et du Portugal,* felt it necessary to include an account of the

Inquisition which contains the statement that "the most common accusation is that of Judaism." A few years earlier the Englishman Veryard, in his rapid passage through Spain, had noted that the Inquisition—"founded to extirpate the remains of the Mahometanism and Judaism, to which the Spaniards *are naturally addicted*"—now meddled in all affairs.[24]

Voltaire was transmitting a generally accepted view when he wrote of the Inquisition:

> Dans Madrid, dans Lisbonne il allume ses feux,
> Ces bûchers solenneles, où les Juifs malheureux
> Sont tous les ans, en pompe, envoyés par des prêtres,
> Pour n'avoir point quitté la foi de leurs ancêtres.

In the eighteenth century the situation was as clear to Voltaire—if perhaps less acceptable—as it had been to Erasmus, Guicciardini, or the Venetian ambassadors two centuries earlier. The Iberian Peninsula was full of secret Jews. They were suppressed by the Inquisition, which was probably the only instrument by which Spain and Portugal could be kept even officially Christian.

In the later sixteenth century English Protestants and French Catholics could agree on two points—one being the danger that the monarchy of Philip II presented to their countries, the other the inferiority of Judaism to their respective versions of Christianity. These two points often came together. The identification in Rabelais of "Marranos" with atheists is typical of much French thought. The belief that secret Jews, who were really atheists, controlled Spain fueled anti-Spanish passions at the time of the League. So a French Catholic writer trying (in 1586) to persuade the future Henri IV (then a Protestant) to become a Catholic, wrote: "Already France is turning Jewish and the [Jews] of Spain hold open traffic here." In the 1590s Antoine Arnauld demanded: "Should these Marranos be our kings?" Another French pamphleteer wrote of Spain: "The Catalans, those of Castile and Portugal are Jews, those of Galicia and Granada Muslims, their prince is an atheist." The very influential *Satire Ménippée* asked: "If [the king of Spain] is so 'Catholic', how can he endure the Jews and Marranos in his lands?" The king in question, addressed by Arnauld as "demi-More, demi-Juif, demi-Sarrazin," was Philip II. When the election of Philip's daughter, the Infanta Isabel, as queen of France was proposed to the Estates of the League in Paris, De Thou tells us that anonymous placards appeared, stating: "If the French hand themselves over to Spain, they are not only traitors but madmen, entrusting their religion to an infidel people, most of whom are Marranos, for whom to ignore God is a minor sin."[25]

By the late seventeenth century the mental confusion in France was such that a dictionary published in 1680 could define "Marrane" as "an insult we apply to Spaniards, which means *a Muslim.*"[26]

Although Englishmen were less eloquent on this subject than the French, they shared many of the latter's convictions. Sir Edwin Sandys (1561–1629), the son of an Elizabethan archbishop of York and a friend of the great political theorists Richard Hooker and Fra Paolo Sarpi, was a prominent politician in his own right. His *Europae Speculum* of 1599, often republished and translated into Dutch, French, and Italian, was principally directed against the papacy, which he saw as a Spanish tool. Sandys assured his readers that religion in Spain was in grave danger from "the pestilent cankers of Mahometisme and Judaisme"; "Marrany, baptised Jews and Moores" often exceeded Christian Spaniards in number.[27]

Like Erasmus and the French pamphleteers I have cited, Sandys had one great advantage; he could write about Spain without having to visit the country. But, as time passed, Sandys's views were reinforced in England by the reports of diplomats and travelers and also by statements by exiled Jews. So Sir Thomas Browne could write (in 1646): "According to good [reports], the Jews forebear not to boast that there are at present many thousand Jews in Spain, France, and England, and some dispensed withall even to the degree of priesthood." Later in the century Launcelot Addison, in his *The Present State of the Jews* (mainly on those in North Africa), cited the concrete example of two Spanish Dominicans, who, on reaching Leghorn from Spain, "instantly changed their Cowle for a Ganephe and of idle Fryers became progging [industrious] Jews. . . . That there are many such Temporising Jews, especially in Spain and Portugal, I have been assured from their own mouths: and what is more observable, some have ventured to affirm that there want not Jews among the Judges of the Inquisition."[28] Given the contempt generally entertained by English churchmen for both Jews and Catholics, it was satisfactory to be able to link the two together and to believe that at heart the great champion of Catholicism, Spain, was run by skeptics who were secretly addicted to another religion than the one they publicly professed.

Those Spaniards of the sixteenth and seventeenth centuries who could take a detached view of the institutions which governed their lives must have wondered at times what purpose these institutions really served. As Farinelli remarks in his study of the term "Marrano," "What use was it to preserve the Faith and 'purity of blood', to support the Inquisition, if, outside Spain, Spaniards could be lumped with the very heretics against whom the Inquisition was set up?" The longer the persecution of secret Jews continued, the more certain many non-Spaniards became that *all* Spaniards were secret Jews. In 1533 Rodrigo Manrique—a son of the then Inquisitor General, wrote to the great self-exiled Spanish humanist, Luis Vives (a man of converso descent): "You are right. Our country is a land of pride and envy; you may add, of barbarism. For now it is clear that one cannot possess any culture without being suspect of heresy, error, and Judaism." It was useless for Manrique's contemporary, Fernández de Oviedo, to protest, remarking of Spain, "it is certain that among all Christian countries there is none whose natives are more clearly distinguished [from others], nor any nation where the nobility and those of good and pure caste (*casta*), nor those suspect of heresy are better known." Non-Spaniards knew better than this. The engine of the Spanish Inquisition had recoiled on those who controlled it.[29]

NOTES

1. The views set out here will be fully documented in my forthcoming book, *The Mirror of Spain (1500–1700): The Formation of a Myth.* The notes that follow only aim to provide some basic references.

2. Erasmus, *Opus epistolarum,* ed. S. Percy and H. M. Allen, 12 vols. (Oxford, 1906–1958), 3.6, 52. See Marcel Bataillon, *Erasmo y España,* 2 vols. (Mexico, 1950), 1.90.

3. José García Mercadal, *Viajes de extranjeros por España y Portugal,* 3 vols. (Madrid, 1952–62), 1.319f, 322, 616f.

4. London, British Library, MS Additional 24180, ff. 50^{v}–51^{r}, 58^{r}, 84^{v}.

5. Ibid., ff. 55^{r}–56^{v}, 64^{v}. *Calendar of Letters and Papers, Foreign and Domestic, Henry VIII,* 15 vols. (London, 1880–1896), 2.2, no. 4660.

6. Emmanuele Antonio Cicogna, *Della vita e delle opere di Andrea Navagero* (Venice, 1855), 340, 344.

7. Johannes Lange, "Die tagebuchartigen Aufzeichnungen," *Archiv für Kulturgeschichte* 5 (1907): 417. Claude de Bronseval, *Peregrinatio hispanica,* 2 vols. (Paris, 1970), 1.58f, 220, 224; 2.640.

8. Pierre de Bourdelle Brantôme, *Oeuvres complètes,* ed. Louis Lalanne, 11 vols. (Paris, 1864–82), 2.109. *Fugger-Zeitungen,* ed. Victor von Klarwill, trans. Pauline de Chary (London, 1924), 17.

9. *De los Judíos y la Santa Inquisición del Reyno de Portugal,* Jerusalem, National Library, MS EH 48 D 26, f. 89^{r}.

10. Eugenio Albèri, ed., *Le relazioni degli ambasciatori veneti al Senato durante il secolo XVI,* 15 vols., Series 1 (Florence, 1839–63), 2.40. García Mercadal, *Viajes de extranjeros por España y Portugal,* 1.860.

11. Joannes Dantiscus, *Acta tomiciana,* ed. S. Gorski, 17 vols. (Poznan, 1852–76), 7.138; 8.301, 348, 362; 10.282.

12. Albèri, *Relazioni,* 5.22, 85, 163; 6.353, 371, 404. Nicolo Barozzi and Giovanni Berchet, eds., *Relazioni degli stati europei lette al Senato dagli ambasciatori veneti nel secolo decismosettimo,* I: *Spagna,* 2 vols. (Florence, 1856–60), 1.75, 145.

13. Jehan Lhermite, *Le passetemps,* ed. Charles Ruelens, 2 vols. (Antwerp, 1890–96), 1.115. Henri Cock, in García Mercadal, *Viajes de extranjeros por España y Portugal,* 1.1305, 1307f, 1334.

14. Hubertus Thomas, *Annales de vita Friderici II* (Frankfort, 1624), 226f.

15. Barthélemy Joly, "Voyage d'Espagne," *Revue hispanique* 20 (1909): 574f.

16. Henry Sauvaire, ed., *Voyage en Espagne d'un ambassadeur marocain (1690–1691)* (Paris, 1884), 116–19.

17. Ann, Lady Fanshawe, *Memoirs* (London, 1907), 116f. Samuel Pepys, *The Life, Journal, and Correspondence,* ed. John Smith, 2 vols. (London, 1841), 1.330.

18. *Lettres de Madame de Villars à Madame de Coulanges,* ed. Alfred de Courtois (Paris, 1868), 132. *Mémoires de la Cour d'Espagne,* ed. Alfred Morel-Fatio (Paris, 1893), 188. Alexander Stanhope, *Spain under Charles II,* ed. Lord Mahon (London, 1844), 17.

19. García Mercadal, *Viajes de extranjeros por España y Portugal,* 1.1097. Maurits Sabbe, *Viaje a España del librero Baltasar Moretus* (Madrid, 1944).

20. François Bertaut, "Journal du Voyage d'Espagne," *Revue hispanique* 47 (1919): 201.

21. Martin van Gelderen, *The Dutch Revolt* (Cambridge, 1993), 17. Jacques Auguste de Thou, *Historiae sui temporis,* 7 vols. (London, 1733), 1.101. Peter Heylin, *Microcosmos* (Oxford, 1621), 35. André Favyn, *Histoire de Navarre* (Paris, 1612), 834.

22. "Relation d'un voyage en Espagne," *Revue hispanique* 59 (1923): 505. Richard Dugdale, in *Harleian Miscellany,* 12 vols. (London, 1808–11), 7.114.

23. Heylin, *Microcosmos;* De Thou, *Historiae sui temporis,* 2.648.

24. "Alvarez de Colmenares," *Les délices de l'Espagne et du Portugal,* 6 vols. (Leiden, 1715), 4.908. Ellis Veryard, *An Account of Diverse Choice Remarks* (London, 1701), 276.

25. Arturo Farinelli, *Marrano (Storia di un vituperio),* Biblioteca del archivum romanicum, Series 2, no. 10 (Geneva, 1925), 53; [Arnauld], *L'Antiespagnol* [1592], in *Le Recueil des excellens et libres discours sur l'estat présent de la France* (Paris, 1606), 22f; *Satire Ménippée* [1594], ed. Charles Labitte (Paris, 1841), 209.

26. Farinelli, *Marrano (Storia di un vituperio),* 56.

27. Edwin Sandys, *Europae speculum* (London, 1638), 239f.

28. Thomas Browne, *Pseudodoxia Epidemica,* 4.10, in *The Works,* ed. Geoffrey Keynes, 6 vols. (London, 1928), 3.44. Addison, *The Present State of the Jews* (London, 1675), 31f.

29. Farinelli, *Marrano (Storia di un vituperio),* 65, 67; Bataillon, *Erasmo y España,* 2.74f.

INDEX

ʿAbdallāh, as family name of Maimonides, 55, 66n69
Abner of Burgos. *See* Alfonso of Valladolid
Abraham Abulafia, 75
Abraham Ibn Ezra, 46, 73, 76–77
Abū ʿĀmir ibn Abī ʿĀmir, 47–48
Abulafia, David, 101, 112, 126
Abū Yaʿqūb Yūsuf (caliph), 49, 65
Academy of Research Historians on Medieval Spain, 96
acculturation, xiii, xvii, 16–17, 274–75; of the Mudejars, 95, 106–8
Acequia de Barxell, 28
Addison, Launcelot, 319
Afers: fulls de recerca i pensament (journal), 103, 120n56
afterlife, Islamic, Alvarus on, 10–11
afterlife, unity of the intellect in, doctrine of accepted by Maimonides, 65n59
Against the Arians (Hilary), 15
agriculture, 26–33, 314; cereals, 26–28, 30, 32; irrigation, 26–29, 30, 32–33
Albornoz, Sánchez, 22
Alcalá de Guadayra, *hereamiento*, 38n42
Alexander of Aphrodisias, 43, 44
Alfonso III of Aragon, 127–29, 136n1
Alfonso IV of Aragon (Alfonso the Benign), 159n43
Alfonso VII of Castile and León, 24
Alfonso X of Castile and León (Alfonso the Wise), 28, 38n42, 144–45
Alfonso of Valladolid (Abner of Burgos), xix, 173–74, 182, 186–91, 193n28, 194n38
Alicante, University of, 98
Alicsend de Tolba and Aytola the Sarracen, story of, 146–47, 149, 157n28
Aljamía (bibliographical bulletin), 98, 104
aljamiado texts, xx, 290–93, 295–99, 304n25
Allāh akbar, Alvarus's interpretation of, 12
allegory, use of in medieval Arabic and Hebrew philosophy, 45–47
Almería (province), 21, 35n6
Almohads, 26, 29, 35n9, 48, 49, 109
Almoravids, 26, 35n9, 48, 49
Alonso, Juan, 299, 305n40
Alpujarras revolt, 31
alquerías (villages)
  González's definition, 25
  parcellization of in process of *Repartimiento*, 26–32
  in rural landscape of Muslim Spain, 21–29, 35nn8, 9; post-*Repartimiento* changes, 27–33
Altmann, Alexander, 67n78
alumbradas (illuminists), 281–82
Alvarus, Paul, xvii, 5, 6–17
American Historical Association, Academy of Research Historians on Medieval Spain as affiliate, 96
American Historical Review, The (journal), 104
al-ʿĀmirī, 72
amulets, Jewish use of, 151, 159n40
Anacephaleosis (Epitome) (Cartagena), 243–44, 255n7
"Anatomy of Ambivalence: Muslims under the Crown of Aragon . . . " (Lourie), 100
al-Andalusī, Abū ʿAbdallah Muḥammad, 296
angels, identification with Intelligences or Intellects, 76–77
Antichrist(s), 5, 7, 14–16; Muḥammad depicted as by Alvarus, xvii, 6, 7–17
Antiochus IV Epiphanes, 14–15
Anuario de estudios medievales (journal), 103, 120n62
Anuario medieval (journal), 104
Aphrodite, pre-Islamic goddesses compared to by Alvarus, 9–10, 19n28

Index

Apocalypse, Book of the, 3–4, 16, 17n2
apocalypticism, implications of Alvarus's identification of Muḥammad with the Antichrist, 14–17
aporia/i: ḥayra translated as, 64n51; Maimonides' interest in, 42, 52, 53–54, 64n51
Arabic language, use of: in anti-Christian polemical texts, 295–99; in efforts to convert Muslims to Christianity, 275, 285n10; legal prohibitions, 268, 274, 276, 279; in Morisco manuscripts found in nineteenth and twentieth centuries, 304n25; in Quranic commentaries, 292–95, 302n11
Aragon, 20, 28, 100, 157n31, 159n43
  archives used to study Muslim-Jewish relations, 125, 127–28, 136n1
  early seventeenth-century Morisco loyalty to the crown, 269
  Jews in, xvii, 105, 128–29; 1492 expulsion, 309; fourteenth-century synagogue, 171–72
  Mudejar society, 98–99, 102, 106–8, 110
  network of *ḥuṣūn,* 23, 36n13
  persecution of minorities, 111, 141–52, 153nn2, 3, 4, 155n16
  religious and sexual boundaries in, 141–52
  rulers: Alfonso III, 127–29, 136n1; Alfonso IV, 159n43; Fernando II and Isabel I, xv, xix, 242, 246, 248–54, 257n18
arboriculture, practiced in the Muslim *alquerías,* 22, 27
Archives of the Kingdom of Majorca, 129
Arévalo, Bishop Rodrigo Sánchez de, 244–45, 247, 256n11
Argemi, Roser, 119n51
Arié, Rachel, 104
Aristotle and Aristotelianism, 45–54, 73, 80n12, 162, 255n9; Averroës's commentaries, 43, 44, 53, 55–59, 65n61; cosmology, xviii, 50–54, 65n58; influence on Maimonides, 43–46, 50–59, 62n27
Arius and Arianism, 6, 293
Arnauld, Antoine, 318
art: Mudejar, 102, 103, 108, 110; used as religious propaganda by Catholics and Protestants, 316–17
Arxiu del Regne de Mallorca, in Palma, registers in the royal patrimony section, 129–30, 138n20
Arxiu de textos catalans antics (journal), 120n62
Asín, Miguel, 299n1
assimilation, xvii, 109
  of Christians into Islamic culture in ninth-century Spain, 5, 16–17
  of conversos into the Catholic Church and society, xix, 211n7, 220–36, 241
  defined, 274–75
  of Moriscos, 267–68, 275–84; failure of as argument for expulsion, 283–84; language as barrier to, 285n9; struggle over, women's role in, xx, 274, 275–84; through intermarriage, 274–75, 280–83
  resistance to, 125, 283
Assís, Yom Tov, 105, 158n39
Association of British Hispanists, Tate's 1985 presidential address, 163–64, 176n6
astronomy, xviii, 41–42, 50–54, 65n58
Athanasius, St., 303n23
atheists, Marranos seen as, 318
Atrosillo, Peregrín de, 33
Auerbach, Erich, 173
Augustine, St., 175, 191n4
Augustinians (religious order), nunneries founded in Toledo, *table* 232
Austria, sixteenth- and seventeenth-century attitudes toward religious minorities, 268, 272
autos-de-fé, 269, 282, 284, 315–16 (*see also* Inquisition)
Avempace. *See* Ibn Bājja, Abū Bakr
Averroës (Ibn Rushd), 40–41, 45, 49, 75; banishment to Lucena and burning of books, 48, 65n60; Borges's story on, 66n63; commentaries on Aristotle, 43–45, 54, 62n27, 65n61; objections to Ptolemaic hypotheses, 51–52
Averroism, xviii, 46–47, 53; doctrine of the unity of the intellect, 65nn59, 61; and Maimonides' philosophy, 45, 54–60, 62n27, 65n59
Avicenna (Ibn Sīnā), 45, 53, 62n27; influence on Maimonides, 43–44, 55–59, 67n77; philosophical mysticism, 71–74, 76–77, 81n17

Index

Ayala, chronicle of, pogroms of 1391 described in, 169–70

Babylon/Jerusalem, as seen in the medieval European imaginary, 171
Baer, Fritz, 161–62, 170, 175n1
Baer, Yitzhak, 142, 193n28
al-Baghdādī, ʿAbd al-Laṭīf, 72, 73, 74
al-Baghdādī, Abuʾl Barakāt, 70, 82n24
Balañà i Abadia, Pere, 101
Balearics, the (*see also* Majorca)
  Mudejars in, 100, 101, 106, 112, 115n12; thirteenth-century Muslim-Jewish relations, 125–36
Baneth, David Hartwig, 55, 61n15
Banū Isrāʾīl, wise men of the, in the *aljamiado* manuscript, 290–91, 292, 293, 295, 303n13
baptism
  of Jews, 225, 309; washing off of infant by conversos following, 216n26
  of Moriscos, 309; Old Christians as godparents of infants, 278
Barceló, Miquel, 105
Barcelona, Spain, missionizing encounter of Friar Paul Christian with Rabbi Moses ben Nahman, 181, 183–85
Barceló Torres, María Carmen, 99, 108, 120n58, 123n84
Barrio Nuevo, in Toledo, 224 (*see also* Judería Mayor)
Barrios Aguilera, Manuel, 31
Bartlett, Robert, 101, 119n47
Basáñez Villaluenga, María Blanca, 99, 101, 124n97
Basel, Council of, Cartagena's 1434 speech before, 243–44
Bataillon, Marcel, 309
bathing the dead, Jewish custom of, observance among conversos, 202–3
bāṭin (nistar) binarity, 45–47 (*see also* esotericism)
Bax, Mart, 289n48
al-Bayḍāwī, ʿAbd Allah ibn ʿUmar, 301n9
Bazzana, André, 22, 105, 107, 120n58
beatas: communities of (*beaterios*) in fifteenth- and sixteenth-century Toledo, 232–34; mystical experiences, 281
Beatas de San Pedro (religious foundation), 232–33
Beatus of Liébana, 3–4, 17, 18n5
Beinart, Haim, 216n27, 219n43
Benedict XIII (antipope), 242
Benedictines, nunneries founded in Toledo, *table* 232
Beni-, place-names in form of, in Muslim Spain, 22, 23–24, 25, 26, 28, 35n8
Bensch, Stephen, 111
Berbers, 4, 23; Almohads, 26, 29, 35n9, 48, 49, 109; Almoravids, 26, 35n9, 48, 49; *alquerías* settled by clans of, 22, 26, 35n8
Berend, Nora, 112–13
Bernáldez, Andrés, 245
Bernat d'Olzet, 133–34
Bertaut, François, 316
Bible, the, 132 (*see also* Old Testament); allusions to in the medieval imaginary, 171–73; Book of the Apocalypse, commentaries on, 3–4, 16, 17n2; Christian missionizing based on, shift to emphasis on reason, 179–80; conflict between text and science downplayed by Maimonides, 52–54; 1 John **2:18** on "many Antichrists," 15; 2 Kings **18:20** as biblical allusion used by Çarça, 168; written Arabic translation of, consulted by al-Biqaʾi, 76
al-Biqaʾi, 76, 84n37
Bishko, Charles Julian, 97
bishops, number at Council of Nicaea, 303n23; in Ibn Kathīr's *tafsīr,* 295
al-Biṭrūji, objections to Ptolemaic hypotheses, 51
Black Prince, the (Edward, Prince of Wales), 168
blasphemy: ninth-century denouncers of Muḥammad executed for, 5–6; notarial formula used in cases of, 147, 157n28
Blau, Joshua, 69
Bleda, Jaime, 266
blessing of children, Jewish custom of, observance among conversos, 203, 205–6
Bloom, Harold, 41
body, human, image of used to express group identity, 145–48
Bohemia, seventeenth-century attitude toward religious minorities, 272
Bonner, Anthony, 87n60
Book of the Circles (Ibn al-Sīd), 75

Index

Book of the Sunna and Sharīʿa, Barceló Torres's edition of, 108, 123n84
Borges, Jorge Luis, 66n63
Boswell, John, 91, 94–95, 99, 127
Bramon, Dolors, 116n24
Brantôme, Pierre de Bourdelle, 312
Brill, E. J., 110
Bronseval, Claude de, 311–12
Browne, Sir Thomas, 319
al-Būnī, 76, 85n50
burial chapels, in fifteenth- and sixteenth-century Toledo, xix, 227–31, 234, 235, 238n16, *table* 229–30
Burns, Robert I., S.J., xviii, 27, 91–124, 126, 127, 137n5, 284n4
Burriel Salcedo, Margarita M., 31
Butzer, Elizabeth, 108, 120n56
Butzer, Karl, 108, 120n56
Byron, Lord, 316

Cagiano de Azevedo, Michelangelo, 172–73
Cagigas, Isidro de las, 114n3
Cairo, Egypt, 74, 75, 84n39
Calls (journal), 105
Cantera Montenegro, Enrique, 105, 119n50
Çarça, Samuel, xix, 163, 164–68, 170–71, 172, 173, 175
Cárcel de amor (San Pedro), 248–50, 257n20, 258nn21, 22
Cardaillac, Denise, 304nn29, 30
Cardaillac, Louis, 103, 298, 305n38
carnivalesque, the, elements of in *Grisel y Mirabella,* 251–52
Cartagena, Bishop Alonso de, 241, 243–44, 246–47, 255n7, 257n18
Casa de Velázquez, 22 (*see also* Bazzana, André; Guichard, Pierre)
Castile (Castile-León), xvi–xvii, 20, 244 (*see also* Toledo)
  1492 expulsion of the Jews, 309
  ḥiṣn/qarya model of agrarian landscape, 24–25
  letrado historiography and political theory during the Trastámara period, 242–47
  Mudejars in, 99–100, 102, 106, 117n33
  rulers: Alfonso VII, 24; Alfonso X, 28, 38n42, 144–45; Enrique II, 164–68, 256n11; Enrique III, 242; Enrique IV, 256nn11, 14; Fernando II and Isabel I, xv, xix, 242, 246, 248–54, 257n18; Juan I, 256n11; Juan II, 175, 242–43, 256n14, 275; Pedro the Cruel, 94, 167–68, 225, 256n11
  1610 expulsion of the Moriscos, 265–66
  1366–1368 Civil War described by Çarça, xix, 163, 164–68, 170
castles (fortified structures; *ḥuṣūn*) (*see also ḥiṣn/qarya* complex): in rural landscape of Muslim Spain, 22–24, 35n8
Castro, Américo, xx n3, 50, 108, 141, 153n1
Castro, Orobio de, 311
Castro, Archbishop Pedro Vaca de, 269
Catalonia, 22–23, 36n13, 96–97, 101, 106
catechism, published in 1498, 226
Catholic Church (*see also* conversion; Inquisition): art used as religious propaganda, 316–17; conversos' roles in, 198, 207, 211n7, 221–36 (*see also* conversos); as important ally in sixteenth-century move toward hegemony, 283; strict adherence to, bypassed by mystical movements, 282
Catholics: Arévalo on Castilian cultural tradition of Gothic Christianity, 245; sixteenth- and early seventeenth-century European, tolerance of Protestants and other religious minorities, 268, 272, 318
Catlos, Brian, 112
Cavalli, 1570 statement on Spain, 313
Ceballos, Jerónimo de, 235
Cédula of September 27, 1571, 31
celestial physics, Aristotelian, 50–54
Celestina (Rojas), 247–48, 258n21
Center for Mudejar and Morisco studies (Teruel), 98, 110; International Symposia of Mudejar Studies series, 100, 102, 107
centuriation, Roman, 25
cereal (grain) culture, 26–28, 30, 32
Chalcedon, Council of (451), 293–94
Chapters on Beatitude (Perakim be-Hazlaha) (attrib. to Maimonides), 73, 77, 83n30
Charfi, Abdelmajid, 303n21
Charles V (Holy Roman emperor), 268, 313
Chazan, Robert, xviii–xix, 179–94
Checa, Jorge, 259n25, 260nn26, 27

Chevedden, Paul E., 113
Chodkiewicz, Michel, 85n50
Christ. *See* Jesus
Christianity: dissension among early sects, referred to in Quranic commentaries, 290–92, 293, 303n13; doctrine on nature of Christ and the nature of the Trinity, Morisco texts on, 290–95, 296
Christianity, medieval, 104, 267 (*see also* Catholic Church)
  conversion to (*see* conversion of Jews to Christianity; conversion of Muslims to Christianity)
  denial of as a defense mechanism among crypto-Jews, 207–9
  polemical literature: early medieval addressed to fellow Christians, 179; twelfth-century shift to addressing the Jews, 179–91
Christians (*see also* Catholics; New Christians; Old Christians; Protestants): attitudes toward slavery, 132–33; as biological parents, children by definition Christian, 144, 156n17; as early converts to Islam, 5, 303n13; interrelations with Jews and Muslims, 77, 105, 109, 141, 145–46; Mozarabic experience, 105–6, 122n72; 711 conquest seen in military and political terms, 4–5
Cicero, *De oratore,* 162–63
Cisneros, Archbishop Francisco Jiménez de, 226, 231–32, 309–10
Civil War, Castilian (1366–1368), Çarça's description of, 164–68, 170–71, 172, 173, 175
clans (tribal segments), *alquerías* settled by, 22, 23, 24, 31
clergy, Catholic (*see also* parish priests): authority of bypassed by mystical movements, 282
Coca Castañer, José Enrique López de, 119n47
Cock, Henri, 314
Códice Pueyo of Majorca, royal charters copied in, 125
collective anxiety, over sexual mixing between Muslim or Jewish men and Christian women, 143–48
Collins, Roger, 96
colonialism, following Catalan conquest of Majorca, 125–26
Commentarium in Danielem (Jerome), 7, 14–16
Commentary on the Apocalypse (Beatus of Liébana), 3–4, 17, 18n5
Commentary on the Mishnah (Maimonides), 56
commerce: conversos of fifteenth- and sixteenth-century Toledo active in, 221–22, 225; relations between Christians, Jews, and Muslims, 145–46
Communities of Violence (Nirenberg), 111
Compendiosa Historia Hispanica (Arévalo), 244–45, 256n11
concubinage, among medieval Jews, 139n32
confessions in Inquisition trials: by crypto-Jews, 197, 210n2, 212nn9, 11, 12, 213nn14–16, 214nn18, 19, 215nn20–24, 216n25; by Moriscas, 280
confessions in sacrament of penance, records kept by priests in fifteenth- and sixteenth-century Toledo, 226
conflict (*see also* violence): role in maintenance of stability, 142, 153n6
Congreso internacional: Encuentro de las tres culturas, 103
consejo real, composition of: changed by Fernando and Isabel in 1480, 246–47, 256n14; in *Grisel y Mirabella,* 260n26
Consejo Superior de Investigaciones Científicas (C.S.I.C.), 101, 106, 124n97
Consolation to the Stranger (Uns al-Gharīb) (Judah ben Nissim), 77
Constable, Olivia Remie, 105
Constantine, Council of Nicaea called by, 293, 295, 299, 303n23
Constantinople, Council of (381), 293, 303n15, 305n40
Contarini, Gasparo, 313
convents. *See* nunneries
conversion: of Christians to Islam, 5, 303n13; of Jews to Islam, 70, 79n7, 303n13; of non-Jews to Judaism, role in emancipation of slaves, 139n32
conversion of Jews to Christianity, 211n7, 241, 285n8 (*see also* conversos; Jews,

conversion of Jews to Christianity (*cont'd*) in Spain, as converts to Christianity); Alfonso of Valladolid's depiction of experience, xix, 182, 186–91; forced baptisms, 225, 309; in 1391, 144, 198–99, 211n7
conversion of Muslims to Christianity, 111, 137n5, 309 (*see also* Moriscos); after fall of Granada in 1492, 275, 277–78; and status of slaves, 131–32, 134; in thirteenth-century Majorca, 126–27
conversos, 226–27, 241–42, 282–83, 318 (*see also* Jews, in Spain, as converts to Christianity)
 crypto-Judaism, 197–210, 211n8, 220–21
 effect of experience on philosophy, 46–47
 in fifteenth- and sixteenth-century Toledo, 222–36, 241; founding and membership in nunneries, xix, 232–34; municipal and church positions, 220–22, 227, 230–31, 238n15; relations with Old Christians, 220–22
 letrado theories of monarchy and religious orthodoxy, 247, 251, 257n18; subversion of in sentimental romances, 242, 248–54, 257n20, 258nn21, 22, 259n25
 sixteenth- and seventeenth-century Spain seen by outsiders as full of, xx, 309–20
 study of, xvi, xix, xx n3, 105
 trials under the Inquisition, 197, 200–207, 208–9, 212nn11, 12, 213–16nn14–25, 28, 217–19nn29–43
convivencia, xv–xvi, 108, 141, 145–46, 148, 157n31; as a central issue in historiography of religious minorities, 141, 153n1; last vestiges of dismantled by presence of conversos as new minority, 241; propensity for among Spanish emigrants, 69
Córdoba: Maimonides and Averroës from, 40; ninth-century Christian denouncers of Muḥammad as martyrs, 5–7, 8, 17; 1367 killing of Jews in Aguilar described by Çarça, 168
Corriente, Federico, 108, 123n83
cosmology, Aristotelian, xviii, 50–54
Counter-Reformation, and Catholic state policies toward minorities, 268
creation-eternity antimony, Maimonides' position on, 52, 54, 65n58
Crescas, Hasdai, description of 1391 violence, xix, 163, 168–71, 172, 173, 175
Crónica Abreviada, 165
Crónica de los reyes de Navarra, 170
Crónica de Pero Niño, 169–70
Crown Archives, used for research, 95, 100–101; on Muslim-Jewish relations, 125, 127–28, 136n1
Crusade and Colonisation (Lourie), 115n12
Cruz Hernández, Miguel, 66n62, 81n17
crypto-Judaism, 197–210, 211n8, 220–21
cuadrillas of peasant land parcels, 20; *alquerías* combined to create, under Christian rule, 28–29
Cuenca, diocese of, 226, 237n13
Cutler, Alan, 154n11
Cyril of Alexandria, 294

Damascus: expatriate colonies of Murcian activists transplanted to, 74, 84n39; Jewish and Muslim Spanish emigrants in, 79n3
dance, Arabic and Muslim, incorporated into Christian liturgy, 275, 285n10
Daniel, Book of, 189
 Alvarus's commentary on, 7–17
 Jerome's commentary on, 7, 14–16
 as key to Jewish doctrine on redemption, 182, 184–85; arguments against, 188–90
 9:24–27, used in argument over coming of the messiah, 184–85
Dantiscus, Joannes, 313
Darby, H. C., 21
Davidson, Herbert A., 65n55
death, deeds punishable by: conversions of Muslim women to the Judaism of their spouses, 127; sexual intercourse between Muslim or Jewish men and Christian women, 142–43, 152, 154n8
Defensorium Unitatis Christianae (Cartagena), 241
Délices de l'Espagne et du Portugal, Les, 317–18
Dellon, 1688 account of Portuguese Inquisition of Goa, 317
De monarchia orbis (Arévalo), 245
De oratore (Cicero), 162–63
De regno dividendo (Arévalo), 245

De Sensu et Sensibili (Kitāb al-Ḥiss wal-Maḥsūs) (Aristotle), 54, 66n65
Deuteronomy **28:15–50,** 165, 166
Deyermond, Alan A., 174
dhimmis: experience in Islam compared with Mozarabic experience, 105–6; status of defined by *sharīʿa,* xiii
dialectical skepticism, of Maimonides, 53–54, 65n58
Díaz de Toledo, Fernán, 241
dietary laws, Jewish, observance of among conversos, 198, 202–6
difference: religion as a marker of, 283; suppression of, 276–77
dispersion of the Moriscos, 312; decreed by Philip II in 1570, 278–79; early seventeenth-century recommendations for, 267–68
divine action, Maimonides on, 59
divine names, Ibn ʿArabi's theory of, 75
divine providence, role in *letrado* interpretation of history and politics, 245–46, 256nn11, 12, 257n18
divine punishment, for miscegenation, 145, 156n23
Domesday Book, compared to the *Libros de Repartimiento,* 20–21, 29, 34n3, 35n5, 36n17
Domínguez Ortiz, Antonio, 267
Dominicans (religious order), 127, 183; nunneries founded in Toledo, 233, *table* 232
Donato, 1573 statement on Spain, 313
Douglas, Mary, 145, 146
dowries, for Moriscas, 281
dream(s), of martyred husband by crypto-Jewish woman, 208, 219n43
dress, distinctive: Islamic, legal prohibition of, 268, 278; required of Jews and Muslims, 143, 154n11
dry farming: in post-*Repartiment* Majorca, 26–27; practiced in the Muslim *alquerías,* 22, 24, 27
Dufourcq, Charles, 105, 115n15
Dugdale, Richard, 317

Early Medieval Spain (Collins), 96
eccentrics, in Ptolemaic astronomy, 50–52
Echaniz, Maria, 124n97
economic activity: of conversos, 221–22, 225, 241; of the Mudejars, 95, 102, 108; relations between Christians, Jews, and Muslims, 108, 145–46
ecumenical councils, convoked by the early Church, 293–95, 296, 303n15
Edward, Prince of Wales (the Black Prince), 168
Egypt, 74, 84n39; time spent in by Maimonides, 40, 41, 49, 56, 75
emotion, emphasis on in Sufi Islam and Christian illuminism, 282
Encyclopedia of Medieval Iberia, 113
England: anti-Spanish traditions, and Anglophone scholars of medieval Spain, 92; land tenure, the *Domesday Book* on, 20–21, 35n6
Enrique II of Castile, 164–68, 256n11
Enrique III of Castile, 242
Enrique IV of Castile, 256nn11, 14
Epalza, Míkel de, 36n13, 98, 105, 111, 113, 122n72, 297–98
epicycles, in Ptolemaic astronomy, 50–52
Epiphanius of Salamis, 303n15
epistemology, twelfth-century Andalusian, 50–54
Epitome (Anacephaleosis) (Cartagena), 243–44, 255n7
Erasmus, 309–10, 318, 319
Escorial Codex, pogroms of 1391 described in, 169–70
esotericism, intellectual, 45–47, 69–78, 80n12; *Ishrāq,* 69, 71–74; Ismaʿilism, 56, 69, 71, 72, 81nn13, 14; Kabbalah, 69–70, 75, 76–78, 79n6; Murcia school of Sufism, 69–70, 74–76; in Spinoza's philosophy, 46–47, 62n31
España: un enigma histórico (Sánchez-Albornoz), 153n1
essence, distinction between existence and, 57–58, 67nn77, 78, 79
Estado social y político de los mudejares de Castilla (Fernández y González), 93, 114n3
Esther **9:5,** used by Çarça, 167
Estudis castellonencs (journal), 103, 120n58
ethnic solidarity, preserved by conversos in fifteenth- and sixteenth-century Toledo, 235–36
etymology, false, recourse to by Alvarus and Isidore, 12–13
Eulogius, 5–6, 13–14
Europae Speculum (Sandys), 319
Eusebius of Caesarea, 303n23

Index

existence, distinction between essence and, 57–58, 67nn77, 78, 79
exotericism, in twelfth-century Andalusian philosophy, 45–47
expulsion of the Jews
  1492, xiv–xv, 141, 241, 265, 309; effect on crypto-Judaism, 199–200
  1498, from Navarre, 309
expulsion of the Moriscos, 31, 33, 112, 283–84, 312; early seventeenth century, 265–72, 280; land transfers following, recorded in early modern *Apeo and Repartimientos,* 21
expulsion of the Mudejars: from the kingdom of Valencia, 106; as a policy of James the Conqueror, 109
extensive archaeology, practice of, 22
extortion, accusations of sexual activity between non-Christian men and Christian women used for, 149–50, 157n33
Extremadura, edict of July 10, 1610, expelling the Moriscos, 266
Ezekiel, Book of:
  3:5 used by Çarça, 164–65;
  23:20 referred to by Alvarus, 10
ᶜ*Ezer ha-Dat* (Polgar), 185–86

faith, 65n61, 255n9
Fakhry, Majid, 81n17
Fanshawe, Lady Ann (wife of Sir Richard Fanshawe), 315
al-Fārābī, Abū Naṣr, 43, 44–45
Farinas, Rev. Juan, 227, 238n15
Farinelli, Arturo, 320
fasting on Yom Kippur, observance of among conversos, 202–6
Favyn, André, 317
Febrer Romaguera, Manuel Vicent, 107, 120n62
Fernández, Paz, 98
Fernández de Angulo, Rev. Lope, 226–27
Fernández y González, Francisco, 93, 114n3
Fernando II of Aragon and Castile, xv, xix, 242, 246, 248–54, 257n18
Ferrer i Mallol, Maria Teresa, 98–99, 101, 107, 108, 114, 119n51, 124n97
feudalism, 22–23, 32–34, 35n12, 39n58
Fez, Morocco, expatriate colonies of Murcian activists, 74, 84n39
fiefs, recorded in the *Domesday Book,* 20
figura (exegetical principle), 170
Fischel, Walter J., 79n7
Flores, Juan de, xix, 257n20, 259n25, 261n28; *Grisel y Mirabella,* xix, 248, 250–53, 257n20, 258n21, 260nn26, 27
folklore: elements of in the *aljamiado* parable, 294–95; significance of number 72, 305n33
Fonseca, Damian, 285n11
Fontaine, Jacques, 173
food: Jewish laws concerning, 198, 202–6; Muslim preparation methods, prohibition of, 278, 279
Foundations of Crusader Valencia (Burns), 100–101
four kingdoms, in Book of Daniel, Alfonso of Valladolid's interpretation, 188–90
Fourth Lateran Council, decrees on segregation of minority men from Christian women, 142–43, 154n10
Fraker, Charles F., 174
France, 97, 271, 316; sixteenth-century policies toward religious minorities, 268, 272; southern, twelfth-century Jewish polemical works composed in, 181–82
Franciscans (religious order), 127; nunneries founded in Toledo, 232–34
Franco del Aguila, Hernán, 234, 239n39
Franco Sánchez, Francisco, 100
Franke, Franz Richard, 19n28
Frederick II (Holy Roman emperor), 74, 76, 82n21
"Free Muslims in the Balearics . . . " (Lourie), 95–96, 126
From Muslim Fortress to Christian Castle (Glick), 110
fruit trees, 21, 30, 35n6
Fuensalida, counts of, 225; burial chapel, 230, 238n20
Fuster, Joan, 108

Gabriel, Alvarus's demonization of, 12
Gaiffier, Baudouin de, 173
Galán Sánchez, Ángel, 91–92
Galen, 59
Galmés de Fuentes, Alvaro, 98
Galut (Baer), 161, 170
García Arenal, Mercedes, 99, 102, 116n24
García Ballester, Luis, 100
García Edo, Vicento, 119n50

Gautier-Daiché, Jean, 115n15
gender: as approach to difference, 277; roles among Moriscos, 275–76
General Historia, 172
geonim, Maimonides on, 41, 60n3
Gerber, Jane, 211n7
Germany, 144, 268, 272
al-Ghazālī, 48, 53
Gideon, Geryon's name changed to in Santa María's history of Spain, 243
Glick, Thomas F., xvii, 4, 20–29, 91, 93–94, 100, 106, 110, 111
God: Aristotelian proof for existence of, 57–58, 67n81; identified by Maimonides with the system of nature, 58–59; revelations from claimed by Muḥammad, Alvarus on, 8
goddesses, pre-Islamic, 9–10
Goitein, Shlomo Dov, 80n8, 133, 139n32
González, Julio, 24–25, 34n3
González Jiménez, Manuel, 29, 33–34, 100, 117n33, 119n47
Goodman, Lenn E., 83n29
Goths, role in Spanish history emphasized by *letrado* writers, 243–44, 245
Grace Period of 1486 in the Inquisition, testimony during, 201–3
grain (cereal) culture, 26–28, 30, 32
Gramsci, Antonio, 276
Granada, 21, 102
  fall of in 1492, xiv; conversion of Muslims to Christianity following, 275, 277–78
  fifteenth-century *Repartimientos* dealing with, 21, 29–31
Granada, Moriscos in
  early sixteenth-century descriptions by foreign visitors, 311
  rebellion of 1568–1570, 312; dispersal following, 278–79; expulsions following, 31, 33, 312
Greece: classical, situation of philosophy in, 49
Gregory I, St. (Gregory the Great), 7
Gregory IX (pope), 134
Grieve, Patricia, 252
Grimalte y Gradissa (Flores), 257n20
Grisel y Mirabella (Flores), xix, 248, 250–53, 257n20, 258n21, 260nn26, 27
Guicciardini, Francesco, 310–11, 318
Guichard, Pierre, 22, 33–34, 35n8, 97, 99, 101, 105, 107, 117n28, 120nn56, 58
Guide of the Perplexed, The (Maimonides), 51–60, 64n51, 72–75
Gutwirth, Eleazar, xviii–xix, 128, 161–78, 211n5
Gwara, Joseph J., 259n25

Habukkuk **1:6,** used by Crescas, 169
hagiography, biblical allusions in, 173
ha'irin, translation of, 64n51
hajj, 12, 13
al-Ḥakam II (caliph), 47–48
Halevi, Judah, 42
Haliczer, Stephen, xx, 265–73
al-Ḥarrālī, ʿAlī, 74, 76, 84n37
Harvey, Leonard Patrick, 101, 284n4, 285n8, 300n5, 301n7
al-Ḥasan, Abū ʿAlī, 42, 60n9
al-ḥayra al-ḥaqīqa ("the true puzzle"), 52–54, 64n51, 65n57
al-Haytham, Ibn, 51, 64n44
Ḥayy ibn Yaqẓān (Ibn Ṭufayl), 73–74, 77
Heath, Peter, 86n57
Hebrew language, knowledge of, Alvarus's lack of, 11, 19n37
hegemony, xii, 244–46, 276–77, 283
Hercules, traditionally the first Spanish king, 243
heresies/y: accusations of among early Christians, discussed in Quranic commentaries, 290–95; as concern of Christians in wake of 711 conquest, 5; discussed by Beatus, 18n5; suspicion of as basis for purging of library of al-Ḥakam II, 48
Hermeticism, 73
Herrera, Juan de, 233–34
Heschel, Joshua, 82n22
Heylin, Peter, 317
al-Ḥikma al-Mashriqiyya (Oriental Wisdom) (Avicenna), 72
Hilary of Poitiers, St., 15
Hillgarth, Jocelyn N., xx, 78, 96, 108, 129, 138n19, 309–22
Hishām (caliph), 47–48
ḥiṣn/qarya complex, 37n32; as model of agrarian landscape, 21–32, 35n8, 36n14
Histoire économique et sociale de l'Espagne chrétienne au moyen âge (Dufourq and Gautier-Daiché), 115n15
Histoire médiévale de la péninsula ibérique (Rucquoi), 115n15

Index

Historia Gothica (Rada), 244, 255n7
Historia inquisitionis (Van Limbosch), 317
historiography
  letrado approach to, 242–47; converso sentimental romances seen as indictment of, 247–54
  medieval Jewish, xviii–xix, 161–62; compared to Christian, 161–64, 172–75; on conditions in the Crown of Aragon, 141–42, 153nn3, 4; use of biblical allusions, xix, 161–75
  on the Mudejars: Anglophone studies, 92–97, 99, 100–101, 104, 106, 110–14; non-Anglophone studies, 96–110, 115n15
History of the Jews in Aragon (Assis, ed.), 136n1
History of the Jews in Christian Spain, A (Baer), 142
History of Medieval Spain (O'Callaghan), 96
Holy Office. See Inquisition, Spanish
Holy Spirit, place in the Trinity established at the Council of Chalcedon, 293–94
holy war, Arévalo's commitment to, 245
hopelessness of Jewish circumstances, role in Christian polemics addressed to the Jews, 180–83, 186–88, 191n4
Horace, 162
Hugo, Victor, 315
Huguenots, 268, 272
humanism, 244, 255n9
humor: of Maimonides, 42–43, 61n15; in verbal exchanges in medieval Spain, 163
Hungary, 113, 268
Hurtado, Rev. Luis, 227, 238n15
ḥuṣūn. See castles; *ḥiṣn/qarya* complex

Iberia and the Mediterranean World of the Middle Ages, 110–11
Ibn Abī Zamānīn, 291, 294, 301n7
Ibn ʿAqnīn, 70
Ibn ʿArabī, 46, 69, 75–78, 84nn39, 41, 85n49; followers of, 75–76, 79nn3, 5, 85n50
Ibn Bājja, Abū Bakr (Avempace), 43, 45, 48, 49, 51, 70; influence on Ibn Ṭufayl, 73, 82n22; influence on Maimonides, 45, 62n27, 65n59, 73, 82n22
Ibn Ḥazm, ʿAlī ibn Aḥmad (Ibn Ḥazm of Córdoba), 48, 296, 297
Ibn Hūd, al-Muʾtamin, 42, 60n9, 74, 84n39
Ibn Kammūna, 70, 74, 82n24
Ibn Kathīr, Ismāʾīl ibn ʿUmar, 292, 294–95, 301n9, 302n11
Ibn Khaldūn, 86n57
Ibn Laṭīf, Israel, 76, 81n14
Ibn Masarra, Muḥammad, 46, 48
Ibn Rushd, Abū al-Walīd. *See* Averroës
Ibn Sabʿīn, 72, 73, 74–75, 76, 79n3, 81n17
Ibn al-Sīd al-Baṭalyawsī, 75
Ibn Sīnā, ʿAlī. *See* Avicenna
Ibn Ṭufayl, 49, 51, 72–74, 81n17, 83n30, 84n39; *Ḥayy ibn Yaqẓān,* 73–74, 77; Ibn Bājja's influence on, 73, 82n22; as a pioneer of Aristotelian revival in Spain, 45, 62n27
Idel, Moshe, 79nn3, 6
identity
  of a group, image of human body used to express, 145–48
  of the Moriscos: loss through assimilation, 279; seen by the Church as a "counter-identity," 283
  religious, challenges to in Muslim and Christian Spain, xiii, xx, 16–17
Ikhwān al-Ṣafāʾ (Sincere Brethren), 44, 56, 62n24
"Illuminationism" *(Ishrāq),* 69, 71–74
illuminism (Christian heresy), 281–82
imaginary, the, in the Middle Ages, studies of, 171–72
imitation, Plato's and Aristotle's theories of, 162
immanence, balance with transcendence, 59–60
Incarnation, the, addressed at Council of Nicaea, 293
incastellamento, Pierre Toubert's conception of, 22
ʿindanā fī l-maghrib: translation of *ʿindanā,* 60n1; used by Maimonides to include Andalusia in Maghrib, 40
Indiculus luminosus (Alvarus), xvii, 5, 6–17
Indigenous Christian Communities in Islamic Lands (symposium), 106
In Iberia and Beyond: Hispanic Jews between Cultures (Cooperman, ed.), 138n19
Inquisition, Portuguese, 268, 272, 317

Inquisition, Spanish, xx, 197–98, 210n2, 230–31, 241–42, 255n9
directed at Moriscos, 269–71, 276, 277–78, 280, 283, 285n12
documents, xv, xvi; use of in study of crypto-Jewish life, 197–200
effects on conversos, 220, 222, 257n20, 260n26
illuminists prosecuted by, 281–82
and the *letrados,* 246–47, 257n16
outsiders' views of, 310–11, 313, 314–20
persecution of Protestant merchants and ambassadors and visiting princes, 314–15
trials: of crypto-Jewish women and their families, 197, 200–207, 208–9, 212nn11, 12, 213–16nn14–25, 28, 217–19nn29–43; parish priests as character witnesses at, 227
insan kamil (Perfect Man), Ibn ᶜArabī's theory of, 85n49
Institute of Medieval Mediterranean Spain, 97, 116n18
Instrucción del relator (Díaz de Toledo), 241
intellect: the undivided soul identified with, 82n21; unity of, 65nn59, 61
Intercultural Debate in the Thirteenth and Fourteenth Centuries, The, 103
intermarriage (*see also* miscegenation): between conversos and Old Christians, 221, 236n4; between Moriscos and Old Christians, 275, 280–81, 285n11, 287n39; as strategy for assimilation, 274–75
International Symposium of Mudejar Studies (Teruel, 1975), 97 (*see also* Center for Mudejar and Morisco Studies)
intertextuality, 162–63; place in medieval Jewish historiography, 161–75
irrigation agriculture in Muslim *alquerías,* 22, 27; changes under the Christians, 26–29, 30, 32–33
Irrigation and Society in Medieval Valencia (Glick), 93–94
Isaac of Acre, 77, 79n3, 84n39
Isaac ibn Laṭīf, 71
Isabel I (queen of Aragon and Castile), xv, xix, 242, 246, 248–54, 257n18
Ishrāq, 69, 71–74
Isidore of Seville, St., 13, 44
Islam, 4, 40, 48–49, 104–5, 267, 305n33 (*see also* Moriscos; Mudejars; Muslims); beliefs and practices taught to children by Moriscas, 276, 279, 285n12; conversion to by Christians, 5, 303n13; conversion to by Jews, 70, 79n7, 303n13; customs, legal prohibition of, 268, 275–76, 278, 279; medieval knowledge of, 6–17; mystical tradition, 282, 288n44
Islamic and Christian Spain in the Early Middle Ages (Glick), 93–94
Islamic Spain, 1250 to 1500 (Harvey), 101
Islam under the Crusaders (Burns), 94
Ismaᶜilism, 56, 69, 71, 72, 81nn13, 14
isolation, of conversos in fifteenth- and sixteenth-century Toledo, 221, 235–36
Israelite Christians
defined, 303n21
on nature of Christ: discussed in *aljamiado* text, 290–91, 292, 294; discussed in Quranic commentaries, 292, 294, 302n11
al-Isrāʾīlī, Abū Sayyid, 70, 84n39
isrāʾiliyyat (traditional lore), 303n13
Italy, 112, 244
Ivry, Alfred, 67n72, 81n13, 82n21

Jābir ibn Aflaḥ, 42, 51, 52, 61n10
Jacob ben Baradai, Bishop, 294
Jacobites, 295, 297, 299
on nature of Christ, 294; discussed in *aljamiado* text, 290–91, 292, 294; discussed in Morisco texts, 292, 296, 302n11
Jaume (James) I (James the Conqueror), 109–10, 113, 136n1; rights granted to Jews, 128, 131–32, 134
Jaume (James) II of Aragon, 128, 136n1, 157n31
Jaume (James) II of Majorca, 128
Jeremiah, Book of: **5:8** cited by Alvarus, 10; **16:4** used by Çarça, 166
Jerome, St., 7, 11, 14–16
Jerusalem, identification of medieval communities with, 171–72
local Hispano-Jewish communities as example, 170–72; for Çarça, 164–67, 170–71; for Crescas, 169–71
Jerusalem school of Jewish historical interpretation, 141–42, 153nn3, 4

Index

Jesus
as the messiah, role in Christian polemics addressed to the Jews, 180, 181, 187–90
nature, 6; doctrine of examined in Morisco texts, 290–95, 298, 302n11
Jesús, Beatriz de, 277, 278–79, 281, 282–83
Jesús Viguera, María, 107
Jewish literature, post-biblical, use of in arguments in Christian missionizing, 179–80
Jews, in Germany, Nuremberg laws of 1935, 144
Jews, in Spain, xii, 225 (*see also* conversos)
circumstances, xii, 241, 247; compared with the Mudejars, 100; role in Christian-Jewish polemical dialogues, 180–83, 191n4
as converts to Islam, 70, 79n7, 303n13
in the Crown of Aragon: accusations of miscegenation, 142–43, 150–52, 158nn36, 39; conditions, 141–52, 153n2
expulsion of (*see* expulsion of the Jews)
interrelations with Christians and Muslims, 50, 69–78, 105, 128–36, 141, 145–46
literacy among women as uncommon, 198, 211n5
sixteenth- and seventeenth-century Spain seen by outsiders as full of, xx, 309–20
in thirteenth-century Majorca, 125–36
in Toledo's Judería Mayor and Judería Menor, 222, 224–25, 236n7, *map* 224
Jews, in Spain, as converts to Christianity (*see also* conversion of Jews to Christianity; conversos): Alfonso of Valladolid's depiction of his experience, xix, 182, 186–91; early Spanish restrictions on descendants of, 144; Israelite Christians as a term for, 303n21; women, Christian men's willingness to marry, 144
Jiménez, José Lozano, 284n4
Job, Book of, discussed in Alvarus's *Indiculus luminosus*, 7, 16
1 John **2:18,** on "many Antichrists," 15
John of Damascus, 19n28
John of Salisbury, 170
Joly, Barthélemy, 315
Joseph b. Judah, 42, 53–55
Joseph ibn Saddiq (Joseph ha-Saddiq), **41,** 43–44
Juan I of Castile, 256n11
Juan II of Castile, 175, 242–43, 256n14, 275
Judah ben Nissim ibn Malkah, 76–77, 84n41
Judah ben Solomon ha-Cohen ibn Malkah, 76
Judah Halevi, 71, 73
Judaism, 41, 303n21, 305n33, 318
medieval culture: attitudes toward slavery, 132–36; studies of, 104–5
Pablo de Santa María's role prior to conversion, 242
polemical literature: early medieval addressed to fellow Jews, 179; responses to Christian polemics from the twelfth-century on, 181–85
situation of philosophy in as blessing in disguise, 48–49
transmission of laws and customs: dominant role in played by men, 198; role of crypto-Jewish women after 1391, xix, 197–210, 211n8
Judaizing, xix, 197–210, 211n8; conversos in fifteenth- and sixteenth-century Toledo accused of, 220–21
Judería Mayor (Barrio Nuevo), in Toledo, 222, 224–25, 236n7, *map* 224
Judería Menor, in Toledo, 225, 236n7, *map* 224
Junta de Tres, 269

Kaʿbah (shrine in Great Mosque of Mecca), 12, 13, 19n28
Kabbalah, 69, 76–78, 79n6; Murcia school of Sufism's influence on, 70, 75
Kagan, Richard L., xx n3
Kalām (Islamic speculative philosophy), 41, 56
Kant, Immanuel, 153n6
Karaites, 41
Kertzer, David I., 289n48
Kimhi, Joseph, 181–82, 192n9
al-Kindi, 9–10, 19n25
2 Kings **18:20,** used by Çarça, 168
Kitāb al-Fiṣal (Ibn Ḥazm), 296, 297
Kitāb al-Ḥiss wal-Maḥsūs (De Sensu et Sensibili), (Aristotle), 54, 66n65
Kraemer, Joel L., xviii, 40–68, 74, 211n5

Kristeller, Paul Oskar, 62n28, 65n61
Kroes, Rob, 107

Labarta, Ana, 108, 123n83
labor, sexual division of, among Moriscos, 275–76
Lacarra, José M., 93, 97
lachrymose school of Jewish historical interpretation, 141–42, 153n4
Ladero Quesada, Miguel Angel, 93, 97, 102
Lamentations, Book of, allusions to: by Çarça, 166; by Crescas, 169
landholding, Andalusi model of, documented in the *Repartimientos,* 21–34
land registers *(Libros de Repartimiento):* produced by Christian conquerors of Muslim Spain, xvii, 20–34; *Repartimiento* before the, 24–25
land registers, of Norman Sicily, 34n2
land tenure, English, the *Domesday Book* on, 20–21
land tenure, in Muslim Spain: documented in the *Repartimientos,* 20–24, 29–30, 35n9; post-*Repartimiento* (Christian), 27–28, 33; post-*Repartimiento* (Moriscos), 31–32
Lange, Johannes, 311
Langermann, Tzvi, 64n44
language (*see also* Arabic language)
  as a barrier to acculturation, 108
  as a barrier to assimilation, 285n9
  Hebrew, knowledge of, Alvarus's lack of, 11, 19n37
  Latin, Spanish Aristotelians translated into, 45
  Maimonides' interest in, 42–43
  as medium of historiography, 164 (*see also* historiography; intertextuality)
  as a prominent element of Mudejar culture, 108, 123n83
  Spanish *(see also aljamiado);* anti-Christian polemical texts written in, 295, 298
Last Supper, blasphemous allusions to in *Grisel y Mirabella,* 252
Lateran Council of 1215, 275
Latin Chronicle of the Kings of Castile, biblical allusions, 173
Latin language, Spanish Aristotelians translated into, 45
Ledesma Rubio, María Luisa, 101
Leibman, Seymour, 211n8
Lent, dietary laws, failure of crypto-Jews to observe, 207
lepers, in the Crown of Aragon and Occitania, persecution of, 111
Leroy, Béatrice, 116n24
letrados
  on *consejo real* as changed by Fernando and Isabel in 1480, 246–47, 256n14
  defined, 242
  writings promoting monarchy and rationalist approach to religious orthodoxy, xix, 242–47; converso sentimental romances as indictment of, 247–54, 260nn26, 27
Letter to Yemen (Maimonides), 40–41
Levine Melammed, Renée, xix, xx, 197–219
Lévi-Strauss, Claude, 146, 147
Lhermite, Jehan, 314
Liber apologeticus martyrum (Eulogius), 5–6
Liber de Causis, 72
library of al-Ḥakam II, purged by Abū ʿĀmir, 47–48
Libros de Habices, 30
Libros de Repartimiento (Llibres del Repartiment): produced by Christian conquerors of Muslim Spain, xvii, 20–34; *Repartimiento* before the, 24–25
limpieza de sangre statute(s). *See* pure blood statute(s)
Linehan, Peter, 35n12, 173–74
lions, symbolism of in *Grisel y Mirabella,* 251–52, 260n27
literacy, among Spanish Jewish women as uncommon, 198, 211n5
liturgy, Christian, Arabic and Muslim dance and music incorporated into, 275, 285n10
Llull, Ramon, 70, 76–78, 79n5, 87n60, 109, 127
logos, 86n57; relationship to *mythos* in Kabbalah, 76–77
Longinus, 162
López de Toledo, Diego, 232, 239n29
López-Morillas, Consuelo, xx, 290–305
Louis XIV (king of France), 268, 272
Lourie, Elena, 91, 95–96, 100, 115n12, 126, 127–28, 158n39
Luna Diaz, Juan André, 31
Lutherans: Spanish, burned at the stake in 1559, 316; as visitors in sixteenth- and seventeenth-century Spain, 314

Index

MacKay, Angus, 91, 96, 119n47
Maghrib, the (North Africa), 105; influence on Maimonides, 40, 41, 43
magical texts, 79n6
al-Maḥallī, Jalāl al-Dīn Muḥammad ibn Aḥmad, 301n9
Maḥazik Emunah (Mordechai ben Jehosapha), 185
Maimonides, Moses, xviii, 40–60, 66n69, 69, 71, 78, 170; and Averroism, 54–60; followers influenced by Sufism, interpretation of Kabbalah, 76–77; Ibn Bājja's influence on, 45, 62n27, 65n59, 73, 82n22; influence on *Ishrāq* and Sufism, 72–75, 85n49; influence on Spinoza, 46, 62n31; *Mishneh Torah,* on slavery, 132, 139n35; *Perakim be-Hazlaha* attributed to, 73, 77, 83n30; position on Ptolemaic astronomy, 50–51, 52–54, 65n58; role in Andalusian revival of Aristotelianism, 43–46, 50–51, 52–54; time spent in Egypt, 40, 41, 49, 56, 75
Maimonides, Ovadya, 77
Maimonides, R. David b. Joshua, 74
Maitland, F. W., 29
Majorca
  great *auto* of 1691, accounts republished in 1931, 316
  ḥiṣn/qarya model of agrarian landscape, 21–22
  Inquisition effects in the seventeenth-century, 315–16
  Repartiment dealing with, 21, 25–27, 34, 36n23
  thirteenth-century, xviii, 20; Muslim-Jewish relations, 125–36
males/men, Jewish, traditional dominant role in transmission of laws and customs, 198, 200; shift in among the Judaizers, 201, 209
al-malkāniyya (Melkites). *See* Melkites
Mancha, La, 1610 expulsion of Moriscos, 266
Manrique, Rodrigo, 320
manumission, medieval attitudes toward: among Christians, 133–35; among Jews, 132–36
Maozim, meaning of in Hebrew, Alvarus's interpretation of, 11–13
marginalization, xii–xiv; of the existence of conversos after the Toledan rebellions, 259n25; of Jewish events in non-Jewish chronicles, reversed by Çarça, 166
Márquez Villanueva, Francisco, 247, 249, 258n22, 259n23
Marranos. *See* conversos; Moriscos
marriage (*see also* intermarriage): emancipation of converted slaves for purpose of, 139n32
Martín-Cleto, Julio Porres, 236n7
martyrs, Judaizers burned at the stake seen as, 208, 219n43
Martz, Linda, xix, 220–40
Mary, mother of Jesus: Morisco anti-Christian polemic on, 293; for Nestorianism, 293; Quranic passage on, commentaries on, 291, 292; treatment by crypto-Jews of images and doctrine of, 207–8
Al-Masāq: studia arabo-islamica mediterranea (journal), 104
masses, for soul of deceased crypto-Jewish husband, 208, 219n43
Massignon, Louis, 74–75
mathematics, Maimonides' knowledge of: Andalusian influence on, 41–42, 60n8; and position on Aristotelian cosmology versus Ptolemaic astronomy, 52–54, 65n58
Matulka, Barbara, 260n27
McVaugh, Michael, 100
medicine. *See* physician(s)
Medieval Colonialism: Postcrusade Exploitation of Islamic Valencia (Burns), 94
Medieval Encounters (journal), 104, 110, 111–12
Medieval Frontier Society (Bartlett and MacKay, eds.), 101, 119n47
Medieval Spains, The (Reilly), 96
Mediterranean Emporium, A (Abulafia), 101
Mediterranean Society, A (Goitein), 133, 139n32
Megilat Ha-Megaleh, 175
Meir bar Simon of Narbonne, 182–83, 192n12
Melkites *(al-malkāniyya),* 294, 297; reference to in Morisco texts, 292, 294, 303n21
Melkites, present-day Syrian, 303n20

Melzetin, M., 170
Memoriale sanctorum (Eulogius), 5–6
mendicant orders, as proselytizers, 241
merchants, Moriscos as, 280
messiah
Jesus as the, role in Christian polemics addressed to the Jews, 180, 181, 184, 187–90
seen as not yet come in Jewish polemical works, 182, 184; Alfonso of Valladolid's response to, 187–90; Nahmanides' prediction of date of coming, 184–85
messianism: in Jerusalem school of Jewish historical interpretation, 141–42; in *letrado* thought, 245, 247
metes and bounds, measurement of *alquerías* by, 29, 38n42
Meyerson, Mark D., xi–xxi, 100, 106, 110–12, 287n28
Miftāḥ al-dīn (al-Qaysī), 296–97, 304n30
Miguel Rodríguez, Juan Carlos, 99–100, 117n33
Milḥamot ha-shem, 181–82, 192n8
Milḥemet Miẓvah (Meir bar Simon), 182–83, 192n12
military aristocracy, dominance on the *consejo real* lost to the *letrados,* 246–47, 256n14
military obligations, effect on Mudejars, 95
military power, 265, 267
Minh-ha, Trinh, 276–77
Minorca, Mudejar society of, 100
"Minorities and Marginalized" colloquy (Pau), 103
miscegenation
definitions and use of term: medieval, 154n9; in the U.S., 147, 154n9
notarial formula used in cases of, 147, 157n28
sexual intercourse between non-Christian men and Christian women as: accusations of, 149–52, 157nn32–34, 158nn37–39, 159nn41, 42; punishment for, 142–45, 150–52, 154n8, 155n13
Mishnah ʿEruvin (Maimonides), 65n56
Mishneh Torah (Maimonides), 52, 56, 132
missionizing, Christian, 127, 181, 183–85; emphasis shifted from the Bible to reason, 179–80; responses to, 181, 183–85, 188
monarchism, *letrado* theories, 244–47; critiqued in converso sentimental romances, 249–50, 253–54; effects on conversos, 247 (*see also* Inquisition, Spanish); shared by Spanish Jews, 257n18
Moncada, Gaston de, Marquis of Aytona, 265
Monophysites, 294, 295
Monter, William, 210n2
Moore, Robert I., 284n5
Moors, African, early seventeenth-century Spain seen as vulnerable to attacks from, 267
Moors and Crusades in Mediterranean Spain (Burns), 95
Mordechai ben Jehosapha, 185
Moretus, description of 1680 *auto-de-fé,* 316
Moriscos, xvi, xix–xx, xx n3, 93, 100, 105, 314 (*see also* conversion of Muslims to Christianity); agriculture patterns, 31; *aljamiado* and Arabic manuscripts, 304n25; *aljamiado* text copied by, 290–93, 295–96, 299n1; anti-Christian polemical texts, 295–99; assimilation (*see* assimilation, of Moriscos); attracted to mystical movements, 281–82; dispersion, 267–68, 278–79, 312; exile in North Africa, 298, 299; expulsions (*see* expulsion of the Moriscos); identity seen by the Church as a "counter-identity," 283; legends, significance of number 72, 305n33; seen as atheists, 318; seen as loyal subjects, 269–72; sixteenth- and seventeenth-century Spain seen by outsiders as full of, xx, 309–20; slaves as, changing status, 131–32; in thirteenth-century Majorca, 126–27; women, Christian men's willingness to marry, 144, 155n15
Moros y judíos en Navarra en la baja edad media (García Arenal and Leroy), 116n24
Moros y moriscos en el levante peninsular (Epalza), 98, 104
Moses ben Nahman. *See* Nahmanides
Moses ibn Ezra, 72, 73
Moshe de Leon, 75, 77
Moshe Narboni, 73, 74, 82n21

Index

Mozarabic experience, 105–6, 122n72
"Mudejar History Today" (Burns), 93
Mudejars, 27–28, 92–93, 106–9
accusations of miscegenation, 142–43, 146–52, 158n37
anti-Christian polemical texts, 296
etymology and use of term, 103
expulsion of, 106, 109
influence on ruling Christian culture, 275, 284n4
persecution of, 111, 141, 142–52
study of, xvi, xvii–xviii, 91–124; Anglophone, 91–97, 99, 100–101, 104, 106, 110–14; non-Anglophone, 96–110, 115n15
in thirteenth-century Majorca, 125–30; relations with Jews, 128–36; as slaves, 126, 128–36
Mudejars of Aragon during the Twelfth and Thirteenth Centuries, The (Thaler), 95
muezzin *(mu'adhdhin)*, 13
Muḥammad: Alvarus's knowledge of revealed in *Indiculus luminosus*, 7–17; depicted as an Antichrist by Andalus, xvii, 6, 7–17; no mention of in Beatus' *Commentary on the Apocalypse*, 4; public denunciations of by ninth-century Cordoban Christians, 5–6
"*Muḥtasib* and *Mustasaf*" (Glick), 94
Mukhtaṣar (al-Taymī), *aljamiado* translation, 291, 300n5
Munk, Solomon, 58, 67n81
Murcia, 102; *Repartiment*, 21, 28–29
Murcia school of Sufism, 69, 70, 74–76
Mūsā ibn Maymūn al-Qurṭubī, Abū ʿImran. *See* Maimonides, Moses
music, Arabic and Muslim, incorporated into Christian liturgy, 285n10
"Muslim-Jewish Relations in the Fourteenth-Century Crown of Aragon" (Nirenberg), 101
Muslims, xii (*see also* Mudejars); as converts to Christianity (*see* conversion of Muslims to Christianity; Moriscos); interrelations with Christians and Jews, 50, 69–78, 105, 141, 145–46; late fifteenth- to early sixteenth-century revolts, 277, 278; sixteenth- and seventeenth-century Spain seen by outsiders as full of, xx, 309–20; in thirteenth-century Hungary, 113
Muslims under Latin Rule (Powell, editor), 101
Musulmans a Catalunya, Els (Balañà i Abadia), 101
al-Mu'tamin ibn Hūd, 42, 60n9, 74, 84n39
Mutgé, Josefa, 101
Myers, David, 153n4
mysticism, 50, 80n12, 281–82, 288n40; *Ishrāq*, 71–74; in medieval esotericism, 46, 62n27; in Sufist interpretation of Kabbalah, 76–77
mythos, relationship to *logos* in Kabbalah, 76–77

Nader, Helen, 246–47, 254n4, 255n9, 256n14, 257n16
Nahmanides (Moses ben Nahman), 46, 70, 170, 181, 183–85, 188
Najm al-Dīn ibn Isrā'īl, 72
names, Christian, forced on Moriscos, and use of Muslim names, 277
Narrative of Unheard of Popish Cruelties, A (Dugdale), 317
naturalism, in Maimonides' thought, 55–57, 58–60
Navagiero, on treatment of New Christians, 313
Navarre: 1498 expulsion of the Jews, 309; Mudejar society, 99, 102, 116n24
Necessary Being (Necessary Existent), God as the, for Maimonides and Avicenna, 57–58, 67n81
Negotiating Cultures: Bilingual Treaties in Muslim-Crusader Spain . . ., 113
Negro, Zuan, 311
Neoaristotelianism, 45
Neoplatonism, 45, 56, 67n79, 80n12; found in Kabbalah, 76–77; influence on *Ishrāq*, 72; in Maimonides' *Guide*, 55–56
Nestorians, 295, 299
on nature of Christ, 293–94; discussed in *aljamiado* text, 290–91, 292, 294; discussed in Morisco texts, 292, 302n11
Nestorius, Bishop of Constantinople, 293
New Castile. *See* Toledo
New Christians (*see also* conversos; Moriscos): attracted to mystical movements, 281–82; flight from the Portuguese Inquisition, 268, 272;

sixteenth- and seventeenth-century foreign visitors' opinions on, 310, 311–12, 313–14, 315
Nicaea, Council of (325), 293, 295, 299
Nicene Creed, 293, 296, 303n15, 305n40
Nicholas of Cusa, 76
nigleh (ẓāhir) binarity, 45–47 (*see also* esotericism)
Nirenberg, David, xviii, 101, 105, 111, 128, 141–60
nistar (bāṭin) binarity, 45–47 (*see also* esotericism)
"Non-Christians in a Medieval Frontier Society" (Berend), 112–13
North Africa
the Maghrib, 105; influence on Maimonides, 40, 41, 43
Moriscos' attempt to escape to, 280
Moriscos' exile in, 298, 299
sixteenth- and seventeenth-century Spanish possessions in, role in Islam's hostility to king of Spain, 267
North American Catalan Society, 96
Nuestra Señora de la Asunción de Bernardas Recoletas (religious foundation), 234
Núñez de Toledo, Bernardo, burial chapel, 230
nunneries, in fifteenth- and sixteenth-century Toledo, 231–35; entrance fees, 233–34; founded and joined by conversos, xix, 232–35
Nuremberg laws of 1935, 144

Obadiah, as family name of Maimonides, 55, 66n69
O'Callaghan, Joseph, 96
Occitania, persecution of minorities in, 111
O'Connor, Isabel Bonet, 112
Old Christians, 257n18, 271; attitude toward conversos, 207, 208, 211n7, 218n41; in convent of Santo Domingo el Real, 233–34; as godparents for Morisco children, 278; intermarriage between men and Moriscas, 275, 280–81, 287n39
Old Testament (*see also* Bible, the; Daniel, Book of): allusions to in medieval Jewish historiography, xix, 161–75; Alvarus's interpretations in *Indiculus luminosus*, 7, 10, 16; commentaries by Hebrew philosophers, esoteric allusions, 46, 47; history, early Spanish history adapted to by Santa María, 243; written Arabic text of the Torah studied by al-Biqaʾi, 84n37
Olivares (Guzmán y Pimental), 272
On the Sublime (Longinus), 162
oral transmission, of Jewish customs and laws among the conversos, 199–200
Oriental Wisdom (al-Ḥikma al-Mashriqiyya) (Avicenna), 72
Orihuela, 99; *Repartiment*, 21, 28–29, 32
Other, the, xii–xiv, 107–9, 146–47
Oviedo, Fernández de, 320
Oviedo, University of, 98
Owens, Joseph, 67n79
Ozaki, Akio, 99

Padilla, Paul, 111
Padrón, Rodríguez del, 248, 253–54, 258n21
Palacios, Asín, 296
Palencia, Alonso de, 245
paper mills and "paper revolution," 36n15
pardons: for charges of miscegenation, 151, 158n39; crimes excluded from, 154n8
parishes, in fifteenth- and sixteenth-century Toledo: conversos in, 222–31, 235–36; *map*, 222, 236n6
parish priests, fifteenth- and sixteenth-century
in Seville, practices of the Moriscos overseen by, 279
in Toledo, 226–27, 228; conversos as, 221, 238n15
training of, 137n13
parody, in conversos sentimental romances, 252–54
Parrilla, Carmen, 259n25
Partner, Nancy, 170
Passover, observance of among conversos, 203–4, 214n20
Paul Christian, Friar, 181, 183–85
Paul V (pope), 234
Paulus Alvarus. *See* Alvarus, Paul
Peace of Augsburg (1555), 268
Peace Treaty of 1604, 315
peasant parcels of land, recorded in the *Repartimientos*, 20
Pedregal y Fantini, José, 114n3

Index

Pedro III of Aragon (Pedro the Great), 136n1
Pedro IV of Aragon (Pedro the Ceremonious), 94, 174
Pedro the Cruel (king of Castile and León), 94, 167–68, 225, 256n11
Pedro de Valencia, memorial for expulsion of the Moriscos, 266–68
Peinado Santella, Rafael G., 30
Pelayo (king of Asturias), 244
Penyafort, Ramon de, 131, 139n29
Perakim be-Hazlaha (Chapters on Beatitude) (attrib. to Maimonides), 73, 77, 83n30
Pérez, Mosen Jaime, 271
Pérez de la Fuente, Hernán, 234
Pérez Viñuales, Pilar, 119n50
Perry, Mary Elizabeth, xx, 274–89
persecution, xii, 111, 283; of Christians by Muslims, 5–7, 8, 16; of Muslims and Jews, 95, 106, 109, 275, 285n8, 320; twelfth-century Andalusian philosophy done under threat of, 47–50
Philip II (king of Spain), 278–79, 316, 318
Philip III (king of Spain), 268
  Moriscos as subjects under, 265–72; expulsion, 265–68, 269–72, 280; loyalty, 269–72
Philip IV (king of Spain), 268, 272
philosophy, 49, 54, 72–74, 80n12
  exoteric-esoteric binarity in, 45–47
  of Maimonides, 41, 43–46, 50–54; relationship to Averroism, 54–60
  twelfth-century Andalusian school of Aristotle studies, 43–54, 62n28
physician(s): interconfessional contacts, 70–71, 80n8; Jewish skills as in thirteenth-century Majorca, 125; Maimonides as a, 40, 41, 49; studies of Mudejar practitioners, 100
pi (π), irrationality of, 65n56
Pines, Shlomo, 53–57, 59, 62n27, 64n42, 65n55, 67nn71, 77
pirate colonies, founded by Moriscos expelled from Spain, 272
Plato and Platonism, 44–45, 162
poetics, on allusion, 163
poetry, 42–43, 46, 61n18, 162
pogroms, 241, 285; described by Crescas, xix, 163, 168–73, 175
Poland, sixteenth-century policies on religious minorities, 268
polemical literature
  Christian: early medieval addressed to fellow Christians, 179; twelfth-century shift to addressing the Jews, 179–91
  Jewish: early medieval addressed to fellow Jews, 179; responses to Christian polemics from the twelfth-century on, 181–85
  Morisco anti-Christian, 295–99
Polgar, Isaac, 185–86, 194n38
political philosophy: *letrado* approach to, 242–47; post-Enlightenment, on conflict and stability, 153n6
politics: active engagement in of Andalusian philosophers, 49; positions held by conversos in fifteenth- and sixteenth-century Toledo, 221
pope of Rome, authority of, accepted by present-day Syrian Melkites, 303n20
Popplau, Nicolaus von, 310
population: depopulation of minority communities through accusations of crime, 151–52, 159nn41, 42; late sixteenth- and early seventeenth-century decline, 267
Portugal
  forced baptism of Jews in 1497, 309
  sixteenth- and seventeenth-century: Inquisition, 268, 272, 317; Protestants seen as a danger, 312–13; seen by outsiders as full of Muslims and Jews, 309–20
Possessing the Land: Aragon's Expansion into Islam's Ebro Frontier . . . (Stall), 110
Poveda Sánchez, Angel, 26, 28
power, shift of, in families of Judaizers, 201, 209
Prescott, William H., xx n3
Present State of the Jews, The (Addison), 319
Prime Mover, Aristotelian proof for, 57
Principles of the Existent Beings (al-Fārābī), 44
prostitutes, 142, 148–49, 157nn31, 32
Protestants: art used as religious propaganda, 316–17; English, late sixteenth-century points of agreement with French Catholics, 318; Huguenots, 268, 272; toleration of by Catholic countries, 268; viewed as dangerous, 312–15
Proverbs **25:11**, 46
Pseudo-Empedoclean traditions, 72
Ptolemaic astronomy, xviii, 50–54, 65n58

Pugio fidei (Raymond Martin), 181
Pulgar, Hernando del, 245, 257n18
Pullan, Brian S., 211n8
pure blood *(limpieza de sangre)* statute(s), 144, 220–21, 235, 241, 259n25, 275; for entry to the Cistercian Order, 311; foreign visitors' opinion of, 316

qarya. See ḥiṣn/qarya complex
Qatāda, *aljamiado* manuscript attributed to, 290–91, 292, 293, 295
al-Qaysī, Muḥammad, 298; *Miftāḥ al-dīn,* 296–97
al-Qiftī, Ibn, 42, 60n8, 70
qiyās (reasoning), 50–51, 53, 64n42
Qur'ān, the, 12; Alvarus's writings on, 9, 11; anti-Trinitarian passages used by Morisco polemicists, 298; commentaries *(tafsīrs),* xx, 290–99, 303n13
al-Qurṭubī, Muḥammad ibn Aḥmad, 292, 301n9

Rábago Hernández, Carmen Díaz de, 101, 120n58
rabbinical studies, school of established by Pablo de Santa María, 242
rabbinic literature, on the messianic era, Alfonso of Valladolid's attacks on, 187–90
Rabelais, 318
Rada, Ximénez de (El Toledano), 244, 255n7
rahal/s (private estates), in Muslim Spain, 22, 26, 27 *(see also alquerías)*
ratiocination, narrative depictions of among Jewish esoteric elites, 76–77
rationalism, approach to religious orthodoxy for *letrados,* xix, 242–47, 251
al-Rāzī, Fakhr al-Dīn Muḥammad ibn ʿUmar, 292, 301n9
reason: arguments from as basis for Christian missionizing, 179–80; distinction between faith and, in Averroism, 65n61
reasoning *(qiyās),* 50–51, 53, 64n42
rebellions (revolts): converso, 259n25; Muslim, 31, 277, 278, 281, 312
Reconquest, the *(Reconquista),* 284n4, 296; myth of in the Alfonsine chronicles, 174; place in Spanish history emphasized by *letrado* writers, 243–44, 245, 247
redemption, corporate, as issue in Christian-Jewish polemics, xix, 179–92
redemption of Muslim slaves, provided for by Jews in thirteenth-century Majorca, 131–36
regidores (city councilors), conversos as in fifteenth- and sixteenth-century Toledo, 221–22, 234
Régné, Jean, 125, 127, 136n1
Reilly, Bernard, 96
religion(s), 283, 288n44 (*see also* Christianity; Islam; Judaism; theology); *Kitāb al-Fiṣal* as a critical and comparative history of, 296; preeminence of philosophy over for twelfth-century philosophers, 48, 49–50
religious foundations, in fifteenth- and sixteenth-century Toledo, xix, 231–34
Repartiment of Mallorca (1232), written on vellum, 36n15
Repartimiento de Almería, 35n6
Repartimientos (see also Libros de Repartimiento): before the *Libros,* 24–25
Révah, Israël Salvator, 211n8
revisionist history on medieval Spain, 100, 105, 111, 122n72
revolts. *See* rebellions
rhymed prose, use by Maimonides, 42–43, 61n18
Ribera, Julián, 299n1
Ribera, Archbishop San Juan de, 266, 268
Río, Fray Nicolás, 274
Risāla al-Nūriyya (Ibn Sabʿīn), 74
Robles, Beatriz de, 277, 280–83
Rohland de Langbehn, Regula, 257n20
Rojas, Fernando de, 247–48, 257n20, 258n21
role reversal, in conversos sentimental romances, 252, 261n28
romances, sentimental, by conversos, xix, 242, 247–54, 258n21
Roman Empire, dissociation of Spain from as topic of Castilian historiography, 243–44
Romans: Muslim persecutors of the church portrayed in terms of, 6; role in Spanish history deemphasized by *letrado* writers, 243–44

Index

Rome meeting of 1978, 22
Rosenau, Helen, 171
Rosenthal, Franz, 85n50
Rosner, Fred, 83n30
Roth, Norman, 105, 153n2
royal charters, on privileges enjoyed by thirteenth-century Majorca's Jews, 125
Royal Treasure, The (Boswell), 94–95
Ruano, Eloy Benito, 236n1
Rubiera, María Jesús, 36n13
Rucquoi, Adeline, 115n15
Rudolf II (Holy Roman Emperor), 272

Sabbath, Christian, failure of crypto-Jews to observe, 207, 208, 216n28
Sabbath, Jewish: observance of among conversos, 202–7, 216n28; women's training in observance of, 198
Sabra, I. A., 53
al-Ṣāʿid al-Andalusī, 47–48
saints, tradition of, as common to Moroccan Jews and Muslims, 288n44
Salamanca, University of: Colegio de San Bartolomé, *letrados* as graduates of, 257n16; theology studies at, 242, 243, 255n9
Samuel ibn Tibbon, 43–45, 54, 55–56
San Antonio de Padua (religious foundation), 232–34
Sánchez-Albornoz, Claudio, 153n1
Sandys, Sir Edwin, 319
San Juan Bautista parish (Toledo), 225–31, *map* 224, *table* 223; burial chapels, 228–30
San Martín parish (Toledo), 222, 224, 236n6, *map* 224
San Miguel de los Angeles (religious foundation), 232–34, 239n29
San Nicolás parish (Toledo), 222, 225–31, *map* 224, *table* 223; burial chapels, 228–30
San Pedro, Diego, 257n20, 258n22, 259n25; *Cárcel de amor,* 248–50, 257n20, 258nn21, 22
Santa Ana (religious foundation), 232–33
Santa Cruz, María de, 232
Santa Leocadia parish (Toledo), 222, 225, *map* 224, *table* 223
Santamaría, Alvaro, 126
Santa María, Bishop Pablo de (Selomó ha-Levi), 175, 242–43, 244, 255n9
Santa María la Blanca (Toledo church, former synagogue), 224
Santo Domingo el Real (religious foundation), 233–34
Santo Tomé parish (Toledo), 222, 224–25, 230, 237n8, *map* 224, *table* 223
San Vicente parish (Toledo), 222, 225–31, *map* 224, *table* 223; burial chapels, 228–30; conversos as parish priests, 227, 238n15
Satire Ménippée (Arnauld), 318
Schmitt, Jean-Claude, 171
scholasticism, 45, 54, 255n9
Scholem, Gershom, 81n13
science, conflict between Aristotelian cosmology and Ptolemaic astronomy, 50–54
scientists, Jewish-Muslim friendships among, 70
Scripture. *See* Bible, the; Old Testament; Qurʾān, the
Sefer ha-Berit (Kimhi), 181–82, 192n9
Sefer ha-Geʾulah (Nahmanides), 185
Seidenspinner-Núñez, Dayle, xix, 241–61
seignioralism, 21, 34
Selomó ha-Levi. *See* Santa María, Pablo de
Sephardic History conference (University of Maryland, 1991), 129, 138n19
72, as number with roots in folklore, 297, 305n33
Seville, 107; Jewish community of attacked in 1391, 168–69; Moriscos sent to, 279, 280–81; *Repartimiento,* 21, 25, 29–30
sexual boundaries, in Christian Spain, xviii, 141–52
  intercourse between non-Christian men and Christian women: accusations of, 149–52, 157nn32–34, 158nn37–39, 159nn41, 42; punishment for, 142–45, 150–52, 154n8, 155n13
sexuality of Muḥammad, discussion of: by al-Kindi, 9–10, 19n25; by Alvarus, 9–11, 19n25
al-Shafra, Muḥammad, 100
Shalom, Joseph, 187–90
sharecroppers, former Muslim slaves as, 133–34
Sharḥ Kitāb al-ʿUqqar (Maimonides), 41
Sharq al-Andalus (journal), 98, 104, 112
Shevet Judah (Baer), 175n1
Shiʿites, Sevener. *See* Ismaʿilism

Shīrāzī, Qutb al-Dīn, 72, 82n21
Sicily: expulsion of Muslims from, 112; Norman, land registers, 34n2
Siervo libre de amor (Padrón), 248, 253–54, 258n21
Siete edades del mundo (Santa María), 242–43
sign of the cross, crypto-Jews' failure to make at appropriate times, 203, 207
Silíceo, Cardinal Juan Martínez, 221
Simeon ben Ẓemah Duran, 133
Simmel, Georg, 153n6
Simon, Larry J., xviii, 111, 125–40
Sincere Brethren (Ikhwān al-Ṣafāʾ), 44, 56, 62n24
Sjoberg, Gideon, 36n13
skepticism, of Maimonides, 53–54, 65n58
slavery (*see also* slaves): medieval Christian attitudes toward, 132–33; medieval Jewish attitudes toward, 132–36; shift to other forms of medieval servitude, 133–34
"Slavery and Solidarity" (Meyerson), 111
"Slavery and the Social Order" (Meyerson), 111
slaves, Muslim, xviii, 111
in thirteenth-century Majorca, 126, 127–28; redemption or manumission of, 131–36; relations with Jews, 128–36; treatment after conversion to Christianity, 131–32, 134–35
social status: burial chapels as symbols of, 228; resting on wealth rather than lineage in fifteenth- and sixteenth-century Granada, 31; stratification following the *Repartiment* of Valencia, 27–28
Society for Spanish and Portuguese Historical Studies, 96
Sol Cabello, María, 100
Solomon ben Abraham Adret, 133
Solomon Ha-Levi, 175
Soto i Company, Ricard, 126
"Spanish and Portuguese Reconquest, 1095–1492" (Bishko), 97
Spanish Kingdoms 1250–1516 (Hillgarth), 96
Spanish language *(see also aljamiado):* anti-Christian polemical texts written in, 295, 298
Speculum (journal), 104
Spinoza, Baruch, 46–47, 58–59, 60, 62n31, 74
Stall, William Clayton, 110
Stanhope, James, 315–16
Still, Judith, 162–63
Strauss, Leo, 80n12
Suárez, Catalina, burial chapel, 230
suffering, as a continuum for Jewish writers, 170
Sufism, 69, 70, 74–76
Suhrawardī, 72–74, 76, 81n17, 82n24
Suma de politica (Arévalo), 245
Summa de poenitentia et matrimonio (Penyafort), 131, 139n29
Sunday as Christian Sabbath, failure of crypto-Jews to observe, 207, 208, 216n28
Sūrat Maryam (Quranic *sūra*), commentary on, 290–91
Sūrat al-Zukhruf (Quranic *sūra*), commentary on, 290–91
al-Suyūṭī, Jalāl al-Dīn ʿAbd al-Raḥmān ibn Abī Bakr, 301–2n9
Sylvester I (pope), 299, 305n40

al-Ṭabarī, Abū Jaʿfar Muhammad ibn Jarīr, 292, 294, 301n9, 302n11, 303n21
al-Tabrīzī, Abū Bakr Muḥammad ibn Muḥammad, 72–73, 82n21
tafsīrs (commentaries on the Qurʾan), 303n13; preserved and translated by Mudejars and Moriscos, 290–92, 295; studied by López-Morillas, xx, 290–99
Talmage, Frank, 45–46
Tapia Sánchez, Serafín, 100
taqiyya: existential esotericism in, 46; practiced by Moriscos, 279
al-Tarjūmān, ʿAbdallah (Anselmo Turmeda), 297
Tate, Brian, 163–64
Tate, Robert B., 254n4, 255n7, 256nn10, 12, 257n18
taxation, accusations of miscegenation used by lords as form of, 151–52
tax-farmers, conversos as in fifteenth- and sixteenth-century Toledo, 222
al-Taymī, Yaḥyā ibn Salām, 291, 300n5
Temple, the: desecration in 168 B.C.E. by Antiochus IV Epiphanes, 14; destruction of the First and Second, used in argument over coming of the messiah, 184
Teresa of Avila, St., 233, 234, 288n44

text(s), 162–63, 170
intertextuality, 162–63; place in medieval Jewish historiography, 161–75
Thaler, Donald, 95
Themistius, 43, 44
theology: *letrado* promotion of rationalist approach, xix, 244–47, 255n9; studied at Paris and Salamanca by Santa María and Cartagena, 242, 243, 255n9
Theology of Aristotle, 72, 73, 75
Thou, Jacques Auguste de, 317, 319
318, theological and biblical significance of figure, 303n23
Todros (thirteenth-century Hebrew poet), 162
Toledo, 24–25, 103
fifteenth- and sixteenth-century: composition of *consejo real* changed in 1480, 246–47, 256n14; conversos in, 222–36, 241; 1499 rebellion, 247; nunneries, xix, 231–34; parishes, 222–31; relations between conversos and Old Christians, 220–22
Torah, written Arabic text of studied by al-Biqaʾi, 84n37
Torres Fontes, Juan, 93, 97
Torró, Josep, 27–28
torture, used to obtain confessions during the Inquisition, 197, 210n2
Toubert, Pierre, 22
Trade and Traders in Muslim Spain (Constable), 105
transcendence, balance with immanence, 59–60
Tránsito, El (Toledo synagogue), 224–25
Trastámara dynasty, 242, 256n11 *(see also individual monarchs);* legitimized by *letrado* writers, 245–47
Tratado catalan medieval de derecho islámico, Un (Barceló Torres, ed.), 123n84
tribalism, 22, 23, 33
Trinity, nature of the: addressed at the Church councils, 293–94; doctrine of examined in Morisco texts, 290–94, 296, 297–98
Triunfo de amor (Flores), 257n20, 261n28
Tuḥfa (Turmeda), 297
Turks, early seventeenth-century Spain seen as vulnerable to attacks from, 267, 270–71
Turmeda, Fray Anselmo (ʿAbdallah al-Tarjūmān), 297
Twelfth Medieval Conference (University of British Columbia, 1981), 106
Tyconius, 3, 17n2

ʿUbaydallāh, as family name of Maimonides, 55, 66n69
Uitti, Karl D., 174
Uns al-Gharīb (Consolation to the Stranger) (Judah ben Nissim), 77
Urvoy, Dominique, 74, 104

Vajda, Georges, 75, 83n30, 84n41
Valencia: *ḥiṣn/qarya* model of agrarian landscape in, 21–22; Mudejars in, 94, 99–103, 106–7, 109, 111, 117n28, 120n56; reassessment of feudalism in, 22–23, 34; *Repartiment,* 21, 23, 27–29, 36n15; 1609 expulsion of the Moriscos, 265; status of Muslims in thirteenth century, 127
Valladolid: burning of described by Çarça, 167; 1559 *auto-de-fé,* 316
Vandenesse, presence at 1559 *auto-de-fé,* 316
Van Koningsveld, P. S., 304nn28, 30, 305n31
Van Limbosch, *Historia inquisitionis,* 317
Vaquero, Mercedes, 174
Vergel de príncipes (Arévalo), 245
Veryard, Ellis, 318
Viator (journal), 93, 97, 101, 104, 111
Vicent Ferrer, St., 224
Villadiego, community of, 1367 killing of Jews in, described by Çarça, 168
villages. *See alquerías*
Vincent, Bernard, 267
vineyards, 26–28, 32
violence, resistance to found in conversos sentimental romances, 251–54
Virgin Mary. *See* Mary, mother of Jesus
Vision of "Spanish Decline" (Galán Sánchez), 91–92
Vives, Luis, 320
Voltaire, 318

Wagner, Klaus, 107
Wansborough, John E., 164
Wasserstrom, Steven M., xviii, 69–87

wealth of converso community, in fifteenth-century Toledo, 225–26, *table* 223
Weissberger, Barbara F., 251–52, 259n25, 260n27
Whinnom, Keith, 258n22
Wiegers, Gerard Albert, 304nn28, 30, 305n31
Williams, John, 3, 18n5
winedrinking, interfaith, 145, 148
wise men of the Banū Isrā'īl, in the *aljamiado* manuscript, 290–91, 292, 293, 295, 303n13
wit, of Maimonides, 42–43, 61n15
witchcraft trials, Pedro de Valencia's memorial on, 266
Wolf, Kenneth Baxter, xvii, 3–19, 122n72
Wolfson, Harry A., 55, 67n77
women, 100, 198, 211n5 (*see also* sexual boundaries); crypto-Jewish (conversas), role in maintaining Jewish life in community and home, xix, 197–210, 211n8; exchange of, 146–47; importance in *Grisel y Mirabella,* 251–53; Moriscas, role in struggle over assimilation, xx, 274, 275–84; religious foundations for in fifteenth- and sixteenth-century Toledo, xix, 231–34
Worton, Michael, 162–63

Yom Kippur, observance of among conversos, 202–6
Yovel, Yirmiahu, 62n31
Yūsuf ibn Hasdai, correspondence with Ibn Bājja, 70

ẓāhir (nigleh) binarity, 45–47 (*see also* esotericism)
al-Zamakhsharī, Maḥmūd ibn ʿUmar, 292, 301n9
zambra, incorporated into Christian liturgy in efforts at converting Muslims, 275
Zohar, 46, 50

www.ingramcontent.com/pod-product-compliance
Lightning Source LLC
Chambersburg PA
CBHW050429240426
43661CB00055B/2318
9780268022631